ISBN: 979-8-9874705-2-7

Library of Congress Control Number: 2023901166

Author: David Jacobson

Editor: L. Pasquale

Illustrations: Shira Jacobson

Also by David Jacobson:

7 1/2 Habits To Help You Become More Humorous, Happier & Healthier
The Jacobson Joy Inventory: A New Look at Measuring Depression

Deadication

(No, that was not a typo.)

I honor all those who, before passing from this life, had an influence on me: my mother, whose kindness, sayings, and wisdom had a profound effect on my leadership style; my sister, Jessica, a wise soul who not only shared her wisdom with me, but constantly gave me praise and support; my brother, Alan, my oldest sibling and the most avid reader I have ever known; and my father, a highly decorated World War II hero who inspired his men and was a natural-born leader who role modeled for me how a leader should act in his positions and at home.

I would also like to deadicate this book to those authors I never met, but greatly admired: Mark Twain, James Thurber, Kurt Vonnegut, George Carlin, and Douglas Adams, to name only a few. Although no longer with us, their writings and their influence remain.

Acknowledgements

I thank all those who helped me on my journey to becoming a leader, including my wife, Laurie Jacobson, who has shared this journey of life with me for the past thirty-eight years and has always been supportive of my advances (or pushed me) into higher leadership positions.

I also thank my editor, without whom this book would have read like a jigsaw puzzle with several pieces missing!

Preface to the Fast Foreward

For those not familiar with a Fast Foreward, in addition to it being an optional button on VHS players and streaming movies, it is also a quick foreward to a book. This is in keeping with my traditional prebook silly format. For those conservative traditional English majors, journalists, book reviewers, and other highly skilled grammarians, I apologize for my discretions, but this is a humorous book, so please cut me some slack. Thank you.

Fast Foreward

While sharing his personal touch, David guides us on a journey to discover the powerful benefits of being a "highly humorous leader." He reaches deep into his decades of experience and brings forth a multitude of stories, anecdotes, and examples of the power of humor to enhance leadership. Throughout the book, David identifies key qualities of highly humorous leaders and provides his "Practice Playshop" which lists clear, simple, and actionable activities to help integrate humor into all leadership styles. Welcome to the journey.

Steven M. Sultanoff, Ph.D.

Past President of the Association for Applied and Therapeutic Humor and recipient of the

2012 Doug Fletcher Lifetime Achievement Award (AATH's Oscar); founder of HumorMatters™

· leadership quality that he role modeled for others. Athletics wa. ing he thought would always be a lifelong hobby, if not a career.

's a natural charismatic leader. He always used humor to win others · to get out of tricky situations. People gravitate toward him. He makes feel better about themselves, the world, or the situation in front of them.

vent to Israel in 1980. He got rheumatic fever and was admitted to an 'e care unit (ICU) in critical condition. Life would never be the same. ult, he left Israel in chronic pain with severe arthritis and less than half ngth of his former athletic physique. Doctors told him he'd be in a iair by the time he was thirty and there was little that could be done t. His rheumatologist said a move to Arizona might help somewhat : of the drier weather. The ultimate diagnosis was severe psoriatic s. Some joints calcified, leaving his wrists and ankles and part of his sed. His fingers were severely deformed, and his hands looked like those ghty-year-old.

ulled himself out of a hell most of us never experience. He did it with He now lives his life using humor every day. We made a lifetime ent that we'd make someone laugh or smile every day, for the rest of s. I'm holding up my end, and I know David is, too.

a forward is supposed to tell you why to read the book. I hope this ' convinces you to. If it didn't, well that's your loss. I'm guessing it did you're still reading.

ok is his best yet. David has an instinct for how to motivate people and em feel better, all using humor. David has held several leadership s as you'll learn more about in this book.

Straight Foreward

I've known David Jacobson for sixty-three years, or thereabouts. I don't remember when we met, but I don't remember him not being in my life. We were inseparable for years at a time, yet, we also had other friends we'd spend a lot of time with, sometimes for months or years at a time, but we always had a special bond and always reconnected. He was the brother I always wanted. I was the brother, he didn't need, having two already.

At nine or ten years of age, we wanted to be blood brothers. We must have seen it on a TV show. We scratched our forearms to draw blood, held the two arms together, and amazing enough, we did not get AIDS, COVID, or develop allergies of some kind.

At twelve or thirteen, we promised each other we'd be best men at each other's weddings, like kids that age have any idea of where they will be ten or fifteen years down the road. Kids say things like that at that age I guess. Oh, we did in fact follow through on those promises.

David was a natural athlete, built like Bruce Lee without even trying too hard. I was more like Baby Huey, always fifteen pounds overweight, good enough in sports, but no athlete. He had a magnetic personality even in younger years, and everyone wanted to be around him.

I was a different person around him. I felt confident, not scared of anything. David was confident, and he was not afraid of anything. Once, we were at a party (we were about eighteen or so), and we were t troublemakers outside who wanted to crash the party. police, the two of us walked into the middle of the gr where the troublemakers were. The four or five toug shrugged and said, "Gee, I think they left." That was th

David's identity through the age of twenty-two was ath sixth grade he broke a county record for the long jump Grammar School Track and Field Championships. Each one champion selected as their best (even though contestant). Another contender from a rival grammar scho David as were most of his opponents, asked David, "Wh school, Midget School?" That same contender after the hand in admiration. David also received The President Award. The award was given to those at or above the ei David scored in the ninety-ninth percentile, the top 1% nati took the fitness test. Also, in high school while on the wr broke a school record for pinning someone in under a hal judo after high school (practicing his new moves on me) a Olympic material. In our spare time we'd go to my basen weight bench set up and we'd push each other to see who more. It wasn't a competition, just two friends pushing each David could push himself to places only Arnold Schwarz medalist Olympian could go. All I had to do was tell him he rep with the extra weight I put on the bar. When he pushed I'd yell that I thought he could do just one more, and he'd alw many "one mores, one after another, after another." His

This book is brilliance. I've worked in banking, car sales, and real estate, and I've rarely come across a real manager whom I could call a leader. David is on top of my "leader list."

David S. Lempert: Master's Public Management, twenty-five years of experience in retail automobile sales, thirteen years in banking; employee of the month and best in sales too many times to count, attributable to my use of humor at work.

To My Readers

As a non-fiction book, the writing within is based on facts, actual events, and real people. Names have been removed and or changed, of course, to protect personal privacy. But erring on the side of caution, I offer this disclaimer:

> *The author is not responsible for any distress or harm as a result of reading or utilizing the suggestions presented in this book.*
>
> *Humor is an art and as such is open to interpretation. That said, not all suggestions will work in all settings, and the author is not responsible for any that don't work or that you personally do not like.*
>
> *Also, please greet with a smile any links or websites that may change over time (as web addresses often do). If the material no longer exists, please forgive any inconvenience.*
>
> *My intent was to write the truth, the whole truth, and nothing but the truth; however, being human, I apologize in advance for any errors on my part. To quote the famous film* Love Story, *"Love means never having to say you're sorry." And hopefully this disclaimer works, too!*

Table of Contents

Preface

"Treat people as if they were what they ought to be, and you help them to become what they are capable of being."

Johann Wolfgang von Goethe

First, let me say that this book is about moving your work culture in the direction of becoming more light, fun, and full of happy comradery. *It should not be used as a substitute for training on general leadership principles, a formal education, or work experience. Even so, I hope that both advanced and novice leaders can find some pearls of wisdom within.*

Fun fact: Oysters make pearls so they can relieve pain. When a grain of sand gets stuck inside their shells, they ease the irritation by coating it with layers of a mineral, and a pearl begins to form. Similarly, grains of sand are present in every workplace. You can help your staff by noticing that sand and coating their pain with humor, protecting them, and allowing healing. Perhaps they themselves will become pearls. And like an oyster bed in the sea, the culture is not created by a leader. Instead, a leader *influences* the culture in the direction he or she would like to see it shift, including choosing new staff. The collective group then ultimately decides what the culture will look like—what pearls are produced—and how members operate or behave.

That was a little heavy. Time for a joke break.

> *A supervisor and two of his employees walk into a bar.*
>
> *The tired bartender says, "What can I get you?"*
>
> *The leader says, "You can get me employees that are more engaged!"*
>
> *The two employees say, "You can get us a leader who is more engaging!"*
>
> *The bartender, nodding off, says, "If you used your sense of humor more often and more appropriately, you'd all be more engaged!"*

What can we learn from this little snippet? First, we could legitimately ask: Why is a supervisor bringing two of his staff to meet in a bar? Why are they asking for more engagement?

Why are bartenders so wise? All interesting questions, but as you'll read, only the second directly ties into the focus of this book!

Numerous articles and books have been written on employee engagement, and even more are being written even as you read. If you found this book in 2023, congratulations, because it's one of the new ones. (If you are reading it later, perhaps I don't yet know how to market very well, and you stumbled upon it accidentally.) Other books also discuss leadership, employee engagement, team building, and related topics; however, since they were not written by me, they will not, in my opinion, be as enjoyable. This matters because laughter promotes learning, so sharing my leadership experiences *should* be as enjoyable as a good conversation.

Even so, creating such a book is a delicate matter, requiring that I share information without pontificating. Which reminds me, leaders should know unusual words so others can think, "Wow, that is why she is a leader, because she knows weird words!" (And now, in order to demonstrate awareness of the term epizeuxis, I will use the word thrice: pontificate, pontificate, pontificate.) If you get nothing else out of this book, perhaps you have learned an unfamiliar word. This brings us to a (very important) leadership tip:

There is always something new to learn.

Before we move on, I would like to express gratitude to my former employees for the privilege of being their leader. Their views may differ from my own, and yours might, too. Whatever the case, I wish all readers success and happiness (whether or not they return that sentiment). In fact, I have found that: 1) even using humor in an uncomfortable way can promote change, and 2) that anyone is capable of changing for the better. If this resonates for you, too, then please, read on!

- David Jacobson, January 2023

Introduction

"A leader is anyone who has two characteristics; first, he is going someplace; second, he is able to persuade other people to go with him."

W.H. Cowley

To this quote I would add: "Humor is the greatest tool of persuasion." To be a great leader it is essential that you have this tool at your disposal. And looking specifically at the effects of eighty-nine studies into whether humor was demonstrably persuasive, Walter et al. (2018) found that humor did have a significant (although technically weak) effect on changing behavioral intentions. (If you'd like to read further about their methods, etc., the findings were published in the journal, *Human Communication Research*, *44*(4), October 2018, pp. 343–373).

A (Very Brief) History of Leadership

Welcome to a post-COVID-19 leadership book! (Not too many authors can say that.) The post-pandemic leader has experienced some big differences, and humor can only help to de-stress staff in this "new normal" world. Many executives and supervisors have learned to lead not only face-to-face, but remotely or virtually as well. Many of the tools, strategies, and habits presented in this book are applicable to all these settings. First, let's see how we got to this point.

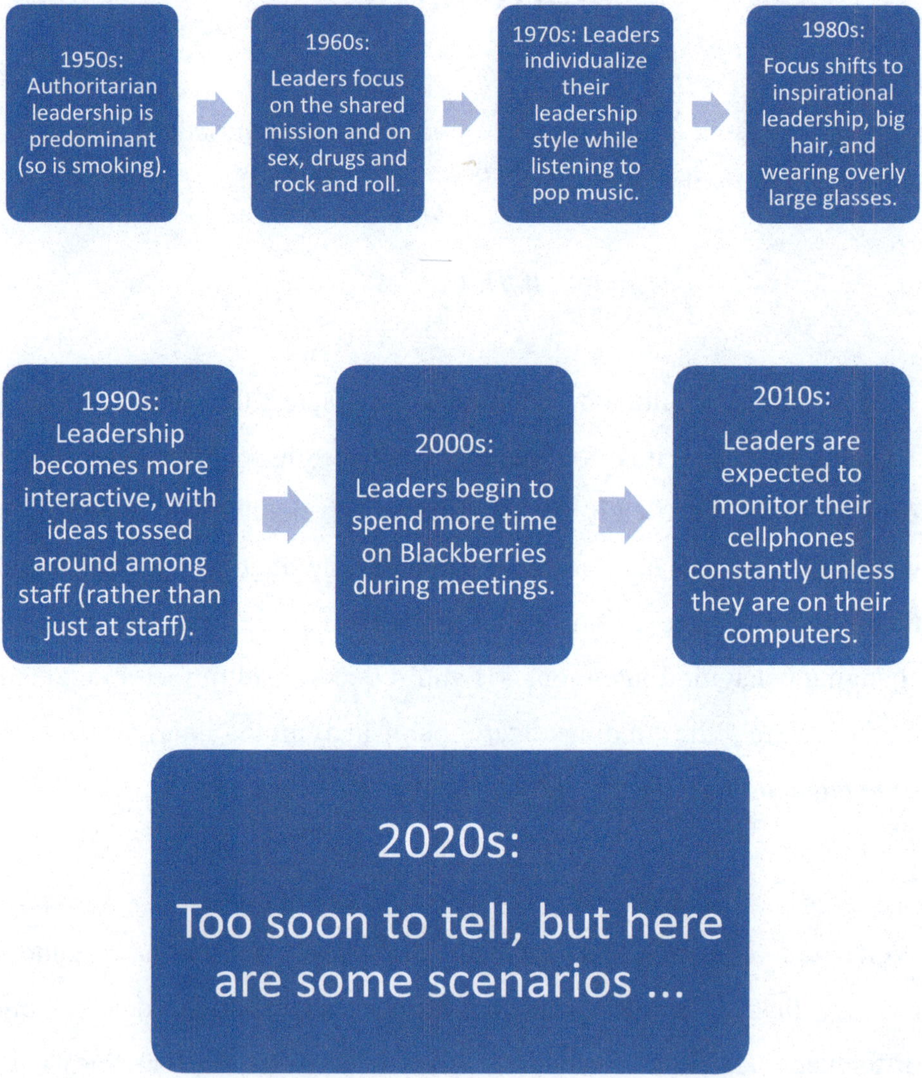

Scenario One: Leaders are mostly unemployed due to pandemics, climate change, and resulting economic distress. Many start their own businesses.
Scenario Two: Leaders return to focusing on productivity, to the neglect of their staff's functioning. Staff quit and find self-employment or start their own businesses.
Scenario Three: Violent conflict breaks out, this time between mega-corporations like Walmart, Royal Dutch Shell, China National Petroleum, Coca-Cola, Microsoft, Amazon, and Exxon. All countries surrender to the CEO of the winning firm.

The more things change, however, the more they stay the same. One-hundred-plus years ago, Mark Twain's wit is pertinent to leaders today. For example:

- "I was gratified to be able to answer promptly, and I did. I said I didn't know." (Leadership Tip: Do not be afraid to admit you do not know something.)
- "The really great (people) make you feel that you, too, can become great." (Leadership Tip: Humorous leaders make their staff feel great!)
- "The right word may be effective, but no word was ever as effective as a rightly timed pause." (Leadership Tip: Be patient when listening to your staff and realize that timing is everything).
- "Courage is resistance to fear, mastery of fear—not absence of fear." (Leadership Tip: It is okay to feel afraid as a leader; just

don't let it rule your decisions, and whenever possible use your sense of humor to overcome your fears).

Based on the following document from the National Archives and Records Administration, someone else saw value in humor. Abbott Washburn, the Deputy Director of the United States Information Agency, attached a note during the clearance process for actor Hal Holbrook's goodwill, humorous tour. He noted that "(the Holbrook presentation) is 90% universal humor. He had all 2,800 guests at the President's birthday press banquet ... enthralled." The response from overseas was positive, and the State Department sponsored Holbrook on an extended European tour. Holbrook represented the United States as a "Humor Ambassador" to the world. Washburn went on to serve as a Commissioner of the Federal Communications Commission from 1974 to 1982.

Do you see where recognizing and sponsoring someone (such as someone on your staff) with a great sense of humor might get you?

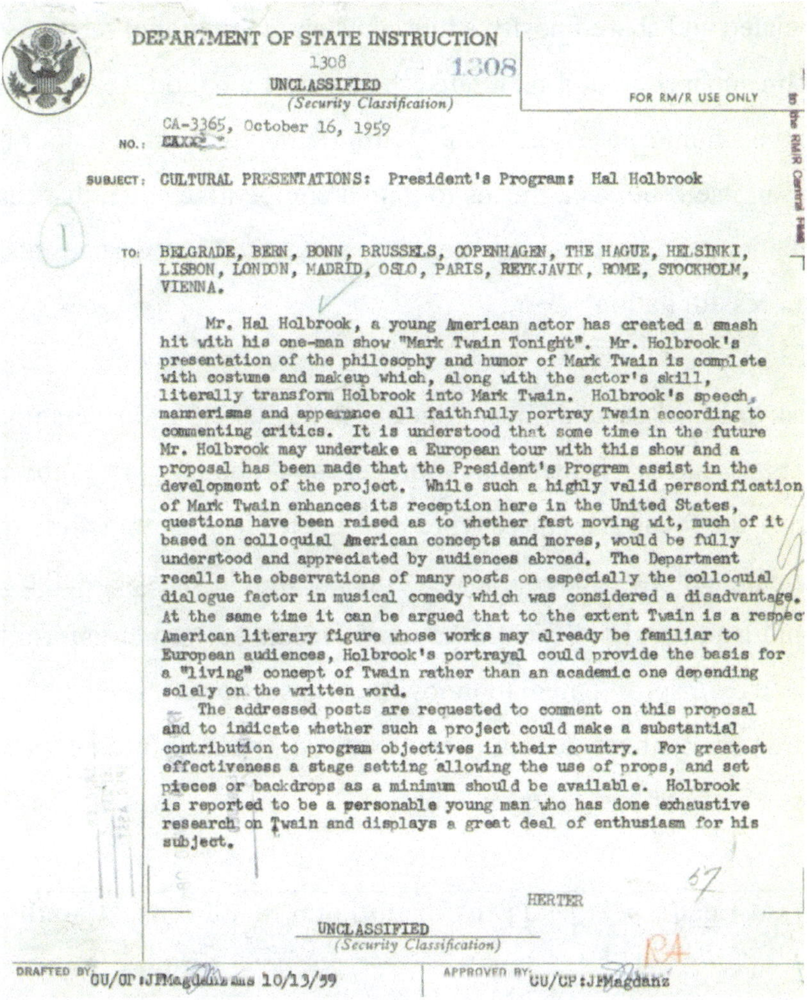

DEPARTMENT OF STATE INSTRUCTION
1308
1308
UNCLASSIFIED
(Security Classification)
FOR RM/R USE ONLY

NO.: CA-3365, October 16, 1959

SUBJECT: CULTURAL PRESENTATIONS: President's Program: Hal Holbrook

TO: BELGRADE, BERN, BONN, BRUSSELS, COPENHAGEN, THE HAGUE, HELSINKI, LISBON, LONDON, MADRID, OSLO, PARIS, REYKJAVIK, ROME, STOCKHOLM, VIENNA.

Mr. Hal Holbrook, a young American actor has created a smash hit with his one-man show "Mark Twain Tonight". Mr. Holbrook's presentation of the philosophy and humor of Mark Twain is complete with costume and makeup which, along with the actor's skill, literally transform Holbrook into Mark Twain. Holbrook's speech, mannerisms and appearance all faithfully portray Twain according to commenting critics. It is understood that some time in the future Mr. Holbrook may undertake a European tour with this show and a proposal has been made that the President's Program assist in the development of the project. While such a highly valid personification of Mark Twain enhances its reception here in the United States, questions have been raised as to whether fast moving wit, much of it based on colloquial American concepts and mores, would be fully understood and appreciated by audiences abroad. The Department recalls the observations of many posts on especially the colloquial dialogue factor in musical comedy which was considered a disadvantage. At the same time it can be argued that to the extent Twain is a respec American literary figure whose works may already be familiar to European audiences, Holbrook's portrayal could provide the basis for a "living" concept of Twain rather than an academic one depending solely on the written word.

The addressed posts are requested to comment on this proposal and to indicate whether such a project could make a substantial contribution to program objectives in their country. For greatest effectiveness a stage setting allowing the use of props, and set pieces or backdrops as a minimum should be available. Holbrook is reported to be a personable young man who has done exhaustive research on Twain and displays a great deal of enthusiasm for his subject.

HERTER

UNCLASSIFIED
(Security Classification)

DRAFTED BY: CU/CP:JPMagdanz:ms 10/13/59 | APPROVED BY: CU/CP:JPMagdanz

Department of State Instruction CA-3365

Subject: Cultural Presentations, President's Program: Hal Holbrook, Oct 16, 1959

From the founding of our nation, a time when Benjamin Franklin went to France to foster an alliance during the Revolutionary War, government leaders have incorporated humor into their leadership styles and have appreciated and shared positive humor as an international relations tool. Franklin supervised and facilitated the birth of a nation with customary wit and his humorous style. In this setting, Franklin valued humor not as an end in itself, but as a means to gain a competitive edge, disseminate information, and promote his agenda to make the United States a strong and successful nation.

Against this background knowledge about the history of leadership, let's talk about current leadership approaches. Although there are many varieties, the focus is on three types: servant leadership, transformational leadership, and transactional leadership. Servant leaders serve the group first and lead second. Transformational leaders seek to transform those they lead by inspiring them to innovate. Transactional leaders hold order and structure as their most important values. This helpful table presents the key characteristics of each approach.

Servant Leaders	**Transformational Leaders**	**Transactional leaders**
• Focus on service to staff, customers, and the organization • Influence by serving the	• Focus on the goals of the organization • Influence by modeling • Use persuasion	• Focus on the role of supervision • Are goal-focused • Concern themselves

needs of others • Promote team problem-solving and individualized development • Motivate by providing staff with autonomy and resources	• Promote individualized influence • Motivate with charisma to attain a common goal	with contractual obligations • Use a corrective response to errors or problems • Use rewards and punishments to motivate others

As with general leadership, there are oodles of books on the topics of servant, transformational, and transactional leadership, so I will not delve into these styles. You're a leader so you don't need me to tell you what leadership books to read, (except this one, of course). If you don't already have a feel for these three leadership styles, select one or two to explore.

The highly humorous leadership style

I propose a fourth style: Take the best of these three and combine that with humor and you get (cue trumpets, and "Ta da!"): a highly humorous leader! In addition to using very large words (see earlier section on pontificating), I have coined this term in the hopes that it will catch on, I will become famous, and I will not have to write more books. Also, while I cannot promise you that by the time you finish this book, you'll instantly be a highly humorous leader, at least you'll know I made up the name.

While reading this book, the left occipito-temporal cortex of your brain will immediately link each written word to its spoken equivalent, so your eyes are immediately converting the words on the page to a voice in your head, as if I am talking to you at this very moment. It's like we are actually having a conversation together about humor and leadership, even though I can't hear your thoughts and it's kind of a one-way conversation. Feel free to respond while you read, perhaps saying things like, "David, please stop coining terms!" (Gee, well, thanks for the feedback, reader.)

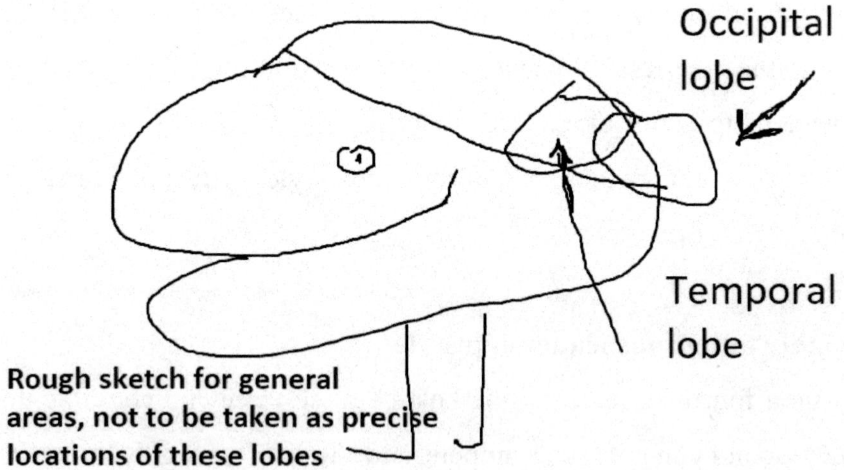

You may ask, "Hey, David, what else can you tell me about highly humorous leaders?" First, they have a vision for their future and for the future of whatever endeavor they are involved in. Second, highly humorous leadership is not necessarily an easy style. It is full of risks, but for every risk, there is a reward. Think of a highly humorous leader as a superhero with enhanced humor powers.

This book emphasizes the benefits of fun, play, and spontaneity, of approaching absurdity with laughter rather than tears. That said, a highly humorous leader learns to use his or her sense of humor in a thoughtful and appropriate way. In fact, I almost coined the term "humor-rational leader," but worried that it wouldn't catch on and stuck with the highly humorous term I've used in the past.

Some leaders use humor ***inappropriately***. (If you've ever encountered them, I'll bet you can still remember their names.) This is unfortunate, especially if they use humor in a detrimental way, to put down their employees, to ridicule staff, or to feel superior to other people. Some are top politicians, some are CEOs, and some are just direct supervisors with a personality defect. The good news, though, is that most leaders like this do not stay around long. Some are found out sooner, others later, but most will eventually lose their leadership positions, having insulted too many people too often (or simply by insulting the wrong person, perhaps the HR Director, once).

Fortunately, other than publishing this book, my current fame is limited to my relatives, friends, and bill collectors. So, I consider my humor to be relatively low-risk. (I also received an invitation to appear on *Lifestyles of the Poor and Unknown*, which took a lot of pressure off during the writing phase.) And that's okay; you do not need a fancy title to be a leader. As my daughter, Shira, reminded me, you *do* need the ability to distinguish a leader from a liter. A liter is 1.05669 quarts. Thank you, Shira!

Here, **we'll define a leader as anyone who takes the lead on anything**. For example, for a family dinner, making the decision about where to eat or persuading the group to choose a certain item on the menu might require influence. You get the idea. In that sense, almost everyone in life gets an opportunity to lead, a reality that makes my latest book perfect for you—or at least justifies my trying to talk you into reading it!

In addition to diffusing tension, humor indicates flexibility, which is a key component in effective leadership. In turn, effective leadership behaviors influence the work culture.

Humor thus enhances your leadership influence *and* the total work environment. Mastering humor will help you be "the one who says that clever thing" instead of "the one who only wishes they said that." Humor is also the thing that helps you say, "I wrote that," instead of "I wish I could write." The following screen capture depicts some questions asked in an (anonymous) staff survey to gauge how effective their leader is:

David Jacobson

:ity: All   Entity Code: All   AU: All   AU Description: All   Job Class: All

Back to top

Leadership Effectiveness

Question	Responses	Distribution
My leader regularly provides feedback that helps me improve my performance.	23	100%
My leader actively helps me achieve my career goals and develop my skills.	23	100%
My leader helps our team balance our workload.	23	100%
My leader uses the strengths of everyone on our team.	23	100%
My leader holds our team accountable for results.	23	100%
My leader takes responsibility for his/her actions.	23	100%
My leader acts with integrity and models Banner's values.	23	100%
My leader makes sure I know what is expected of me	23	100%

I would have also liked to see questions like, "My leader puts a smile on my face on a regular basis during our interactions."

More good news: According to the following graphic, in 2019, my leadership effectiveness rating was 99%, and 91% of my staff were actively engaged!

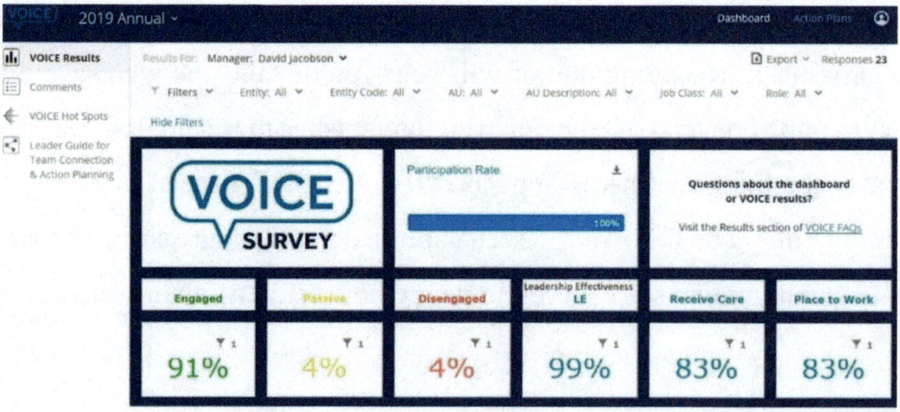

National averages? Not so hot:

> "Currently, 36% of US employees are engaged in their work and workplace.
> Globally, 20% of employees are engaged at work (Gallup, 2020)."

Wow! Should we really be encouraged and excited about employee engagement below 40%?

What if your staff could reach 50%, 60%, or even 70% engaged? That's what this book is designed to help you, the leader, to achieve. It's not all attributable to humor of course, but for me and my staff, humor was a central contributing factor.

As Abraham Lincoln said, "A leader without humor is a jackass."

Okay, he did not say that, but can't you picture him saying that? Of course, you can! Because President Lincoln was known as a great and highly humorous leader (even if he did die 156 years before I coined this term). For instance, Lincoln began a speech to a group of newspaper editors by stating that he lacked the credentials to speak to such a distinguished group. He told them he felt much like he did when he was a traveling judge visiting courts to preside over cases. On one such journey he passed a woman on horseback. As he turned his horse to the side to let her pass, she gazed intently at him and said, “I do believe you are the ugliest man I ever saw!”

“Madam,” he replied, “I expect you’re right, but I just can’t help it.”

“No,” she said, “You can’t help it, but you could stay home.”

Lincoln’s sense of humor enhanced his abilities of persuasion. Lincoln also used his sense of humor to cope with the unimaginably heavy burdens of his office and the great loss of life during the Civil War. In the classic best seller: *Lincoln on Leadership: Executive Strategies for Tough Times* by Donald T. Phillips, he writes about how Lincoln used humor to

capture the audience's attention and keep them entertained, and how humor allowed him to bring levity to these stressful situations as well as keep the audience's attention. Philips also introduced us to the term Management by Walking Around (MBWA). Lincoln liked walking around the White House, government buildings, and even battlefields to get a sense of what was happening. He was diligent about setting a good example since countless people looked to him as a leader. This book originally written in the early 1990s has now been revisited in his newer book from 2017, *Lincoln on Leadership for Today: Abraham Lincoln's Approach to 21st-Century Issues*. In it he explains how Lincoln attempted to avoid provocation whenever possible by looking at the humorous side of any potentially hazardous situation and goes on to say that Lincoln "would also be entertaining in his own right by applying humor or telling stories that would place partisan attacks in a slightly different light. He would get people to laugh about it- and when people laugh you know they're with you. Lincoln knew that and had a real knack for getting voters to respond to his humorous yarns." The song: "Always Look on the Bright Side of Life
Song" by Monty Python is reflective of Lincoln's perspective on life.

More good news: Humor skills can be learned. And it's worth it! If you enhance your sense of humor and humor leadership style, it can result in:

- Increased positive emotions
- Decreased negative emotions
- Increased ability to cope with life stressors

- A happier, more connected, supportive, and productive workforce
- An increased sense of belonging, which improves morale, enhanced group cohesiveness, and improved communication
- Better relationships
- Staff empowerment, and
- A positive impact on larger organizational outcomes

Some leaders who enhanced their leadership style have even won cars and other valuable prizes, but this is not the norm.

As noted by C.W. Metcalf in his book *Lighten Up: Survival Skills for People Under Pressure* (1992), one of the main things that holds us back from using our sense of humor is our fear of looking foolish. You must get over this fear (or at least learn to control it) to be successful as a highly humorous leader. Consider, perhaps, that a sense of humor is a universal human trait. (So are arrogance, deception, dishonesty, ego, envy, greed, hatred, immorality, lying, and selfishness, but those are not the subject of this book, and not traits of the good leader, anyway.)

A Word About Burnout

"Apple's Employee Retention Plan didn't work, perhaps because Apple Turnovers are so good."

When you look at any staff member, think of them as a fire that is burning. Their fire is their passion and purpose. And fires always need fuel. Your passion can be your fire, and fire spreads with the proper fuel. With every interaction you have, the other should walk away with their fire burning at least a little stronger, rather than being dampened or burned out.

Leadership Tip: Highly Humorous Leaders use humor to:
Take initiatives and risks
Remain calm during crises
Worry less about making mistakes
Focus on opportunities
Smile often
Experiment and embrace change

The world is struggling with one of the greatest pandemics of the last 100 years, which as of this writing, the World Health Organization (WHO) estimates to have killed fifteen million people (as reported in *The New York Times*, May 5, 2022). The mind struggles to comprehend this number. As a result, as is natural in human nature, humor arose as one of the greatest ways to survive this crisis. Comedians, highly humorous leaders, and others who use humor to cope have applied their skills to confront this crisis and to deal with their own stress and fears, as well as the fears of those they interact with.

Leaders with the ability to infuse humor into this strange, new world are the ones truly helping their employees to make it through. For example, a CEO "accidentally" left his screen-share on during a companywide Zoom call as he typed "things inspirational CEOs say in challenging times" into Google, leaving the words for his audience to read. During challenging times, such creative leaders are truly helping their employees to cope.

Chapter One:
The Importance of Humor at Work

"I find the great thing in this world is not so much where we stand, as in what direction we are moving ..."

Oliver Windell Holmes Sr.

Have you ever considered creating a leadership development plan? If so, what part is humor going to play? If you haven't put a plan in place, what can you do today to ensure that humor plays a role in your leadership activities? Hint: The answer might be closer than you think. ("Today, I am going to read a chapter in Jacobson's book as part of my development plan.")

Highly Humorous Leaders can use humor to:

- Acknowledge their weaknesses
- Absorb setbacks, learn from them, and turn them to their advantage
- Improve their self-confidence and thus, the confidence employees have in them

- Express their passion in a genuine way (rather than the latest business guru's idea of what passion looks like)
- Be (or become) real, authentic, and grounded, remaining humble and not letting the power of their ego get the best of them
- Be more proactive, less reactive, and more patient

Let us begin with a caveat. Sorry, that's not caviar, which can't be served through an app, although you might consider humor a delicacy that can be used as a garnish sprinkled through your leadership actions ... Back to caveat, which comes from the Latin verb *cavēre,* meaning to be on guard. A caveat suggests caution or awareness. As a caveat, wise authors will share their own perspectives, so readers can understand how to mindfully apply information.

My own areas of experience and expertise have mostly been in behavioral health and social work. My tiles have included Behavioral Health Director and Chief of Social Work (not Director or Chief of Stand-Up Routines). I have always been balanced with my use of humor, as doing so prevents me from going overboard or using humor excessively.

Another caveat: Do not force the use of humor. If you try too hard to be "funny," your humor will fall flat. If you have something humorous to say that helps make a point, do so. Do not, though, use a joke or a one-liner merely to impress. Remember that you are seeking to be authentic.

In addition, use *extreme* caution with gags and practical jokes. Only use them with those you are closest to and when you are 99.9% sure the person on the receiving end will find them funny, too. Most important, know the difference between appropriate and inappropriate humor. (We will delve into those differences later in the chapter.) It might not take deep wisdom to know the difference between appropriate and inappropriate humor, but it *does* require common sense, which might be the least common commodity of all.

Now that the caveats have been addressed, let's get to the heart of the matter.

Staff Rhymes with Laugh!

Rhymes help us remember better so now when you think "staff," think "laugh," as follows:

It is important every now and then to take a break from your leadership responsibilities and just have fun with your staff. What does this look like? These are goal-free interactions, without a hidden agenda, *no matter how helpful or productive you might think that agenda is*. Annual retreats that involve sitting around with crayons and magic markers, designing the organization's future, for example, are not "fun." They can be enjoyable, creative, even inspiring, of course, but they are usually leader-driven or at least completely goal-directed (you're trying to produce a long-range plan, perhaps). So, take time during relatively low-stress times to relax and simply enjoy a meal or take a walk together.

Staff whom with their leaders laugh,
are so much better at their craft!

A 2003 study by American researcher Fabio Sala, a consultant with the Hay Group's McClelland Centre for Research and Innovation in Boston, Massachusetts, found a positive correlation between the size of executives' bonuses and their use of humor. In other words, big bonuses and humor were linked. Additionally, Sala found that outstanding executives use humor more than twice as often as the so-called average executives—237% more, to be exact! (To evaluate for yourself whether the data mean that income creates joy, please see the resource section at the end of the book for more information.)

Humor can be used to lift your mood and boost your staff's morale by helping you become more aware of your own feelings and those of your staff. Today, when something goes wrong, I usually do not take it too seriously, because in the future, it may become just another anecdote, something to look back on and laugh. So, if you don't believe an event will have an impact next month or next year, *teach your staff* how to laugh it off starting today!

Physiological benefits

The physiological benefits of laughter are well-documented. Dr. Lee S. Berk is a pioneering medical researcher who studies the neuroendocrine and immune effects of positive emotions. Berk has been studying the effect of laughter on the body since 1988, appearing in media outlets from *TIME* and *USA Today* to *Forbes*, NBC, and even the illustrious *Tucson Jacobson Scoop* newsletter. Dr. Berk and I also appeared together in a documentary on the healing power of humor (produced by the Korean Broadcasting System in the early 1990s). For more information on the physiological benefits of laughter, see CNN.com, "Seriously, researchers are trying to determine whether laughter heals" (2000) at http://www.cnn.com/2000/HEALTH/alternative/05/08/laughter.health.wmd/index.html or http://www.dr-lee-berk.com/).

According to the Mayo Clinic (https://www.mayoclinic.org/healthy-lifestyle/stress-management/in-depth/stress-relief/art-20044456), when you have a hearty laugh, you experience:

- Deep breathing: Laughing oxygenates the blood. Laughter helps to provide longer exhalations, thus ridding the lungs of residual air and enriching the blood with ample supplies of oxygen. It also decreases the chances of someone calling you an old windbag.

- Decreased muscle tension.
- Stimulated circulation in the body (just like exercise but without the sweat, which is not appealing during a staff meeting—save it for the gym!): This sudden stimulus increases **oxygen** levels while also increasing levels of endorphins (often called "feel-good hormones") and reducing levels of cortisol, epinephrine, and other stress-related or immune-inhibiting hormones.
- Decreased blood pressure: Blood pressure decreases, after an initial rise, and those who laugh heartily on a regular basis have naturally lower standing blood pressures than the average population. (Mine is extremely low, but perhaps that is because I don't take my medications correctly.)
- Fewer muscle aches: Did you ever laugh so hard that your stomach hurt? Laughter is much preferred over doing too many push-ups. It's also extremely helpful for people like me with chronic pain.
- Improved digestion: A full-blown, pee-your-pants belly laugh activates and strengthens more than 400 muscles! (I would name them all, but that would be pretty boring, and I don't know all their names anyway.) Laughter can also reduce blood levels of fatty acids (Is it possible the acids are just heavy-set?)
- Brain-released endorphins

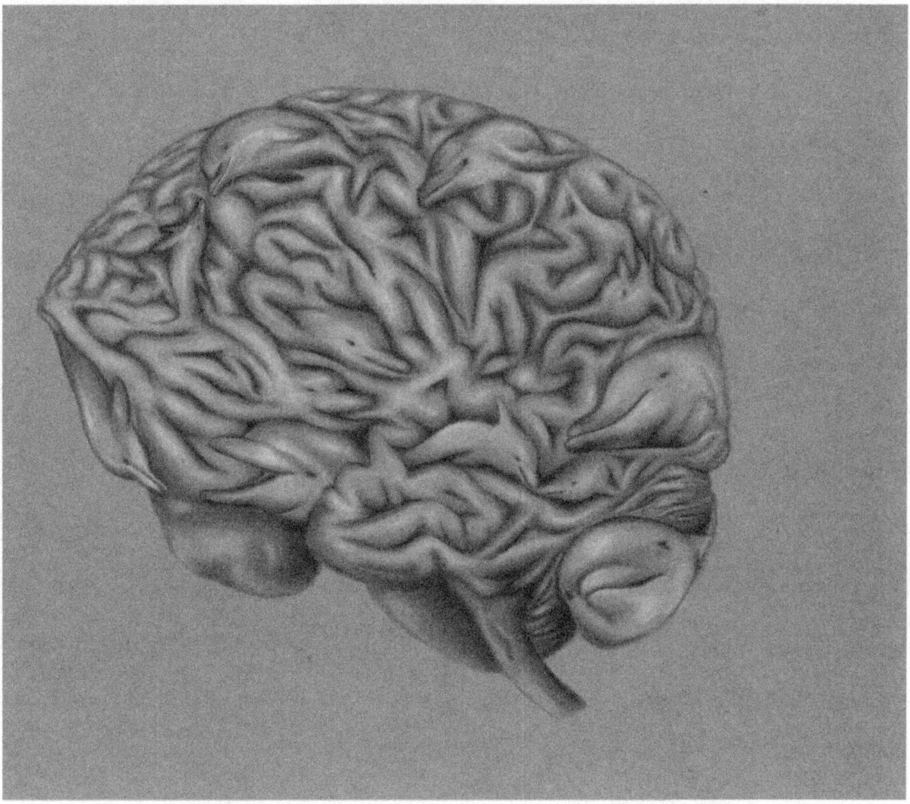

What endorphins in thc brain look like

Psychological Benefits of Humor for Leaders

Oodles of articles have also been written on this topic. (I think “oodles” sounds funnier than “numerous,” don’t you?) The resource section of this book contains links to a few. Included among the benefits: humor helps when recouping losses. Leaders experience loss along with change on a regular basis. When facing losses, humor can soften the blow. For example, our corporate office informed all departments that they had to reduce their budgets by 10% and then present the plan to their department administrator by the end of the day. Of course, I did comply with the request, but I also took the humorous road and gave my administrator a copy of my budget that I reduced on the copier to make the image 10% smaller. Sounds like a silly little thing, but in the end my department did not have to make budget cuts. (Did that silly little gesture have anything to do with it?)

Humor also helps with addressing setbacks and/or disappointments, as mentioned previously. Making jokes about a setback can indicate to colleagues that you are confident and calm. And when leaders use humor to address setbacks, they can strengthen their leadership position on the team and promote the respect of others. Appropriate jokes can set staff at ease and make it easier for them, too, to accept delays or setbacks.

True story: Years ago, despite my severe arthritis, I received some media attention for getting a silver medal in the "El Tour de Tucson." The El Tour is a 110-mile bicycle tour around the perimeter of the city. My plan was to "go for the gold" the following year; however, I had many setbacks when I started training. My knee was constantly filling with fluid and needed to be drained by a rheumatologist. In addition, I could not ride more than a mile or two without severe pain. There was *no way* I was going to ride in the event that year.

Yet, a local paper scheduled an interview with me in only a few weeks' time to discuss my plans for the event. Using my sense of humor, I brainstormed alternative and "silly" ideas to get the creative juices flowing and to relieve some of the pressure I felt. I started with, "Hmm, maybe I could take my fishing pole and hook onto another rider's bike, or try steroids, or maybe ride my unicycle instead." That last idea, though sounding silly, was something that really got me thinking …

So, I got on my unicycle more as a joke and for fun rather than as an alternate plan, but found my back was not as painful because I was sitting upright rather than being hunched over the handlebars. In addition, the range of motion of my knees was much more tolerable on the unicycle than on the bike. The result? I was able to ride the unicycle fifty miles on the El Tour that year! A struggle was transformed into a wonderful way to address a setback with humor and to find a great alternative.

As in this story, a sense of humor is the key to resilience. It helps you take hardships in stride (if you do not live in the town of Stride, it helps you take hardships wherever you live). It helps you weather disappointment (whether disappointed or not!) and helps you bounce back from adversity and loss (even without a pogo stick).

Humor helps us see things from a new perspective. You still don't believe me? Leadership Tip: A picture is worth a thousand words. (But I won't charge for this one.)

Photo by Laurie Anne Jacobson

You might say, "Okay, David, but as a leader I typically don't have to ride a bike or even a unicycle for that matter. Can you give me some examples of addressing setbacks in **my** workplace through humor?"

Good point, reader. I can tell you about my worst setback in leadership and how I addressed it. It's kind of a long story, but I think it's worth sharing.

Opportunity knocks

I had the opportunity to move to Texas to a newer VA Healthcare System and help create a culture and department reflective of highly humorous leadership. As Chief of Social Work, I was new to the agency and had a lot to learn about being a federal employee, but I caught on quickly and created a smooth-running machine.

David Jacobson, Chief of Social Work

(In background an image of his father, a highly decorated WWII Veteran)

Sadly, all organizations have employees who make it difficult to create a healthy culture. All a leader can do is try to protect the staff and help unengaged employees get to a place more suited for them. As I saw it, I was a highly humorous leader who discarded all the "dead wood" within the first six months. (Despite the legends, it is a myth that federal employees cannot be fired. I let go the four worst employees who seemingly did not care about Veterans or themselves. Sorry, but no punch line here. These decisions were tough.)

Ultimately, we got national recognition for best practices. On second thought, I should not say "we." My **staff** did all the work. Our system was, for instance, one of the leaders in housing for homeless Veterans. I led dedicated, passionate social workers who would do anything for their clients. Also at this time, the VA's National Suicide Hotline Center in Canandaigua, New York, was grossly understaffed. My staff did not have the time to go and volunteer there, as we had only recently reached full staffing, and I did not want to burn out any staff who already worked overtime. A message went out across the country asking for volunteers. So, I volunteered to go there myself.

It turned out that I was the only "chief" in the country to do so, and having an experienced social worker on the phones was greatly appreciated. For this reason, and with staff more playful and happier than in any other system in the country, I was recognized as one of the best Chiefs of Social Work. I was also approached by the National Office of Mental Health Operations to share my best practices and was sent to Minnesota for training and certification to inspect other VA Healthcare

Systems. I jumped at the opportunity! (More accurately, I was having an arthritis flare, so I limped.)

Our office was called the:

VA Office of Mental Health and Suicide Prevention

Our team reviewed several VA Healthcare Systems and provided suggestions to improve their mental health services. As a leader, you are likely to be familiar with inspections from regulatory agencies and other types of reviews—not usually a humorous situation! On the contrary, they typically are unpleasant and, more often than not, are very stressful for all involved. As you might have guessed, my approach to the inspections was quite different. I used my sense of humor to build rapport, to put those participating in the reviews at ease, and to help staff see that I was truly there to help and not simply to criticize them. The result was that these reviews seemed more enjoyable for all, and suggestions made were much more likely to be implemented.

My staff also had the freedom to work independently, rather than having to get permission from their chief to do their own jobs! An example, I met the leader of the local Housing and Urban Development (HUD) office and developed a "playful" relationship with him. My staff (not me) chose to escort Veterans to the HUD office to register for low-income housing. My staff would personally visit each Veteran wherever they were, whether under the bridge, in a homeless camp, in their car, etc. Veterans began to trust us more. We began to house more homeless Veterans than most healthcare systems in the country, because of the personal touch and involvement. Our Suicide Prevention Coordinator was remarkable; she watched and knew all the suicidal Veterans in her care. As a result, we had a lower rate of Veteran suicide than most.

Bottom line: After these experiences and having made a name for myself within the VA social work community and on national committees, I was actively recruited by the Phoenix VA Healthcare System. They knew I was working with best practices, and our Texas health care system had become the national spotlight for housing Veterans. Again, this was my staff's doing, not mine. I was truly blessed to have incredible and passionately devoted employees on the team. Eventually, the Phoenix VA made me an offer I could not refuse. (And to be transparent, my sons also wanted to go to the University of Arizona with only in-state tuition costs!)

This promotion came with higher pay and more responsibility. Looking back, I had no idea what I was getting into. It would become the most challenging leadership position of my life. Shortly after I arrived, I discovered how dysfunctional, disorganized, under-budgeted, and under-staffed the organization was, rife with unhappy employees and extremely high attrition rates, and with very little social work and mental health leadership in place. I could be more specific, but ... (I will stop here, as I am "walking the talk" of common sense!)

At this point in my (long) story, you might be wondering, "What does all this have to do with highly humorous leadership?" Well, I obviously took my sense of humor with me to this new position, and from the start, I began to use it. Humor gave me the courage to face crises and rough times. For instance, I was introduced to colleagues at our daily chief-only leadership meetings. The Medical Director said, "This is David Jacobson. He is our new Chief of Social Work. David, would you like to tell us a little about you?" I said, "Yes, but I would rather show you," and I unicycled around the board room. It did not cost me any professional credibility or respect. Quite the opposite…this open, light-hearted moment kind of brought us closer.

Establishing that your sense of humor is an *integral* part of your leadership style is important for all other leaders and superiors to know. The sooner you let it be known by all, the sooner you will have room to use humor and to worry less that it will be misinterpreted. Others will know where you are coming from—a place of humor, compassion, and caring rather than from a place of ego or indifference.

Back to the Phoenix VA: Within months of my arrival, our VA and I became the center of a national scandal. Whistle-blowers revealed that our scheduling department was 'hiding' Veterans on waiting lists. Why? Because it was mandated that patients be seen within a certain amount of time, and with such poor staffing, the mandate could not be met. The scope of this problem included mental health appointments that were my responsibility. The late Senator John McCain (himself a decorated Veteran), Senator Krysten Sinema, and on up to the President wanted to know (warning: incoming language ahead) what the *hell* was going on at the Phoenix VA! It later came to light that most VA systems in the country were struggling with this same issue, but that did not solve our problem.

Five months later, after our VA office was on the front page of major newspapers across the country, a news bulletin was released:

"Veterans Affairs secret waiting list"

According to reports by CNN in 2014, Veterans' hospitals across the country were delaying care of Veteran patients, at times to the point that some Veteran's conditions deteriorated vastly, or that they died due to the wait times. To cover for the long delays, some hospitals resorted to "secret lists" for patients awaiting care in order to keep their official wait times down. President Barack Obama launched a probe into the extent of that problem period. On May 15, 2014, he named Deputy White House Chief of Staff Rob Nabors to lead the probe. Following repeated calls for his resignation, US Secretary of Veterans Affairs Eric Shinseki stepped down on May 30, 2014.

At this point, let me be clear: humor is **not** appropriate in every situation. When the scandal first hit, it was a time of legitimate concern, damage control, and some unilateral decisions that I made as chief. For instance, I mandated cross-training so that more staff could help cover the emergency department and ensure 7-days-a-week/24-hour mental health coverage. I included *myself* in the mandate and helped cover shifts. My assistant chief did also (covering many more shifts than I did) and was my greatest support during this time. It was also my responsibility to address the authorities about our response. I began my presentation with the following slide and said, "Here's where we are with the fix as of today."

Golda Meir, Prime Minister of Israel from 1969 to 1974, said, "You can't shake hands with a closed fist." This little humorous picture opened the hands of those present. Breaking the tension put us in a state of mind to explore options and to think creatively. Funds and resources were provided to boost staff levels. The Obama administration made leadership changes at the top of the VHA system and congress provided additional funding. I went from a staff of 125 to nearly 200 within the next six months. I had playful relationships with all the local leaders of our Medicaid system, psychiatric hospitals, and our mental health organizations and centers, the city, county agencies, etc. After some time passed, and improvements were in place, we were able to decompress and to joke (a little bit) about the scandal. When visiting local leaders, I would sometimes carry a piece of paper in my pocket, pull it out, and say, "Hey, I found the secret list!" After the discovery that these long waiting lists were occurring across the country, the VA abandoned its 14-day wait time goal after deeming it was unrealistic with the resources available.

The effort to de-escalate stress paid off. I was given more autonomy and empowered to make changes quickly. One of the biggest changes I played a critical part in, was getting an agreement with Mercy Maricopa Integrated Care, the county's largest behavioral health system, to help with treatment of Veterans; some Vets were afraid to come to the VA after the media outlets told them that they would die if they received treatment at our centers. (In case you haven't been watching TV recently, let me explain that news outlets can sometimes focus more on sensationalism rather than facts.) The Mercy Maricopa agreement was a tremendous success and helped so many Veterans. It is still in place. I cannot say for sure that it was because of my sense of humor that the Mercy Maricopa protocol was completed so quickly, or that so much progress was made, but it did not hurt. On the contrary, using humor to help address all the corrections needed to improve services, made the whole process less painful for me, my staff, and everyone involved!

Link to full protocol

https://www.mercycareaz.org/assets/pdf/rbha-providers/rbha-forms/Collaborative%20Protocol%20with%20Phoenix%20VA%20Health%20Care%20System%20(PVAHCS)%20Scanned.pdf

mercy maricopa
integrated care

Collaborative Protocol with Phoenix VA Health Care System (PVAHCS)

Procedures to identify and address joint training needs
• As training needs arise, Mercy Maricopa will work with the Phoenix Veterans Health Care Administration to identify and develop trainings for Mercy Maricopa staff and providers as well as the Phoenix Veterans Health Care Administration. • Mercy Maricopa will invite the Phoenix Veterans Health Care Administration to participate in relevant online and in person trainings facilitated by the RBHA free of charge. • Both Mercy Maricopa and the Phoenix Veterans Health Care Administration will encourage and support family members as participants and co-facilitators of trainings.

This protocol outlines the joint commitments of both parties in our service to the community.

Eddy Broadway, Chief Executive Officer, Mercy Maricopa Integrated Care — Date 03-16-16

David Jacobson, LCSW Chief of Social Work Phoenix VA Health Care System — Date 3/16/16

Fast-forward (I said this was a long story!), the Veterans who knew me and my staff mostly loved us. Others, however, hated us after the news broke. Nurses and other staff were actually spit on by disgruntled patients while on their way to or from the hospital. And while there were honest whistleblowers, there were others who were about to be let go that jumped on thc whistleblower protection band wagon to try to save their jobs.

I was personally subject to an intense, expansive, and thorough investigation, which was conducted by the VA's Office of Inspector General. One result of the inquiry revealed that my action plan, the actions I had already taken and those I was in the process of taking made great strides in improving services provided to Veterans.

Since the problem was found to be nationwide, new outpatient scheduling policies and directives have been put in place with more realistic goals and expectations. New improvements continue. The most recent update was just completed this past June of 2022 with new changes to outpatient scheduling directive: VHA DIRECTIVE 1230.

On an organizational level, as a result of congressional funding provided after the scandal, our homeless Veteran program (previously understaffed and in disarray) became another best-practice example for the country. Our suicide prevention program doubled in size and also became one of the best. Our PTSD programs grew, doubling the number of Veterans who could be treated, thanks to the (playful) collaboration between myself and the psychologist in charge of the PTSD program.

Finally, our Homeless Standdown event, which provided donated material support and services to Veterans, became one of the largest in the country. In the following year, we helped more than 2,500 Veterans, many of whom came from out of state after hearing about these great, free resources! Best of all, despite the stress and negative stories in the media, the staff remained passionate and dedicated.

Okay, that was a lot of material! Time to get playful.

Practice Playshop

Part I: Diffusing anger

When facing an argument from a staff member, do you engage and argue back? Instead, try a humorous fantasy. For example, pretend they have a bowl of spaghetti on their head and see the sauce dripping down.

Practice:

Envision a recent difficult exchange, and see what visual images, music, sounds, or other thoughts pop up as a harmless and humorous response!

Part II: Diffusing unrealistic expectations

Unrealistic expectations can cause stress. For example:

Unrealistic expectation: My workdays should go the way I would want!

My inner response: I abdicated as king here at work, so I should expect some days are not going to go my way.

Practice:

Expectation: I must receive approval from my staff every day.

Your Response:

Expectation: I should be able to obtain the highest results in every project.

Your Response:

Expectation: I must not experience disagreements or conflict with others at work.

Your Response:

Humor helps us improve our level of leadership confidence. Despite the good that came out of our crisis at the VA, we were bombarded with Congressional inquiries, and I needed to spend more time responding to these inquiries than developing and expanding Veterans' programs. The confidence I formerly got from physical activities and achievements now came through leadership, as I began to use my sense of humor with my staff and colleagues. Even though the use of humor is ultimately for the benefit of staff (and not the leader), the confidence the leader might feel is a nice byproduct.

In general, humor helps us feel better about ourselves. In our first meeting, staff asked how my first week of management went. Words couldn't describe that week, as it was extremely difficult. So, instead of explaining all this verbally, I responded to the question by collapsing on the floor. Staff responded by chuckling. Not only did their response help **my** confidence, but it also boosted my self-esteem, because I knew that I made a boring meeting more fun. After that, the interactions in our office were usually playful.

The benefits of humor grow over time. Humor can increase meeting involvement by making the ambiance more relaxed, so that employees feel comfortable speaking up or asking questions. At work, humor helped change the culture in our department, especially changes related to preventing mistakes. As a leader you have an opportunity to model how to handle mistakes. Handle them with honesty and humor, and there's a good chance your staff may handle mistakes that way. Instead of hiding them or ignoring errors, we celebrated them as teachable moments! Instead of looking for excuses, the focus became, "How can I help prevent my coworkers from making the same mistake?" The staff member who made the biggest mistake was recognized with a silly prize. The team could then see mistakes as lessons that helped them quickly reach their goals. The result: of all hospital departments, ours received the highest scores on team audits from the state, from Medicare, from the Joint Commission (a healthcare accreditor), etc.

Humor helps you become more flexible. Without humor, we can become like a glass that shatters on impact. Humor can act as a pillow, so that when the glass lands, it lands *softly*. And as a leader you take responsibility for all issues and incidents in your department. That is a lot of stress to absorb. Let's add another image: think of yourself as a sponge and stress as water. When the water saturates the sponge, there comes a point where no more water (stress) can be absorbed. Humor is the hand that squeezes out some of the water (stress), so the leader can absorb more without feeling overwhelmed.

According to an old story about Albert Einstein (or another scientist—there are several versions of the story), a reporter at his lab office in Princeton, New Jersey, was surprised to see a large horseshoe hanging over the professor's doorway. "Professor Einstein," she asked, "you're a great scientist. Surely you don't believe a horseshoe will bring good luck." "Of course, I don't," he replied." Then why is the horseshoe up there?" the reporter pressed. Einstein said, "Because luck works whether you believe it or not." As illustrated by Einstein's replies, humor gets rid of the stress that often blocks us from seeing things from a different angle. In other sources, Albert Einstein is said to have directly attributed his brilliance to a child-like sense of humor. If you can change the way you think, you can change the way you feel, and humor is (in my book!) the best tool to help you change your thinking. It works whether you believe in it or not!

Reflecting for a moment on theory, in psychology and social work, changing one's perspective is called reframing. For example, you might ask how a *comedian* (perhaps Tina Fey, George Lopez, Groucho Marx, Trevor Noah, or Jerry Seinfeld) would see this situation. Seeing challenges from a unique perspective helps you regain self-control, which will also help to ease tension.

Social benefits

"A smile is a curve that sets everything straight."

Phyllis Diller

You cannot be angry and happy at the same time, can you? And humor can move you from a place of anger to a place of happiness. Here are some examples of the social benefits of humor:

- Humor can diffuse anger and decrease conflict and fighting: It is hard to argue when you are enjoying a good laugh with someone. When conflict and fighting threaten your relationship, humor can help ease the tension and playfully restore a sense of connection. Some lighthearted humor (used appropriately) can quickly turn a conflict into an opportunity for shared playful banter.
- Humor clears the air: It allows you to get your point across without hurting others' feelings. For example, I am retired, so I am now home almost all the time. My wife, Laurie, has told me numerous times that it drives her crazy that I have piles and piles of papers all over the place. Today, instead of complaining, she smiled and said to me, "You know, it's husbands like you who

turn wives into nags." I laughed and began to organize my papers for a change. Message received!

- Humor decreases fear: A 2011 Stanford University study called "Humor as emotion regulation: The differential consequences of negative versus positive humor" (conducted by Andrea C. Samson and James J. Gross) revealed that positive humor can decrease fear. (I was afraid to share this information, but since I used my sense of humor while writing, I was able to overcome that fear!)
- Humor makes group activities more fun: If you are bored of getting dragged into dull meetings, then become a change agent using humor! So many group activities use humor that I am not going to list them here. Think "Charades," for example, or simply do a quick internet search using the keywords "fun group activities."

On a more serious note, *our happiness and our health are contingent upon the quality of our relationships.* Our ability to see and appreciate humor and our ability to laugh easily builds rapport and binds people together, all without the use of ropes or duct tape!

Putting things into perspective

A leader who uses humor can address the most sensitive issues, such as poor work performance, communication issues, tardiness, hygiene, and even bad breath. I have used humor in all these areas and would give examples, but that would only make this book longer. (I am not trying for a Pulitzer here!) In fact, most situations are not as bleak as they appear when looked at from a playful and humorous point of view. Humor can help you reframe problems that might otherwise seem overwhelming and perhaps damage a relationship.

Lift your spirits!

In addition to physiological, psychological, and social benefits, humor benefits the human spirit. Or perhaps that should be "the humor spirit?" (I cannot prove that a humor spirit exists, but I love the idea that there is one.) I have found that laughter helps balance the mind, body, and spirit. Whether you believe you have a "humor spirit" or not does not really matter. It is more about how you *feel* after a hearty laugh, one that grounds you and helps you to feel more content.

Because laughter is a universal part of the human experience, it can even help decrease prejudice. Humor makes it so very clear that we have much more in common than we might think. We might say that laughter reveals connections. When laughing with someone else or in a group, you naturally feel more connected.

As we've seen, highly humorous leaders are sincere, and their colleagues *know* they are. How do they know? Because their leader has taken the time to get to know THEM. They have done this with sincerity and with humor. They ensure that some of the time they spend with their staff is **fun**! Staff know their leader does not have much free time, so they appreciate it and enjoy the fact that that it's not a time for criticism; rather, it's time for being playful, for acknowledging their importance to the leader and to the organization. What does this look like in practical terms? Perhaps…

- A celebratory lunch
- A drop-in visit (not baring your teeth, but with a heartfelt smile, please, leaders!)
- An acknowledgement or recognition of a job well-done
- Sharing a joke or coffee *for no reason at all*!

This next bit is important: These activities are not “canned and planned.” The biweekly rah-rah meeting, complete with PowerPoint slides, might be necessary, but compared with the other approaches we’ve reviewed, it lacks at least five key elements of effective humor:

- **The leader is not vulnerable.**
- **The leader is not spontaneous.**
- **The leader is not personable or supportive (meaning that he or she is doing little to boost the individual team member, or vice versa).**
- **The leader is not leaving room for input or a response from staff (aka the “audience response”) let alone a good laugh.**
- **And, perhaps most important (some fanfare here): *it is just not fun!* Not for the leader preparing slides or for those viewing them.**

Rather than these claustrophobic encounters, the highly humorous leader builds fun, playful memories over dozens of times throughout the year, all while enjoying every experience. To those he/she leads, some of these memories will be unforgettable.

Leaders who do not take time for fun are not using humor to the maximum to help build their relationships. I would even propose that they are building mediocre relationships at best. On the other hand, if you ask a highly humorous leader what one of their most outstanding employees is like (out of dozens and sometimes hundreds of staff), that leader will be able to describe the employee—in fact, the person as a whole—in detail.

Staff retention

Many mediocre leaders spend the least time with their outstanding staff, perhaps thinking that they are independent and productive, and do not need their guidance. Yet this is often far from true. Consider, instead, that these employees are the ones being recruited by other organizations, and that they may just go if you do not demonstrate you are serious about *their* development by … (Guesses? Anyone? Bueller?) *investing your time in them*! Your time is of great value, a reward, not to be spent only with unengaged employees already halfway out the door.

This principle applies to leaders no matter the number of staff. When I led forty staff, I made sure I knew my top twenty percent; and when I had 200 staff, I still knew my top twenty percent. Today, CEOs with thousands of staff have survey tools available to become more aware of their top performers' abilities, concerns, and interests. Especially in today's labor market, it is in your best interest to have fun and get to know your staff!

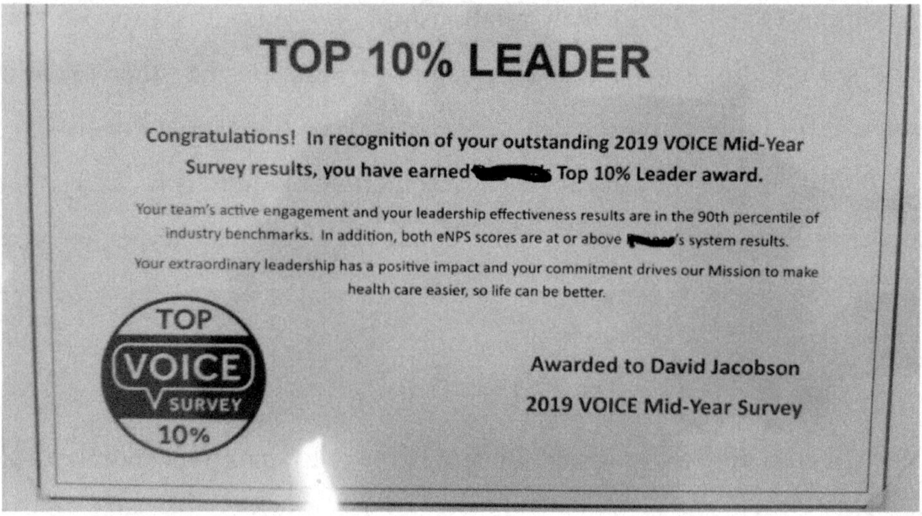

Does the highly humorous leader worry about staff loyalty? Yes, of course! They are highly humorous, so they are observant, attuned to everything around them. Asked if they are confident that they have the loyalty of their staff, without flinching, the leader's response can be, "Absolutely." If asked how they know, they can show you a dozen (or perhaps even hundreds) of emails, letters, phone messages, photos of the latest birthday party or company picnic, and notes of appreciation that all point to this truth.

Sincerity

A highly humorous leader can look anyone in the eye and with true sincerity say, "Thank you for your effort in fulfilling our purpose." And as great as I'd like my advice to be…you just cannot get sincerity out of a book! You must have it in your heart. No way to fake this, either; if you're putting on a "happy face" with other motives, your employees will smell it. (For any sensitive souls, I hope that came across as tactful!) Those with that same purpose will KNOW you do, and that is why they're willing to follow your direction to help manifest that purpose into reality.

When I was a new, young Master of Social Work, I was fighting the chronic pain of severe arthritis. This is not a crime, of course, but I wanted to use it as an excuse for being mediocre or just lazy at times. My boss, a highly humorous leader with both HIV and cerebral palsy, would call me out on being anything less than excellent. For example, if I arrived a little late:

> Me: I am having an arthritis flare and had to soak in the tub before coming in.
>
> Boss: You could have gotten up earlier and done that. I get up at five a.m. to take care of my extra health needs. That is no excuse!
>
> Me (so busted): You are right.
>
> Boss (smiling): Yes, I agree!

Same conversation with two mediocre leaders:

> Me: I am having an arthritis flare and had to soak in the tub before coming in.
>
> Mediocre boss: Oh, I completely understand. In fact, any time you need to come in a little late, I will understand.
>
> (Me, internal monologue: "Sah-weeet!")
>
> (Mediocre boss, internal monologue: "Why is he grinning?")

The first, highly humorous leader served as a role model for me and other followers. Because followers trust and respect this type of leader, they are more likely to emulate that person and internalize his or her ideals. Such leaders have an impact on their community as well. In Tucson, they named the Cerebral Palsy Foundation after my boss, and even changed its name to "The Easter Seal Blake Foundation." He was and is a great leader, but not the first I have met.

A true story

The first highly humorous leader in my life was my father. He was well-known as the City of Rochester's most decorated WWII Veteran. He was very charismatic, and many politicians wanted to befriend him in order to advance their careers. When he was fighting terminal stage-four cancer, the city held a dinner in his honor. The mayor gave him the Key to the City. The Chief of Police spoke at the dinner in his honor. My father, among other qualities, had two qualities a leader should strive for:

1. A good sense of humor, and
2. Charisma.

The two messages I got when I was growing up were, “You are great,” AND “You are a failure.” The "You are great" message came from my father before he died, when I was eight years old. All I heard growing up was how great my dad was, and how lucky I was to be a Jacobson, because, as they said, “That Jacobson family is great."

As you can probably guess, my father’s death at the VA’s Buffalo hospital was a great blow to the entire Jacobson clan, as my father was the center of it. It devastated my family. And I became a “behavioral problem” in school. (ADHD might have had something to do with it, but it was not commonly diagnosed in the mid-1960s. This was an era when children were routinely fed sugary cereals and then sent outside to burn off extra energy by climbing trees or tearing through the neighbors’ yards.) At one point our home even became violent; one of my siblings would choke me unconscious on occasion.

After I flunked third grade, one sibling would call me “failure.” I heard it all the time, but I also recalled something else. When I was called a failure, a loser, etc., I could *still* hear my father's voice in my head, saying, "You are great! You are a Jacobson!"

So, who was I? A failure to some and great to others. But who was I *to myself*? That is when I decided which message to take in. Your staff members have the same choice so make sure that hearing how great they are from you, their leader, is an option for them.

Moral of the story

Today, I wish for you to take the leadership message from my father, and now from me: **you *are* great!** Also, what you will do with your life cannot be measured or even fully expressed in words, and very few can do what *you* do. Finding your purpose, your message to share, can inspire others and have a significant impact on their lives. You can even help them on their own journey.

We've probably all heard the saying even the strongest chain is only as strong as its weakest link. Sometimes you must remove the weak link to make the chain that much stronger. Highly humorous leaders know how to do so *without generating unnecessary stress*. They first try to strengthen the weakest link, giving it every opportunity to become stronger. If that doesn't happen, they can help the "link" (the employee) to move on. If the highly humorous leader can help the employee to find joy, perspective, a reason to laugh, or permission to explore other options, that leader might also give him or her the boost needed to find greatness elsewhere. Sometimes that weak link will then get stronger; often it does not. But either way, the chain itself continues to strengthen.

My father had a vision for me, as all great leaders have a vision. They also choose the right message to listen to. If you find such a leader, cling to them. They will help you reach your potential. You, in return, will do the same for others. This is how leaders forge the continuing links of the strongest chain.

Humor requires intelligence

Although it can be hard to imagine a rodeo clown joining MENSA, the comprehension and invention of humor requires some cognitive abilities. A highly humorous leader must have at least the *minimum* of intelligence and common sense, not only intellectual intelligence, but emotional intelligence as well. The leader does not have to be a genius [although, in my experience, it didn't hurt! ☺]. They ***do*** need to know their subject matter, as well as their subject matter experts, and be smart enough to know if any of their experts are making big, irreparable mistakes. Ideally, your relationships with the team will reach a level where your experts will *tell* you if they have discovered any mistakes that they or any others might be making.

Let's be realistic: we know there are stupid leaders out there. You have probably dealt with one or more. And as the old saying goes, "Empty wagons make the most noise," so they are easy to spot. They often lack basic competence in their field, are clumsy in their use of humor, and tend to offend rather than to enlighten. As another old saying goes, "If you lie down with dogs, you get up with fleas." Although you would cling to the effective, highly humorous leader, avoid stupid leaders like … well … the plague, or COVID-19. Or, if you are a highly humorous employee, put some gas in your clown car and leave that three-ring circus!

Making humor your own

Leaders may use many styles of interpersonal humor. My Association for Applied and Therapeutic Humor (AATH) colleague, Professor Rod A. Martin, has narrowed it down to four (more information and links to the four styles are in the resource section, and Chapter Four is also devoted to exploring these styles). They are:

1. Affiliative
2. Self-enhancing
3. Self-defeating
4. Aggressive

Highly humorous leaders adopt the **affiliative** and **self-enhancing** styles of humor and engage in non-hostile joking behavior. They relate funny stories about themselves, aiding in relationship-building with their staff. Self-enhancing humor is a coping mechanism for reducing the impact of stressful events on both the leader and staff. In general, people who exhibit self-enhancing humor are not overly distressed by the experience of ambiguous life events, and as a result they maintain a positive perspective on life.

One of the most frequent questions I have gotten as a professional speaker and consultant on leadership is: how do you distinguish appropriate from inappropriate humor? Both affiliative and self-enhancing humor are appropriate and safe to use. The other two styles fall into the inappropriate category.

Aggressive humor involves "put-downs," and racist, ethnic, ageist, or sexist humor, as well as sarcasm, teasing, and mocking humorous expressions. This style of humor may insult and humiliate other people, increasing their anxiety and at the same time reducing their perception of well-being. And these are NOT the mark of a highly humorous leader. Instead, this is a sign that the individual in authority needs constant attention and reassurance, like a two-year-old. Needy leaders will *never* be able to transform themselves or an organization, and will likely choose to compete with, not to support, a productive employee. That is, until they become more self-aware and self-confident (rather than self-centered!).

The key to being a highly humorous leader is to know the difference between negative humor and positive. Ideally, a highly humorous leader is the same person at home or at work. And, of course, self-defeating humor has no place in the workplace or in the home; therefore, such leaders encourage family members, supporting them in their journey to become all that they can be.

Highly humorous leaders understand both control and resistance. While spending their time with staff they have more control, and their sincerity overcomes the resistance. A highly humorous leader uses humor to level the playing field, so staff do not feel intimidated by those higher up in the organization, but empowered to speak with them on the same level. Those who trust such a leader are not afraid to offer feedback or even criticism. Why? Because that criticism is just what a highly humorous leader would want to hear! They are secure enough to know that, overall, staff feedback will improve their leadership abilities, and they reinforce to staff that critical feedback is appreciated. And once again, sincerity is key. (An "open door policy" that is merely an excuse for gossip or a first-class ticket to the human resources department is NOT going to fool anyone!)

When you get feedback about how you are doing, reward the employee immediately for offering that gift, perhaps with a comment like, "I'm so grateful that you're not afraid to provide me with feedback! It helps me be a better leader," or better yet, demonstrate that you mean it. This is the perfect opportunity for humor, perhaps in an email about their idea for better productivity, or an impromptu coffee or lunch (your treat, leaders!).

Practice Playshop: Smile!

Many leaders feel that smiling will undermine their authority and they won't appear as strong. In fact, the opposite is true: we are naturally drawn to people who smile, and smiling helps you look more confident, not less. When you smile at your staff, staff tend to smile back. This helps to spread a more positive and trusting culture. Now:

- Think of something that makes you feel happy, or if alone, do something silly that makes you smile.
- Look at pictures of yourself when angry or tired, versus when having fun. Which version of you is more approachable?
- Draw a picture of an angry leader, and then of a smiling leader that you have personally worked with. (We're not talking Mona Lisa here—just a doodle would be fine.) Feel free to crumple and toss the former image and keep the latter where you can see it.

Practice this playshop alone or with others.

Conclusion

Humor is a core component of everyone's work and home life. It is present in daily activities and behaviors. Within the workplace context, leadership humor may result in both employee and employer benefits.

Leaders use their sense of humor to help improve the work environment, to help release employees' creativity, and to reinforce their innate capabilities. This type of leadership exerts a positive effect on employee's psychological safety to help them feel empowered to improve their own work environment. Using humor also reaffirms long-standing employees' trust in their leader.

Always keep in mind that every humorous interaction you have could possibly be offensive to someone. That said, make sure that the humor tool you use is also the *right* one for the situation. Review the affiliative and self-enhancing styles of humor, or try out the material with a trusted friend, just to be sure.

Bottom line: Use the appropriate tool for the job!

Chapter Two: The Half Habit of Highly Humorous Leaders

Mastering your thoughts

"The best way to deal with adversity is to find the humor hidden within it."

David Jacobson

(Yeah, that's me.)

I discussed this topic in my previous book *7 ½ Habits to Help you Become More Humorous, Happier & Healthier*. This next "half habit" may be the most important: you only need to do it half the time to enhance your ability to be an effective leader. I'm referring to the half habit of changing your perception of any given situation.

Since you started reading this book, you've probably been talking with yourself. "Hey, it's okay. Everyone does it. Everyone makes mistakes." (Or you might even be thinking right now, "Gee, I'm talking to myself.") Notice your thoughts. Don't let a common, detrimental thought rule your life, as in, "I suck as a leader." Rather, let this thought be replaced with a steady guide, such as: "I don't suck as a leader—and I enjoy chocolate!"

Think of the "future you," one year from now. Looking back, would you rather have ruminated on thousands of negative thoughts, perhaps mistakes you have made, mistakes that stressed you and your staff out and affected everyone's health, well-being, attitude, feelings, and behaviors? OR—would you rather have cut your negative thoughts in half (and ruminated on only 500 or so negative thoughts)?

As I said, this is the type of habit you don't need to do all of the time for it to be effective. Yet even this half habit can be quite a challenge. Why? Because the mind is very busy, perpetually. Even if we're physically lazy, our mind is churning out thoughts, perhaps negative ones about how lazy we are.

As a leader you will face one challenging situation after another. Would you like to find another way to deal with those challenging situations? All of us at one time or another thought that a situation we were in was bad, but then it turned out to be much better than we expected.

It is impossible to have only positive thoughts all the time. It's human nature to have unhealthy thoughts when we feel down. But if you can change just half of your detrimental thoughts, you'll be a better leader, happier, and healthier (and sexier—my wife said so!).

Practice Playshop: Choosing Our Thoughts

It might not be easy to just abruptly stop disturbing thoughts, so they must be replaced. We must consciously think about this at first. Undesirable self-talk statements (I hope you are suitably impressed by this use of jargon) make us feel sad or angry, and the result is increased stress and tension. Let's start right now playing with examples of how you can change a disturbing thought to one that feels better:

"My staff don't like me" can change to
"I'm hiring a new employee next week, so maybe there's still a chance," or "Hmmmm … staffing cuts … guess the lattes are on me!"

"My staff think I'm boring" can change to
"The staff who think I'm boring don't really know me, or is that just my spouse talking?"

When we notice our thoughts, we can switch them to something that feels better in every way!

When you awaken tomorrow, what kind of day will it be? It is your choice. Just as we dress based on the weather, we clothe ourselves with thoughts based on how we're feeling. If I'm feeling like I am not good enough or that I don't think I'll ever be a great leader, I can catch and change those thoughts to "I am not there yet, but I am well on my way."

Again, think of the "future you," this time at the pinnacle of your leadership career. Looking back, would you rather have ruminated on *even more* challenging matters that stressed you out, affected your health, well-being, attitude, feelings, and behaviors? Or would you rather have ruminated on only fifty percent of those issues? Or a quarter of them? (If this math problem stumped you, too, I'll let you borrow my calculator!)

A good beginning

Humor can make job candidates feel more at ease and decrease their stress levels by lightening the mood during interviews. This can also help the candidate understand what the work culture is like and show the interviewee how they might fit in. Let me illustrate. At this moment, I am going to give you an opportunity to respond to an executive interview question:

> "We here at Make Us Money Corporation pride ourselves on our ability to make money while smoking cigars and using our sense of humor. Can you think of a time when you were faced with a challenging situation and were able to use humor to turn it into

something beneficial?"

I suggest you really think about that. If you can produce an example, then you are on your way to becoming a highly humorous leader.

Tenderizing tough decisions

As a leader you are faced with challenges daily. How you view those challenges will determine how you address them. Using your sense of humor can help you become proactive and less reactive. How does this work? Through this equation:

Humor + Patience = Time

I often use my sense of humor to give me time to ponder a situation rather than react to it. For example:

> Staff: "David, there's a law enforcement officer downstairs who wants to serve a subpoena to one of our psychiatric patients. Should we let him?"
> Me: "Depends. Can he ride a unicycle?"
> Staff: "Do you want me to ask him?"
> Me: "Not really. Is the subpoena related to court-ordered treatment for his mental illness?"
> Staff: "No."
> Me: "Give me a minute to talk to his psychiatrist, who has the

final say. But for now, no, do not let him in to see the patient."

So unicycling had nothing to do with it, but a quip gave me a chance to get some distance, take a breath, and to really think about the purpose of the subpoena and whether this would be detrimental to the patient's treatment or not. (By the way, his psychiatrist backed me up on this, and we did not permit the subpoena to be served while the individual was an inpatient.)

As a leader, you need to be able to make hard decisions that are responsive, not reactive. Especially in healthcare, these sensitive or urgent matters happen daily. If you use your sense of humor, you will give yourself an opportunity to step back and not make a knee-jerk, bad decision. This does not mean you'll hold off indefinitely on hard decisions. A lack of decisiveness can negatively impact your team. Hard choices are also sometimes necessary without much time to reflect, such as in a true, life-threatening emergency. In those cases, use your sense of humor to step back, get some distance, and then make the best decision you can at the time, based on the available information.

And speaking of critical situations...

As leaders we are pulled in different directions. Our employers rarely give us a compass to help. Again, if you can change just half of your negative thoughts or dismiss half those crises and challenges from your ongoing thinking, you will be happier, healthier, and sexier. Okay, the first time my wife mentioned this; I just threw the "sexier" in again because sex sells books like it sells everything else.

But seriously, folks, sexual relationships do sometimes begin in the workplace. In fact, many people meet their future spouses on the job. Unfortunately, some of these relationships can be toxic. Despite the "Me Too" movement (and more long-standing attempts by women to advocate for themselves at work), sexual harassment laws, education, and training, sexual harassment is still common. Therefore, it is *critical* that you as a leader are approachable for any staff to discuss such matters.

To be clear, **there is no place at work for sexual harassment, and if leaders try to use humor to dodge responsibility, or to take personal, perverted advantage, then depending on the severity, they deserve to be fired, publicly mocked, or at least required to sit in a corner with a cone of shame on their head.** The "I was just joking" defense does not fly. In fact, it can't even limp.

From lemons to lemonade

I once had a patient who, at only eighteen years old, was on his way to a neo-Nazi camp in Kingman, Arizona. (That fact does not merit a punch line.) While on his way there from Louisiana, he had a motorcycle crash, resulting in a compound fracture of his leg. One of our physicians, Dr. Benjamin, operated, and the patient then needed to recuperate before being discharged. **(Note: The rest of this story contains an actual**

account of bigotry and includes ethnic slurs, so please feel free to skip to "Moral of the story," if you prefer.)

I introduced myself, saying, "Hi, I'm David." He then asked my last name. (Sorry to say, my dear reader, that his answer might not surprise you.) He said, "Oh, so not only my surgeon, but you're a f***ing Jew, too?" Taking a breath, I replied, "Well, I do have an intimate relationship with my wife."

He paused, thought for a moment, and chuckled a bit. Then he told me he was on his way to a skinhead camp, and asked if I still wanted to help him to get there. I said, "If that's where you want to go, I'll help you get there." That was the end of the conversation.

A physical therapist worked with the patient for the next five days. My job, as his social worker was to help him get the resources he needed and get back on his way. So, I told him I ordered a walker to take with him and arranged for a Greyhound bus to Kingman. The day before his discharge, the patient asked me to come see him. He told me he had been thinking about what he was always told about Jews, and that Dr. Benjamin and I were the first Jews he had ever actually met. He had seen for himself that we weren't who he had been taught that we were, so he had to rethink where he was going and why.

The patient then asked me if I could help him stay in Tucson; he didn't want to go to that camp, and instead, he appreciated me and Dr. Benjamin. I told him I could help him do that. Then I asked him what changed his mind. (Here comes the good stuff!) He said, "Both you and Dr. Benjamin made me laugh and helped to heal me." And he could not negate those facts, that we had treated him even though we both saw his Nazi tattoos and *had every right to decline helping him*.

Moral of the story

Now if you think I didn't judge him or even feel hatred, you're wrong. I did. But my highly humorous leader *made* me work with him! In fact, I had initially told my boss to reassign the patient to someone else, but he refused, and said, "David, you can work with him, and when he gets to know you, he'll know your intentions are good."

I offer two lessons from this experience:

1. My boss was right not to take me off this case.
2. My sense of humor was invaluable in changing the patient's mind.

My sense of humor turned this challenging situation into a more beneficial one for all involved. Through humor, I learned that one can decrease prejudice, and even become optimistic in the face of it. There is no guarantee that this will always work, but in this case, it did. These principles not only apply to work situations, but to our personal lives as well.

Turning the tables

Reader, do you believe someone can use humor to turn a situation for you? I once came home after a challenging day. I was having an arthritis flare up, was in pain, and just wanted to take a hot bath. My wife was in the bathroom and in front of the mirror, admiring herself. I asked her what she was doing, and she said she just had her annual appointment with her doctor, who told her she had the shape of a thirty-year-old. I said, “Oh, did she mention your fifty-year-old ass, too?” She stopped, looked at me, and without missing a beat, said, “No, your name never came up.” (I just love my wife!)

What does all this have to do with leadership? Whether in your personal life or at work, humor is a way to take a challenging conflict, look for humor in the situation, and diffuse it, sometimes even regaining the upper hand!

Another example: After the tragic Tucson shooting (when U.S. Representative Gabby Giffords and eighteen others were shot), part of my job was to organize all arriving family members of the survivors coming to the hospital, so they could get updated information on their loved ones from the trauma doctors. I did so, and I also brought many of the survivors’ family members to see their loved ones after their surgeries. I escorted one husband to meet his wife after her surgery, just as she was on her way back.

When she was wheeled into her hospital room, I introduced myself. "Hello, I'm David Jacobson, manager of the social work depart…" That's as far as I got before she said, "Oh, shut up, and let me rest." I turned to her husband and said, "Oh, her communications skills are very intact. That's a good sign." And he smiled and said, "Yes, that's how she talks to me, too. I think she's going to be okay." After the initial trauma had worn off (including my own!), I assisted them both in using their sense of humor as a coping skill.

To be clear, I'm not asking you to respond to numerous situations like this. In fact, that last one could be a challenge even for the most humorous leader! I'm only asking you for one. If you can address just one difficult situation, it means you are able to generate humor in many others. If you haven't yet, maybe it's time to try?

Facing Adversities

All leaders face adversarial situations. They help build our strength. Challenges are the steps we climb to reach higher levels of competency. In fact, I have a shoe box at home filled with more than forty letters of rejection from hiring managers. I kept those rejections because I knew that someday I would get a job in the social service field that I loved, and I would be able to show others those letters and say, "See, if you're determined and don't give up, things will be just great!" This is not some allegory or metaphor. This is a reality. (Full disclosure: I just looked up "allegory" in the Thesaurus, and it came back with "metaphor.") I still have those letters, but I did not let them stop me (as I've said many times now!).

This is not just a trite response on my part. Had I not been rejected from every application, I would not have applied for vocational rehabilitation. After reviewing my vocational rehabilitation application, my vocational rehabilitation counselor told me that due to the severity of my arthritis, I qualified for full vocational rehabilitation benefits. She asked me, "If you could be anything, what would you want to be?" I answered, "A social worker." Arizona's State vocational rehabilitation agency paid for me to go to graduate school for my master's in social work. (In return, I paid forty years of state taxes, so they got their money back and then some! Too bad programs like these were the first to be cut by subsequent administrations.)

The list of such experiences goes on. Had I not gotten arthritis, I would not have done my fifty-mile unicycle ride fundraiser for the Arthritis Foundation, thereby raising tons of money, and becoming an inspiration to children and young adults with the disease. My first standing ovation was when I spoke at an Arthritis Foundation National Hero Overcoming Arthritis event in Atlanta at their fiftieth anniversary celebration. That speech launched my professional speaking career and later inspired me to write my first book.

Had I not been involved in addressing the community's needs after the horrible Tucson shooting, I would not have learned to utilize my skills to help survivors and their families. I cannot emphasize enough the impact this tragedy had on those involved. No words suffice to describe the devastation. Working with the survivors, we had to focus on anything positive, and many were ultimately able to develop stronger coping skills.

Had I not worked at the Phoenix VA as Chief of Social Work, I would not have enhanced my therapeutic humor skills for trauma-informed care, which then gave me the ability to enhance my cognitive processing therapy with therapeutic humor to treat Veterans with PTSD. I've even had the opportunity to do "humor consults" for Veterans interested in humor as a coping skill. This work, in turn, resulted in a new, federally approved governmental Veterans Administration humor consultation referral process (though limited to just our VA Healthcare System as I was the only one who received humor consult referrals).

What do you see in your current role as leader? Will you look for the good in every challenging situation? Will you enhance your leadership style by using your sense of humor to change the way you are thinking, so you can change your feelings to a more positive state? As a leader, you are expected to manage your thoughts and emotions. Do you engage in this self-management of your thoughts? If not, are you ready to try? Do you now see the need? If perhaps your leadership survey scores could use improvement, have you considered how humor might help? Have you weighed the pros and cons? (And, critically, do you know how much they weigh? Do you have a scale, and is it digital, or the old needle one that you never really know if it is accurate or not?) You can use your humor scale to weigh your thoughts and ensure the balance skews toward the positive. I am optimistic that you can do so. Why? Because you are still here reading. The half habit of leadership can propel you to the next level.

If you are into video games (as of this printing of the book, are they still called video games?), one of the main reasons you play is to get to the next level. Hey, that is okay, because we all need to relax, and if games work, then more power to you. Yet these arbitrary game levels are meaningless as compared to the next level of leadership. Imagine if you took that same pleasure in improving your work as you do in your game! That is what humor can do for you! Imagine that you could help staff, the wonderful people you care so much about, to get to their next level, all because you used your sense of humor to help get them there. WOW! Put a value on that!

Here is the most important piece of wisdom I can offer: replace every "highly humorous leader" in every sentence in this book with the word "jerk." Not only will this make the reading more amusing, but it will quiet your ego, and help you see that, in some way, we are all jerks…that is, just regular people with human frailties who have the potential to influence others and to make the world a better place.

If you haven't seen the classic film called *It's a Wonderful Life,* I suggest you watch it to get an idea of how much difference one person can make. I genuinely believe that you have the power and opportunity to change your corner of the world (even though, technically, the world is round and doesn't have corners). You do not need to know how you've changed it. Instead, just be in love with the idea that the world is better because you treaded—or in my case limped—on it!

Cognitive Processing Therapy (CPT): using humor to heal

At this point, I hope you are excited enough about the change process to tackle some theory. (Again, anyone? Anyone? Bueller?) CPT was developed by Patricia Resick in the early 1990s. It combines cognitive therapy and trauma processing (additional information is presented in the resources section). Conducted via individual or group therapy, CPT is often completed in twelve weekly sessions. Cognitive therapy helps individuals to "understand how certain thoughts about your trauma cause your stress and make your symptoms worse" (www.VA.gov/PTSD, 2009). It also helps to identify negative thoughts, replace them, and cope with the upsetting feelings.

As discussed earlier, positive thinking and many other components of highly humorous leadership can be done as half habits. The importance of the half habit—of changing your thoughts to change your view by using your sense of humor—cannot be over emphasized. In Cognitive Processing Therapy (CPT), they call these thoughts that prevent us from knowing reality "stuck points." For example, you might get stuck on the idea that "If I let anyone get close to me, I will get hurt," or "I can never trust my judgment." These are global statements, and we must peel back the layers of that onion. Humor is one tool to help. (A good paring knife is also handy for literally peeling vegetables. Not so hot for metaphors.)

Combining my knowledge of therapeutic humor with my knowledge of CPT, I was able to enhance my therapy work with Veterans. I recall one therapy group for combat Veterans. The goal of the group was to learn to better cope with the symptoms of PTSD. In the first session, I asked them all to introduce themselves and to share something, like the name of a favorite pet, how many children or grandchildren they had, their favorite food or hobby, etc. As we went around the room, the Veterans became more relaxed and seemed to like getting to know each other, until one statement caused an awkward moment.

A Veteran said, "Hi, my name is John, and I saw my best buddy have his legs blown off right in front of me."

The group became silent. After a few distressing moments, I said "Well, I was hoping you'd share something a little more traumatic or personal about yourself." The group, including John, began to laugh, and the uncomfortable moment dissipated. I followed with, "John, I appreciate that you shared this life experience with us, and over the next twelve weeks, we'll be delving deeper into how all of us can better cope with our traumatic experiences."

Back to half habits and stuck places. Are the rules you have made to live by based on facts, and are they true? Let's take our earlier example, "If I let anyone get close to me, I will get hurt." Trust, in fact, exists on a continuum. The levels vary. And when we make global statements, we discount the facts of what we can trust, or how much we can trust. How much can you trust your friends? You may have a friend whom you could not trust with your money, or your sister, or your wife, but could trust them to guard your physical safety.

Or instead of facts, are your thoughts based on unusual or traumatic events? For example, "If I go to the store, how do I know that the person behind me will not smash me in back of my head?" While doing CPT, I worked with one Veteran who was traumatized by being struck in back of his head with a bat (or similar object). He said he could never enter a retail store again, because he could not let anyone stand behind him and perchance attack him. It was about our third session, and I suggested he walk into a store, and while in the store, turn to the person behind him and ask, "Are you going to smash me in the back of my head?"

Perhaps this sounds absurd, but that was his fear, so he did just that. He went into a store for the first time in years. He then took the courageous risk and turned to the person behind him and thought of asking that question in his head. At that point, he could not help but smile at the absurdity, and after he smiled, they started a conversation and had a good interaction. At that moment, his greatest fear turned into a positive encounter with a stranger. As silly as it was, it helped him open a dialogue and overcome one of his greatest fears because he saw the humor in the situation. He was able to intentionally change the way he thought so he could change the way he felt.

Leaders need to do that daily. They can never acquiesce to their own assumptions. As previously mentioned, humor helps you respond rather than react. By using the half habit to change your thoughts on the situation, you can get some distance so you can respond appropriately.

Here is a challenging question: As a leader, are you psychic? Can you prevent every bad thing from happening? If I believe that "I failed to prevent my staff member from getting injured by that patient," is that based in fact, or merely a conclusion, idea, or thought I am telling myself? Consider:

> Fact: My staff member was assaulted on the unit by a delusional patient.
>
> My thought: If I knew it was going to happen, I could have prevented it.

Factually, there was nothing I could have done to prevent this occurrence. My staff know that, too, and they know I genuinely care about them and felt horrible that this happened. So, this is an erroneous conclusion, not based in reality.

Time to pause.

- Can you think of any situations at work where you used or could have used the half habit to change your perspective?
- What situation is bothering you at work right now?
- Can you try the half habit this week at work?

Here's a simple guideline for knowing if/when to act. Leaders understand that if they can't let it go within a reasonable timeframe (say a half hour), that situation has now become—rightly or wrongly—their problem, and in order to move forward, the leader will probably need to directly address it. In that process, the half habit of changing your thoughts is a great way to determine if it is your problem and not someone else's. One leadership motto of mine is, "Poor planning on your (staff member's) part does not make a crisis on my part." If you as leader *make* it your crisis, then your staff will not learn how to cope for themselves.

Practice Playshop: Empowering Staff through Humor

You can help your staff practice the half habit by modeling (not yodeling, though—that would be distracting) the use of humor to change the way they think, so they can change the way they feel. Help them become aware of:

- Thinking in all-or-nothing terms: "Either I take on the requested project or I refuse."
- Confusing a habit with a fact? Habit: "I always say yes and then get in over my head." Fact: "I have alternatives. I could say no, or maybe, I could jump up and down and have a tantrum while saying no! Perhaps I could do the project jointly with a colleague." (That last one might be a realistic option.)
- Inaccurate interpretations of the situation: "That coworker of mine looked at me funny. He must hate me." Ask your troubled staff member: "What is the evidence for and against this idea?" The humorous side: "Maybe your coworker's face looked like that because he was trying not to pass gas."

You'll know if your use of humor is helping if the attitude of your staff improves!

Addressing trauma on the job

One of the most traumatic experiences anyone can experience is a physical assault, and lately, healthcare workers have experienced an elevated risk. Because these situations in themselves are **not** funny, I will not make a joke (appropriate use of humor, right?). Instead, I refer the reader to documented accounts of emergency medical staff and ER nurses and physicians in particular, who put themselves in harm's way to provide care during the pandemic. As a leader, it's important to know what resources are available to help staff deal with the physical or psychological impacts.

Where does the humor come into play? As the leader you can recognize the assaulted staff member by awarding them a Purple Heart medal. As the leader you must also help your staff come to terms with their fears and create a perspective that helps them carry on the duties they are so passionate about. And please, leave psychotherapy to professionals outside the workplace! Instead, *after* the acute effects of stress have passed (for example, the staff member reports not eating or sleeping, or needs to take personal leave), swing into humorous action!

When and if the staff person seems open to it, help them to put their experience into perspective, and into the past. "Okay, you got assaulted and joined the 'we got assaulted' club, a very exclusive group of staff passionate about their jobs, who share amazing stories about extreme situations." You can give them a "hit me" sign to tape to their back, etc.

What about presenting them with a cardboard shield? Consider what the individual (as a highly humorous leader, you've already gotten to know the individual, right?) might enjoy, their personal comfort level. This acknowledges what happened but also lets them move forward to continue doing what they love.

Fun fact: *M.A.S.H.* was one of the longest-running sitcoms on television and is still in syndication. Could it be because the doctors and nurses on the show used humor *while on the front lines*? Equipped with your sense of humor, and helping your staff equip themselves, you can also support your unit, as they continue to carry out their mission with a smile, and to overcome fears that could otherwise have stopped them in their tracks.

In conclusion (well, to this section, anyway)

There's more to this chapter, but readers like it when I conclude!

We each have at least 60,00 thousand thoughts a day, and although emotions should not be categorized as negative or positive (because all emotions are real to the individual and not meant to be labeled or packaged for others), some emotions are health-enhancing and others diminish those health-enhancing factors. Things like lower blood pressure, healthier heart rate, and improved respiration are physiological benefits of laughter. Increasing the positive thoughts and decreasing the negative makes us twice as healthy and twice as happy.

You might think, "But if I use more humor, then I might be seen as not serious about my job." What is the evidence for and against this idea? This book you're reading is providing you with evidence that the *opposite* is true. We have choices about how to face leadership challenges, just as we have choices on how to face anything else, like surgery:

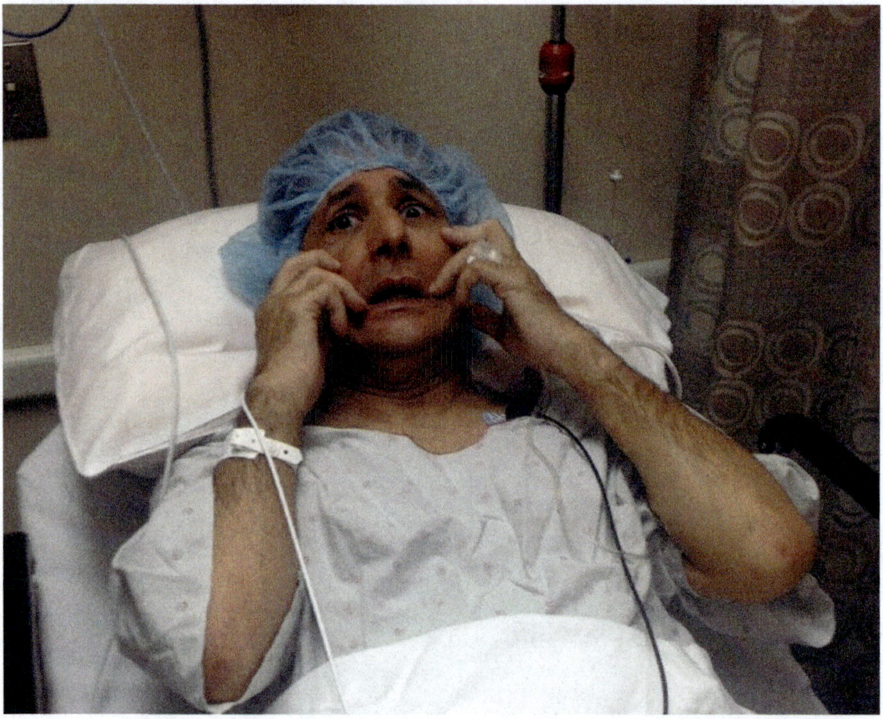

What is your leadership style under extreme stress? Would you like to be able to handle that stress even better? Remember that your staff watch you. You are their role model. Your staff will adopt the model you portray. They can see the reflection of your attitude in the actions that you take. If they see a humorous attitude, it puts them at ease. It restores confidence. If they see you worried and stressed, it will increase their own worry and stress. Now that you've been reading this book for a while (wow, you are tough!), you are learning the power of creating *hope through humor*. Like this:

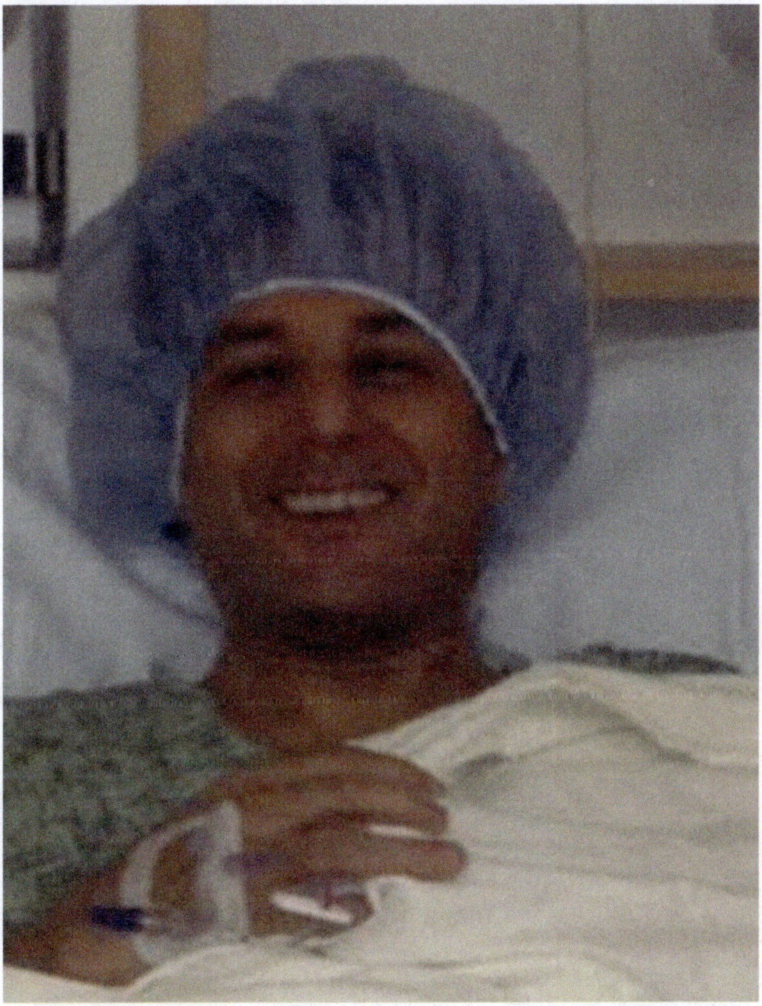

(Thanks goes to my wife Laurie for taking both pictures.)

I was still nervous in this second picture, but the smile alleviated some of the anxiety and helped me to practice what I preach!

Humorous fantasies are our friends!

Humorous fantasies can also help change your thoughts from negative to positive, helping you to master this half habit. For example, I was under pressure and stressed out and had to inform staff that our whole electronic health record system was changing to a software system that (of course) they were going to have to learn to use, after *years* of using a system they were comfortable with. Rumors about the change were flying and needed to be addressed, and I sensed this was not going to be a pleasant meeting. On the way, I took the elevator, which was empty. This rarely happens in the hustle and bustle of the hospital. I was the only one in there, so I celebrated! I jumped up and down and danced, singing out loud, “Hurray, the elevator’s empty!”

When the doors opened, I had a big smile on my face, truly feeling the spirit of humor. When I walked into the meeting room, I was glowing with happiness—not pasting on a phony smile but authentically happy. This affected all those in the room. No, my joy did not change the fact that our health record system was changing, but it did help to elevate the mood, so we could discuss the change from a place of confidence rather than fear.

The elevator dance is an example of indulging a type of humorous fantasy. Leaders can use these fantasies to keep their own fears and concerns under control and not to freak out staff by exhibiting worry. But now I wonder … was there a security camera in the elevator? I should have asked for the tape in case I need another mood boost!

Anger is natural. We all experience it. Someone once said that it's just our body's way of alerting us that a boundary has been crossed. At work, though, a leader openly expressing their anger (raising their voice, appearing agitated, etc.) or passive-aggressively leaking their anger (nasty-grams, unreasonable work requests, blaming) is *very* threatening to staff. (Because they kind of need the paychecks, right?) Hostile thoughts also lead to physiological arousal (the fight or flight syndrome) and could result in inappropriate behaviors *by you* as a leader.

Responding with humor when others expect anger is the most powerful response a leader can model.

This doesn't mean laughing in someone's face, but rather responding with a humorous diffusion of the situation. And humorous fantasies can be used to decrease the anger and also to diffuse conflicts.

As an example, several years ago, I was invited to give a guest sermon at a Universalist Unitarian Church on the subject of "humor and spirituality." (That was a "transitional sentence." I hope you liked it!) The church was on the other side of the city, and I was running late. On my way there, I was driving, stressed out in traffic, and watching the time, when a guy cut in my lane directly in front of me, so that his back bumper barely missed my front bumper. We were heading for the stop light, and I was furious! I couldn't wait to pull up next to him, so I could give him "the look" (the equivalent of "flipping the bird," except with a facial expression instead—classy).

Then, as I approached the stop light, I thought about where I was going. I decided a different tactic would be more in line with my sermon and my purpose in life. So, when we reached the light, I put my disabled placard on the mirror, pulled my arms out of my sleeves and tucked them in my shirt, and bit the steering wheel with my teeth.

The other driver turned to see me, the person he just cut off in traffic. His eyes grew wide as I slightly turned toward him, grinned at him with my teeth still holding the steering wheel, and nodded my head. He had a shocked look and appeared to feel awful for cutting off "the poor, pathetic armless guy." But I wasn't mad anymore, and he wasn't either. Instead, because I was able to come up with this humorous fantasy, a potentially explosive situation turned into a milder and much more humorous situation that was totally non-threatening to both parties. Makes a better story, don't you think?

Practice Playshop: Practicing the Half Habit

Detrimental thoughts could be limiting you or your staff. The half habit will help you find another, more positive way to see the situation. Think of some silly, humorous fantasies of your own that you can use to gain perspective, elevate your mood, take a fresh look at the issue, and model your positive outlook.

Here are two examples:

1. "I know the best way to do things, because I am older and have more experience than my staff." Those with this attitude can change it to "Maybe my staff know a better way to accomplish their task than I do. Besides if I make them do it my way, they might fail and think I'm a jerk."
2. "I do not like when my staff criticize me." Switch to "If I take their feedback to heart, instead of falling on the floor and crying, they will know I truly listen to them. If I handle it more lightheartedly, I'll receive more feedback to make me better at my job."

Now pick one of the thoughts below and come up with a more positive way of looking at it:

- **"I may fail if I try my staff's suggestion."**
- **"I'm not really good enough for my leadership position."**

- **"My communication skills are not good enough to lead my staff."**

If you are fanatical about making this work for you, you could even write out responses to all the negative thoughts above and the humorous, alternate thoughts. If not, just do one or two in your head—and don't turn that into a negative thought, like "Oh, duh, gee, I guess I'm not that serious about using humor as a leader because I don't feel like writing it down. "

Chapter Three: Humor in Daily Communication

"Inform all the troops that communications have completely broken down."

Ashleigh Brilliant

How often do you use humor intentionally at work? Many companies are known for their use of humor with their customers. Southwest Airlines, for instance, has been repeatedly acknowledged for their successful implementation of humor in daily work activities. Their preflight announcements, for example, are more closely attended to due to the often-hilarious way they present instructions.

So back to my original question: how often do you use humor? Monthly? Weekly? Daily? When I used my sense of humor daily it helped to change the culture of all my departments for the better. How did I do it? Through emails, meetings, encounters, instant messages, door signs, posters, videos, and weekly Monday Messages; through song lyrics, nursery rhymes, and customized poems to staff members; and through routine face-to-face interactions.

You don’t have to churn out lots of memos, though. Simply pay attention to the nature and the tone of your emails to staff. Do you only email staff when there is a problem? How often do you compliment them? How often do you reach out just to put a smile on their faces?

While you ponder those deep, deep questions, let me bring you back to the very first time I can recall using humor to cope. I was in the fourth grade. Due to my ADHD, after about an hour in class, I would be bouncing off the walls. This was not by choice. I simply could not stay still. Lucky for me, my teacher had a good sense of humor and balanced it with her responsibilities for keeping the class under control. A usual punishment for disrupting the class was to have to sit in the clothes closet where we hung our winter coats (that was just the way we did things, folks!), which was located on the inside wall of the classroom, with doors that pulled down like window shades.

On one occasion when I was disruptive, and in the closet, I quickly became bored. I slowly closed the closet door while the teacher was talking, so that no one was aware of what I had done. Once the door was closed, I climbed into my winter coat, put my arms in the sleeves, and then got stuck in the coat and dangled helplessly on the coat hook. The teacher finally noticed the closed door and said, “David, come out of there!” I yelled, “I can’t. I’m stuck!”

The teacher came over, opened the closet, and the whole class saw me dangling in my coat, arms flailing. Everyone cracked up, including the teacher. At that moment, I had found my calling. The laughter was a great reward for my efforts, and although I accidentally tumbled into the situation, it became the first lesson in intentionally using humor to influence others.

This is a simple, significant lesson that a leader can take to heart. Use your sense of humor to endear yourself to others, to lift their spirits, and to move them closer to a place of happiness, and you will have a loyal following. Treat humor as a necessity, and the habit of using your sense of humor daily will grow stronger and stronger, until you reach the point of becoming your own Hercules of Humor.

One of the biggest myths about humor is that you must be "naturally funny" to use humor. Not true. I am not primarily a comedian or joke-teller. I am much more of a humorist, an observer of human activity, but through the years I have learned not only to identify humorous situations, but to share my observations with others. If a leader can do that, then they can master the art of seeing the world through humor-filtered glasses.

Another fun example: The year after my "great awakening," I was in the fifth grade and had a wonderful, understanding teacher (thank you, Ms. Jordan at Martin B. Anderson School, # 1 in Rochester, New York). She made a deal with me, that if I could stay in my seat and sit most of the day without disrupting others (she permitted me to get up and walk around the room when I really needed to), then for the last ten minutes of the day I could do my stand-up for the class. She would put a slide show on the wall, and I would be allowed to comment on the pictures.

Little David's Editorial Humor

Picture of a St. Bernard dog: "Hi, I'm Big Bertha, the Drooling Dog. Can I slobber on your face?"

Picture of a pig: "I'm into tie dying, vegetarian food, and cooked broccoli. Call me."

Picture of a farmer in the wheat: "Oh, she's outstanding in her field, so we gave her a desk." And so on. Get the picture? (Ha, ha.)

Like my amazing teacher, leaders find ways to channel disruptive behavior into creativity. I once supervised a manager who simply did not have the skill set to manage. He wasn't a bad person; he just was not ready yet. I had him come in for a talk. He knew he was screwing up, and his first question was, "Are you going to fire me?" I said, "No, I think we can find something you love to do that is not your current job." This lowered his stress level, and we started to humorously banter about different jobs. I asked him what he liked to do, thinking that if he liked to cook, perhaps he could be the designated department chef. He said maybe he could be the designated department therapist for all our staff.

This led us to a very lively discussion about therapy. He said he loved doing therapy more than any other position he ever had. We decided that he would take a shot at being a therapist at one of our clinics not far from his home. The trial period went well, and he *thrived* in his new position. So, instead of firing him and letting all his knowledge and experience (and the time-consuming process of hiring and training a new employee) go to waste, through humor, we found a niche for him that turned into a real win-win.

Back in college I volunteered to do a year of national service. As an example of an early leadership experience, in mid-January 1978, I was selected from all the students in the University Year for Action program (a part of Volunteers in Service to America, or VISTA) in Monroe County, New York, to represent all students in the program. The Council consisted of all the CEOs of the local social service agencies. At this first meeting that I attended, the tensions were high. The United Way had just released their contributions for the year to each of these agencies; some were big winners, and some were losers. Before the start of the meeting, I had heard some of the CEO's grumble to each other about how their agencies had not received much of an allocation.

Then the meeting began, and it was time for me to introduce myself to the CEOs. I gave my name and the agency of my placement (New York State Division for Youth), and I ended by saying that I personally had not received one dime from the United Way! This broke the tension over funding, and all attendees started laughing. Afterwards, some said hello and told me they were glad I was the student representative, and they could see why I was chosen. This was my very first encounter with a leadership board *per se* (yet another impressive phrase, meaning "as such" or "I said that specific thing on purpose"), and I was already learning the power of humor to enhance interactions with others!

Modes of communication: Instant Messaging (IM)

Every leader needs a source of support. My old boss was one of mine. I was lucky to have a boss who had a great sense of humor and supported mine, often through instant chat messages that took only a few seconds to send.

> IM - Me: "Tell me a joke."
> IM – Boss: "I'm really busy right now. I'll get back to you later."
> IM – Me: "That's hysterical—tell me another!"

Now, I would not use such a response with any of my colleagues or staff (only those above me). Remember the adage "Complain up, support down." Actually, I do not know if that's an adage. "Fish and visitors stink after three days" is, but that one, as my editor might say, is "outside the scope of this book."

Modes of communication: Door signs

One of the managers I supervised had an office directly across the hall from me. She put the following sign on her door:

Seeing that, I felt compelled to put up a sign of my own:

Practice Playshop: Door Signs

Think of some humorous messages you might put on your door (the front or the back) or on your desk.

Modes of communication: Email

Every week, I used to send a "Monday Message," an inspirational, humorous, or motivational email just for my staff. They looked forward to these, and I usually received positive comments. In fact, if I missed a week, I often got an email asking where the message was. The following are some examples from various leadership positions I have held. Please feel free to use them, if appropriate, with your staff. Some might not be appropriate for your current work culture, so be cautious or test the waters before deciding which ones to use.

Over time, I also learned to shorten these messages, so I edited them here to keep them briefer. Here's one of my earlier ones from back in the 1990s:

From: Hospital Manager of the Social Work Department
Subject: The Social Work Profession

> We are social workers by profession, other things by choice. Did we really choose social work, or did it choose us?

For all of us, that path has steered us toward helping our patient population. We seek to make a difference; to enable others to move out of poverty, despair, hopelessness into some level of economic stability; or to gain hope and a sense of personal fulfillment. Yet when we look at all these areas, there are serious challenges to the practice of social work. We now have even fewer resources to meet our patient's needs. (It can become aggravating, though, and makes you wonder: "Why didn't I just go into a profession where people actually make money?")

I am also quite aware that many of you will be faced with burnout. It is an inherent part of our profession. Over the past two years, you've expressed this with me, sometimes feeling like, "Why bother? No matter what I do, nothing seems to change. I cannot move the entire system forward."

So now, to address the burnout, *you must take some time off.* Take that vacation. Do not feel that you cannot leave because if you do the building will collapse. Guess what? When you come back, that building is still going to be there. (In fact, depending on how much vacation time you've saved, there may even be a new one!)

Or take a day off. Get a new hobby. Start exercising or learning about nutrition. Re-energize yourself!

I remain hopeful that we can overcome discouragement, because there have been times—far more difficult—that our parents, our grandparents, and others experienced. Yet they came through it all, even though they often had even fewer resources than we do today.

So (just this once!) please, do as I say, and find ways to connect with your peers. Do not decline those lunch offers (unless the person is someone you just can't stand, or the cafeteria is serving meatloaf again) and start inviting others to join you! And know that others like me appreciate your work, support you, and are proud of all that you do for our patients.

Have a great week!

Here are a few more to consider:

From: Hospital Manager of the Social Work Department
Subject: Conference Session

I just returned from a board meeting of the Association of Applied and Therapeutic Humor. Now, with a name like that, you wouldn't think the participants would have any worries or challenges. Not true.

Our facilitator, Carol Weisman, had us take a moment to reflect and write down five problems that each of us were facing. Then she asked us to fold the papers and place them in a basket she was passing around. She mixed them up and then passed the basket around again, this time instructing us to remove a paper from the basket and quietly read it.

Finally, she asked if anyone in the room would exchange their own problems for those listed on the paper they had drawn. No one did, because no one felt that their problems were worse than the ones experienced by the author of the list they had selected.

I'm going to take that experience with me this week.

To: All Staff
Subject: Behavioral Health Director's Monday Message

Have you ever wondered why, a lot of times, you just cannot seem to make progress in life despite the fact that you know so much about what it takes to succeed? There just seems to be a gap between what you know and what you do. You may think of this space in between as the Twilight Zone, but it is actually the "gap between knowledge and action." (For more information, you might even check out *The Bulletin of the World Health Organization*, 2006;84:603-607, the article entitled "Bridging the gap between knowledge and action for health: case studies" by Visanu Thamlikitkul.)

Sometimes what holds us back is fear of looking foolish. (Even the person who said, "Today is the tomorrow you worried about yesterday" may have been afraid to be quoted, because it was attributed to "Anonymous.") In order to counteract this tendency, find ways to deal with fears you are aware of. Knowing the origins of your fears is useful.

Next, practice overcoming fear. Even silly little things can help you feel more confident. On Friday, I was at a festival in a park, and a band was playing some great music. The crowd was listening, but no one danced. Without planning to, I jumped up and danced and really enjoyed the music. When the song ended several people clapped for me. If I had feared looking foolish, I would have lost out on a fun-filled memory of my (baffled, but amused) thirteen-year-old son watching his father (and perhaps wondering why I had to be *his* father). In the end, dancing turned into a lesson on role modeling and coaching, presenting an example of taking a risk and seizing an opportunity in the moment.

Here is a link to a two-minute video of Mo Cheeks, an American professional basketball coach, helping a girl sing the national anthem. He offers an immensely powerful lesson on coaching/helping another in need: https://www.youtube.com/watch?v=ZXnT84Eu-oA&t=7s

Let us continue this week to be there when the moment of need arises.

From: Chief of Social Work
Subject: Some only you can reach

You may have heard the story of the Cherokee grandfather teaching his grandson about life. "A fight is going on inside me," he said to the boy. "It is a terrible fight, and it is between two wolves. One is evil; he is anger, envy, sorrow, regret, greed, arrogance, self-pity, guilt, resentment, inferiority, lies, false pride, superiority, and ego."

He continued, "The other is good; he is joy, peace, love, hope, serenity, humility, kindness, benevolence, empathy, generosity, truth, compassion, and faith. This same fight is going on inside you, and inside every other person, too."

The grandson thought about it for a minute and then asked his grandfather, "Which wolf will win?"

The old Cherokee simply replied, “The one you feed.”

At this very moment, there are Veterans that only you can reach, and differences in their lives that only you can make. The work you do is very special, perhaps even sacred, and should be approached with that concept in mind. So today, while going about your daily tasks, take a moment to reflect and recall why you are here, doing what you are doing. Ask yourself if what you are doing is enriching your life. If so, I’m guessing you are feeding the right wolf.

> *“It is one of the most beautiful compensations of this life that you cannot sincerely try to help another without helping yourself.”*
>
> *Ralph Waldo Emerson (“Where’s Waldo” Emerson to his friends)*

To: Social Work Department
From: VA Chief of Social Work

Social work, much like nursing, is a nurturing profession, and as such was first associated with women more so than with men. In fact, most of the founders of the professional and the inspirational social workers of our time have been women, although today men also hold such positions. And our work today still deals with the “messiness” of life and emotions. The psychosocial situations we face can be overwhelmingly complex with no simple solution, and sometimes so bizarre that truth becomes stranger than fiction Yet social workers often do their best work in situations of uncertainty and precariousness. For me it comes down to using two tools:

1. Maintaining my sense of humor, the source of my positive perspective.
2. Using gentle kindness.

Compassion is what often unravels the overwhelming, complex problems that people find themselves in, and in most cases, it even lights the way to their own solutions. Very often, this does not take long. Sometimes within minutes, a solution arises, or at the very least, the realization that their situations could be different or perhaps even *better*. But without you, that realization may never come.

As we move closer to Social Work Month, acknowledge to yourself that because of what you do, day in and day out, the world is a better place. Give yourself a pat on the back for being part of the solution, rather than the problem.

Thank you for serving our Veterans and making the world a better place *for them*!

From: Chief of Social Work

Subject: Checking the Tires

This story starts on the weekend. My wife looked at my front tire and said it didn't look good, and that I should take it in and replace it. I was on my way to McAllen this morning, to work on our "decrease waiting lines" project, when the tire blew as I drove on Highway 83. I called AAA, they got the spare on, and I was quickly on my way, but all I could think was "Why didn't I take the time to replace it over the weekend? Why did I risk an accident to 'save' an hour of my time?"

Laurie's caution should have been all it took to bring my awareness back to the moment and what was needed to remedy the situation. For you today, it may not be a tire, but your health, nutrition, a relationship, or self-growth calling for your attention. On this hectic Monday, take the time you need to assess your priorities for this week. Don't wait for a senseless "blow out" before taking care of a matter that may seem trivial, but with a little thought, could be addressed to prevent a larger problem.

And as always, have a great week!

At this point, reader, you might be wondering how these messages were received. Were they helpful and appreciated, or just one more email message needing to be read? Here is one example of a response from staff:

From: Staff Member

Subject: RE: Monday's Message

Chief,

I want to thank you for having started the "Monday's Message." Every time I read them, I tell myself, "Please respond and tell him how you feel about it," but then I get busy and forget. Well, today I will make time to tell you: Thank you!

I look forward to reading them. They bring me laughter, motivation, and blessing, but most importantly, a sense of being appreciated. I value the time you take every Monday to send us the message; it has sort of become one of my meals to chew for my week. Keep them coming.

Respectfully,

M.T.

Finally, here's a message I sometimes send to myself that never fails:

To: David Jacobson

Dear Mr. Jacobson,

I see that you are having a stressful day today. I just want you to know that you are doing a great job!

Take a humor break and then get back at it! There's a good chance tomorrow will be better.

Jest-fully yours,

Yourself

I use the above example of emailing yourself in workshops I do about humor and leadership. A friend of mine, Martha, a humor communication trainer among other wonderful things, who lives in Japan, is also a member of AATH and attended one of my AATH workshops and graciously translated the email above into Japanese for her humor group and her popular blog. (Thank you, Masako "Martha" Kusakari!)

So, for all my Japanese readers (possibly the majority of you!), I'm including it here:

親愛なるデービッド　ジャコブソンさん

今日はストレスの多い一日だったようですね。

あなたはよく頑張っていますよ。

ユーモアで一息ついてから、また挑戦してください。

明日はきっといいことがありますよ。

Modes of communication: Listening

While we're on the topic of Japanese translations, Martha also translated a poem of mine that contains a good message for leaders. It is called "A Place for Pain." I present it here with her permission:

A Place for Pain 痛みの居場所

I open the door 扉を開けると

pain walks in 痛みが歩み入り

filling my home with darkness and discontent 家を暗闇と不満で埋め尽くす

I open the door 扉を開けると

faith walks in 信頼が歩み入り

illuminating my living room 居間を明るく照らしてくれる

I open the door 扉を開けると

hope walks in 希望が歩み入り

filling the kitchen with wonderful smells キッチンをいい香りで満たす

I open the door ドアを開けると

joy walks in 喜びが入ってくるので

I explain that she has the wrong address 住所を間違えているよ

she should be next door 隣の家だろうと伝える

She comes in anyway 喜びはお構いなしに入ってくる
joy, like pain 喜びは　痛みと同じで

knows not of manners or proper protocol 礼儀作法をわきまえない。

I open the door ドアを開けると

humor walks in ユーモアが入り、

It fills the empty spaces 空っぽの空間を埋めてくれる

Pain is still here 痛みはまだいる

But, it has little room しかし居場所はほとんどない。

Not only humor but connection with *all* the positive emotions should be encouraged by leaders to help their staff diminish the pain they must face in their work environment, and to reduce the room it has to fill their workday. Essential to this process is learning to listen.

Practice Playshop: Listening

This playshop, if done correctly, is challenging but extremely rewarding! Also, I can't remember who I stole this version from, but this is the one I like to use, so I thank the *many* authors to whom it is attributed!

1. Divide your team into pairs. Each person should then think of a fun-filled memory.
2. Have the pair decide who will go first (or come up with a creative way to choose who goes first or just flip a coin).
3. For two minutes (one minute if they have a fear of public speaking!), have each person share the memory with their partner. During that minute, have the listener ignore them, as if it's the most boring thing they ever heard. They should be looking away, checking their phone, looking at their watch, yawning, etc.
4. Next, have them share the experience with the entire group.
5. Then, have them repeat the same story to their paired partner, but this time they should receive it as the most fascinating thing

they have ever heard. They can ask questions, listen with 100% of their energy, give great eye contact, smile, never look away, etc.

6. Again, have them share the experience with the group.
7. Switch roles and repeat Steps 3 through 6.
8. Debrief with the entire group (or if you're not a consultant, just ask them to talk about what happened).

Modes of communication: Song lyrics

Song lyrics are another fun thing you can play with. Take a popular song and change the words to relate it to your work. Here is an example of song lyrics I invented for professional meeting planners, to be sung to the tune of "Hey, Jude." (By the Beatles, of course!)

Hey, Dude, the contract's bad.
Ask the DOS to make it better.
Remember to change the center piece art,
Then you can start to make it better.

Hey, Dude, interns don't get paid.
They were supposed to be here earlier, to meet her.
You just feel like punching them all on the chin.
That would begin to make you feel better.

And anytime you re-schedule a plane,
Hey, Dude, refrain
Don't carry the plans upon your shoulders.
For well you know that it's a fool
Who plays it cool
When losing his client's CRM folder.

Nah-na-na, na na, na na, na na, YEAH!
Nahhh, na-na, na na na na, etc.

Okay, if you are a meeting planner it makes sense, but if you're not, then maybe not so much. (Good news: You'll see another song lyric example in Chapter Six under "Humor and Trust.") And that is the beauty of songs: you can make them unique to your workplace and have an "inside joke" that only your team may understand. This makes them feel part of an exclusive club.

Modes of communication: Nursery rhymes

These rhymes are from an Arthritis Foundation conference:

RUB A DUB DUB

Rub a dub dub
Three men soaking in a tub,
And who has arthritis here?

The butcher, the baker, the candlestick maker,
Because arthritis does not discriminate when it comes to occupations.
Clearly, this lyric was not written at a meeting of English majors.

THREE LITTLE KITTENS

Three little kittens, they lost their med records, and they began to cry, "Oh, receptionist dear, we sadly fear, our records we have lost. "
"What! Lost your records, you silly kittens? Then you shall have no appointment.
Mee-ow, mee-ow, mee-ow. No, you shall have no appointment."
The three little kittens, they found their records, and they began to cry, "Oh, receptionist dear, see here, see here: our records we have found!"
"Hand me your records, you happy kittens, and you shall have an appointment! Purr-r, purr-r, purr-r, and you shall have an appointment."

The three little kittens gave over their records and got an appointment **… four months later.**

You get the idea. While these should probably be burned after reading, nursery rhymes have a way of cutting problems down to size (much like the butcher's wife with her carving knife—you know the one).

Modes of communication: Face-to-face

As I've said, you do not need to do stand-up comedy or have amazing humor skills to let your staff know you care and to be playful with them. In daily interactions you can simply ask your staff …

- What skills and talents do you have?
- What are some challenges you have overcome?
- What things do you do that make you feel happy?
- What do you think others like about you?
- Who's your favorite comedian?
- What's your favorite funny movie?
- In a movie about you, what actor would play your part?

Practice Playshop: Getting to Know You

While having your one-on-one conversations with staff, ask them some of the questions in the preceding paragraph and also share what you like about them.

Alternative (or bonus?) Playshop

1. Organize staff into pairs.
2. Let them decide who will go first and who will go second.
3. Instruct them to spend a few minutes asking each other these questions:
    - What are you proud of that you have done?
    - What do you like about yourself?
4. Be sure to set some ground rules (such as no judgements, only supportive comments, no disagreeing with each other's statements), and state that they can also share what they like about the other person, if so desired.

Chapter Four: The Four Styles of Humor

"We lead by being human beings. We do not lead by being corporate, professional, or institutional."

Paul Hawken

Leaders use humor to help their staff see their compassionate side and reveal how truly human they are. Deep bonds also form when staff feel understood and valued. Some styles of humor assist with this, while others sabotage any chance of accomplishing this bonding. As presented earlier in this book, I often refer to four primary styles of humor. Let's review.

Four Styles of Humor

(from Rod Martin)

Affiliative Humor - Making others feel better.

Aggressive Humor - Making other's feel worse.

Self Enhancing Humor Making oneself feel better.

Self-Defeating Humor - Making oneself feel worse.

Affiliative humor: "I often joke around with my friends."
Affiliative humor is a type of humor that most everyone might find funny and makes one more likeable. Highly humorous leaders use affiliative humor to amuse others as one way to improve and facilitate their relationships. If you are popular because of the type of humor you use, it is usually because you are using affiliative (or self-enhancing) humor. Affiliative humor points out some universal faults or tendencies that we as humans have and how silly they sometimes are. Think of observational humor and the comedians who use it. Comedians like:

- Woody Allen: "Dying is one of the few things that can be done as easily lying down."
- George Carlin: "Some people see things that are and ask, 'Why?' Some people dream of things that never were and ask, 'Why not?' Some people must go to work and do not have time for all that."
- Sid Caesar (my favorite of his quotes): "The best thing about humor is that it shows people they are not alone." (While we are on the subject of Sid Caesar, here is an example of affiliative humor that stands the test of time: https://youtu.be/qOjn5_1Y-Jg "Sid Caesar: The Bavarian Clock" (from *Your Show of Shows*, September 26, 1953)

- Ellen DeGeneres: "Follow your passion. Stay true to yourself. Never follow someone else's path, unless you are in the woods and you're lost, and you see a path. By all means, you should follow that."
- Jim Gaffigan: "You ever talk about a movie with someone that read the book? They are always so condescending. 'Ah, the book was much better than the movie.' Oh, really? What I enjoyed about the movie: no reading."
- Will Rogers: "There are three kinds of men. The one that learns by reading. The few who learn by observation. The rest of them have to pee on the electric fence for themselves."
- Jerry Seinfeld: "If you have something, anything, an ability of some kind, you want to use it. That, I think, is the essence of human living … The idea is to do more in life … Money is nice, but it is not what really makes you feel good." (My editor mentioned stuff about the importance of mastery in psychological development, but I told her it was beyond the scope of my book.)

Affiliative humor can reduce prejudice. The playshop features an actual example of affiliative humor that gives insight into the connections we all have as humans, as well as how we have so much more in common than we think.

Practice Playshop: Affiliative Humor

This deceptively simple playshop will quickly build staff rapport:

1. Ask one staff member to identify a second staff member whom they feel they know the least about.
2. For two minutes, invite them both to count off as many things as possible that they both have in common.
3. Ask the first person to choose another staff member whom they don't know well and list their commonalities.
4. Repeat as often as needed!

While in Jerusalem many years ago, as I boarded the city bus one day, I noticed a Palestinian mom with her three young sons. She gave each of them some chocolate. The boy, who looked about four years old, immediately crammed his chocolate bar into his mouth. Then he glanced at his six-year-old brother, grabbed his chocolate bar right out of his hand, and shoved it into his already-stuffed mouth. The shocked brother glared at him in disbelief, jumped up and down, and began yelling and shouting. The oldest brother fell to the ground cracking up laughing. As the bus drove off, I was laughing as well. I had enjoyed a humorous scene of a mom and her kids that could have been *any* mom, your mom, a neighbor's mom, and children anywhere on the globe.

Similarly, affiliative humor will enhance your relationships with staff through its positive, nonjudgmental, nurturing tone. If you know your staff well, you understand the types of humor they appreciate, and you can use it spontaneously to ease tensions. Affiliative humor is associated with happiness, while self-defeating and aggressive humor were related to lower levels of happiness. There is a ton of research now that bears this out. As a leader modeling affiliative humor, you can help staff find that they have so much more in common with co-workers than differences.

Affiliative humor is useful for creating a high-quality relationship with the majority of your staff. Keep in mind, as I stated at the outset, that every type of humor isn’t for everyone. One of the biggest mistakes a leader can make is using humor with a staff member who doesn't appreciate their style. No problem! Other positive approaches can be used to inspire others, to bond, and to feel understood (such as the active listening playshop from the previous chapter).

Summary: Benefits of Affiliative Humor

- Reduces tension by joking about universal human faults
- Encourages people to relax and laugh
- Unites people
- Creates a supportive atmosphere of fun and caring
- Includes everyone in the good time

- Builds rapport
- Highlights the positive aspects of human relationships

Aggressive humor: "When telling jokes or saying other 'funny things,' I don't care how I might affect others."

This style typically involves put downs or insults against others, and is often used by bullies, thereby increasing their opportunities for hostility. Leaders use aggressive humor to disparage others as a way of manipulating them. Leaders who use this style often provoke fear and intimidation and then pawn it off as being done "jokingly," while they belittle, humiliate, and embarrass their staff. Such leaders fall into all demographics. Sadly, most who rely on this style have (incredibly) little or no self-awareness of what they are doing. In contrast, leaders using affiliative and self-enhancing humor are often quite aware of themselves and their impact on others.

Comedians who are known for using aggressive humor include:

- Jeff Ross: "You have such a huge career ... behind you."
- Jimmy Carr: "I'm not being condescending. I'm too busy thinking about far more important things you wouldn't understand."

Still, a few comedians have been able to use aggressive humor successfully. One example is Don Rickles.

Don Rickles commented on being labeled an insult comic by saying, "An insult comic is the title I was given. What I do is exaggeration. I make fun of people, at life, of myself and my surroundings." Peter McGraw and Caleb Warren worked together to develop and research what they call The Benign Violation Theory, which proposes that for something to considered humorous it needs to violate existing beliefs of what is normal but must also be considered benign (nonthreatening). These factors must also occur simultaneously. Rickles' successful use of aggressive humor may be explained because he overturns social norms (beliefs, attitudes, and behaviors that are acceptable within a culture) in a way that is *nonthreatening*.

Here is a handy diagram to put it all together:

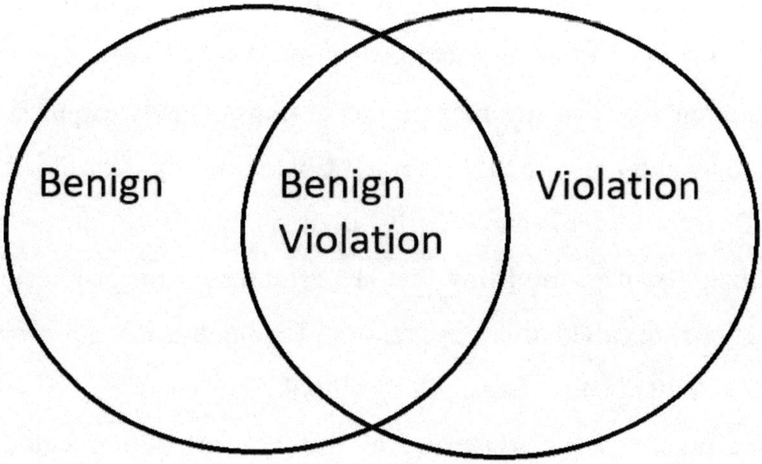

If Don Rickles insults an audience member, that is a violation, but at the same time, if they've paid to see Don Rickles, they know he doesn't mean it, that he's playing, and—pay attention to this part—that he does not have any control over them or their livelihood. (In other words, there isn't a vast power discrepancy, a subject which, as I told my editor, is also outside the scope of this book!) That's the benign (safe) part. So, in the hands of an expert performer, without any power over his audience members, who were there *by choice* and free to leave at any time, even an insult could be funny. Those familiar with Don Rickles' life also knew how loving and compassionate he was, so most could separate his comedy persona from him as a person.

The difference between the humor Don Rickles used and aggressive humor used by a leader is that the leader's humor is *not* benign. Because the workplace is not a comedy club or the World Wrestling Entertainment (WWE), the statements are taken at face value. As such, aggression at work or in other public settings is used to put staff and others down and to make them feel inferior. Similarly, jabs about highly personal information, particularly if it is sensitive or potentially stigmatizing (that is, **anything** that HR requires training about) are **not okay**! These are called micro-aggressions (again, this is a topic in its own right, and outside the scope of this book, but plenty of research is available on this issue). Overuse of this type of humor could be an indication of mental health issues and/or poor self-esteem.

To summarize, aggressive humor:

- Puts others down and pokes fun at other people's shortcomings.
- Reflects the anger of the person wielding the insults
- Is often racist, sexist, ageist, etc.
- Offends with inappropriate use of sexual references or profanity.
- Uses stereotypes to denigrate a person or group.
- Creates a cruel, abusive, offensive atmosphere and is insensitive to others.
- Is divisive and detrimental to teamwork.

Most of you are familiar with the so-called "slap heard around the world," when Will Smith slapped Chris Rock on stage at the Oscars ceremony. Smith himself said it was "shocking, painful and inexcusable."

As a leader your role is not to judge, but to try to understand when inappropriate instances occur in the workplace. When staff come into conflict with each other, your focus should be on understanding where each of the staff members in conflict are coming from. As the leader it is better to avoid taking sides and telling your staff that one was right and the other wrong. The incident at the Oscars provides an opportunity to discuss with staff their feelings on the occurrence.

Smith's wife, has a medical condition, and the question to ask is: Did Chris Rock's joke cross the line? Many would agree it did, but what is the proper response to that? Obviously, physical violence crosses the line as an appropriate response. I cannot say I know how I would have reacted if it was my wife being insulted, but I like to think I have enough control to respond verbally rather than physically. Rock's joke was inappropriate and would be considered put-down, aggressive humor, but it was not physical. Imagine a staff member responding to their leader using aggressive humor toward them by slapping them (as much as they'd probably love to). Who would be disciplined in this situation? There are ways to address aggressive humor without a physical response. This incident is just one example you could use to open a discussion with staff about what kind of humor and what kind of behavior is okay and what is not okay. Incidences like that can be used by leaders as opportunities for fruitful discussions. Take advantage of occurrences involving humor to open conversations on appropriate and inappropriate humor.

Ensure that your staff are well-educated on the differences between appropriate and inappropriate humor. As a leader you'll need to respond if you hear any staff using aggressive humor. You could say something like: "I'm not sure you're aware of how mean-spirited what you said just sounded." Use your response to educate them. For example, if it was a joke about a certain group (race, religion, etc.) of people, ask them to tell it again, but this time use their own group. That could be an "aha" moment for them to realize that it's not funny.

I also want to make sure I clearly communicate the differences between dark humor and aggressive humor. The difference is intent. Aggressive humor is used intentionally by leaders who rule by fear and intimidation. Dark humor is used to handle the stress of the most dangerous and traumatic jobs. Typically, you find the use of dark humor in jobs where the most disastrous situations can occur—police, military, firefighting, emergency rooms, etc. (Again, think of the characters Hawkeye Pierce or Trapper John in *M.A.S.H.*) And as I am sure you know by now, the use of affiliative and self-enhancing humor indicates the person has great coping skills and is often used by those with high self-esteem, high confidence, a good amount of social intelligence, and high resiliency.

Self-enhancing humor: Know your weaknesses and turn them into strengths. "If I am feeling upset about something stupid I did, I usually try to think of something funny about the situation to make myself and others feel better."
Be able to laugh at yourself. Find amusement in life's hardships and stay positive. Poke fun at yourself when something bad happens to you, if done in a good-natured way. As you may notice, I use it often in this book, because it comes from a place of confidence and high self-esteem. Use of self-enhancing humor is also indicative of being able to put yourself into someone else's place and see their perspective. Statements like "I cannot believe how well you're holding up, considering how much stress you're under" is an example.

Research bears out the correlation between self-enhancing humor and high cognitive empathy. Leaders who utilize both assets can truly understand the struggles of their staff, and their staff not only know it, but they also feel safer, more secure, and more comfortable going to their leader to discuss their challenges. For example, I recall falling off my unicycle once in front of several people. Of course, they were concerned I might have gotten hurt. While they were approaching me to help, I got up, picked up the unicycle, and yelled at it, “That’s not funny! If you’re mad at me, just tell me next time!” Not hilarious or even particularly funny, but those near me got the message that I was not hurt. More about that:

> Sid Caesar: “When I did comedy, I made fun of myself. If there was a buffoon, I played the buffoon. And people looked at me and said, ‘Gee, that's like Uncle David,’ or ‘That's like a friend of mine.’ And they related through that. I did not make fun of them. I made fun of *me*.”
>
> David Jacobson (who has severe arthritis): “I went into a bar to get a drink. The bartender said, ‘Sorry, we don’t serve arthritics here.’ I replied, ‘Well, I’ll just have to find a replacement for this joint.’ “

Opportunities for self-enhancing humor often arise from embarrassing moments. The ability to use self-enhancing humor to overcome embarrassment is so much more powerful than you could ever imagine. C.W. Metcalf talks about this in his book *Lighten Up: Survival Skills for People Under Pressure.* The things we say when we have been embarrassed are unbelievably extreme when you really think about it. "Oh, I was so embarrassed I wish I were dead." Pretty strong reaction, don't you think? The sooner you can overcome your embarrassment the better, and highly humorous leaders are very quick to do so.

As mentioned, those who make self-enhancing jokes do not have low self-esteem, nor are they prone to depression. They may, in fact, be happier and better socially adjusted than most people. Those with self-esteem issues, however, should be cautious in using this type of humor and not overdo it. To be able to laugh at oneself, one has to overcome any negative self-concepts or self-perceptions. In other words, you need to like yourself!

Abraham Lincoln: Master of humor

President Lincoln often used self-enhancing or self-effacing humor. For example, on one occasion an angry man thrust a pistol into his face. Lincoln at once concluded that any attempt at debate or argument was a waste of time and words. So, he told a joke:

> "What seems to be the matter?" Lincoln asked with as much calm as he could gather.
>
> "Well, some years ago I swore an oath that if I ever came across an uglier man than myself, I'd shoot him on the spot."

> "Shoot me," he said to the stranger; "for if I am an uglier man than you, I don't want to live."

Lincoln was a master storyteller. Often, he focused on his awkward gait, and his not very photogenic face, using these characteristics to make himself the butt of his own jokes. His sense of humor was very disarming to anyone who came into contact with him. Lincoln often visited hospitals in the Washington, DC area, for example, and he asked wounded soldiers about their health and entertained the patients with his stories. There is an (unsubstantiated) story that after one such visit, a journalist followed him to the same hospital and heard wounded soldiers laughing and talking about the President. The soldiers seemed in such good spirits that the journalist was curious; one soldier was overheard to say that even though he lost a leg, he would be glad to lose the other if he could hear more of the President's stories.

I might not give an arm or leg for humor, but I know its importance. I trust you are developing that understanding as well. If not, please shut this book, open it at page one, and begin again.

A true self-enhancing humor story

When my wife and I were visiting my brother in Flagstaff, I had my own embarrassing moment. As you know, I have psoriatic arthritis. Another chronic illness I have is (dun dun dun DUN) the heart break of psoriasis.

Sometimes this skin affliction affects … umh … sensitive parts of the body.

That night as we were going to bed, my groin started to itch. I went to the medicine cabinet and the only thing I found to apply was Bactine®. I sprayed some on. It seemed to cool the area, and I went off to bed. Later in the night, I felt a burn in the area, so I went back to the medicine cabinet for more. A few hours later, I woke up with my groin area really burning. I sprayed on even more but could not go back to sleep with the burn getting worse and worse. I tried to wait until morning, but finally reached the point of the burning sensation driving me crazy!

Laurie awoke to me jumping up and down, holding my groin, and yelling, "I need to go to the hospital." She raced me to the emergency room. At the ER, when the clerk started asking the insurance questions, and while holding my groin with a waiting room full of people, I screamed for them to kill me or knock me out. They quickly put me in a room and a doctor finally gave me a shot. He explained that I gave myself a chemical burn with the antiseptic and just kept making it worse by pouring on more.

I felt like such an idiot. Terrible at the time, funny story now. My brother says this story always reminds him of that Jerry Lee Lewis song "Goodness gracious!" (You know the next line, and if you don't, ask a good friend). The good news is that the more risks you take, the more self-enhancing stories you are likely to experience and have available to share!

Self-enhancing humor

Let's start this section with a visual aid. Here's what I think I look like:

Here's what I might actually look like as I finish this chapter:

What can I say? Writing is not for sissies!

If you are not laughing at yourself and your own mistakes or shortcomings, I can guarantee that someone else is. Leaders who laugh at their mistakes create an atmosphere where risk-taking is okay. This is another time when you can be a role model for your staff, so they can laugh at their mistakes as well. The safest focus of humor is oneself. It is important to laugh at what you *do*, (your actions), not at who you *are*.

As a leader you should be well aware of your own baggage. For example, if you think to yourself, "He looks like [that person] I hate," then unfinished business can get in the way. We cannot listen to our staff when our ears or our hands are filled with our own resentment. Projections onto our staff ("She is so rude; I'm not listening to her.") can very well be tendencies that we do not want to see in ourselves. Our projections may be based on our leadership expectations, realistic or not. As leaders we should be aware that these projections lead to judgments such as, "I don't like it when I am rude, so when one of my staff is rude, I can just project my anger toward myself onto them!"

Judgements are also perceptions that can keep us from knowing reality and are based on beliefs we've been taught. They are usually designed to keep us safe. Here's a statement based on a belief: "I'll never lose my job because I always have excellent reviews." Is this reality? How many excellent employees became unemployed because of the pandemic? Because of prejudice? Because of a boss who feared competition? Because of a merger?

Perceptions are our own personal attitudes, toward ourselves or things outside ourselves. "I know the best way to do things, because it worked for me when I was in my staff's position." This perception will set the tone for the level of sharing with your staff; most people will not go any deeper into conversation than you are willing to go. If you don't examine your assumptions or habits, neither will they.

The good news is that you can use self-enhancing humor to acknowledge that some of the baggage (judgements, projections, and perceptions) you carry is baggage that can otherwise influence how you treat your staff. Knowing that they are false assumptions, on the other hand, you can use your sense of humor to overcome and distance yourself from that baggage. Your sense of humor can help you become more objective and see your own personal biases.

Practice Playshop: Perceiving Reality

Try this playshop: close your eyes … well, close them after you read all this … and with your eyes closed, picture a truck going down the road.

Next, pretend you are on the witness stand in court, and the lawyer is asking you to describe the truck.

- "How fast is it going?"
- "What color is it?"
- "How big is it?"

Now it's your employee's turn to "get on the stand" and describe the truck that *they* saw.

Finally, be the "jury." If there are differences in your descriptions, consider:

- Was each person looking at an entirely different truck?
- "Whose truck is "right" and whose truck is "wrong"?

Of course, both trucks, both sets of responses are "accurate," because we all have our own perceptions. But when it comes to our values, we like to think our value (that is, our truck) is right, and that our employees' value (their truck) is wrong, or at least "less right."

And that playshop shows us the crux of most conflicts at work. Sometimes there isn't an absolutely right or wrong way to see or do things, rather just a personal opinion on how things should be done. And sometimes both ways can be right, but we can only clearly see *our* way. When in doubt, remember that you aren't perfect, they aren't perfect, and that sometimes two heads are better than one (unless you have two heads and start talking to yourself.)

You can even get to the point (and I do this with my sense of humor) of acknowledging that maybe, for the other person, their way is right; if the end result is that the task is accomplished, no matter which way is chosen, then you can have even more respect for your employee's choice. Give them a chance, and if need be, let them fail, so when you really want them to do it your way, they can take time to understand why and will be committed to doing it that way (or maybe vice versa: when you see their way works, you just shut up and let them do it).

To effectively use self-effacing humor, you must come from a place of confidence—a place where your strength emanates and overshadows any doubts your staff could have of you. They love that you joke about yourself because they truly know the real you, the you that cares, and who is more concerned with them than yourself. It's the you that wants and helps them to succeed.

Self-defeating humor: "If I am having problems or feeling unhappy, I often cover it up by joking around, so that even my closest friends do not know how I really feel."

This style involves putting yourself down in an aggressive or a "poor me" fashion. It's saying funny things at your own expense. The late, great comedian, Rodney Dangerfield, used this type the most. He was famous for his "I don't get no respect" or "I was an ugly baby" jokes. Yet psychologically, this can be an unhealthy form of humor, and is often used by the targets of bullies to try to avoid attacks. In a sense, this means making ourselves the butt of jokes before others put us down.

There are exceptions, of course (I do not think the highly successful entertainer Rodney Dangerfield was hurt by using it), but generally, those who use self-defeating humor do so at their own expense. They might make themselves the butt of their own jokes and make fun of themselves to gain approval from others. They'll even laugh with everyone when others put them down. Sadly, most of those in the habit of using self-defeating humor have very poor self-esteem or think they are in one way or another unworthy.

Being human, we all at one time or another may have used this type of humor (or even aggressive humor). What is important is to recognize it and be aware when it is being used by you or anyone else. As you now know, of these four styles, the self-enhancing and affiliative humor are the positive types that leaders should focus on, and self-defeating and aggressive humor are detriments to your team and workplace. That knowledge empowers you to be both an effective and a funny leader!

Chapter Five: Humor and Empowerment

"It's kind of fun to do the impossible."

Walt Disney

At this point, you're about two-thirds of the way through this book (yay, go, you!). Let's check in:

- Is my goal of enhancing my leadership style with my sense of humor reasonable or "impossible"? (My boss tells me I'm great all the time and gives me the freedom to make the choices I need to make to do my job excellently! He's also pretty funny, which gives me another incentive to practice humor in my work as well.)

- If it's attainable, then what am I doing to reach this goal? (I'm reading this book!)

We have already discussed what humor is, so moving on to empowerment, let's use the most credible choice for its definition. In this case, I cite the coveted book that I have referred to in previous writings, namely the *Winston Dictionary for Schools, Shorter Edition*, by the John C. Winston Company (unfortunately, this 1957 edition did not list the word "empowerment," but this is close enough): "Empower: To give authority to."

When I think of my use of empowerment as a leader, two ways come to mind:

1. A leader shares knowledge regarding the employee's performance and understanding of their job.
2. A leader provides psychological empowerment, increasing how safe and comfortable the employee feels at work.

Regarding Item #1, a leader may use humor to enhance an employee's confidence in four major areas:

a. Provide information regarding the employee's performance. If you make a mistake, you will not get into trouble; in fact, let's find a fun or funny way to share it with others, so they avoid it.

b. Recognize an employee for doing something good: reward those who use humor appropriately.
c. Provide the employee with knowledge in an entertaining way that will enhance their ability to do their job.
d. Empower the employee to make decisions that influence how they do their jobs as well as the direction of the whole department.

Regarding Point B: Psychological safety is obtained through psychological empowerment in four important ways (coincidentally, there are four major areas here, too. I did not make these up; I read them somewhere):

1. Meaning: Value of the task to you as a leader and to your staff. "On my list of priorities of 1 to 375, I would put this task at number…"
2. Competence: How capable is the staff member of completing the task? "Who feels confident in doing this task, and who feels like they suck at it? Don't answer now, just share with me later."
3. Self-determination: Is the task optional or mandatory? If mandatory, have you enhanced the staff member's ability to use self-enhancing humor so they are not overly stressed out by the task?

4. Okay, I was wrong. There are not four areas here, only three.

The four styles of humor (previously mentioned) will either have a negative or positive impact on receptivity to knowledge shared by the leader and an impact on their psychological safety. Affiliative humor and self-enhancing humor will positively affect psychological safety and knowledge-sharing receptivity. Aggressive humor and self-defeating humor will have a negative impact on those two components. Think of any bully you know, including those in the news, and how they use "humor," and these points will become clear.

Leveling the playing field

On the playing field there is higher ground and lower ground. Leaders have the higher ground, and in terms of power in the organization, their staff have the lower ground. Humor is like a tiller that helps you level the hierarchal difference between leader and staff. The greater the difference in power, the more it helps with the leveling. (Oh, I guess power distance IS in the scope of this book after all!)

For example, if you are a GS-14 chief in the federal government, with staff from GS-7 to GS-13, humor can be used to de-stress those staff in lower pay grades, who may feel even more intimidated by the chain-of-command differences. In other arenas outside federal agencies, this might be like comparing a CEO or director to their senior managers, supervisors, lead staff, and line staff. Leaders who are adept at using humor to level the playing field will have not only better relationships at all levels of their organization but will have the added gift of hearing from line staff about concerns they may not normally be willing to share with those at top levels. Incidentally, I never call staff "line staff," unless they are standing in a line or line dancing. Also, I never call staff "frontline staff," unless they are standing at the front of the line dance.

Modeling humor helps staff to improve their own sense of humor. I have found that my staff go out of their way to use humor more often after knowing how much I appreciate it. I have seen staff go from barely being able to use humor to becoming quite adept at it over time with encouragement.

New staff assimilated into a culture that regularly uses humor seem to adapt more quickly to its use and also appreciate it even more than seasoned staff who are already used to a "laughter mode." The positive relationship between a leader's affirming humor and an employee's psychological empowerment is not a novelty, but remains steady over the long-term relationship. For example, workplace banter and playfulness become a regular part of meetings, resulting in more attentiveness, more interactions, and better participation. A leadership style that incorporates humor encourages employees to use the freedom their leader offers to make independent decisions and commitments, and they perceive their leader as someone who supports their decision-making and provides them with the tools to carry out those plans.

If staff are empowered to implement actions without direct supervision or intervention, then humor also fosters creativity. The team that plays together, stays together. Most people will work even harder for the team they work and play with than they will for themselves. Why? Because people are even more inspired and motivated by their peers than they are by money. This is the positive form of peer pressure. (If you're not sure about that, consider behavior outside of work. How much time does a teen spend trying to act or look like their friends? How much energy is devoted to keep the yard looking tidy, even when you're not the one who sees it all day—your neighbor does!)

One of the most crucial actions a leader can take is to praise, praise, praise their staff! If you have humor in your arsenal of tools, use it to praise your staff. Almost everyone likes to be recognized for a job well-done. If you can make it joyous or fun as well, it may turn into an indelible memory. Recognize achievements of staff, even if only at corporate events.

"I can last two months on a good compliment."

Mark Twain

The following are several examples of how to recognize and compliment staff. After you've read them, do the playshop activity that follows.

- "As you know my position is very challenging, but without you and the amazing job you do, it would be virtually impossible." - This one must be truly genuine and come from your heart.

- "I think the hardest part about being your leader is pretending as though I like my other staff as much as I like you**."** - Just don't say this one within earshot of your other staff and say it to **all** your staff (or as many as you sincerely can!).
- "Our department is a more joyful place with you in it. Thanks for the laughter you regularly generate!" Or "Talking to you is the best part of my day, aside from time with my wife, when I'm sleeping, and when I'm eating ice cream." - Learn to use the trifecta (in this example, it's my wife, sleep, and ice cream) that makes your praise light-hearted and more effective.
- For staff who are good and have potential, but often doubt themselves, you can still honestly say: "It's too bad you don't see what I see; if you did, you'd smile and realize all the skills you already have and the amazing potential you have to become a great leader."
- "You know what's awesome? Chocolate cake, oh, and the job you do every day!" - What's more complimentary than being compared to chocolate cake!?! "Your sense of humor makes coming to work a joyful experience. Thank you for inspiring us and keeping our spirits high!"
- Or "You are just so strange sometimes. It's great." – You can use this when the humor starts to get extreme or out of hand, in order to bring both you and your staff back to their tasks.
- When your humor gets just a little weird and you catch it, try, "Thank you for understanding me, even though I'm weird. I mean,

we both know I'm weird, but you accept it, and that makes me happy."

- "The only thing better than your support and the job you do is being friends with a talking stork." - Use this one with your staff who just get you.
- "Only an exemplary employee with a fantastic sense of humor inspires her leader on a daily basis. You are that employee. Thank you for setting such a great example for everyone on our team!"
- And praise for you, my dear reader, because you've made it to this page in the book: "Your interest and motivation in further developing your sense of humor as a leader is amazing. Not many can compare!"

Sorry to say, but we're just not used to speaking positively, so now that you're warmed up—on to the next playshop!

Practice Playshop: Positive Statements for Staff

Write down three light-hearted praise phrases or statements that you could use with your staff.

Tip: Think of your best workers and what you admire about them. Even better, if it is something they do better than you, get silly and compare their ability with yours, so that THEY look good:

"When you _____________, you make it look so easy! When I try to do the same, I look like ________."

Say this phrase until it feels natural!

Your sense of humor is powerful enough to impact another's life, and most likely, you'll be unaware when it does. So, if you find yourself spending more time with just a few staff who have highly-developed senses of humor, then you might need to learn to be more self-aware. *All* your staff have a sense of humor, and the ones who express interest in further developing theirs need more of your time!

Setting expectations with a smile

"If love means never having to say you are sorry,
humor means never having to be disciplined for
making a minor mistake."

The Author (aka Me)

> "Employees' experiences and perceptions of a humorous work climate enhance trust, further relationships, and empower staff to make changes to improve the work environment. Staff feel empowered in the resulting warm, creative, and humorous environment. Empowerment means employees can bend and break rules, eliminate rules, and offer changes to existing rules and for creating new ones. Research shows that higher-humorous work cultures were significantly more innovative than those that reported lower-humorous work cultures." (read more in "Organizational climate for creativity and innovation," G. Ekvall, in the *European Journal of Work and Organizational Psychology*, Vol. 5, No. 1, pp. 105-23).

For the reality described in Ekvall's research to occur, the leader often must step out of the way and permit staff to mold the "humor culture" based on their own ideas, practices, and comfort levels! The sooner you shake off the false notion that you as the leader have more answers, better answers—even all the answers—or better ideas than your staff, the sooner you'll discover how great your team can truly be when you: a) listen to your staff, and b) adopt their ideas.

Is humor a natural part of how staff communicate with each other? Yes, but just as important is an intentional focus on creating and sustaining a more humorous work culture. The internet, for example, allows access to a vast ocean of ideas to enhance the humor culture. If you are a leader with arthritis, like me, then you may not need an ocean of ideas, just a creek. (Or a creak?) At the same time, too much humor can be counterproductive; it is much better to sit at a productive table with just the right amount of humor. You may think that a focus on humor would be too time-consuming. This is not true (unless you eat your watch).

Is humor a natural part of how staff communicate with each other? Yes, we all have different tastes in humor (and watches); what one considers funny, another does not. My sense of humor is not for everybody, and particularly not for the people who started reading this book but have already stopped. (Luckily for me that is not you.) If you're understaffed, maybe it's time to use humor in hiring. Bring in a couple of dummies, put them in chairs, and say they are here to help because you are understaffed. (Also, they cannot catch any viruses.) Add a question or two to get a sense of how solid their sense of humor is. I find that those with a good or profound sense of humor usually make better employees, because they know how to have fun on the job and are typically self-motivators.

Let's get specific. With Michael Kerr's permission, I am sharing his fifteen ideas to get the humor ball rolling, and this link to the article on his website: https://mikekerr.com/free-articles/humour-in-the-workplace-articles/humor-in-the-workplace-tips-how-to-get-the-humor-at-work-ball-rolling/ and https://mikekerr.com

Humor at Work: How to Start Adding More Humor into Your Workplace

(From Michael Kerr)

"Do you want to add more fun into your workplace? Looking to create a more passionate, humor-filled culture but not sure how to get started? Here are fifteen ideas to get the humor ball rolling in your workplace:

1. Create a "Humor at Work Team" or "Culture Squad" to coordinate and implement fun at work ideas.
2. Have a meeting to specifically address morale in the workplace and to brainstorm some simple ways to create a more fun work environment. Ask what it is that people fear about using humor

in the workplace to make sure potential roadblocks are discussed and dealt with effectively.

3. Commit to two or three specific goals per quarter for adding more fun into the workplace.

4. Create a FUN "humor in the workplace code of conduct" to remind people of the importance of having fun, but in a safe, professional way.

5. Start a humor at work library to encourage people to read (or watch) about the topic.

6. Create a humor at work bulletin board to post fun announcements, funny quotes, fun photos, and fun thoughts of the day

7. Create a few simple rituals or traditions that encourage people to have fun and lighten up. Rituals and fun workplace traditions create a sense of shared history and shared team experience, and they give employees something to look forward to and something to reminisce about.

8. Set aside time in every meeting for a bit of fun. Encourage people to share funny work-related anecdotes or funny work-related jokes.

9. Use a rotating "corporate jester" position to spearhead fun activities. Rotate the position every three months to give everyone a chance at taking on the role, and to make sure no one burns out trying to do everything themselves.

10. Create a humor room or a humor first aid kit stockpiled with funny props, costume parts, and books that people can access when they need a break.
11. Dedicate a part of your internal intranet website for fun and use it as a resource section where people can share best practices and fun ideas.
12. Start a shared inventory of everyone's favorite funny books, TV shows, and movies.
13. Create a mascot that will serve as a permanent reminder to everyone to lighten up.
14. Create a fun slogan that will remind everyone to lighten up.
15. Give people explicit permission to have more fun at work; do not assume they know this already!"

Humor and forgiveness

Forgiveness, like humor, is very empowering. William Hampes conducted a research study which found that self-enhancing humor was positively correlated with perspective-taking empathy, and aggressive humor was negatively correlated with perspective-taking empathy. This study also revealed that self-enhancing humor was significantly *and* positively correlated with all of the forgiveness measures used, while aggressive humor and self-defeating humor were significantly and negatively correlated with some of the forgiveness measures. Affiliative humor was not significantly correlated with any of the forgiveness measures (guess you can't win 'em all!). (For more detail, see "The

Relationship Between Humor Styles and Forgiveness" in the *European Journal of Psychology,* August 2016, Volume 12, Number 3, pp. 338–347). So, forgiveness and all its benefits go hand-in-hand with humor!

Handling difficult situations with tact (and humor)

Conflicts and difficult situations are going to happen. That is a fact and part of human interaction. Let's face it—my needs will sometimes conflict with those of others. It's no one's fault and is quite normal.

For example, two staff have a conflict, and it begins to escalate. You could step in and say, "I have one question for both of you." They are likely to want to hear it. Ask them, "What would you name your airplane if you had one?" Sounds ridiculous, but it will distract them for a moment, just long enough to lower their stress levels and help them to be in a slightly better state of mind, to regain control over their emotions, and to be prepared at least to *attempt* to understand each other.

When they are able to focus and listen, remind them of their shared purpose on the team. Their conflict with each other could be a great opportunity to teach them about humorous fantasies. Have them both come up with a humorous fantasy to visualize a win-win outcome. This may help them regain the mutual respect they should have for each other.

Respect is like air. You don't really notice it until it's not there—and then it's all you notice.

Practice Playshop: Hindsight is 20-20

- Think of a challenging situation you experienced. Was there anything inherently humorous about the situation?
- In hindsight, is there anything you could have done to *add* humor?
- Think of a highly humorous leader you know (or knew) and write down some behaviors they exhibited during a conflict or difficult situation.
- Finally, think of a situation in which the conflict wasn't resolved. What was the impact? Was it worth the stress?

Influence through humor

Even a court jester has the ability to influence the outcome of a situation. Through humor, we too, can move events in a more positive direction. That is, if it is within our area of control. For example, if the staff having a conflict report to you, they really must respond to you. If they choose not to accept guidance, then perhaps there is another issue brewing … and another opportunity to use humor!

With issues that are concerning to us, but outside of our area of control, we will probably not be able to use the power of humor to gain influence. The course of COVID-19, for example, is outside our area of control. We can use our sense of humor to help ourselves and our staff cope with it, but we have no power on a global scale to eliminate it or make it go away. Even so, we can change *our part*, that is, our actions and decisions.

And especially in healthcare, focusing on things like protocols and personal protective equipment use at the individual level is crucial!

What could make us hesitate when considering the use of humor? Perhaps the conflict was unexpected, and we were taken by surprise. Or perhaps we fear the humor backfiring and then being disliked or rejected. If we fear creating anger, we might think we'll make the situation even worse. Perhaps we have never witnessed the use of humor to diffuse a conflict; and therefore, we had no leader to model how to do it or no chance to practice.

When we face conflict, we often relapse to a more primitive state. Even though we may no longer have to run from a lion, we can still experience the fight or flight syndrome. And physiological fight or flight response is more detrimental than useful in these modern times. We are human, not Vulcan. (And even Spock had his moments!) More often than not we are emotional beings, rather than logical ones.

So, I find it amusing that, when we meet, the first question often seems to be, "What do you do?" instead of, "How are you being?" We are never referred to as human doings; we are human beings. *Feeling in a humorous mood is a state of being, not doing.* (How am I being right now? I am laughing while trying not to lose bladder control, which is my present state of being and one of my favorite states of being.) Leaders can benefit from using humor to become more aware of their state of being and their feelings, thus becoming more in control of their behaviors. The more you can use humor for introspection, the more self-aware you will become.

Think now of a challenging work relationship, someone you just don't get along with. How do you typically communicate with that person, knowing that you can never predict how they will respond? What do you do in those situations? Avoid them? Face them, but handle the situation poorly because anger bubbles up or you get anxious? There's a third option. You can face them, using a humorous fantasy or other leadership humor skill to better handle the situation. Once the other person sees you smile, they know you are in control of your emotions and not in a state of either anger or fear.

Ponder these questions (or, if it's Friday afternoon, answer them right away!):

- How do you currently handle conflict?
- Do you attempt to keep the peace?
- Do you have a need to be right and get your own way?
- Do you simply avoid conflict as much as possible?
- Do you sugarcoat the issue, perhaps because you're afraid to hurt someone's feelings?
- Do you try to force the other person to change their mind?

Practice Playshop: Humorous Fantasy Technique

1. Focus on yourself and on your breathing. Are your muscles tense or relaxed?
2. Close your eyes and imagine Homer Simpson counting down from ten to one. When he reaches one, try to think of a time when you were cracking up laughing. What were you feeling at that time? What was going on that made you start laughing?
3. Recall that feeling, and *in the present*, try to sustain it for about one minute. When you can use your imagination to make yourself laugh by conjuring up some silly scenario, then you will have mastered the art of the humorous fantasy.
4. If this feels foreign to you, write down the experience of laughter and keep it handy for the next time a stressful situation occurs.
5. In addition, the very next time you crack up, you can write it down, and while still in a humorous state, ask yourself some self-introspection questions: What did you find so funny about the incident? Was this the kind of incident that caused you to crack up every time you recalled it?
6. Finally, start a humor journal where you can keep humorous fantasies and uplifting incidents of laughter for future reference.

Chapter Six: Finishing Touches

Laurie Jacobson and youngest child

(I do not know what this picture has to do with Humor and Leadership, and there are so many books that have sunset pictures in them, but it looks like they're enjoying the sunset, and I felt the need to have an image at the beginning of this final chapter.)

Before we wrap up our work together, I'll share some juicy tidbits to help you put the finishing touches on your use of humor in the workplace.

Humor and trust

Here is an example of a song I wrote as a behavioral health leader, sung to the tune of "Do You Love Me?" from *Fiddler on the Roof.*

"Golde, do you trust me?

Do I what?

Do you trust me?

Do I trust you?
With our profits getting buried,
and our census going down,
You're upset, you're worn out,
take a break, walk around!
Maybe it's congestion.

Golde, I'm asking you a question: Do you trust me?

You're a fool.

I know … but do you trust me?

Do I trust you?
For almost five years I've worked for you,
wrote your reports, made changes you've asked
Given you work plans, worked on the C.O.W. [computer on wheels]
After almost five years, why talk about trust right now?

Golde, the first time I met you was on your interview day.
I was stressed.
I was shy.
I was nervous.

So was I.

But my CEO and his brother
Said we'd learn to trust each other.
And now I'm asking, Golde …
Do you trust me?

I'm your employee.

I know, but … do you trust me?

Do I trust him?
For almost five years I've worked for him
Fought with him, reported to him,

for almost five years my work results are his.
If that's not trust, what is?

Then you trust me?

I suppose I do.

And I suppose I trust you, too.

It doesn't change a thing,
But even so,
After almost five years,
It's nice to know."

Let me ask you this question: Do you know if your staff trust you? The question isn't, "Do you think your staff trust you?" The question is, "Do you KNOW that your staff trust you?"

Practice Playshop: Humorous Songs

- What are staff members dealing with? Is it trust? Rudeness? Gossip and rumors? Performance issues? Tardiness? Coworker conflicts?
- Write song lyrics or a parody about the issue.
- Share the drafts with each other or have a contest to see whose is voted best!

Forming connections

As seen in our humorous song, trust is the cornerstone of leadership. Leaders who start interactions with a humorous experience will enhance their interpersonal trust with their staff, and their other interactions will be more fun, too. Beyond that, staff will be empowered to do better work! A 2007 U.S.-based study required participants to laugh for fifteen minutes per day for fifteen consecutive days. Data showed that levels of competency doubled. Even more interesting, participants continued to show an improvement three months later!

Since the beginning of the twenty-first century, we have witnessed a series of shocking events (consider the 2008 housing bubble bust and subsequent financial crisis; the Fukushima Power Plant nuclear disaster in 2011; and the storming of the U.S. Capitol Building in 2021, as well as the investigation of the presidential administration then in place). Again, this is not the right place for a joke, because as a result of these events and others, our global trust in our leaders has been severely damaged, if not completely destroyed. This decline of trust in leadership has also changed employees' perspectives of their employers.

A 2019 *Harvard Business Review* survey, for example, found that 58 percent of employees trust a complete stranger *more* than their own boss. How important is this lack of trust, and does it affect work performance? The same survey found that 45% of employees cited their lack of trust in leadership as the single biggest issue impacting their performance at work.

Think of a leader you have worked with who has a great sense of humor. How did your level of trust toward this person affect your ability to do your job? If you'd like, write down their name and your answer to this question. (And if it was me, let me know. 😊) Now, recall a leader you have worked with who had very little sense of humor. Did your level of trust toward this person affect your ability to do your job? How? If you want, write down their name and your answer to this question. (If it was me, do not email me your response—unless it's humorous!)

Trust, humor, and straight talk

Practice becoming adept at mixing humor with the facts. Humor is a character strength that is respected. Those who use it appropriately are showing respect toward the people they work with. It's essential those staff members understand that your humorous comments come from a place of caring and are never intended to offend (though there is always that risk). As a leader, let your staff get to know your motivations; those who know your intentions are less likely to become offended, and even if they do, they are more likely to be forgiving.

Sincerity + (Time and a Dab of Humor) = Loyalty

Let me conclude with an anecdote about Abraham, the first highly humorous Jewish leader (I just invented this story, so please, no fact-checking.)

> Abraham: Lord, why have you chosen me?
>
> The Almighty: Because I like your sense of humor, and you're a big ass.
>
> Abraham: That's because you told me to tie my ass to a tree and walk forty miles.
>
> The Almighty: Ha, ha! See what I mean?

Humor and morale-building

Chapter Three was all about using humor to boost morale, but morale is such a critical component of work culture that I wanted to expand on the topic here. One historical example of using humor to build morale is *The Wipers Times*, an ersatz newspaper (Thesaurus time: "ersatz" means "bogus" or "faux" … which means "fake" … which means—oh, you get the idea) put together by British soldiers fighting in Flanders during World War I. Its name originated in a mispronunciation of Ypres (https://en.wikipedia.org/wiki/The_Wipers_Times). *The Wiper Times* reported on the doings of the soldiers as they battled terror on the one hand and boredom on the other; and it served as a pressure valve to vent frustration by incorporating humor.

Most British army units also staged makeshift musical reviews that played the hardships for laughs, as well as providing opportunities for the troops to listen to songs that reminded them of their sweethearts back home. Similarly, the United Service Organizations (USO), which began in 1941, entertain the armed forces to this day. Big-name entertainers beginning with Bob Hope and Bing Crosby volunteered their services. Hope himself made it an annual Christmas tradition to visit the troops. Comedy was the staple, but so were skits and music.

Even for civilians, laughter in times of crisis is *essential* to good morale and reducing stress, allowing folks to relax and take their minds off immediate problems and return to their work more refreshed and positive. In contrast, signs that your staff are experiencing morale issues include negative attitudes, decreased performance, and poorer quality work and an increase in the spread of rumors. If you note any of these trends, here are some additional ways to utilize your sense of humor to address the issues:

- Staff don't expect your meetings to be hilarious, but if you add even a little humor, it can have a great impact.
- For negative attitudes, it would be helpful to talk one-to-one with each of your direct reports. If you're working remotely, set up a video call so the discussion is face-to-face.
- First and foremost, you need to know if the bad attitude is coming from a work-related or a personal issue. If it's work related, you can mentor the staff member on some humor strategies that could

help them improve their attitude. If it's personal, encourage the staff member to take time off to better address the issue.

- For performance issues, use the humor techniques discussed in Chapter Three to foster a milieu (Thesaurus says "setting") in which staff are encouraged to do the same.
- Be a role model and teach the humor techniques to your staff.
- If possible, have a humor skills retreat for your entire staff. If you're not sure how to conduct it, contact me and I'll come. Better yet check out the www.aath.com website for speakers/facilitators who are reasonably priced.
- Let staff clearly know your performance expectations, and make sure they also know you expect them to take the initiative in improving their coping skills to address the workplace challenges. Then offer your assistance in helping them use humor as one of those coping mechanisms. Don't wait for them to ask!
- Too much gossip? With a decrease in negative attitudes and improvement in performance, rumors will likely dissipate.

Humor and productivity

Sometime between 2000 and 2020, one department of mine (which will remain anonymous) was losing more than a million dollars a year in insurance claims denials. This was at least partly a productivity issue. The staff handling claims felt that their previous leader did not care about them or the work they did. So, I spent time with them, heard their grievances, had frequent and playful interactions, and earned their respect.

The result was an average of over 100% productivity for the departments under my supervision as seen in the chart below. If you're wondering how productivity could be higher than 100%, it is because staff were so dedicated that they would stay a little longer than their assigned shifts, even though they were encouraged to leave on time. We ended the year with a monthly average of 100.5%.

484-[redacted]--[redacted] Campus
Pay Period Productivity Trending
Workforce Analytics Dashboard

1174230-Social Svcs Beh Hlth-Hosp

2018 Productivity $/UOS

Metric	03/10/18	03/24/18	04/07/18	04/21/18	05/05/18	05/19/18	YTD
Prod $/UOS (includes shift diff, incentive pay)	$ 33.61	$ 32.13	$ 38.93	$ 35.31	$ 35.02	$ 39.89	$ 34.52
Target $/UOS (Based on McKesson Budget)	$ 35.25	$ 35.25	$ 35.25	$ 35.25	$ 35.25	$ 35.25	$ 35.25
Productivity Index	104.9%	109.7%	90.5%	99.8%	100.7%	88.4%	102.1%
$ Variance	$ 2,629	$ 5,002	$ (5,309)	$ (95)	$ 376	$ (7,157)	$ 11,663
Volume (*YTD =average PPE)	1,605	1,601	1,442	1,594	1,617	1,544	*

I also made changes to give them more freedom to do the important work that they did for our employer. Many of their daily data entry tasks were unbelievably repetitive and boring. Humor helped them find ways to enjoy their tasks more, so they could work on them longer without feeling bored. I also permitted them to work from home (pre-pandemic!) on some days of the week because most of their tasks were computer- and phone-based. By now, you will probably not be surprised to learn that being happier, more empowered, and enjoying their jobs more, resulted in a *drastic* decrease in insurance claims denials. In other words, the department's effectiveness skyrocketed!

Productivity takes energy, and it doesn't matter how much time is spent if staff cannot be productive with their time. In just one year after taking over leadership of their department, they (not me—I did not have a clue how they did it) reduced denial payments by **$879,214.64.** My boss was so happy, she let me keep the .64 cents! The next year, my budget was raised to hire two additional staff to help them save even more. And, of course, they happily did! In addition to productivity, a Wharton School of Business study found that laughter promotes creativity and greater analytical precision. So, not only are your employees inspired to perform, but they also perform *better.* Our department's figures speak for themselves (if you're an accountant or budget analyst; if not, you might want to call one):

Denial reason by Reimbursement and Year

	Annual denials	
Sum of PAID amount		
Row Labels	**20[redacted]**	**20[redacted]**
Billing Issue	$ 72,470.00	$ 7,416.00
Date Range Issue	$ 2,059.00	$ 27,845.00
Denied for Medical Records	$ 279,771.00	$ 111,020.00
Denied no COE criteria	$ 940.00	
Diagnosis Code	$ 12,682.00	$ 16,023.00
No Auth Admission Clinical	$ 2,998.00	
No Auth Admission Technical	$ 84,799.00	$ 41,728.00
No Auth Continued Stay	$ 176,928.00	$ 20,319.00
No MD Documentation	$ 16,980.00	
[redacted] County Packet not received	$ 356,762.00	
Placement related	$ 8,673.64	
Requiring Retro Review	$ 114,641.00	$ 141,724.00
Rev Code Issue	$ 100,038.00	$ 1,673.00
Unbillable/Unappeasable Resource Management		
Untimely Admission Notification		
untimely appeal		
Untimely Documentation Submission		$ 8,365.00
Untimely Processing of Required Information	$ 115.00	
Wrong Plan Code Entered	$ 19,222.00	$ 9,812.00
(blank)	$ 55,492.00	$ 39,431.00
Grand Total	**$ 1,304,570.64**	**$ 425,356.00**

Humor and creativity

"Be outrageous! People who achieve mastery have the ability to be outrageous."

Gita Bellin

By reading this book you've allowed yourself to be unconstrained and are considering new ways to develop your leadership style. Congratulations on this bold move!

Now let's check out our new corporate promotional materials:

Here's an illustration of a job interview, where the boss is seeking creative candidates.

At this point in your reading, you've earned a story break:

One night, a Delta twin-engine puddle jumper was flying somewhere above New Jersey. There were four people on board: the pilot, a venture capitalist, the Dalai Lama, and a young college student. Suddenly, an illegal oxygen generator exploded loudly in the luggage compartment, and the cabin began to fill with smoke. The cockpit door opened, and the pilot burst in.

"Passengers," he shouted, "I have good news and bad news. The bad news is that we're about to crash. The good news is that there are three parachutes, and I have one of them!" With that, the pilot threw open the door and jumped from the plane.

The venture capitalist immediately went into action. "Ladies and gentlemen, I am the world's top venture capitalist, and probably the smartest person in the world. Obviously, I need a parachute." Grabbing a pack, the capitalist jumped.

The Dalai Lama and the student looked at one another. Finally, the Dalai Lama spoke, "My friend, I have lived a satisfying life and have known the bliss of True Enlightenment. You still have your life ahead of you, so you should take a parachute, and I'll go down with the plane."

The student smiled and said, "Hey, don't worry, Your Holiness. The smartest person in the world just jumped out with my backpack."

If that didn't make you laugh, or at least smile, then our senses of humor are really divergent (totally fine, but please do not give me a rating on Amazon). Our tastes in humor vary as much as the foods we like and dislike. (And if you enjoy my type of humor then, please, *do* write an Amazon review!)

Research also suggests that humor and creativity go together, probably because in both cases, we're tying things together in a new way, seeing new connections. Divergent thinking is basically about having the ability to think about whatever issue is troubling you from a fresh and different perspective. Humor gives us a chance to see things from a new perspective and so to develop our divergent thinking capabilities.

If you as a leader really want to develop your ability to use humor as a creative process, I suggest you take an improv class. Improvisational humor hones skills like empathy, problem-solving, and divergent thinking. Improv also gives you the ability to connect seemingly unrelated ideas and come up with creative solutions that otherwise would have never even been considered. And you get to interact with new people in a new setting—kind of like starting a new job or hiring a new employee. In many cities, classes are available on improv. If you have no interest or are too shy to try a class, books are also helpful.

Practice Playshop: "These are three things"- An Improv Game

Have staff stand in a circle: You as leader turn to the person on your right and give them a category of three things (three things you love to eat). They will list three things as quickly as they can.

"Ice cream." Everyone responds, "One!"

"Chicken." All respond, "Two!"

"Cupcakes." All respond, "Three!"

Then everyone says in unison, "These are three things!"

The person who just gave their list turns to the person to their right and gives them a category (three things in the water…). The game continues until you have gone all the way around the circle. Be sure to include yourself at the end.

It's a fun warm-up exercise before a brainstorming session or just to get the blood pumping during any kind of meeting.

Essential improv takeaway:

"Yes, and…"

My most important learning from improv is the concept of "Yes, and…" When ideas or suggestions are made, it's very common to respond with why it *won't* work, such as:

> Staff member A: "We could try rotating staff on different units."
> Staff member B: "No, that probably won't work."

(Would you be encouraged to work with Staff Member B on anything?) Instead, in improv the response is always: "Yes, and …," which opens up other options. For example, instead of finding fault with assigning staff to difference units, Staff Member B could have said:

> "**Yes, and** perhaps staff would *voluntarily* like to try working on a different unit. That way it is up to them."
> "**Yes, and** we could also offer some *incentives* for those who are willing to volunteer."

You can see how this gets the creative juices flowing rather than shutting them down with a "no, that won't work" response. (**Yes, and** additional information about improv is listed in the resource section of the book!)

A clear sign of a successful brainstorming session is lots of laughter and lots of positive ideas.
Karuna Subramaniam and her colleagues at Northwestern University found that boosting the mood of volunteers increased their likelihood of having an "aha! Moment" that helped solve a word association puzzle. Specifically, volunteers who watched a Robin Williams comedy special did measurably better at the task using insight than those who watched a quantum electronics talk or a scary movie. Laughter is also one of the best stress management tools leaders can use for themselves and their staff. As the Mayo Clinic reports, laughter increases the release of endorphins, reduces tension, and helps us connect with others

(http://www.mayoclinic.org/healthy-living/stress-management/in-depth/stress-relief/art-20044456?pg=1).

That said, there is a difference between laughter and humor. As we know, humor is personal and based on one's worldview. Laughter is more of a physical response to that humor. According to friend and former Association for Applied and Therapeutic Humor (AATH) President Steven Sultanoff, "A sense of humor can be defined as the ability to perceive one or more of the universal characteristics. Therefore, one's sense of humor involves the capacity to appreciate incongruity, absurdity, an unexpected future, a pleasant surprise, a startle, getting it and/or emotional chaos remembered in tranquility … Once a stimulus is perceived as humorous, it will trigger a reaction within the individual. This reaction may be physiological (laughter) cognitive (wit), or emotional (mirth)." For the rest of us, that means: "Laughter is a physical response to humor."

Put another way, humor is the condition of *being or seeing funny things*. Laughter is the *physical manifestation*. "Laughs" take many forms. My colleague, Paul McGhee, says there are fifteen stages of laughter (check out his website to learn more: https://www.laughterremedy.com). Humor is a sort of elixir, a tonic that is good for mind and spirit. Laughter is documented to be good for the body. "Some early research suggests that humor and laughter activate our bodies to turn down the stress hormones (cortisol and epinephrine) and turn up the happiness hormones (oxytocin and dopamine) as well as the natural pain killers (endorphins)," according to Dr. David Fessell, Professor of Radiology at the University of Michigan.

At this point, now that we're clear on the many forms and benefits of humor, let me throw in a caution: leaders who have little sense of humor or who are uncomfortable using humor should *not* do so. Even if you are usually comfortable doing so, if something in your gut says "no" or if the person in front of you literally says, "No," then you might want to change course. Why? Because this might foster an inauthentic display of humor, which would fail its intention or make the relationship between leaders and followers even worse. An inauthentic display of humor may also have negative consequences for the leaders themselves, such as surface acting. Surface acting is one form of emotional labor, which fosters psychological strain, burnout, and even psychosomatic complaints, and also decreases job satisfaction and commitment.

How can we know the limits? First, humor guidelines prevent leaders and staff from using aggressive humor. Second, humor is not a necessary requirement to become a transformational or other kind of leader. Other things can also support staff and help them feel cared for by their leader (such as the "Monday Memos," having lunch, etc.) Here are a few:

DO:

- Be open to new ways of thinking
- Be an active listener
- Be a risk-taker
- Be willing to accept responsibility
- Give credit to your staff whenever possible
- Trust your staff

DON'T:

- Be condescending
- Use sarcasm
- Act like a know-it-all

Most importantly, understand that only one man in ten is a true leader (the other nine true leaders are probably women!). Consider the two charts below. The first illustrates measurement of a leader's sense of humor as opposed to leaders who don't use their sense of humor.

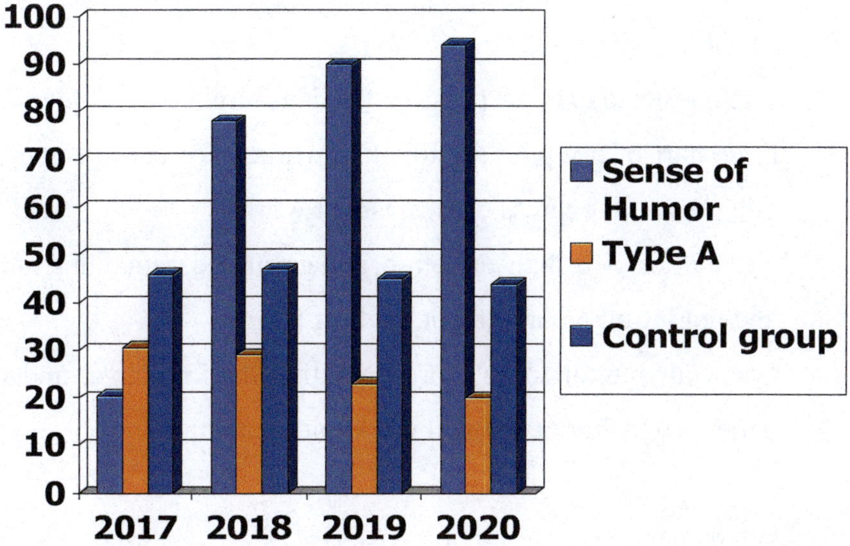

Just kidding! Actually, this bar chart is not properly labeled. The image clearly does not mean anything, but my editor recommended graphics, so I added this. Also, this was the smallest chapter, so it helps to balance it out.

Okay, back to the real input!

To be a top 10 % leader, one must possess or at least work on acquiring certain abilities. There are many, in fact, but obtaining these are a priority:

1. Recognize and acknowledge your weaknesses.
2. Use humor to learn from setbacks and turn them to your advantage.

3. Use humor to improve your self-confidence and thus earn the confidence of those you lead.
4. Use humor to express passion. (Because my sense of humor is a large part of my passion, this has worked for me, but there are other ways to express enthusiasm at work.)
5. Use humor to be real, authentic, and grounded, remaining humble and not letting your ego get the best of you.
6. Use your humor to be more proactive, less reactive, and more patient (whether or not you work with patients).

Most leaders have the ability to master at least one of the abilities mentioned above. The more your humor comes from a place of kindness, grace, gratitude, and sincere appreciation for the daily dedication of staff, the more effective you will be at mastering these abilities.

Leaders should do their best to be healthy role models. I always did my best to be effective, even when my pain levels were quite high. The very last thing you want is for your staff to feel sorry for you, or to worry that you aren't caring for yourself properly. If they think you are having overwhelming challenges, why would they approach you with theirs? This is not about denial; it's about personal responsibility.

Practice Playshop: Why Use Humor?

For this playshop, we'll look at the intention behind the humor, and the difference that makes.

1. If you are already a highly humorous leader, you can apply the following questions to yourself. If not, recall a great leader you've met. If you've never known any (and that is a shame!), recall an ineffective leader.
2. What is your (or their) purpose for using humor? Is it coping? Reframing a problem? Celebrating an achievement? Improving a confusing communication? To destress? Something else?
3. Which intention seemed to be the most beneficial, either for the leader or for staff in general?
4. Which intent did *not* seem to be met through humor?
5. How did the effect of those two intentions differ, and why?

My experience indicates that a positive, humor-enhanced leadership style is more admirable than attractiveness, physical abilities, or intellect. (Otherwise, why would I spend time writing this book?!) Leaders should use their humor to address problems and address conflicts, not to avoid them. I recommend a focus on humor at work for two primary purposes:

1. Inspiring trust.

2. Unleashing staff creativity.

Leaders can learn to develop a playful attitude, to look for humor in everyday life, to use humor for stress relief, and to help others learn to do the same.

Keep in mind that a positive intent is essential, especially in case the humor goes wrong, because it is much more likely you'll be forgiven for your mistake. Consider: if this action or statement were taken out of context, would it stand on its own, on your reputation, or would you suffer from "bad optics" (there's more great jargon!)? It is also important that top executives or your supervisors support its use; otherwise, staff could get mixed messages. As mentioned, I had "permission" to use my sense of humor from others in leadership.

Humor and emotional intelligence (EI)

Emotional intelligence (EI) is a term (coined by Daniel Goleman) to describe our ability to regulate our impulses, empathize with others, and increase our resiliency when facing adversity. Austrian researchers have found that higher emotional intelligence is present in people who *appropriately* use dark humor. Their research bears out that humor-processing is a complex task, one that is dependent on cognitive and emotional aspects. The researchers suggest that these processes allow the frame-shifting and conceptual blending (creating new meanings out of old) that underlie humor processing. They concluded that highly humorous people have both higher verbal and non-verbal intelligence, and that they score lower in mood disturbance and aggressiveness. (For more details and correlational data, see the citation in the resource section).

"Knowing others is wisdom; knowing yourself is enlightenment."

Lao-tzu, Philosopher, 6th century BCE

When humor is used, it enhances our emotional intelligence (EI) and helps us increase our awareness of ourselves and others, as well as provides the spark to apply self-management and to use social skills. One way humor can enhance our EI is through the use of our humorous fantasies. Recall that humorous fantasies come from our imagination, and when we think of them, we become distracted just long enough to decrease our stress level and to separate ourselves emotionally from the anger or frustration over the situation.

It is virtually impossible to stay angry when you are thinking of something humorous. Have you ever been in a situation where the colleague you were arguing with made you laugh? Perhaps you tried not to, because you "wanted to stay angry" at them, but just couldn't? Using your sense of humor to develop your EI will also help you enhance your leadership abilities, enrich your relationships, extend your sphere of influence, and so expand the resources at your disposal to face leadership challenges. When you utilize your sense of humor and your EI, you'll realize that to mock others means you don't know them, to laugh with others is to understand, and to laugh at your own antics means that you know yourself.

Humor and Spirituality

"The attempt to develop a sense of humor and to see things in a humorous light is some kind of a trick learned while mastering the art of living."

Viktor Frankl, Man's Search for Meaning

Viktor Frankl was a Holocaust survivor and founder of a school of psychotherapy called logotherapy. He also said, "Humor, more than anything else in the human makeup, can afford an aloofness and an ability to rise above any situation, if only for a few seconds." And a few seconds is all it takes for an "aha" moment to occur. Laughter has afforded me such moments, moments that have transformed my life. That is how powerful *your* sense of humor can be.

The *many* theories of humor include: the superiority theory, the relief theory, the incongruence theory, and the solidarity theory. Let's review them briefly. The superiority theory assumes that humor serves to advance the humorist at the expense of the "butt of the joke." The relief theory assumes that humor serves to stimulate and then release tension in the individual and in society by mixing things up, activating people while ultimately providing a positive experience that serves as a release from the tension, such as that created by the suspense of a story. The incongruence theory assumes that humor "messes with people's minds," surprising them in subtle or challenging ways. The solidarity theory assumes that humor serves to bring people together, introducing and bonding them in a common cause, or for no cause at all, but simply because they share the ludicrous condition of being human.

Now let's delve into my very own Humor Spirit Theory. Humor has emotional, cognitive, and physical aspects. I find that humor also has a spiritual aspect, and when we laugh uncontrollably, we are experiencing the spiritual aspect. Many spiritual beliefs also incorporate humor in some way. I'm not referring to adherence to a specific religious denomination, but rather your own personal belief system and the role of spirit within it. For instance, the Baal Shem Tov, founder of the Jewish Hasidic movement, noted, "Humor is that thing that ushers a person's mind from a place of constricted consciousness to a place of expanded consciousness." Very deep!

A highly humorous leader, as we've learned, has mastered or is on their way to mastering what I will call their humor spirit. They can take a challenging situation and transform it into a totally different and more positive situation; they often use their humor spirit, whether they are aware of it or not. My Humor Spirit Theory also assumes that when we laugh heartily, we are feeling and experiencing the true spirit of humor.

In other words, humor is an integral part of our soul, and we laugh because we have been moved by our humor spirit.

I have difficulty distinguishing between my sense of humor and my spiritual self, which are really two sides of the same coin. One cannot exist without the other. Your humor spirit, I believe, also helps you become more aware of the spiritual aspects of your personal sense of humor. In *Star Wars*, they call it "The Force."

Masters of the humor spirit (think of them as Humor Jedi) have mastered "The Humor Force," which gives them the ability to manifest their humor spirit's presence at will. Highly humorous leaders have a keen awareness of the humorous aspects of their leadership style and personality. If you asked a highly humorous leader who their favorite comedians are, they could rattle the answer off in seconds. They could easily tell you their favorite types of humor, be it dark, slapstick, self-enhancing, improv, word play, topical, observational, or bodily function (potty) humor, to name just a few. Perhaps you are in that group as well! Dave Chappell, Jerry Seinfeld, Ellen DeGeneres, as well as late, great legends like George Carlin, Richard Pryor, Lucille Ball, Rodney Dangerfield, Robin Williams, and many others are or were Humor Jedis.

Most of the time we can control our humor spirit, but we have all probably experienced a time when the spirit of humor overtook us, and we laughed uncontrollably. No matter how hard we tried we simply couldn't stop that force. When that happens, you have given yourself over to your humor spirit! You are in a state of bliss. If you are laughing uncontrollably with another, then your humor spirits have connected and perhaps intertwined, and you feel closer to each other. While there is no tangible proof that a humor spirit exists, if you've felt that connection with another during hearty laughter, then you experienced a very unique kind of connection. When you think of those you are attracted to and like to spend time with, their humor spirit could likely be one of the reasons why.

"I never lose sight of the fact that just being is fun."

Katherine Hepburn

Practice Playshop: Wrap Up

This week, you can wrap up this learning in real life:

1. When funny moments happen at work, jot them down each day, even those you may think are insignificant.
2. At the end of the week (and again at the end of the month, quarter, or year), review and mark any of the instances you initiated.
3. Savor and celebrate those moments, and any success that resulted!

In closing:

This book is not intended to have been read only once and forgotten about.

Revisit it as a humor leadership manual that is always available.

I myself need the friendly reminders herein, on occasion, to maintain my positive attitude.

Samuel Jacobson, son of author and pretty funny guy.

Congratulations you have just about completed reading this book!

Appendix B
(Appendix A had to be removed)

Motivational steps to becoming a highly humorous leader

This was intended to be Appendix A, but that was removed during emergency surgery, so I decided to go with the duodenum instead. A duodenum is like an addendum (or at least sounds similar), but there are two in this one addendum. (Either that, or it's the first part of the small intestine. You be the judge!) Having read the book, consider these suggestions to go even farther.

1. Self-reflection

If you've seen *Fiddler on the Roof*, think (again) of Tevye. (If you haven't seen it, well watch it! Use a streaming service or contact your library and check out the DVD!) At the times he goes go into the "witness state" as I call it. Things freeze for a moment, and he stops and has a discussion with himself about a decision he has to make. You can also look at yourself as a leader, asking:

- What am I doing to help my staff?
- What could I do to be even more helpful?

- What am a doing for my own satisfaction rather than for my staff?
- Taking a deep look at our team processes, what are my staff doing that is a time drain, but a necessary component of their job?
- How can I alleviate some of that tedious work?
- Do I take myself too seriously?
- Are our meetings enjoyable?
- Do I spend lots of time bad-mouthing our corporate office? Why?
- Am I generally pleasant?
- What am I doing to enhance team-building?
- Do I seem to be uptight, angry, or upset by things, and do I show that to my staff?

Consider your answer to these questions in any order you like.

Now, to help complete the reflection, here are some humor***less*** attitudes and beliefs that would need to change in order to move your work culture out of these boxes and in a more positive direction:

Work is a struggle to be endured.	I only work to earn money to use when I am away from work.	If I use humor, my staff will take advantage of me.
The work setting is not a place to have fun.	As leader, I have to be tough and distant.	Using my sense of humor makes me look foolish.

2. **Motivation: Convince yourself that change is needed, and that you CAN learn to utilize humor to help your team move forward.**

After self-reflection, it is time to decide that a change is necessary to move your culture into a more positive state. To do so, you must believe that you have the ability to learn how to use humor as a strong tool to assist you with the effort. Take a moment now—perhaps reviewing what you learned through the playshops, or times when humor was a positive force at work—to convince yourself that humor is one tool for positive change.

3. **Lightening up the workplace.**

"Do the thing you fear, and death of fear is certain."

Emerson

Like all other skills, being humorous requires education, development, and practice. Strange as it seems (or strange as I might seem!), we have to *learn* how to be more informal and lighten up. It starts with overcoming our fear of looking foolish. C. W. Metcalf does a great job addressing this (https://www.amazon.com/Lighten-Up-Survival-Skills-Pressure/dp/0201622394). Once you get past the fear, you can practice humor techniques to help you and your team lighten up.

To acquire the ability to utilize humor as a leader, you'll need to be willing to stand outside your comfort zone. There, the humor you use or are strengthening becomes a new leadership skill in your leadership toolbox.

4. **Challenge yourself!**

Take ownership of your role as the leader of your team, department(s), sections, or whomever you supervise. Talk honestly and openly with other leaders, letting them know that you intend to use more humor to help shape the workplace culture and would appreciate their support. Trust other leaders to do so, and then in turn, offer your support to them. Share the humorous messages you offer employees, so other leaders can share with their own staff. Incorporate your sense of humor into your work with all those you come in contact with. Practice smiling, greeting people each day, making eye contact, reaching out to others, and letting your face tell people you are happy. Make humor inclusive: work deliberately to get everyone involved and encourage them to use their own sense(s) of humor.

The nuts and bolts

If you have not read the book yet, a good way to cheat is by taking this post-reading quiz:

Having a great sense of humor has caused people to:

A. Become very angry over little things.
B. Become very defensive when asked an appropriate question.
C. Become more emotionally well-balanced.

Leaders who appropriately use humor at work:

A. Are terminated within two weeks.
B. Have more sexual harassment suits than other leaders.
C. Are perceived as more trustworthy and typically have higher rates of employee retention.

You have just hired a new employee. During their first week of orientation, it is:

A. Best not to use any humor. Orientation is serious business, and you do not want to give them the wrong idea.
B. It is important to use and role model appropriate humor during the first week to orient them to the culture where using appropriate humor is not only permissible but encouraged.
C. It's best to use aggressive and put-down humor on your new staff, to provide intimidating job descriptions, and/or to brag about your intense workout routine and what type of car you drive, so they know what to expect.

Humor:

A. Increases conflict, damages trust, and damages employee engagement.
B. Connects us with others and reduces status and power differentials.
C. Increases stress, and turnover, and discourages people from working together.

(Hint: A and C of the last question are the opposite of the truth.)

Answers: Okay, really? If you need an answer key, please, read the book.

Hooray—you have done it! You have completed the book and are now ready to implement the new humor skills! With this information to draw from, I hope you will be more comfortable trying out different humor techniques and feel good about your journey to becoming a highly humorous leader!

Sources, Outsources, Resources, and Courses (and of course, Fake References)

References that I Wish Existed

Adams, J. (1790). *Freedom is not a laughing matter (no matter what Jefferson says)*. Braintree, MA.

Alexander The Great (325 BCE). *How to use humor to appease a conquered world.* Babylon, Mesopotamia.

Buddha, G. (500 BCE). *How I used humor to spread Buddhism around the world.* Kushinagar, India.

Churchill, W. (1960). The *role of humor in winning World War II (which, overall, was not too bloody funny).* London, UK.

Crebicus, A. (23 CE). *A centurion's use of humor with their infantry groups*. Rome, The Roman Empire.

Cromwell, O. (1657). *Why I regret not using humor as leader during my brief political career and unsuccessful trial defence.* Huntingdon, UK.

Einstein, A. (1950). *Leadership = (humor)*$^{2.}$ Plainsboro Township, NJ.

Franklin, B. (1788). *Why I love fart jokes.* Philadelphia, PA.

Jefferson, T. (1789). *Why I, too, love fart jokes.* Monticello, VA.

Lincoln, A. (1862). *The role of humor in my decision to remove McClellan from command of the Union Army*. Washington. DC.

McClellan, G. (1861). *The failed use of leadership humor at the Battle of Antietam*. Sharpsburg, MD.

Tzu, S. (490 BCE). *The art of humor*. Zhou Kingdom, China.

Washington, G. (1783) *The role of humor in leadership, Volume One: Revolutionary wars, and Volume Two: Why presidents should not use fart jokes*. Mount Vernon, VA.

Real References

Thousands of articles are available on humor and leadership. If you would like to delve further into this topic, consider using a database (such as Google Scholar or perhaps one available through a local university) or your favorite search method. Try key words "humor" and "leadership," or regional variants such as "big Kahuna," "The Dude," or "Royal Majesty."

The number one resource for all therapeutic humor information in the world is the Association for Applied and Therapeutic Humor (AATH) at www.aath.org. Members have access to *The Humor Research Library*, including a searchable database designed to locate peer-reviewed and other academic research articles specifically focused on humor and laughter.

There seems to be a mandatory requirement that all leadership books that mention humor must also cite the Robert Half survey, which found that 91% of executives believe a sense of humor is important for career advancement, and 84% feel that people with a good sense of humor do a better job. (I do not know why they call it Half. It was a complete survey.) You will find the link to the survey in the recommendations below.

Recommended Articles, Authors, Books, and Links

American Association of Therapeutic Humor (AATH)

https://www.aath.org (free) and https://aath.memberclicks.net/aath-authors (must be a member; if you are serious about humor in leadership, it is worth joining).

Cognitive Processing Therapy

Resick, P., Monson, C., Chard, K. (2008). *Cognitive processing therapist group manual: Veteran/military version.* Washington, DC: Department of Veterans Affairs.

Resick, P., Monson, C., Chard, K. (2008). *Cognitive processing therapy veteran/military version: Therapist and patient materials manual.* Washington, DC: Department of Veterans Affairs.

Marc Gelkopf (2011). The use of humor in serious mental illness: A review. *Evidence-Based Complementary Alternative Medicine*, 2011: 342837. https://www.ncbi.nlm.nih.gov/pmc/articles/PMC3135316/

Ulrike Willinger, et al. (2016). Cognitive and emotional demands of black humor processing: the role of intelligence, aggressiveness and mood. *Journal of Cognitive Processing, 18*:159–167 DOI 10.1007/s10339-016-0789-y https://link.springer.com/content/pdf/10.1007%2Fs10339-016-0789-y.pdf

Humor and Grief

Allen Klein (1989). *The Healing Power of Humor: Techniques for Getting Through Loss, Setbacks, Upsets, Disappointments, Difficulties, Trials, Tribulations, and All That Not-So-Funny Stuff.* https://www.amazon.com/Healing-Power-Humor-Disappointments-Difficulties/dp/0874775191

Humor and Leadership

Esther Blumenfeld and Lynne Alpern (1994). *Humor at Work: The Guaranteed, Bottom Line, Low Cost, High Efficiency Guide to Success Through Humor.* Peachtree Publishers. https://www.amazon.com/Humor-Work-Guaranteed-Efficiency-Success/dp/1561450855

John Boldoni's website: *Leading with humor: Laughter Is an affirmation of humanity.* https://www.smartbrief.com/original/2020/07/leading-humor-laughter-affirmation-humanity

Karyn Buxman's website: (Neurohumorist, Speaker Hall of Famer & past President AATH)
https://www.karynbuxman.com/

P.S. Fry (1995). Perfectionism, humor, and optimism as moderators of health outcomes and determinants of coping styles of women executives. *Genetic, Social, and General Psychology*

Monographs, 121(2), 211–245.
https://psycnet.apa.org/record/1995-45550-001

Wayne H. Decker and Denise M. Rotondo
https://www.jstor.org/stable/40604364
Relationships Among Gender, Type Of Humor, And Perceived Leader Effectiveness

P. Gkorezis, L. Hatzithomas and E. Petridou
https://www.jstor.org/stable/25822539
The Impact of Leader's Humor on Employees' Psychological Empowerment: the Moderating Role of Tenure

Scholarly Articles Published in 2022

Effect of humor leadership on inventiveness of employees and administrative reliability

Leading through affiliation: the effect of humor type and gender on likelihood of being perceived as a leader

The Impact of Leader Humor on Team Creativity

Beyond formal exchange: An informal perspective on the role of leader humor on employee OCB

Research on the mechanism of leader aggressive humor on employee silence

Leader self-deprecating humor and employee creativity at workplace: a longitudinal study

Laughing with me or laughing at me? The differential effects of leader humor expressions on follower status and influence at work

Leader Humor and Followers' Change-Oriented Organizational Citizenship Behavior: The Role of Leader Machiavellianism

Learning from Fun Leadership Experiences

Impact of Leader-Member Exchange on Innovative Work Behavior: Role of Employee-Based Brand Equity, Humor, and Humble Leadership

David Jacobson. Several interesting articles on humor and leadership topics at Articles on Humorous Leadership - Highly Humorous Leadership

David Jacobson. Several interesting articles on therapeutic humor-related topics at https://davidmjacobson.com/interesting-articles-on-therapeutic-humor-related-topics/

Humor Research Lab (n.d.) *Benign Violation Theory* https://humorresearchlab.com/benign-violation-theory/

The International Society for Humor Studies http://www.humorstudies.org/ (By the way, Rod Martin is a former president of this organization).

Martin, R. A. (2010). *The Psychology of Humor: An Integrative Approach.* Elsevier. https://www.amazon.com/Psychology-

Humor-Integrative-Approach-ebook-dp-B005XJ4MC0/dp/B005XJ4MC0

Mary Kay Morrison (2010). (A wonderfully supportive friend and past President AATH, amazing educator, and a great, great grandma, too! I mean she's great at being a grandma as well as being a great grandma) Here's two of her best but check them all out. They're all great! *Using Humor to Maximize Learning: The Links between Positive Emotions and Education.* R&L Education. Lead With a Sense of Humor (Vol. 2): Why (and How to) Be a Funnier and More Effective Educational Leader and Laugh All the Way to Your Institution The Curious Academic Publishing (January 31, 2022)

Fabio Sala (2003), "Laughing all the way to the bank." *Harvard Business Review* https://hbr.org/2003/09/laughing-all-the-way-to-the-bank

Steven M. Sultanoff, Ph.D. (Adjunct Professor on the faculty of Pepperdine University and past President of AATH among other things) has several articles and other wonderful things on his website: http://www.humormatters.com/articles.htm

The Four Styles of Humor

https://www.researchgate.net/publication/235289206_Empowering_leadership_and_the_influence_of_a_humorous_work_climate_on_service_employees%27_creativity_and_innovative_behaviour_in_frontline_service_jobs (Spoiler alert: Empowering leadership and the influence of a humorous work climate on service employees' creativity and innovative behavior in frontline service jobs.)

Humor and Emotional Intelligence

Ed Dunkelblau past President AATH and Director of the Institute for Emotionally Intelligent Learning **http://www.teacheq.com**

Paul McGhee, Ph.D.

https://www.laughterremedy.com/article_pdfs/Emotional%20Intelligence.pdf

Comedy Skills

Judy Carter (2021) *The New Comedy Bible: The Ultimate Guide to Writing and Performing Stand-Up Comedy* (Audiobook). https://www.amazon.com/New-Comedy-Bible-Ultimate-Performing/dp/B08SHZGGX4

Matt Walsh, Ian Roberts, and Matt Besser *(January 1, 2013) Upright Citizens Brigade Comedy Improvisation Manual* (Paperback).

Classes and Courses

If you are serious about enhancing your leadership style, I ***highly*** recommend the Association for Applied and Therapeutic Humor's *Humor Academy*. (I'm not just saying that because I am on their leadership team.) The Humor Academy is a three-year, college-level program focused on the science, benefits, and application of humor. Each level of the Humor Academy lasts one year, and those who complete all three years earn the distinction of Certified Humor Professional (CHP). Continuing education credits are also available. www.aath.org https://www.aath.org/humoracademy

Courses

Humor is now being recognized as a serious component of any good leader's toolbox. At the time of this writing, the Stanford School of Business offers a course:

> https://humor-seriousbusiness.stanford.edu/
>
> Remotely Humorous: Build Joyful and Resilient Virtual Teams with Humor Professional Certificate | edX

Employee Incentives

> https://packedwithpurpose.gifts/corporate-gifts

Improv Training

If you're in LA, Chicago, or NYC, I dare you NOT to find an improv class!

https://magnettheater.com/

https://www.secondcity.com/courses/chicago/adult/

https://www.ucbtraininigcenter.com/

Please reach out by email: humorhorizons@gmail.com or visit his LinkedIn page at

https://www.linkedin.com/in/david-jacobson-9989062

Never forget the importance of play!

ABOUT THE AUTHOR

David M. Jacobson, LCSW, CHP is a professional speaker, author and consultant on leadership, team building, humor and health, and overcoming trauma. David has served on many boards including the Board of Directors of the Arthritis Foundation Southern Arizona Chapter, Board of Directors NASW, Arizona Chapter, and the Board of Directors of the Association for Applied and Therapeutic Humor (AATH). He is a Certified Humor Professional through their AATH Humor Academy. He also served as a cook at Arthur Treacher's Fish and Chips© and voted in an HOA meeting once. David M. Jacobson, LCSW, CHP rose to the top of the companies he worked for, including his own. This book explains how his humorous approach became the most essential part of his leadership style. It details the specific techniques he used and how you, too, can use them to rise to the top. Under his highly humorous leadership, his departments attained the highest employee engagement, productivity, creativity, retention, revenue generation and happiness in their places of work. David is a former Hospital Director, Federal Chief of Service, and Executive National Director at an Internet company. He has been married for over thirty-eight years and attributes this to not getting divorced. He and Laurie have four children, who are now adults and most of whom are less dysfunctional than David.

Author website: https://authordmjacobson.com/

Printed in Dunstable, United Kingdom

73148336R00127

19 [illegible] 2

Crimson

ARCHITECTURAL HISTORIANS

Too Blessed to be Depressed

ROTTERDAM-MAASKANT FOUNDATION

010 PUBLISHERS, ROTTERDAM 2002

2

Contents

FOREWORD

In awarding the ninth Rotterdam-Maaskant Prize for Young Architects to Wouter Vanstiphout, it is as though the major Rotterdam-Maaskant Prize and the Young Architects award have been rolled into one. Young though he is, Vanstiphout, together with his colleagues at Crimson Architectural Historians, has already achieved much in the way of publishing, teaching and other stimulative work to further the cultural and/or social cause of architecture, urban design and landscape architecture - the very criteria for eligibility for the 'major Maaskant'. Yet by tunnelling deep into the practice of building and planning, Crimson also has the attributes of a design office. The 'young Maaskant' is an incentive prize for designers up to the age of 35 that up till now has focused on the architectural work, whether this be three-dimensional or on paper. Vanstiphout's young predecessors - Körmeling, Mecanoo, Arets, Neutelings, Van der Pol, Geuze, Rapp and the occasional consortium of Bindels, Gietema, Hartzema and Klok - were almost all practicing architects.

As an architectural historian and a pupil of Ed Taverne, winner of the 1984 major Rotterdam-Maaskant Prize, Wouter Vanstiphout has carried historical research into the arena of current professional practice. The lack of a descriptive historical awareness in the design disciplines and, conversely, that of a design attitude in the historical department, have been synthetized by Crimson and Vanstiphout into a way of working. Both disciplines thus gain a worthy supplement, which Vanstiphout continues to unstintingly furnish, that lends relevance to the incentive to press on and expand, not just for the prizewinner but even more so for the two professional groups.

'Too Blessed To Be Depressed' gives a foretaste of the compelling integration and confrontation we can expect to see between the various branches of the profession. Viewed in this light, Maaskant would not have wished for a more fitting recipient for the award he helped instigate.

Ivo W. Opstelten *Chairman of the Rotterdam-Maaskant Foundation*

History

The Crimson Architectural Historians are sitting in a three-room office on the fourth floor of a fifties building in downtown Rotterdam with their backs to a window on a canal. Not your beautiful, leafy, old, elegant, rustic 17th century Amsterdam canal, but a big, bare, ugly motherfucker of a canal, flanked by brutish buildings of concrete and glass. There's a greasy downward smudge on one of the windows left by a cormorant who flew into it some days ago. Funny animals, cormorants, sitting there on a floating tyre, spreading out their wings in the wind to dry, squawking at each other. They say that in Japan fishermen put a metal ring around their necks, attach the ring to a chain and release the bird into the water. It swims around and catches a fish; the ring stops it from swallowing the fish and when the bird is back on board, all the fisherman has to do is reach inside and pull the flip-flopping fish out of the squirming bird and throw it in his basket, and back in the water goes the cormorant.

You guessed it: cormorants are like architectural historians; history is the fish. Either through academic values and regulations, or through an architects' and planners' monopoly on getting things done, historians have to operate with a ring around their throat. They are allowed to search out the historical data, can even make analyses, but have to fit them into research programmes, present their research using academic standards, not say anything that cannot be checked or even proven and at all costs avoid being partisan, emotive, fanatical. They have to gather the historical data, give their verdict on historical importance, and then pass on their conclusions to the planning commissions and architects who decide what to do with the said historical building, mediaeval trench, twenties social housing, rusty old steelmill etc. Crimson likes to catch its fish and swallow it too. We don't want to choke it up to the fisherman, who cuts it open, throws away the guts, the brains and the spine, filets the meat and sells it only to be cooked in a stew with carrots.

Stranded in the sad, stupid city of Rotterdam we realize that urban planning and architecture, like war, are continuations of writing history by other means. Take the jubilee of 1995, when fifty years of reconstruction was celebrated. Architectural historians went into a frenzy of writing books and brochures about this particular period, fixating the events of bombing, burning and building in definitive essays, books, and exhibitions, emancipating the stark fifties and sixties architecture in an architectural period-style worth conserving. Behind or underneath the buildings something else was found: a riveting psychodrama that proves the transformative powers of writing history. The archives showed that from the thirties onward, the form of the city was rhetorically divorced from its 'true meaning'. The city was described by its planners, businessmen, architects and critics not as a form but as spirit of change, and subsequently physically attacked with enormous demolition and building projects. 'The reconstruction of Rotterdam' started before the bombings, we noticed. The reason for Rotterdam to so radically draw the ultimate conclusions from the devastation caused by the German bombing, was caused by the rewriting of its historical identity before the war. The rewriting of Rotterdam's history reached fever pitch during the war and developed into the worship of its emptiness, and into an urban project bent on avoiding any kind of fixation. Rather than placing this partly ideological, partly technocratic operation in its appropriate historical context and criticizing it, we dived straight in. History to us became not a clear-cut period in the past, but a total panoramic experience in which mythology and truth, writing and building and demolition all blur into each other. And we had no inclination whatsoever to put distance between ourselves and this panorama. If you mythologize the emptiness of Rotterdam so strongly that it actually becomes part of the urban planning, myth does become fact.

The reconstruction research led us to conceive of our job as painting panoramas of possibilities. And Rotterdam in our mind became much, much more than the existing panorama of old and new; it became a hallucination of what was, never was, could have been, should have been, should not have been, might still become and can be made to be believed by some that it actually is.

On a more practical level, history became incredibly useful, because the confrontation with it means the possibility of adding something to a programme or a project that is new and wild. Depending on what kind of old stuff you have to deal with as an architect, a planner or a writer, there is a wild, unpredictable offering of themes, images and ideas: they can be about death, crime, sex, poverty, destruction, beauty, love, religion, ideology, nature or even about architecture. History becomes the random factor in what are usually stalely conventional programmes. The success of a new project for an old building depends on the narrative abilities of the architect, with which he mobilizes the historical offerings. Differently put: being able to tell a good story, a gripping story, a touching, exciting, spectacular story is the core of designing and planning.

Learning to swallow the fish ourselves, is the main theme of this first chapter. It is about taking a resolute turn towards engagement and away from critical distance, it is about trying to paint the panorama of war-torn Rotterdam from many different angles and using many different 'techniques': historical writing, pictorial collage, counter-factual parallel history. It is about uncovering the narrative possibilities of dealing with historical context again by writing about it in our 'normal' role as critics, but also by winging our way through two actual urban design commissions, one for a 17th century harbour-fragment, the other for a 19th century panopticon jail. But probably it is mostly about bringing down the walls between the mythological and the real, by giving the myths real presence in our physical experience of the city. We believe in the use of history to animate the dead stones and empty spaces of the city with a whole gamut of human sentiment: from righteous indignation to homesickness and back again.

Substance and Tenacity

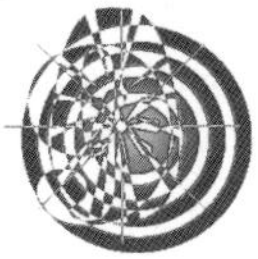

In 1946, six years after the devastating bombing of the centre, *the Basic Plan for the Reconstruction of Rotterdam* was presented to the city's residents in the form of a dreary-looking brochure on poor-quality paper with the title The New Heart of Rotterdam. The plan had been supervised by Cornelis van Traa, Rotterdam's director of urban planning. The psychology of the introduction to this brochure is breathtaking. In romantic and almost nostalgic terms, Van Traa asked: *'Citizen of Rotterdam, do you ever think back on your old town?'* He continued by evoking collective memories of the peculiarities of the pre-war city and the pain of the bombing. But then it stops. The reader is rudely awakened from his reflection with the admonition: *'Do you realize, citizen of Rotterdam, that many of the fondest memories of what was lost in the May bombardment were attached to what were frankly mere shortcomings in our old city? The chaotic circumstances on Coolsingel, the impossible traffic problems, the formlessness of Hofplein, the singular entertainment on the Dijk, the period of high water, the obsolete uniforms of our unsurpassed Marines? With all this, the great fire has swept away, violently and at one fell swoop, that tension of which we spoke. It has removed what we, citizens of Rotterdam, could not or did not wish to discard at an earlier date, regardless of how little it conformed to the material requirements of the present day.'*[1]

The tension to which Van Traa refers is that between the dynamics of developments in society and the stubbornness of urban morphology.

So much had become clear during the thirties, when urban planners tried frantically to transform the old centre into an effervescent inner city that would fit the new status of Rotterdam as the world's principal port. But the core of this metropolis didn't look the way one would expect: the original triangle of town had been built and colonized solid and was now shot through with stinking ditches. The main streets with their chic department stores and grand cafés supplying the entire agglomeration with entertainment, bordered directly on dank alleyways where the most destitute lived. By driving channels through this most densely packed urban mass to carry the traffic, and by classifying and rearranging the morphology, the planning authorities hoped to create a representative heart for the industrial city and thus rid Rotterdam of its inferiority complex (no single inhabitant or tourist regarded this 'work-city' as a beautiful place).

Urban planners in Rotterdam saw only one major advantage in their city when compared to Amsterdam: its lack of tradition and absence of consideration for valuable monuments. Rotterdam knew only the physical dilemma of historical obstacles and it pondered upon a way in which to shake these off. The shortcomings of the inner city were formulated as an issue of too much substance and too little spiritual and cultural content; as a disparity between the form and content of the city. In its transformation, both plastic surgery and open-heart operations were deployed in a persistent, refined struggle *against* the 'resistance of the stone' and *for* a dynamic urban substance.

Penetrating the mass

Because the redevelopment of the inner city was a matter of reconstruction dependent on the purchase and expropriation of ground, every intervention required enormous effort and vast sums of money. At the start of the 20th century redevelopment began in the western, most run-down part of the inner city, which was designated to become the new centre. The Coolsingel waterway was filled in and a series of monumental buildings rose on the new site: a City Hall (H. Evers, 1909-1915), a Post Office (C. Bremer, 1915-1923), and a Stock Exchange (J.F. Staal, 1936-1940). To this purpose, an entire, originally mediaeval working-class area was demolished in one high-powered operation. After the trilogy of monumental public buildings was implanted in the periphery of the inner city, people became aware of the rather bizarre fact that this fragment of the City Beautiful lay completely isolated on a boulevard that went nowhere. Accordingly, a start was made on creating a square at each extremity: Hofplein and Van Hogendorpplein. Hofplein was intended to become the representative entrance plaza, but this notion was far removed from reality. 'Plein' (square, plaza) was a flattering name for the random collection of spaces surrounded by waterways, roads and rail tracks that were mutually connected in some vague way by high bridges. Besides being a traffic junction, it was also a hub of nightlife. At the beginning of the 20th century, these two functions were no longer compatible. Between 1915 and 1946, a phenomenal total of 40 plans were drawn up for the 'plein'. This continuing story can partly be ascribed to the contradictions in the brief. It turned out to be almost impossible to draw a design for a monumental square that would function as a 'reception room for the city' and also fulfil the requirements of an increasing volume of traffic. Plans that had been formulated according to an architectural approach often involved much expropriation and thus were very expensive; in addition, they were soon outdated in terms of traffic needs. It is therefore no surprise that people sought ways of separating the different functions of the squares. This led in 1936 to a plan (by Witteveen, director of urban planning before he was replaced by Van Traa) in which the traffic configuration was the main determining factor in the square's layout. The international tendency in urban planning, in which car traffic demanded an increasingly prominent role, also played a role here. In a way very uncharacteristic of Witteveen's aesthetic urban design he chose a solution which in its designation of traffic as the epicentre of urban planning anticipated the preferred solution in the post-war period.

An unpredictable game of chess

Witteveen's closest colleague Angenot was responsible for economic-demographic research on urban planning. He compared it to a game of chess; *'A programme for urban improvement resembles a game of chess in which the execution of a certain move is dependent on a series of previous moves.'*[2] In actual practice, the urban process was much more uncontrollable. A domino effect occurred with interventions that succeeded one another without there being a total plan at the basis. Witteveen's plan, however, was never realized. Inner-city schemes for Rotterdam display a coherence whose ground plan can only be drawn later, just like the Haussmann plan in Paris could only be reconstructed at a later date, despite its apparent unity.

Urban architecture

The conversion of Van Hogendorpplein at the other extremity of Coolsingel was largely informed by the architectural work of two celebrated architects, J.F. Staal and W. Dudok. This intervention proceeded quite differently to that of Hofplein. Except for traffic chaos, the two squares had little in common. Hofplein was indisputably the centre of gravity of the city and had major significance for urban life. But there was also the 'Great Breakthrough', a part of the Van Hogendorpplein scheme that was to connect two existing traffic arteries. The 1913 expropriation plan for Van Hogendorpplein was based on property relationships and existing plot boundaries and was exclusively intended to create a breach in the dense mass without providing a picture or an idea of how the frayed ends would be dealt with. Around the 17th-century Schielandshuis, which stood with its rear to the new urban boulevard, building blocks were truncated, streets widened and canals filled in. The question of which developments would replace the voids was regarded as being of secondary importance and a matter of private initiative. With the monumental and astoundingly beautiful department store De Bijenkorf (1929) and the Hollandse Bank Unie building (1940), the architect Dudok accentuated the two main directions of the square. The crystal tower of De Bijenkorf formed the termination of Coolsingel. This building testified to the new scale and status of the square. Its characteristic sculptural form was an advertisement for the company. With this 'shining' design, Dudok attempted to find a typology for the department store that would make it recognizable as such. The building was a sensation, due not only to the architecture, the lunchroom and the roof garden, but also to the technical equipment, the assortment of articles and the seduction tactics deployed. The architect A.J. van der Steur wrote: *'In this work, the vital, vibrating tension of our nervous era is solidified into a fragile but crystal-clear balance that holds its own, with the delicate but unshakeable resolution of its spiritual superiority, against the brute force of the harbour's bustle.'* [3]

The prominent, protruding Hollandse Bank Unie building could be seen from all along Coolsingel. It marked the corner with Blaak and celebrated the fact that the east-west breakthrough would finally be realized. The route was a component of the traffic circuit with roundabouts, which the urban planning department wished to construct around the inner city and which would be included in the post-war reconstruction plan a few years later. The next step in this circuit was a link to the eastern edge of the city. This required the demolition of the old Town Hall on Hoogstraat and the beautiful Plan-C retail building. The Schielandshuis, which stood right in the middle of the ideal path of the Blaak piercement, could be saved only at the very last moment (in 1933). These three buildings belonged to the rare objects that until then had been referred to as the pride of the city. Now people were prepared to demolish them in favour of car traffic.

Another prestigious project was the competition held in 1926 to design the Exchange Building for siting next to the Post Office. It had a very demanding programme, combining offices, an exchange hall, a restaurant, a bargemen's coffee house, garages and shops. Though the winner, J.F. Staal, managed to design a fine building, the competition became notorious for its remarkable course of events. After the first round, in which eight architects participated (including Oud, Dudok, Kromhout, Meischke and Schmidt, Mertens and Staal) all merits and clever ideas from the submitted designs were gathered together and further elaborated by a selected trio. Oud, who was rejected to his great anger, produced the model with the Exchange Building parallel to Coolsingel, clad on three sides by offices, with each function in its own building part, and an entrance on Beursplein. This solution was adopted into the second-round design by Staal. More sickening still was the fact that the building, which was eventually built in the first year of the war, was much more modern, austere and sober than Staal's definitive competition-winning design, and actually displayed a great resemblance to Oud's concept, which had been discarded on stylistic grounds. A constant factor in the development of Staal's building was the office wing on Coolsingel with a distinctive feature at the corner with Beursplein which, in the last version, assumed the shape of a volume on slim supports with a glass bay window and a slender green belfry for the Chamber of Commerce. The modernity of the building, expressed in the enormous underground car park and the impressive steel trusses of the Exchange Hall, made it a symbol of the way in which Rotterdam business life could overcome even the crisis years.

▲ Hofplein in the thirties ▼ Pre-war Rotterdam, with the Laurenskerk in the background

▲ Rotterdam City Hall under construction on Coolsingel, before this was filled in ▼ Coolsingel in the forties, with on the left the City Hall, Post Office, Exchange Building, HBU office building and, majestically terminating the axis, De Bijenkorf department store

One of the numerous small channels in pre-war Rotterdam that were to make way for the modernization of the centre

Van Hogendorpplein
Hofplein
Stadhuis
Coolsingel
VEN

Spiritual and cultural vacuum

In addition to the physical substance and density of the centre that demanded 'urban clearance' and the ugliness that requested 'urban beautification' there was a great 'mental void' that the inner city of Rotterdam represented to its inhabitants. People tended to see Rotterdam as a void in the middle of four or five (annexed) provincial towns. It had become lost among the sea of houses that had swelled around it. The centre had literally been sucked out: it had become a workplace instead of a dwelling place. The changing social structure of the city also contributed to the reduced eloquence of the inner city as a communal centre. In Zuid, the part of the city south of the river, the population was made up of workers originating from the Province of Brabant and the islands in Zeeland. Not only did people live far from the centre in geographical terms, the various population groups were also encapsulated and lived within their own social infrastructure, clubs, bars and churches. There was no feeling of the 'common good' that could be given shape in a mental or cultural centre. This was partly due to the new form the city was gradually assuming, a large-scale agglomeration in which the historical heart was no longer even the geographical centre.

In the twenties a change occurred when people began to regard the rise of cultural organizations and institutes as an important means to neutralize the insignificance of the inner city and thus transcend the image of Rotterdam as a working town. The new mentality was somewhat ironically described by the Rotterdam novelist Ben Stroman: *'Times have changed. Rotterdam has suddenly come to a shocking realization. People have vilified Rotterdam as the dirty, a-cultural dogsbody for so long now that it has been shocked during working hours. And now it wishes to make up for the damage incurred. Rotterdam is busy with a major cleaning operation. The city now realizes that for years it has only been engaged in digging harbours without paying any attention to the fact that people had to live and enjoy themselves in these centres of heavy work. Rotterdam is breaking down its core. And, to prove that our city does not spurn culture, it is building a concert hall and a new Exchange. To prove that it values the testimonies of old culture, it is dismantling the Delftse Poort to re-erect it carefully a few dozen metres further on. The old Boijmans Museum is being restored to its original state and there are voices in favour of saving the old exchange building. Rotterdam has acquired a mind for culture.'*[4]

The business world suddenly emerged as the new patron. It began to feel responsible for the cultural elevation of the city to which it owed its riches. The Club of Rotterdam, a fraternity centred on C.H. van der Leeuw (who commissioned the Van Nelle factory) and composed of heavyweights from the port and industry, was capable of engaging the urban planners in dialogue, grounded as it was in philosophy, economics and architecture. It also gave a solid basis to the enormous power wielded by the business world during the reconstruction, which was strong enough to force a change of course.

'The new psyche of Rotterdam' was the

collective term for all expressions of the general upturn of the city in the pre-war years; it was the name with which people referred to the expansion of unilateral economic development allied to attention for cultural amenities and a communal centre. To this belonged an approach that regarded the city not only as a machine but also as an aesthetic artefact. The chronicle of the modern spirit of the times was the *De Maastunnel* journal, founded to report on the progress of the work on the new tunnel under the Maas and all the other important Rotterdam building projects. In it, the top brass in this process described what it was that expressed this new psyche. Mayor P. Droogleever Fortuyn observed an almost poignant interest in higher values, a pursuit of mental civilization: *'The city's wholeness is formed by its external beauty and its mental life and, in both respects, Rotterdam has completely revised itself.'*[5] By reinforcing one another and conveying this optimism to a large public, there arose a heady atmosphere in which everyone was convinced of the imminent resurrection of Rotterdam, which was intended to be celebrated with a great exhibition in the city's Park in 1941. At that point, Hofplein, Coolsingel, Van Hogendorpplein, the Maas Tunnel and the plans for Diergaarde Blijdorp (the new zoo) would have been completed, along with important cultural amenities such as the new buildings for the Boijmans Museum and the Volksuniversiteit. Then the city could be appraised in terms of what it was and not in terms of what it would become.

Depending on their political colour, the media reacted with either admiration or horror. The liberal *Telegraaf* newspaper (1939) was full of praise for the initiatives to strengthen the cultural basis of Rotterdam. Whereas Amsterdam had driven away or restricted its patriciate and thus forfeited both its tradition and its future, Rotterdam gained an increasingly magical allure for *Telegraaf* journalists. Not very surprisingly, the socialists regarded Rotterdam as a 'horrible product of young, unbridled liberalism'. And the members of the Dutch CIAM group 'de 8 en Opbouw' perceived the link between the liberal character of Rotterdam and the nature of the urban beautification of its centre. Willem van Tijen called Rotterdam '*the typically liberal city, liberal in each of its expressions of that attitude of mind, and invariably in the most outspoken manner. ...'Liberalism also means lack of culture. Nowhere will one see that more clearly than here.'*[6] Van Tijen did not regard lack of culture *a priori* as a threat, except where people tried to prove the opposite and wished to keep up this pretence, as if the city did actually possess a certain amount of material and spiritual culture. 'If one does attempt it anyway, the most mortifying failures generally follow. A drama such as that of the City Hall, the Bijenkorf, which is a mere shadow of the broad gesture of its counterpart in The Hague, and an Exchange that is a weak emulation of Oud's project which was rejected due to a total lack of understanding.' The alternative to false monumentality was demonstrated by the architects of 'de 8 en Opbouw' in a great many projects for the city centre, of which not one was realized. The only exception was the 'cardboard' facade of the De Unie (on Coolsingel) and even here the originally hard and brightly-coloured image between the chic Passage and the traditional Gymnasium was tolerated for only a few years. Van der Vlugt's tower for Van Hogendorpplein, Van den Broek's arcade on Coolsingel, Oud's design for the Exchange, Van der Vlugt's theatre, and Van Loghem's development for the Meent all remained unexecuted. The Modern Movement's field of activity was forcibly confined to housing; the form they sought for monumental construction was apparently regarded as being too deviant, taking into account the jury's remarks on Oud's Exchange design. The monumentality that J.J.P. Oud sought for the Exchange was based on a formal articulation of the various components of the complex in naked, cubist volumes. This way the closed symmetry and representative decoration would have disappeared from the third building in the City Hall-Post Office-Exchange trilogy in a rather alarming fashion. Van den Broek and Van der Vlugt pushed this concept further, so that the building as a finished and autonomous object dissolves. In 1933, Van den Broek designed an arcade cinema on Coolsingel, near Hofplein. In its final form, this building would emphasize the corner with Hofplein with a high-rise apartment block. However, this final stage seemed less important to Van den Broek than the preliminary stage which was designed in anticipation of the expropriations to be made in the context of Witteveen's Hofplein plan. Here a shapeless building is squeezed aggressively between existing parcels and an arcade hewn through the middle. The premises to be demolished on Hofplein were attacked from the rear with an accumulation of shops, an arcade and a cinema (on the upper floor). The design celebrates the congestion and multifunctionality of the *Großstadt* and contributes urban components rather than a building. This new way of giving, or rather withholding, metropolitan form would be further explored by Van den Broek during the post-war reconstruction period.

Post-war reconstruction plan

Many prestigious urban projects were being carried out at the time of the bombing in May 1940. Reorganization of Hofplein was in full swing, the Maas Tunnel and the Exchange Building were almost finished. The festive celebration of New Rotterdam – due to take place in 1941 – was in sight. All improvement plans that had been custom-fitted into the existing environment with all the compromises this brought along, were suddenly torn from their context by the bombardment. The Meent, which had been hacked through the most densely built quarter of the inner city like a jungle path, was all at once the only recognizable street in an otherwise empty area. The latest and most modern buildings, each of which had been designed as the termination of a boulevard or as an infill in an elevation of a square, now stood as unassailable monuments. Their isolated shapes, grown out of a previous situation, had become incomprehensible. The city appeared as the photographic negative of the pre-war clearance maps on which the blocks to be demolished were marked blank; after the removal of the rubble in 1940 only the buildings on the white areas remained standing.

Now that we know how much the old town was detested before the war, with its congested centre, confined streets, narrow canals and poor housing, the most remarkable element of Witteveen's reconstruction plan is that it did not follow this tendency - that is, the cult of renewal and urge for destruction regarding the old centre. He did not seize the opportunity to delete all traces of the old city within the new one, although the circumstances justified this: all physical remains above ground and even below it were carried off in a communal effort by 36,000 Rotterdam rubble-clearers. All administrative restrictions were counterbalanced by general expropriation; moreover, all relevant material (maps and information) was lost when the Stadstimmerhuis, the local works office, burned down. Nevertheless, Witteveen stated that the essence of the city lay in its physical ground plan and that this should again be made visible. He posed the rhetorical question: 'Can we ignore the past completely and, if not, which principles should be the leitmotif when designing a new city? The more we deliberated on such issues, the more we felt bound hand and foot. There was seemingly great freedom of movement but in reality there was a surprising restraint.'[7] The post-war reconstruction plan was formulated by Witteveen and his department on the basis of recollections of the old city. The structure of the bombed city was still visible in the streets whose outlines lay as ditches in the rubble. Witteveen spoke of breakthroughs while the houses were only a metres-high mountain of debris. Although no street lay on the site of its pre-war equivalent in Witteveen's plan, the new routes were broadened derivatives of these.[8] The city that had disappeared was reanimated in a refined and modernized form, and not radically conceived anew.

Witteveen was most innovative and rigorous in the particular field of reconstruction to which he first turned his attention: the great infrastructural issues of the railways, dyke reinforcement, canal links, and the road traffic system. As all these issues had been on the agenda before the war, this was the area in which he was most convincing and most successful. As a civil engineer with the national railways, it had been his task to harmonize municipal urban plans with the railway tracks. He was accustomed to looking at the mutual coherence of infrastructure and urban planning and, accordingly, it was in the line of expectation that this part of the city design would become his hobbyhorse. The solution to the one issue presented the solution to the next, as it were. By having the railway lines from Amsterdam and Utrecht converge in one central station, Maas Station became superfluous and the site of its burnt-out building could be used to realize another essential change: extinguishing the division of the centre into a 'land' and a 'water' city. The dyke of Hoogstraat was relocated to the riverbank and the Maasboulevard became the new dyke. Similar to Rose's Water Project, Witteveen combined typical civil-engineering work with urban beautification by adding 'an element of beauty', a promenade along the shore of the Maas. Subsequently, the old

De Bijenkorf department store by W.M. Dudok, 1929

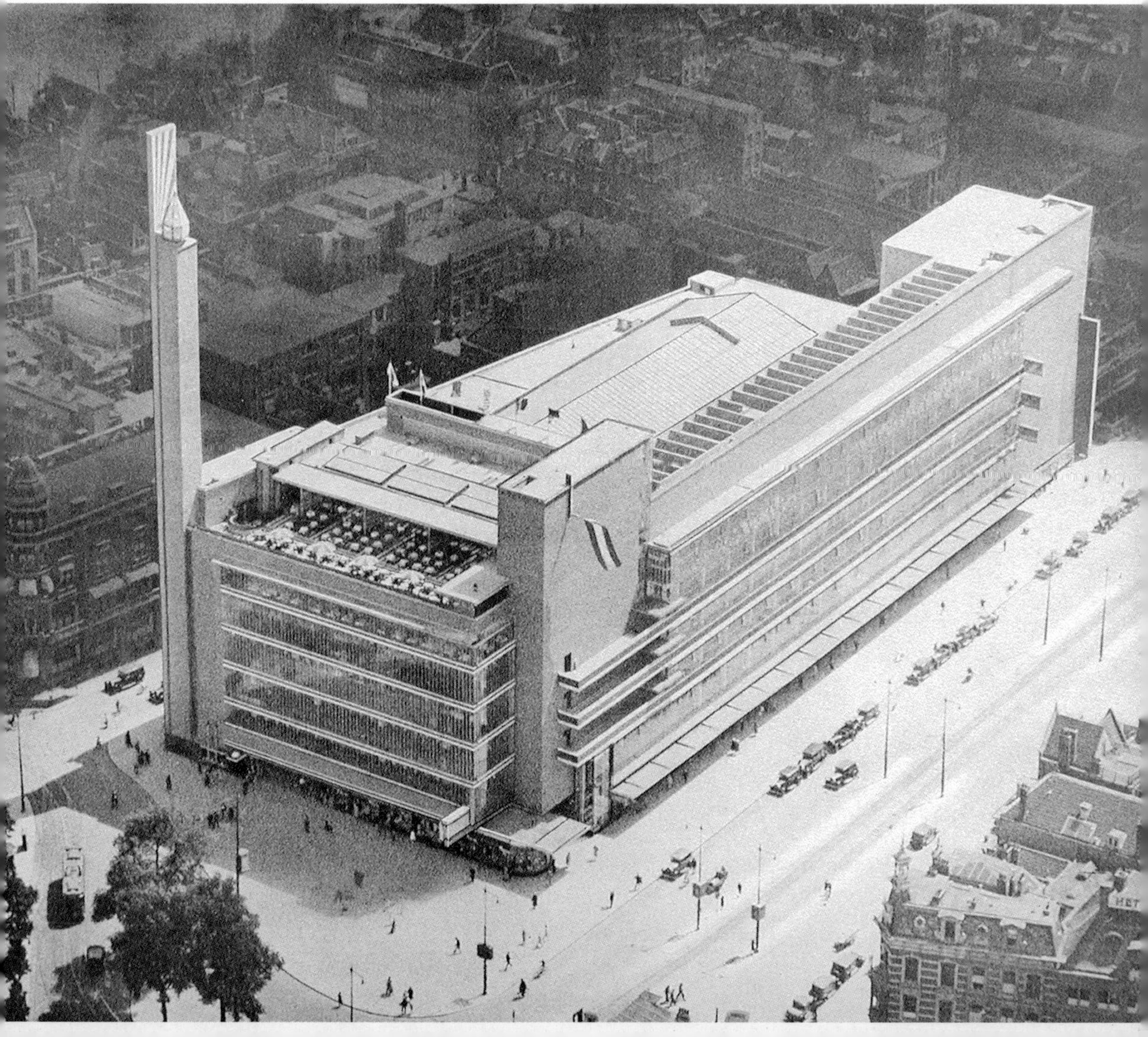

Downtown Rotterdam during the war

▲ 'Street 55', the initial try-out of Witteveen's new traffic circuit against the background of housing blocks by Jan Wils (1940-1943)
▼ Dr. A. Seyss-Inquart, the highest German official for occupied Holland, examines Witteveen's reconstruction plan

Witteveen's first accomplishments: new quay walls and bridges along the inner-city water infrastructure

harbours along Leuvehaven were modernized to become an inland shipping centre and the canal to the Rotte was revamped into a wider version of the small pre-war canal. In addition, the connection with the Rotte was relocated to the south, to below Hofplein. The decision to retain inland navigation in the inner city was not rational in economic and planning terms. However, Witteveen wished to keep the attractiveness of the water and the bustle of the harbours visible in the future city. It was his way of staging what would later occur metaphorically in the 'Basic Plan' by means of the 'Window on the River'. The bridges and quaysides were erected in restrained brickwork; small squares adjoining the water were designed at the head of Leuvehaven and in front of the Laurenskerk, giving a view of the passing barges.

Another aspect of the plan that arose from considerations other than economic or rational ones was the redefinition of the urban triangle. Witteveen regarded this as an essential feature of the centre, as an inviolable genetic property. During the design of the road network (1940), it had been a difficult task to reconcile the introduction of a modern traffic system with the desire to restore the triangular urban form. The road network consisted of boulevards, 52 metres wide, adapted to car traffic. The old routes of Coolsingel, Goudsesingel and Blaak formed the main arteries, while Hofplein was the primary point of distribution whose status was emphasized by the architecture of its elevations and layout. With the 1942 design competition for the Hofplein-Blaak development, the entry by 'de 8' unerringly improved the contradictory combination of nostalgia for the historical urban triangle and the modern road system. The solution presented by 'de 8' for the traffic system rested upon practical traffic requirements and furnished a model that would return in the Basic Plan. This plan, in which Van Eesteren played a major role, further rationalized the parcelling of the urban section to the west of Coolsingel into a system of rectangular blocks. The complicated hub at Hofplein was reduced to a simple roundabout, analogous to other vertices of the traffic system. This plan was highly esteemed by the Club of Rotterdam and particularly by Van der Leeuw who attempted, in vain, to get Van Eesteren to draw up a entirely new plan for the city in the autumn of 1944.

Believers

On 30-6-1940 the reconstruction got underway with a full-scale try-out of the traffic circuit around the inner city. A 100-metre section of 'straat 55', as people referred to the current Mariniersweg, was laid on. Extensive research had resulted in the definitive profile and technical implementation. The roads were assigned a free tram lane, a separate strip for parked cars, and wide pavements. They were founded on the rubble of the bombed houses and covered with cobblestones. The section of road ended at Goudsesingel, where the apartment complex designed by Jan Wils provided a foretaste of the tall street elevations that would rise along the traffic circuit, with 'hefty commercial premises, banks, maybe grand cafés and hotels'. Between the traffic routes, Witteveen's plan furnished the conditions for a modern city from which residents and industry were excluded. With this, he introduced two prewar tendencies, core formation and the banishment of industry to areas beyond the centre, 'in one grand gesture to their logical conclusion'. Little of this could be realized in the first years of the war. After the crisis-management priorities of rubble clearance, expropriation and plan-making, an organization was set up to execute the reconstruction. Specially formed departments (DIWERO, ASRO) were engaged in the elaboration of the reconstruction plan, area zoning, the creation of block maps, the issuing of plots, etc. Much has been published on the vicissitudes and achievements of the Witteveen plan; however, the sheer size of the 'paper city' designed during the war years has only recently come to light.[9] A hierarchical system of supervision was set up with Witteveen, as urban planner, at the apex of the pyramid. This was necessary in order to guarantee that the intentions of the masterplan were upheld. Witteveen's general directions were elaborated by supervisors in charge of a certain area. The Architect's Committee checked the selection of architects in advance on the basis of a 'top five': a classification of architects into five categories. Van Traa adopted this system and even fine-tuned it further. A persistent issue among all those involved was the question of how strongly the new city was to be bound by regulations. The dividing line between believers and non-believers cut clear across the architectural schools of thought: 'moderns' like Oud and Van Traa believed in precisely worded rules that were to ensure that the masterplan was filled in harmoniously, whereas a 'traditional' architect like Berghoef was an avowed opponent of this strategy. The leadership of the major industrialist Van der Leeuw, who became the general authorized representative for the reconstruction in 1944 and who would contribute to the replacement of Witteveen as Director of Municipal Public Works by Van Traa, saw to it that this discussion was soon obsolete. The cards were reshuffled and urban planners no longer stood at the peak of the new order but had to share their position in the 'dynamic force field' with politicians, civil servants, and above all with the business world. Urban development as a design issue was replaced by urban development as a process. The typically Rotterdam liberalist tradition, 'in the sense that the hindrance of any expression whatsoever should be avoided at all costs, that one should not reject the bad when this does not occur of its own accord, and that the good and worthwhile is only achievable by free growth and never by regulation' (the words are Van Tijen's) was given urbanistic expression in the *Basic Plan.*

Rotterdam, dynamic city

Van Traa's role in redeveloping the inner city had already begun shortly before the bombing, when Witteveen appointed him for this purpose. In 1938 he redefined in the magazine *De Maastunnel* the 'cityscape of Rotterdam'. He scarcely mentioned a desirable physical or aesthetic picture but described all the more emphatically what he saw as the character of the city. In his view, the city was completely subordinate to the harbour: 'Every object here has a directly demonstrable goal and displays its own function. Where is pure beauty shown more clearly? The city lies behind it. The city was not the main issue, it had no cause of it own, it was a result.'[10] He saw the ease with which the city renewed itself, replacing the old, as the most important character trait: 'The youth of the city, the young force, that sees no further than itself, with little attention to old beauty handed down; this was the decisive factor, choosing the new out of distrust of the old.' On the basis of the last plan for Hofplein, which was primarily a traffic plan, he stated that the city did not possess the concordant will to 'prefer a beautiful form to free and flexible growth. It is as if here too the young city remained suspicious of fixed and unchanging shapes, regardless of how beautiful and impressive the promised beauty might be.' Between the lines, we can observe a sigh of relief that the lead weight of the harmonious cityscape had fallen from the shoulders of urban planning. Now Van Traa could begin to seek a new way to steer the anarchy latent in the development of Rotterdam.

The Basic Plan could only originate in a city that had a deep-rooted resistance to its own physical form and wished to get rid of it; in a city that believed that it was an ugly duckling at the point of turning – with a little help – into a swan. Van Traa was the first to see something positive in the constant negative appraisal of the city, which ran as a leitmotif through its 20th-century history, and in the mutilations of the urban fabric and the corresponding destructive tendencies. He regarded this as an unremitting drive for renewal. The lack of respect for the old he saw as a positive bias for the new, and drew attention to the urban dynamic as the core of Rotterdam's *genius loci.* With this, every link with the past, with the historical city, had become spurious; it was a form of nostalgia that belonged to the likes of Amsterdam but not to Rotterdam. Whereas Witteveen concluded that the *genius loci* could be found in the city plan, and in the combination of its physical attributes of water, harbours and shipping, Van Traa postulated that the character of Rotterdam could not be described formally. It could only be expressed in terms of attitude; only the aesthetics of mutation, of more, better, newer, more modern, could be applied here. As soon as the opportunity arose to celebrate this urge, the city would seize it as never before. All obstacles would be pushed aside. The fact is, Van Traa had begun the reconstruction even before the bombing.

Notes

1 *Het nieuwe hart van Rotterdam Toelichting op het basisplan voor den herbouw van de binnenstad van Rotterdam,* Rotterdam 1946 **2** L.H.J. Angenot, 'De stadsverbeteringen in Rotterdam', *Economisch-statistische berichten,* 19-4-1939 **3** A.J. van der Steur, 'De Rotterdamsche Bijenkorf', *Bouwkundig Weekblad* 1929 no. 16, 122 **4** B. Stroman, 'De culturele bezinning van een havenstad', *De Maastunnel* 1938, 173-174 **5** 'De nieuwe psyche van Rotterdam (een onderhoud met onze burgemeester)', *De Maastunnel,* 1938, 147-148 **6** W. van Tijen, 'Rotterdam en het bouwen', *de 8 en Opbouw*, 1936 no. 9, 97 **7** Elucidation by W.G. Witteveen of the reconstruction plan in: *Het opbouwplan van Rotterdam in het museum Boymans,* Rotterdam 1941, 3 **8** See the research and maps by Gioconda Jager-Mina Quiñonez, in: C. Wagenaar, *Die neue Stadt. Rotterdam im 20. Jahrhundert. Utopie und Realität,* Münster 1993. **9** See the research by A. Tijhuis in: *Een stad voor het leven. Wederopbouw Rotterdam 1940-1965*, Rotterdam 1995. **10** C. van Traa, 'Het stadsbeeld van Rotterdam', *De Maastunnel* 1938, 37-41.

Rotterdam 1940-1960

INTERIOR THE TWENTSCHE BANK, A. VAN DER STEUR, 1945

>> Uma cidade totalmente devastada. Dois homens. Homem 1: Estamos a testemunhar a morte da nossa grande cidade. Homem 2: Certamente que nã
>> *One utterly destroyed town. Two men. Man 1: we are witnessing the death of our great city. Man 2: Absolutely not! We ar*

Panorama 1

> Rotterdam 1940-1960

LIJNBAANBUILDING, H.A. MAASKANT, 1954

CENTRAL STATION, S.J. VAN RAVES

ão! Estamos a testemunhar a sua glória. Às bombas e aos incêndios sucederam-se cinco anos de terraplanagens e limpeza até que os detritos produziram uma supe

e witnessing its glory. The bombs and fires were followed by five years of flattening and cleaning until the debris had yielded a perfect

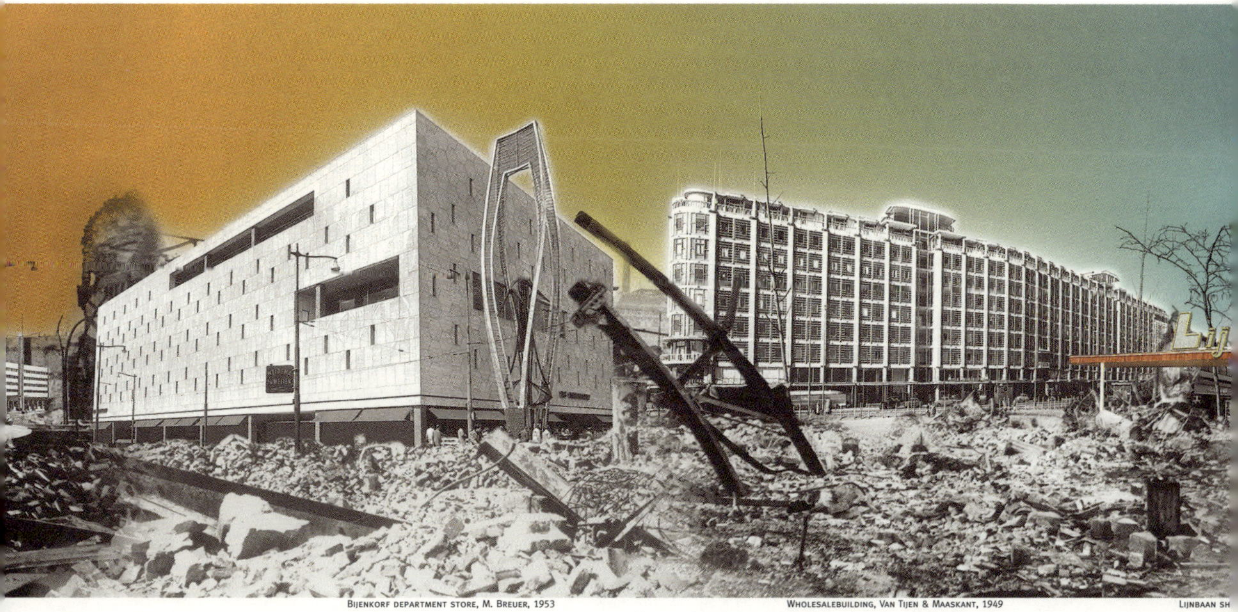

Bijenkorf department store, M. Breuer, 1953 Wholesalebuilding, Van Tijen & Maaskant, 1949 Lijnbaan sh

perfeitamente abstracta. Foram precisos mais dez anos para conquistar o vazio com uma colecção de objectos completamente novos. O branco nunca foi mais br

plane. It took another ten years to conquer the emptiness with a collection of perfectly new objects. White was never whiter, concrete

-> Rotterdam 1940-1960

HOPPING CENTRE, VAN DEN BROEK EN BAKEMA, 1949 — GROENENDAAL APARTMENTS, H.A. MAASKANT, 1953 — MAN WITHOUT HEART, O. ZADKINE, 1946

ranco, o betão nunca foi tão cinzento-rato como o cinzento dos edifícios lançados de pára-quedas no vazio criado pela destruição de Roterdão.

e never as mousegrey than that of the buildings parachuted on the emptiness created by the destruction of Rotterdam.

Emptiness

The mound of Kuyunjik, site of the ruins of Nineveh near Mosul (Iraq). Probably drawn by Austen Henry Layard, ca. 1842

For years after the bombing of May 1940 all that was left standing of old Rotterdam were a handful of historic buildings. These were the coordinates along which you could measure just how empty the city had become, how much space the old city had occupied all that time. The Laurenskerk, the Witte Huis, the Exchange, the Post Office, the City Hall and the Schielandshuis played the same role as had the Palais Royal, the Opéra and the Place Vendôme between the glass skyscrapers of Corbu's Plan Voisin. The emptiness of Rotterdam had been dictated by the Germans because the rubble was a hindrance to them; it was made possible by the actions of J.A. Ringers, the general authority for the reconstruction process, who immediately ordered complete expropriation of the ground, and was physically created by all of Rotterdam's 32,000 unemployed under the supervision of the Director of Municipal Public Works, W.G. Witteveen.(1) Witteveen was also responsible for drawing up an urban masterplan for the new centre within a few weeks. Yet these two projects were not in any way connected. There were no priorities, hierarchies or even points of application with which one could anticipate a newly designed city. The emptiness was a pure emptiness, an innocent emptiness, an emptiness without content, a very empty emptiness.

During the war years, two ideal cities were formulated, one a carefully documented city that presented an ideal extrapolation of the ambitions and ideas of 15 years of urban planning in Rotterdam, and the other an utterly smooth urban expanse that projected only emptiness where an intense fullness had once stood. This second city would undermine the realization of the first and destabilize all subsequent cities.

Sixty years later, the emptiness that was visible in its totality for a few years still lies beneath the buildings. Each time a building in Rotterdam is torn down, the emptiness reappears, only to vanish again almost immediately. This is why buildings in Rotterdam can be demolished with comparative ease; they lack all connection with an urban substructure, whether this be mental or physical. We are dealing with a phenomenon that is the exact opposite of the resistance that new interventions usually encounter in cities with a historical sediment, where, after a difficult period of settling in, even the most radical building

becomes an inextricable component of the old city. Take the Palace on Dam Square in Amsterdam designed by Jacob van Campen. A new building in Rotterdam, regardless of how radical it may be, scarcely meets any resistance from the city. However, just as there is no period of acclimatization, there is equally no possibility of attachment. As a consequence – right up to the present day – a building can be removed just as easily as it was built.
Buildings in Rotterdam will always remain objects that nudge the emptiness temporarily out of sight. The demolition of a building is each time something of a relief, which dissolves after some months with the construction of something new. We should really ask ourselves what made Rotterdam so susceptible to the emptiness that lay under the smouldering rubble. Clearing this rubble – the removal of cellars, foundations, piping and ducting, the levelling and the expropriation – was the most significant urbanistic project since the damming of the Rotte at the Maas in the 12th century. Everything that occurred after this ought to be seen in the light of this emptiness. It bestows continuity on the recent history of the city; it is the identity of Rotterdam. Emptiness is that which always returns.

'An emptiness of the mind'; authors and the ravaged city

Besides a physical reality, the emptiness of Rotterdam was also a rhetorical construct, assembled out of poetic elements. The reconstruction of Rotterdam arguably began when people started to write about its destruction rather than when the first plans were fixed for its future reappearance. In retrospect, one may speak of a writers' school around the journalist Ben Stroman, a literary laboratory where, between 1940 and 1941, writers attempted to place the bombing, the rubble, the emptiness and the reconstruction in an integrated narrative on the identity of Rotterdam. The bombing compelled them to describe a city that existed no longer and at the same time still had to come into being. Besides Stroman, several other names repeatedly arose in the construction of this imaginary city. One was Leo Ott, a renowned journalist and author. His name is also associated with the monograph on the genesis of the Wholesale Building, itself a mythical event both in the real and in the imaginary Rotterdam.[2] Furthermore, there was M.J. Brusse who was also a journalist and was exceptionally skilled in expansive narratives about the 'world-class port' of Rotterdam being 'its true soul'. Finally, there was Anton Koolhaas, later renowned as a writer of books on animals, as Director of the Film Museum and father of the architect Rem Koolhaas who would celebrate the urbanistic emptiness of Rotterdam in the seventies and eighties.[3]
Immediately after the bombing of 1940, Anton Koolhaas organized together with poets J.H. Speenhoff and Jan Musch Het Hart van Rotterdam (The heart of Rotterdam), a cabaret complete with dancing girls, with contributions by other Rotterdam authors.[4] This is interesting because Koolhaas had never assumed a position as a chronicler of the metropolis, neither before nor after the war. Yet here he seems to have taken the lead in generating a specific attitude towards the destruction and reconstruction of the city. Although Het Hart van Rotterdam was performed on 1 September 1941, the libretto was never published.[5] The piece consists of five scenes, each written by a different writer. It is garnished with poems, songs, music, ballet, slides, etc., all conceived by well-known artists. The scenes were borrowed from the city's past, present and future: the building of the Laurenskerk in the late Middle Ages, the great days of the port in the 19th

century, clearing the rubble after the bombing, city life during the war, and finally the businessmen and shipowners who found a new elan in the Exchange Building on Coolsingel. The prologue is a giddy account of an imaginary journey through time from the destroyed city to its roots in the Middle Ages.

The manuscript contains an introduction by Ben Stroman, describing the background to Koolhaas's revue. Shortly after the bombing, when rubble clearing was in full swing, four writer-journalist friends received the same mysterious telephone call from Anton Koolhaas: 'Anton Koolhaas speaking – I have something to tell you' ... Outside the dull thud of rubble being detonated. There was work afoot. There was haste to liberate the city for the new era, an era of reflection and building. Koolhaas's plan turned out to be an idea to write, jointly, a piece about the reconstruction of Rotterdam. To Stroman's questions concerning why and for what purpose, Koolhaas replied: 'To play, of course. To give work to stricken artists. As many-sided as can be, stage set painters, musicians, dancers... A play with a revue-like character.' Just like the clearance of rubble itself, the musical was also a form of unemployment relief. However, the four invited authors reacted in a somewhat shocked manner to Koolhaas's idea of creating a cheerful piece about the drama of Rotterdam. They also expressed their concern about their impotence as writers in the light of recent events and wondered what suitable literary response they could give. The conclusion was that they could not write the piece without also involving the suffering, the destruction, in short, the rubble. Koolhaas added: 'But we mustn't stop at the rubble; it must be a piece born of the rubble yet it has to look further than that, to the future.' The challenge of creating a vision on Rotterdam's future, implanted in its destruction, stimulated a number of the writers to reveal their aesthetic fascination for the rubble. This 'coming out' was described by Stroman as follows: 'Then arose a quiet voice with a noticeable trembling of emotion, a sensation different to that of memory: "The rubble is not ugly at all when seen in bright sunlight against a clear blue sky or at dusk under the red horizontal glow...".' Stroman describes the reactions of an artist to the rubble: 'I drew Hoogstraat and it may be mad to confess but for the very first time I thought Hoogstraat attractive'. Koolhaas himself fought against a purely melancholic fascination with the rubble. Stroman heard him say: 'The rubble is most certainly indispensable, but for a new prospect'. The discussion that followed was also recorded by the writer: 'Beautiful rubble then?' 'Not <u>beautiful</u> rubble, no.' 'Rough, hard, astonishing rubble then?' 'How could the play be cheerful in such a case?' The group fell into deliberation again. What a strange assignment: a play based on rubble, but not beautiful rubble, and not horrid rubble either... Then the initiator came with the words of deliverance: 'The pain that has been endured should have grown over the rubble and soothed it, like soft moss.' A few months after Koolhaas had made these utterances, the piles of rubble had been levelled and a tundra-like plain covered with grass and weeds lay on the site of what had been the centre. The ragged three-dimensional scars etched against the sky had made way for an alienating, uniform space. The destruction of the city lost its drama; an expectant quiet took its place.

The play shows that Koolhaas and his colleagues wished to integrate the violent destruction of the city in a historical continuum spanning the genesis of the city and the expansion of the city and its port. The brusque changes in 19th century Rotterdam largely brought by heavy technology were linked with the equally abrupt changes the city underwent from spring 1940 onwards. This was the first step in the city's reconciliation with its destruction. In order to visualize this urban history, Koolhaas and his colleagues envisaged the use of various techniques, some of which originated in the 19th century diorama.

While the accompanying music swells, the screen splits in two to reveal the projection screen upon which a kaleidoscopic picture of the growing city passes by. Two projectors conjure up the pictures. These they project onto the screen in green and red a few centimetres apart, causing a fantastic play of colour. Spectators first see the old city, visited by cog boats, and then ships from our country's golden age, the 17th century. The city, ever renewing, pushes onwards. Proud buildings pass by. Bridges and cranes unfold a high-powered image of prosperity. The apotheosis comes with the 'Nieuw Amsterdam', which steams through the projection with illuminated portholes, accompanied by a grand upsurge of the music.
The Choir sings:

We ram piles, build in brick, demolish and break
    Reconstruct the city
    We hammer, put together, dig and rake
    Extending the city

The song of the builders of the pre-war city could as easily have been sung by the tens of thousands of rubble clearers levelling it in the spring of 1940.
While the rubble-writers initially interpreted the bombing, the clearance and the future reconstruction as components of a continuous transformation, a few people soon realized that something had happened that in many respects was the complete opposite of everything that had occurred in the previous period. After the rubble had been cleared but before reconstruction had begun, silence took over. Instead of the constant change, there was only a green field from which a few buildings protruded. Almost nothing of this field changed for a period of five years. The inner city had not known such a period without alteration for at least a century and would not have one again. As the emptiness manifested itself, the disappearance of the old city was experienced as a relief. The renowned poet J.C. Bloem was asked to write a poem for the musical with the destruction of the city as its theme.[6] In his poem he captured the pastoral feeling that descended upon the city when the rubble was cleared.

Rotterdam

How strangely the city lies open now,
    How miraculous and light:
    The streets devoid of houses run
    From nought to nought, yet not in flight
The heavens glow as ne'er before
    Upon the work of ages gone -
    The summer is as bright as ever,
    The sun as it has always shone.
We sink in innermost retreat,
    Rememb'ring how it used to be,
    And find ourselves to our great wonder
    Not so much aghast as shy.
Complain not, still the gardens bloom,
    Above mortality and despair:
    A shepherd kisses on the stones
    Of Babylon and Nineveh.

Photograph of Rotterdam taken by RAF spy-plane, 1944

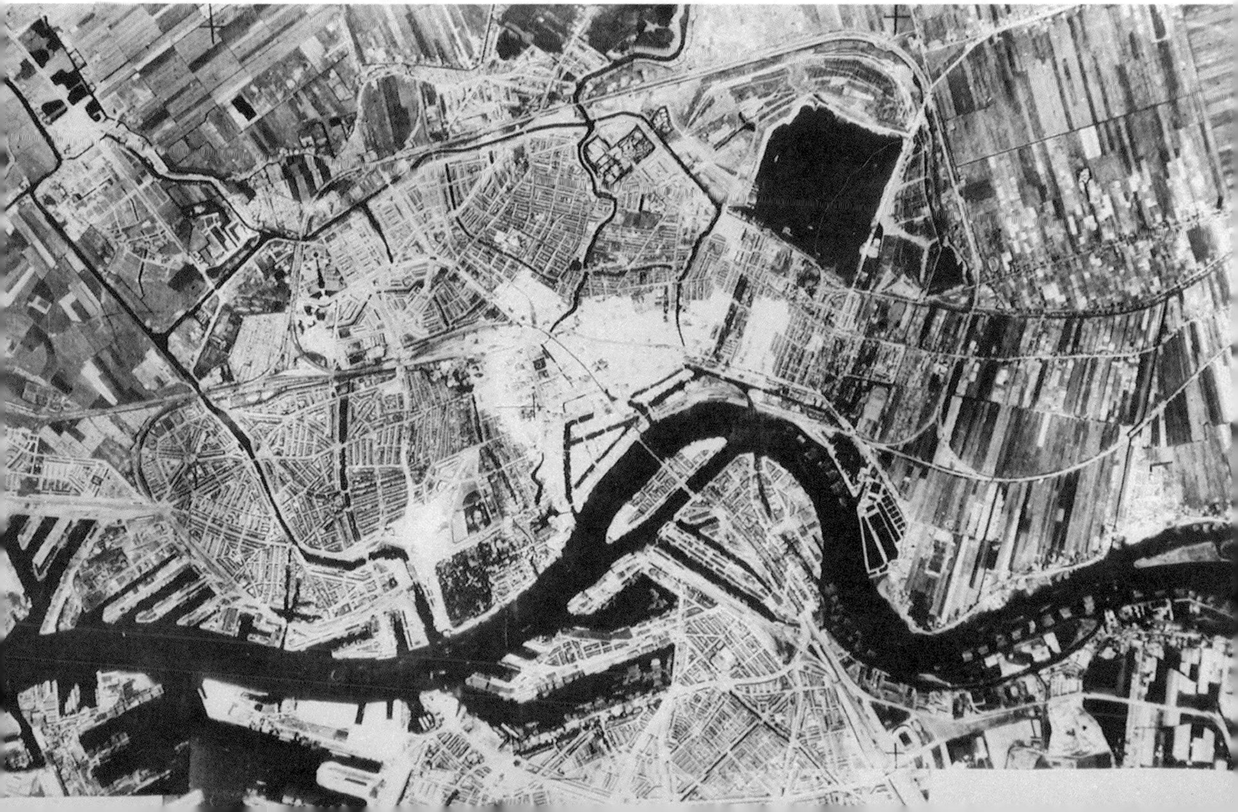

Amateur photos of downtown Rotterdam the week after the bombing, May 1940. Clockwise;
1 Post office on Coolsingel 2 Boompjes embankment 3 Westersingel 4 Oude Binnenweg looking towards De Bijenkorf department store (W.M. Dudok 1929)
5 Leuvehaven 6 Oude Binnenweg, looking towards De Bijenkorf and HBU office building (W.M. Dudok 1938)

^^ Clearing the rubble, ca. 1941 ^ Clearing the rubble, ca. 1940

Growing wheat in the eastern part of downtown Mariniersweg, ca. 1944

Bloem actually wrote the poem a few weeks after the bombing while the city itself was still a smouldering ruin, dramatically outlined against the sky. The poet was already one step further. He focused not upon the destruction but upon the emptiness that would follow.

The texts on rubble and emptiness were not a private response by a group of authors to an urban disaster. Rather, they documented the 'time out' that had been forced upon the urban development of Rotterdam. Not only could people do little else than deliberate for years on end, the disappearance of the centre demanded a fundamental reconsideration of the relation between form and content in urban planning. Up until that time, urban development had subsisted on the coincidence of the mental and organizational content of the city with its physical, three-dimensional form. Directly after the bombing the rubble-writers took as their theme the unhitching of city form from city substance. This was inevitable due to the fact that the idea of the city seemed to live on whereas the city as a material artefact had in fact vanished. The difference between form and content of the urban identity would be the central theme for the entrepreneurs, architects and administrators who grouped together to prepare, in an entirely new manner, the genesis of a new centre. This kind of disassociation could only take place if there was a physical, organizational and mental openness at all levels in the centre of the city. This process grew to maturity in the years immediately after the destruction. Under Witteveen's supervision, the physical remains of Rotterdam were smoothed away. With one stroke of the pen, Ringers removed the administrative remnants. The rubble-writers did likewise with the images and ideas that clung to the historical city.

During a reading for the M.I.T. in 1960, when the reconstruction of Rotterdam was at its peak, C. van Traa, the author of the 'basic plan for the reconstruction of Rotterdam' (Basisplan voor de Wederopbouw van Rotterdam) said: 'The role of the town planner is a very dynamic one, his proposals are for a living society, changing, growing, dying. Therefore his work is mainly based on indications, functional developments, directions which must be aimed at. His task is at least a four-dimensional one.' Van Traa's notion of urban planning as a companion to dynamic processes is the outcome of a process that was launched immediately after the bombing: the detachment of the city's identity from its history and physical reality. The emptiness of Rotterdam was simultaneously that which furnished this new form of urbanity and the platform on which urban planning and even architecture were redefined as being primarily immaterial processes.

The one-dimensional city

In the catalogue for the 1947 exhibition Rotterdam Straks (Rotterdam in the Near Future) in the Boijmans Museum, we can read the following: 'What is urban planning? It is not the building of cities.' The Basisplan, as ratified in 1946, was the result of a shadow urbanism wielded by a group of Rotterdam entrepreneurs and architects, in opposition to the reconstruction plan of City Architect Witteveen, who was officially in charge up until 1944. This group suffered from a collective horror pleni; they were afraid that refilling the emptiness would purge the city of all dynamics, for they had discovered that the city existed despite its physical form. This group was afraid of the moment of congealment and sought to postpone it as long as possible.

The core of the opposition to Witteveen's plan was the so-called Kleine Kring (Inner Circle) or the 'Club of Rotterdam', a group of leading Rotterdam entrepreneurs who met fairly regularly to discuss current business and economic matters. After the bombing, they had a topic with more immediate relevance: the economic reconstruction and the future of Rotterdam as a port. Under the leadership of C.H. van der Leeuw, the meetings were held with great discretion in the tea pavilion of his Van Nelle factory, the factory of the future, the symbol of the capitalist-social society envisioned by the mystic cum tycoon cum reformer Van der Leeuw.(7)

It started off quite innocently with a discussion of a number of points of specific interest to them in anticipation of the time when the war would be over and the world economy back in motion: these were the layout of the port, inland shipping and the connection to the Rhine, and ocean-going merchant shipping. The points on the agenda subsequently became more ambitious, broader and yet at the same time more specific. They foresaw the future of Rotterdam as a world-class port and a city with a million residents; they anticipated – four years prior to the advent of Marshall Aid – receiving substantial development funds from the USA, and changing relations with the Dutch East Indies, which had up till then been an important factor in bringing Rotterdam to full flower.(8)

As the Club of Rotterdam became more visionary, it acquired ever clearer ideas on how the new centre was to be designed. In line with this development, Van der Leeuw drew up a list of twelve new urban elements that would be open and representative in their nature: a Centre Maritime to accommodate a wide range of maritime matters; a Centre Artistique, an extension of the Boijmans Museum; a large city theatre; a commercial college; an exhibition centre; a theatre for Rotterdam-Zuid; a country golf hotel in Kralingen; the Maas Bastion – a terrace across the river; a park in Zestienhoven; a park in De Esch near Kralingen; and a water and riding sports centre.(9)

It gradually became apparent that the vehicle they wished to use to carry their ideas into the practice of reconstruction was that of increasingly aggressive criticism of Witteveen's plan. The entrepreneurs had strong objections to upholding the old town triangle as the basic form for the new centre. They were opposed to the parkways, the green wedges importing traffic and nature into the city. They disapproved of the preservation of the Schielandshuis and the Willems bridge. They challenged the system of supervisors by which Witteveen divided the city into sectors whose designs would be monitored and checked by a renowned architect. Finally, they protested against a city where the signature of a single urban designer would be recognized everywhere.(10)

In retrospect, we can recognize a strategy of disconnection in the collective criticism by the Club of Rotterdam. The link between the new city and the ground plan with attributes of the old has been abandoned; the trajectory from masterplan via detailed sector plans to the elaboration of individual buildings has been shot through; the infrastructure is dealt with quite independently of the morphology of town and country. Finally, individual creativity is resolutely refused access to urban design. What was taking place here was the dismantling of urban planning as it was traditionally known, as an integral whole reaching from organization to realization. Even more important was the dismantling of the urban concept to which Witteveen held on grimly: that of the city as a synthesis of history and future, overall form and components, function and representation.

As time passed, the activities of the Club became increasingly concrete. They founded a secret committee, OpRo, as a kind of shadow cabinet to AsRo, the official advisory organ that supervised the reconstruction of Rotterdam. OpRo

subsequently established an Architects' Study Group. Under the leadership of the architect J.H. van den Broek, these specific proposals for changes to the reconstruction plan were further elaborated. Up until the last moment, Van der Leeuw toyed with the idea of generating a wholly new masterplan in which the radical ideas of the Club of Rotterdam were deployed right from the outset. In 1944, when Van der Leeuw became the governmental authority for the reconstruction, he asked Mart Stam – just about the most radical Dutch architect available at that time and who had had considerable and exacting experience with urban planning in the Soviet Union – to draw up a proposal. However, before the scheme could be developed, the Government had already approved of many of the amendments to the original reconstruction plan. Therefore Stam's plan never materialized.[11] The 'basic reconstruction plan' that was finally approved in 1946 ought to be regarded as an almost coincidental cross-section through the dismantling process of a previous plan. This Basisplan – in contrast to what would have been a *pure* plan by Mart Stam – is an archaeological field that documents a period in time when urban planning cast off, and was stripped of, all its certainties and the city was liberated from the solidarity with its history and physical form.
The ideas of OpRo basically asserted that in no way whatsoever should urban planning be an obstacle to the future of the city. The group saw the city as a dynamic process, in this case one that would become increasingly strong and grand after the war. Both urban planning and architecture had to reformulate themselves as an organizational or analytical model with which this dynamic could be immediately exploited and made visible.
Urban planning, therefore, could do little more than arrange or rather equip a city in such a way that its spatiality remained neutral, that it remained devoid of spatial determinants. It was an urban planning that made things possible and continued to make them possible. The grid of traffic roads that was laid through Rotterdam and gave short shrift to the idea of the town triangle ought to be seen as irrigating a desert without abandoning its most important features (or non-features). The square traffic grid allowed Rotterdam to transcend its site-specificity, since it can be viewed as a slice from a network of human and freight flows that covers the entire world. This is also indicated by the way in which Van Traa allowed the traffic grid to become a part of a regional network of national trunk roads that was constructed around the harbours like a net, between Capelle and the North Sea. All at once the geometry of the inner city could be explained in terms of a much larger organism in which it took up a small and relatively insignificant position.[12]
At the moment when urban form is no longer an integral three-dimensional composition and a city's significance no longer coincides with its physical shape, the urban form can only be described in terms of something other than itself. This goes far beyond simply describing the city in terms of the activities that take place there; it means – and here we touch upon an underestimated aspect in Rotterdam's reconstruction – that the city is filled with stories, with narrative lines and points. Now that buildings and urban elements could no longer draw their significance from a general ground plan, they were artificially charged with rhetorical utterances on the identity of Rotterdam. For instance, Backx, a shipping magnate and a member of the Inner Circle, requested a design that would manifest the historical relationship of the city with the port.[13] By providing a cross-section through an ocean liner for his *Centre Maritime* project, Van den Broek drew merchant shipping into the heart of the city. J.J.P. Oud wished to allow only the

spire of the Laurenskerk to remain standing in order to create a monument to the mutilation of Rotterdam. The surface area of Rotterdam had no shape and no content. It presented a screen for all projections of a still imaginary Rotterdam, or a neutral table on which poetical utterances and centres of intensity could be jotted down.

Urban planning

One of the most lucid of the drawings with which the Basisplan had been presented from 1946 on, was the scheme for the functional zoning of the city centre, formulated in 1953. Where the centre had once stood, there was now a programmatic pudding, a pattern of splotches without any formal definition. Each splotch represented a function: housing, open-air market, banks and offices, inland shipping, etc. The pattern represented a random freeze-frame in a constantly fluent, thickening and diluting, mixing and curdling programmatic tub. Over this was laid the grid of a traffic system in a few sweeping inked lines with circles specifying the important nodes.

What we see here is a force field. The programme is regarded as something with a fixed surface area but certainly no fixed form: there was a puddle of shops, a puddle of houses, or a puddle of offices. Traffic was regarded as something with a certain form but no surface area: it was a line, or a flow. The shape of the lines issued from a collective search for the path of least resistance and the shortest distance; this produced the whiplash route. The traffic affected the fluid puddles by attracting some programmes and repelling others. Finally, the function-puddles also differed intrinsically from one another; some had the tendency to remain as compact as possible, such as the entertainment zone, for example. Others, such as the shops, spilled throughout the entire area.

Van den Broek's laboratory

In the laboratory work that Van den Broek performed during the war, we can see an intense concentration on the hubs in the traffic network. Hofplein, the cause of the legendary rumpus between Witteveen and Oud concerning the relationship between Architecture and Urban Design, was regarded by Van Traa and OpRo as a purely technical and thus organizational problem.[14] Van den Broek, however, said that form was more important to Hofplein than function. With this, he was not retreating towards a monumental urban square as envisaged by Berlage, Witteveen and Oud, but extending the radical standpoint of OpRo until it became a principal design issue.[15]

OpRo and Van Traa for their part were of the opinion that Hofplein ought to become a simple nucleus in the grid instead of an urban square. But to Van den Broek, this raised the following set of questions: how does an urban nucleus work, what kind of urban design does it demand, and what form does this elicit? In January 1945, he presented a study on 'traffic and urban squares, and Hofplein in particular' (Verkeer en pleinvorm, in het bijzonder van het Hofplein).[16] It opened with the following sentences: 'In the most recent studies of Hofplein, this has been seen in traffic terms as the junction of two traffic routes. In general, a road intersection can be reduced to one or more of these junctions, for which the most perfect unravelling of the traffic flow can be researched. If the ideal solution to this issue can be found, the question arises as to the extent to which this perfect solution can be the basis of the urbanistic shaping of the square, not only in the sense that traffic can be ideally arranged within its elevations but also in the sense of a concept from which a truly functional form can be derived.'

General Authority for the Reconstruction J.A. Ringers (second from left) being shown the OpRo amendments to the reconstruction plan after having been liberated from German custody. Photograph taken by C.H. van der Leeuw in his office at the Van Nelle factory, July 1945. From left to right: W.H. Mouton, Ringers, S.J. van Embden, A. van der Goot and (crouching) C. van Traa

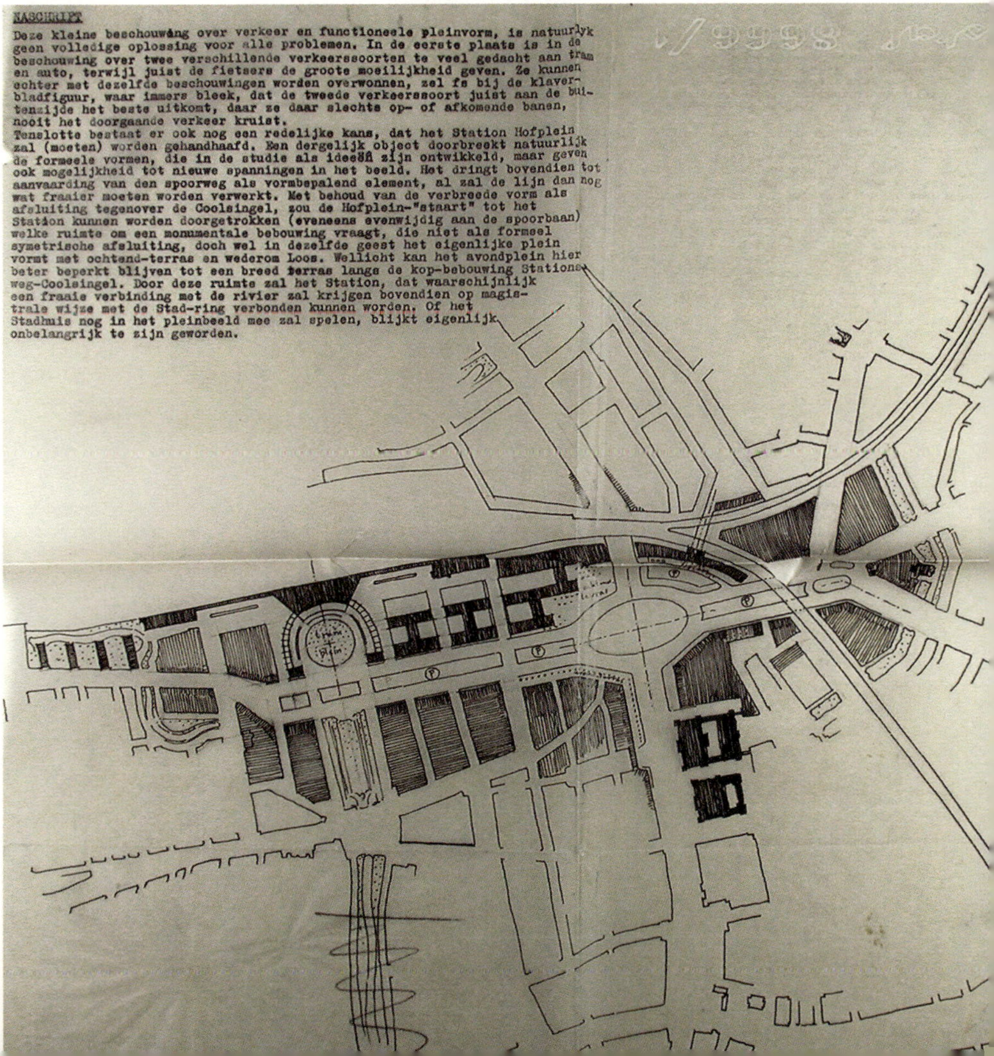

'Traffic and the shape of the square, in particular Hofplein', design study by J.H. van den Broek for OpRo, 1945

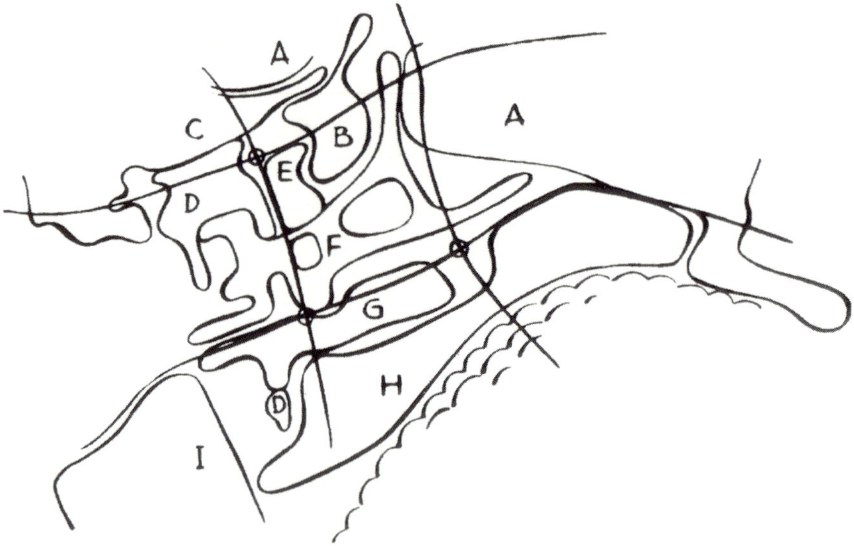

Scheme for the functional zoning of the city centre, 1953

- A Houses
- B Market grounds
- C Railway/trade
- D Theatres, hotels and restaurants
- E Government buildings
- F Shops
- G Banks and offices
- H Riverboats
- I Social and cultural institutions

A — woningen
B — marktwezen
C — spoorwegen, handel
D — theaters, hotels en restaurants
E — overheidsgebouwen
F — winkels
G — banken en kantoren
H — binnenbeurtvaartgebieden
I — sociale en culturele instellingen

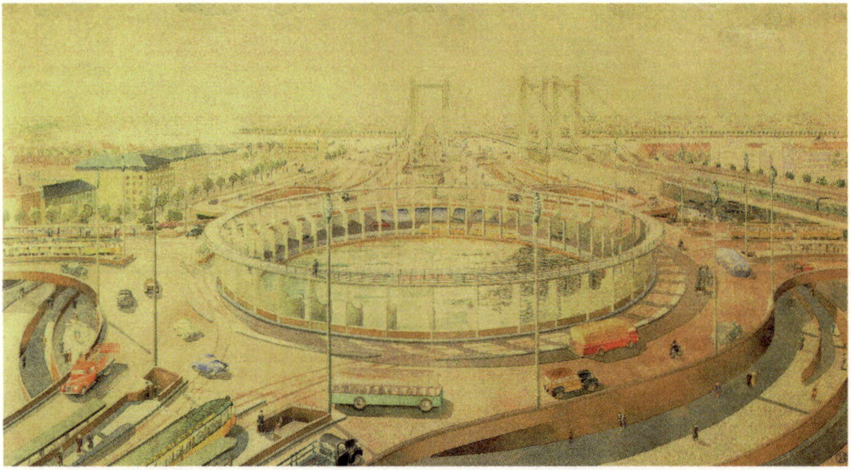

Double roundabout design for Oude Haven, ASRO 1946

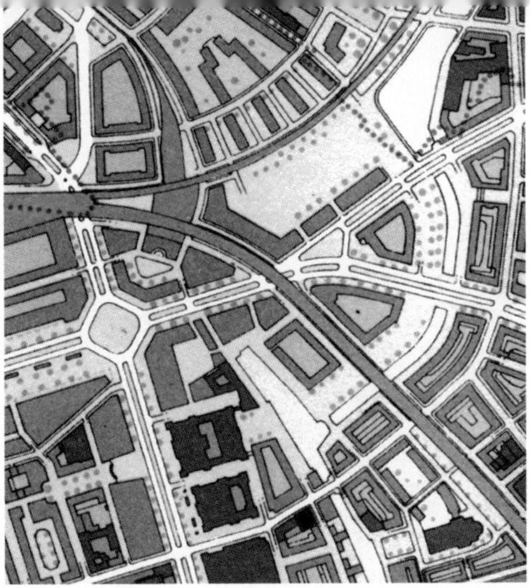

^ Basic Plan for the Reconstruction, 1946, area around Hofplein

The same area in the Basic Plan a few years later

v The Heliport east of Hofplein, ca. 1955

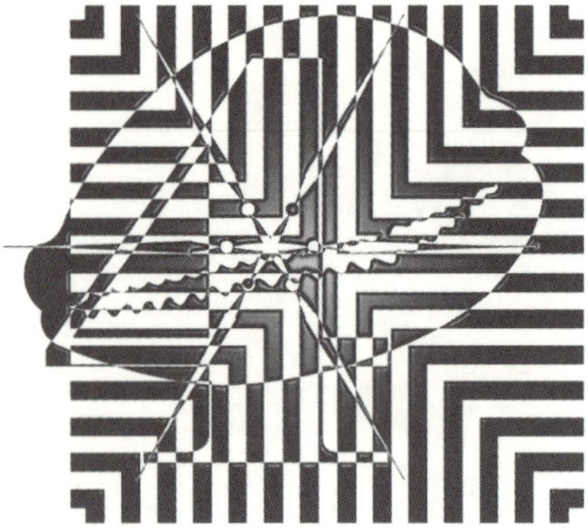

Oude Haven in 1999, with on the left 'het Witte Huis'

Van den Broek subsequently presented page after page of traffic schemes, circular junctions, cloverleaf figures, single- and multi-level crossings and so on. Additionally, the number of branches of each traffic arm were counted, formulas were tested to calculate traffic intensity and moments of comparative quiet in certain models, etc. In short, Van den Broek was engaged in traffic engineering. Very slowly, almost unobserved, it filtered into the design. Van den Broek refused to fall into the trap of Berlagian 'accents at salient points' but attempted to distil a form from the idea of the traffic function and its solution.[17] He first of all referred to the form of the structural work itself, especially that of the cloverleaf. However, 'their own significance is so great that they not only tolerate the grand and even background of nature, they actually need it.'[18]
Thus, in the city, the form of a traffic nucleus was not to be sought in the sculptural qualities of the object itself but in the urbanistic qualities of the surrounding buildings. Van den Broek ultimately was looking for a thing that was thought to have been rendered impossible: a synthetic approach to infrastructure, buildings, public space and image. Van den Broek proposed that the entertainment and catering functions of the square should be used to keep its elevations at a distance, to push them away from the square and thus furnish Coolsingel with a yielding rear elevation of its own. However, he was quick to point out that he was not concerned with classic urbanist geometry, oriented towards the centre of the square, but with a new geometry, that of modern-day urban traffic: 'one with the diagonal values of centrifugal roads.'[19] The oval shape he designed for Hofplein should accordingly be seen as a radical statement against every kind of concentric city form. City form is no longer defined by a hierarchical relationship to a central point but by a dynamic relation to the flows that surge through the city.
Van den Broek saw the dismantling of urban planning and the dissection of the physical form of the city as a reason for fundamentally rearranging the relationship between urban content and urban form. Van Traa regarded the form-less city simply as the paradigm within which he chose to work. Van den Broek reorganized town planning around the dynamics of traffic, Van Traa saw traffic as an autonomous element by means of which one could command the scale and functioning of the entire city. Van den Broek's work during and just after the war had an enormous influence on Van Traa's Basisplan. Many components of the plan can be found in their original form in the studies that Van den Broek made for OpRo. However, Van Traa did not adopt the subtext of Van den Broek's work – reconstructing town planning as a synthetic discipline. In other words, Van den Broek's theory disappeared under Van Traa's empiricism.

Traffic gave Van Traa the opportunity to develop a three-dimensional physical structure as large as the whole of Rotterdam, which could be defined as lines and points, and to irrigate the city with flows of people and goods without erecting any form of spatial centrality or hierarchy whatsoever. Finally, Van Traa did exactly what Van den Broek disapproved of: he deposited large autonomous structures in the landscape that would simply impose their image and sculptural nature on the other elements.
Van Traa's instruments were the city map, in which he sought traces of a grid of roads, and the vertical zoning of traffic types, a principle taken from the Maas Tunnel. By extending the Weena in a straight line from Hofplein to the Station, extending Blaak to Churchillplein – sweeping away Dudok's Bijenkorf department store in the process – and filling in the waters of Westersingel and

extending it to the Maas, Van Traa succeeded in drenching the city with a balanced dosage of traffic while simultaneously constructing an internal skeleton.
The traffic network in the Basisplan consists of extremely broad boulevards with trees on either side and grass in the middle. The traffic is vertically divided into cars wishing to cross the city at high speed and those wishing to turn off somewhere. For this purpose, the fast cars can seek out the central lanes that carry them under junctions while the slower traffic remains above ground and can change direction or stop. The pre-sorting of traffic at points of increasing intensity has led to an elegant and lucid design. The concrete cladding panels and pale yellow tiles of the traffic channels, the steel railings, the oval pavements around the air shafts, the street lamps and the trees are attributes of the highly symmetrical and even monumental compositions that very much bring to mind elements of the work of Van Traa's boss, Witteveen.
The climax of Van Traa's traffic network ought to have been Oude Haven. The Maas was crossed via a new four-track suspension bridge for railway traffic on the site of the old one, and a new suspension bridge for road traffic to the east of the railway bridge. Traffic would access the much higher bridge by means of a double roundabout. The traffic remaining in the northern section would take the lower roundabout, the traffic heading for the south of the city would take the upper one. Planned on the site of Oude Haven was a gigantic coliseum-like structure for moving cars. The Witte Huis would be the only building from the pre-war row to remain, standing like a traffic policeman between the new bridges. This would give the building the ultra-metropolitan context that it seemed to have been demanding for fifty years. The double roundabout with a diameter of almost 200 metres was of emphatically monumental design. In the sketches we can distinguish a large pond – or is it a lawn? – at the centre. The lamp posts, pillars and railings all contribute to the upcoming style of infra-classicism, with which Van Traa converted a traffic hub into an urban building with a civil authority like that of a church, city hall, court of justice or corrida.
At Hofplein too, which did get implemented according to Van Traa's plan, representation, classicism and monumentality were found to be concentrated at the places where there were the most cars. If Van den Broek sought a centrifugal geometry for the buildings around the junction, Van Traa concentrated on the junction alone and did not flinch from monumentalizing the central point by means of a large fountain, zoomorphic ornamentation and all. This was a solution also named by Van den Broek but then as an example of what should not be done.
As Michelle Provoost has demonstrated, we should ultimately regard Van Traa's traffic network as a transcendental project.[20] The 1955 road network clarifies what Van Traa had in mind. This map shows the Roads and Waterways Department's tangential highway structure around Rotterdam's central city. Rotterdam's traffic network within this structure proves to be a refined version of a regional, national and even continental network of lines and points.
The most important property of this traffic structure is that it is not a circle. This means that a city has been defined as a point on a neutral grid, instead of a 'totemic' unit fixed to its location and history for ever, with highways pointed at it and then draped around it. By thinking in terms of grids around the city instead of rings, one can transcend the city and strip it of its territoriality.
The true context of Van Traa's town planning increasingly shifted away from Rotterdam towards the network of state highways and as a result the port and

its hinterland. This has led to a miraculous state of affairs: the form of Rotterdam speaks less of Rotterdam than of something else, maybe world trade, Europe, the future, 'every family its own car', democracy, prosperity, technology, happiness?

The Plan 1946-1955

Even although the plan itself had been set aside, the first buildings that arose after the war were designed within Witteveen's urban plan and derived their urbanist position and architectural identity from it. In 1944, H. Mertens began work on the Amro Bank on Coolsingel, an impressive brick building which formed the east side of an otherwise uncompleted city block from the Witteveen plan. It was erected on a Coolsingel that was initially planned to head in the direction of Schiedamse Vest. However, Van Traa had Coolsingel bend towards Leuvehaven to open 'the window on the river', which explains the curious broadening of the boulevard opposite the Amro Bank.

It was not only Witteveen's plan that allowed hard rudiments to bob about in the emptiness that was Rotterdam in 1946, various sections of the Basisplan itself were very close to its abandoned predecessor. Much of the development to the east of the overhead railway, between Meent and Goudsesingel, consists of the large city blocks – shops and commercial premises below and housing above around a service courtyard – with which Witteveen equipped the modern city with a formal and functional hierarchy and thus with a normal city form; they were just a little more widely spaced than in the first plan.

The classical planning and Witteveenian components of the 1946 Basisplan are largely absent from the 1955 version of the plan. It is striking that the only element which scarcely altered was the traffic network, the grid in Van Traa's scheme. The programmatic pudding – the buildings between the principal roads – had undergone many and substantial modifications, both in its consistency and its texture. The rectangular building blocks with service courts to the west of Coolsingel, for example, have been blended into the elementarist composition of the Lijnbaan; the corner development around Hofplein has fragmented into a number of detached elements of extremely varied size and shape. Furthermore, a number of major interventions, which all at once reorganized a large chunk of the city, have disappeared. An example of this is the complete revamping of Muizenpolder, Parklaan and Zocherspark, a project that seems to have vanished from the Basisplan somewhere between 1946 and 1955.

It turns out that the carefully reproduced planning prescriptions in the 1946 Basisplan, such as alignments, construction heights and building blocks, were merely codes whose sole function was to clarify a future urban programme in a way comprehensible to everyone. A city block in Van Traa's plan had quite another significance than it had in Witteveen's, even if it was identical. In Witteveen's plan, it was a normative proto-object, in Van Traa's an invitation to total deconstruction of the type. In this way, the Basisplan redeemed its promise and furnished a solution to the paradox of non-formal urban planning. Planning can no longer coincide with a form but only with a partly unpredictable production of forms and images. The Basisplan suddenly seems to have become an analytical model instead of a forecast. The development of Rotterdam presented itself in the series of amended 'Basisplans', each of which formed a freeze-frame in the constant flow of realizations and ambitions.

So the Basisplan was hollow; but what about the emptiness of the situation in

1940? Was this also included in the plans? In fact, it was still very prominent in 1955. The records show how the reconstruction of the inner city really only gained momentum at the beginning of the fifties and how it first concentrated on the centre of the pudding, far away from the main traffic network even though this was the most attractive element by far. The 1955 Basisplan indicates, however, that most transformations to the original took place at the lines and points of the traffic grid. Where a generic city block had originally been set down in the 1946 plan, an office complex or high-rise block of flats was now projected, standing there in splendid isolation. However, in reality, there was nothing as yet. This is evidence of the cunning way in which Van Traa used the emptiness as a strategic means to prevent the form of the city being completely determined by the economic circumstances in a certain period. The zones that fell within the magnetic force fields of the traffic were kept empty as long as no customer arrived who could profit from the site to the maximum. The blocks around Blaak and Hofplein in the 1946 plan were merely disguises; the discrete objects in the 1955 version illustrate the true intentions: large buildings that are not impaired by urban planning.
In that sense, the 1955 plan is much bolder that its predecessor. It dared to leave large segments open, without having to set down a building, park or complex for diplomatic reasons. The candid treatment of emptiness was a symptom of the approaching end of the sobriety and caution of the early reconstruction. The emptiness began to acquire independent and concrete urban significance and an extraordinary visuality when the immense cobbled expanse behind Hofplein was used for the Heli-port, not just a powerful symbol of the modern cosmopolitan port and industrial city, but most of all a monument to the life-giving urban emptiness of Rotterdam.

Notes

1 E. Roelofsz, **De Wederopbouw van de in Mei 1940 verwoeste delen van de binnenstad, Kralingen en het Noordereiland van Rotterdam 1940-1950**, Rotterdam 1989, 17 **2** L. Ott, **Van luchtkasteel tot koopmansburcht**, Rotterdam 1969 **3** Rem Koolhaas, **S,M,L,XL**, 010 Publishers, Rotterdam 1995, 204-209; 518-541 **4** Jef Bonten, **Anton Koolhaas**, Uitgeverij B. Gottmer, Nijmegen/ Bruges 1980, 18 **5** A.L. Sötemann, **Een dichter en zijn wereld. Over J.C. Bloem**, Historische Uitgeverij, Groningen 1994, 101 **6** Sötemann, 64 **7** C. Wagenaar, **Welvaartsstad in wording: de Wederopbouw van Rotterdam 1940-1952**, Rotterdam 1993, 215-217 **8** E. Roelofsz, op. cit., 133-134 **9** Ibid., 134 **10** Ibid., 136 **11** Ibid., 141 **12** M. Provoost, **De stad als Verkeersmachine: de Ruit om Rotterdam**, Rotterdam 1994 **13** C. Wagenaar, op. cit., 218 **14** Ibid., 195-207 **15** Ibid., 235 **16** J.H. van den Broek, **Verkeer en Pleinvorm in het bijzonder van het Hofplein**, manuscript 1945, archives of Van den Broek & Bakema **17** Ibid., 1 **18** Ibid., 3 **19** Ibid., 6 **20** M. Provoost, op. cit., 31-35

What if?

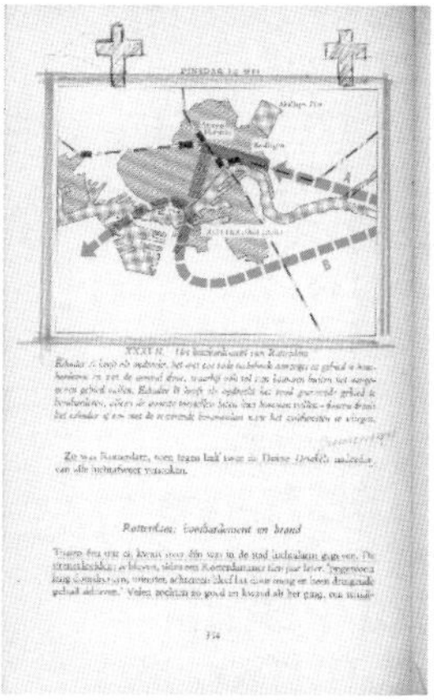

Diagram of the bombing of Rotterdam, 14 May 1940. Squadron A drops its bombs, squadron B gets called off at the last moment. Taken from a copy of Lou de Jong's *The Kingdom of the Netherlands in the Second World War* in the Municipal Library, Rotterdam

Diagram of the bombing of Rotterdam, 14 May 1940, What If? version. Squadron A drops its bombs, then squadron B drops its bombs

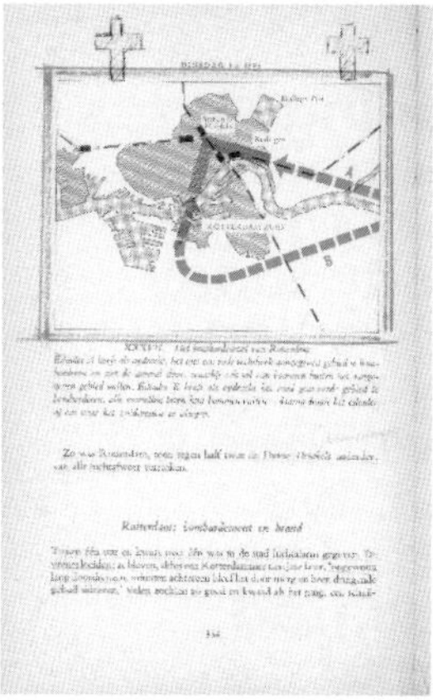

The Boijmans Van Beuningen Museum plays a major role in the cultural life of Rotterdam. Situated close to an attractive water course at walking distance from Central Station and the river Maas, it occupies a prominent place on the 'cultural axis' of Rotterdam. It owes this central position to the historical decisions and struggles that have shaped Rotterdam. But what if history had taken a different turn? *Where* would Boijmans have been then - literally and metaphorically - in Rotterdam?

Rotterdam came within a hair's breadth of being even more heavily devastated by the German bombing on 14 May 1940 than it in fact was. This much is clear from volume four of Dr L. de Jong's book *The Kingdom of the Netherlands in the Second World War.* Just seconds before the second wave of bombers was due to drop its load of bombs, it veered away and flew back to base. Unlike the first squadron, it had noticed in time that the city had surrendered and that further bombing was therefore unnecessary. What would have happened if the destruction of the city centre had been complete and a disaster comparable to that which later overcame Dresden, Hamburg and Darmstadt had taken place?

What if the first newspaper reports of ten thousand killed in Rotterdam had been accurate? What if not only buildings but also the entire administrative apparatus had been wiped out, and the whole idea of centre had

been burned away by the magnitude and horror of the destruction? Might people not have reacted in typical Rotterdam fashion by making a virtue of necessity and grasping this opportunity to realize pre-war plans for a *Greater Rotterdam*? In which case an alternative reconstruction scenario would have come into force. Greater Rotterdam: the annexation of Vlaardingen and Schiedam, a city with over a million inhabitants and a world-class harbour, a true metropolis on the Maas. Because of the awful trauma associated with the site of the historical centre, the new centre would have been built on a completely different spot, more to the west around the current industrial area of Marconiplein: more in the centre of *Greater Rotterdam*. The old town centre would have been dug out to make a harbour basin. What would the city have looked like then and where would Boijmans have ended up in the new scheme of things?

Extrapolating from historical events that very nearly happened is not restricted to film and literature. Historians, too, practice research by writing counterfactual histories. The act of thinking out alternative historical scenarios throws an exceptionally bright light on the processes that have shaped our present world. It reveals that historical decisions and struggles that have had tremendous impact were actually touch and go up to the last minute. Only by posing the 'what if' question can we really penetrate to the pivotal moments in the history of a person, a city or the world.

For the exhibition in the Boijmans Van Beuningen Museum we decided to stick as close as possible to the pictures and documents everyone knows: the bombing, the post-war reconstruction, the city today and the museum. The exhibition was no more science fiction than developments then and now. By manipulating reality in tiny and specific ways we sketched a parallel history as if it had really taken place. We produced urban design schemes as if they had been made at that time and, in a series of manipulated snapshots, we gave a hyper-realistic picture of

Rotterdam and Boijmans in that parallel history. The exhibition consisted of four elements. The counterfactual post-war reconstruction scenario was related on 406 A4 sheets containing text and pictures which together formed a tableau of 3 by 9 metres. Hanging on the same wall was Han van Meegeren's wartime Vermeer forgery, *Christ at Emmaus*. On the magenta-coloured wall opposite these two elements was an installation: a window with a picture of the museum courtyard (which is on the other side of this wall) as the 'toleration zone' for heroin prostitutes it would have become in the parallel history, because in Greater Rotterdam the museum would have found itself on the outskirts of town. Finally, J.C. Bloem's poem *Rotterdam*, written in one continuous line, divided the floor in half along its length.

Our aim in exhibiting in the Boijmans Museum a history that would not have left the museum itself unaffected, was to confront the museum as a setting and as an institution with an alternative course of events. An alternative that was not implausible. The exhibition demonstrated that the prestige the museum currently enjoys as a centrally located metropolitan cultural shrine is by no means self-evident.

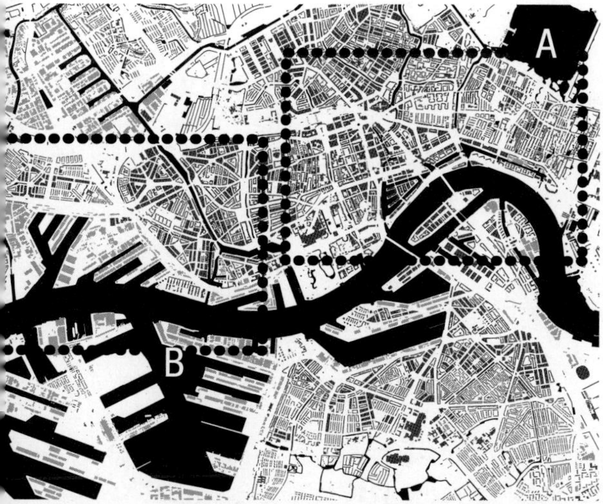

Crimson assumes that if the bombing of Rotterdam had gone as originally planned, the devastation and death count would have been so great that the city would have decided not to rebuild a new centre on the site of the old one, but dig out a huge harbour basin where the heart of Rotterdam used to be: (A). The new centre would be moved to the west, so that it would take a more fitting position in the agglomeration that had been moving westward for decades and would continue doing so after the war. A perfect location would have been the area around today's Vierhavengebied: (B). We carefully dismantled the Basic Plan for the reconstruction of the centre of Rotterdam (1946) that had been drawn up for the site of the old centre and reassembled it on the new site. From there on we imagined how the city and its buildings would have evolved. What would have happened to institutions that were built near the centre, but after the war found themselves near the port? What would the centre of Rotterdam have been like, had it been much more connected to the river, as would have been the case in our scenario?

^ The Boijmans Van Beuningen Museum (A. van der Steur, 1935), finished a few years before the war, stands just outside the reconstructed centre of Rotterdam, having escaped the bombing by a short distance. Over the last decade it has become the centre of a cluster of museums and cultural institutions and parks, all designed by distinguished architects: the Netherlands Architecture institute (Jo Coenen, 1993), Museum Park (Yves Brunier & OMA, 1993) and the Kunsthal (Rem Koolhaas, 1992)

v The once grim and stony Schouwburgplein (theatre square), intended to be the social condenser for the new centre of Rotterdam, was redesigned some years ago in a spectacular way by landscape architect Adriaan Geuze and architect Koen van Velsen. Geuze turned the square into a steel, rubber and wood platform above a parking garage. Van Velsen lowered an enormous plastic cinema complex onto the square. The giant moving lamp-posts remind the skaters, breakdancers and cinema-goers of the harbour cranes that exist far away from the centre

^ The Basic Plan for the Reconstruction of the Centre of Rotterdam, 1946

v The Schielandshuis (Jacob Lois & Pieter Post, 1665), one of the sole survivors of the bombing, now holding its own in-between the skyscrapers of Wim Quist, Pi de Bruijn and Helmut Jahn

^ The Boijmans Van Beuningen Museum (A. van der Steur, 1935) left the area long ago and thus also its building which had served it for less than twenty years. The area around the old Boijmans Museum has evolved into the very antithesis of the centre: a hybrid, urbanistically grey area. The long warehouse sheds belonging to shipping agents Van Gend en Loos and Pakhoed have stood empty for years, while the harbour railway carries at best two locomotives a day. Other activities are thriving though: the harbour offices and warehouses have been taken over by architects, graphic designers and artists. Here, too, are the louche bars, the lock-up garages with dubious contents and rusting vessels with obscure African registrations...

v The once grim and stony Havenplein (harbour square) was intended as a wide open window on the bustling harbour, positioning the port activities firmly within the social and cultural heart of the city. Some years ago it was redesigned in a spectacular way by landscape architect Adriaan Geuze and architect Koen van Velsen. Geuze turned the square into a steel, rubber and wood platform that mirrored the containers, ships and machines moving through the late 20th-century port. Van Velsen lowered an enormous plastic cinema complex on the square, as if it were itself a vessel. The giant moving lamp-posts vie with the movements of the real cranes for the attention of the skaters, breakdancers and cinema-goers

^ The Basic Plan for the New Centre of Rotterdam, 1946

v A final remnant of the old city, in the middle of Rottehaven – the harbour basin dug out on the site of old Rotterdam - is the Schielandshuis (Jacob Lois & Pieter Post, 1665). After 14 May 1940, the Schielandshuis was restored to its original 17th-century classicist state. Now it stands as an alien fragment among the sheds, ships, cranes and containers of Pier 2 in Rottehaven. It houses the Historical Museum of old Rotterdam where an exhaustive archive and a somewhat tatty exhibition about the rise and fall of old Rotterdam attracts few visitors but many researchers...

^ The museum stands as a beacon in this economically and socially marginal area. In the 1980s it was appropriated by artists who set up studios here. The city council recently legalized this use and sold an entire wing to Atelier van Lieshout, thereby tacitly acknowledging that the building is an outlet for activities which are regarded as awkward in the handsome and lucrative city centre and the socially sensitive residential areas, but which are nonetheless part and parcel of a big city. The clearest example of this policy is to be found discreetly tucked away in the courtyard of the old Boijmans building: a toleration zone for heroin prostitutes. This urban facility consists of traffic signs, planters, asphalt, white arrows, red neon lights, railings, awnings, partitions, official and unofficial rules, all designed to facilitate traffic and transactions. It opens at six in the evening and attracts an average of 200 visitors a day at 50 guilders a turn ...

v The Crimson team standing in front of the 'What If?' installation in Museum Boijmans van Beuningen

Re-Arch

New designs for old buildings

What do architects mean when they talk about history? If we regard 'history' solely as an idea and as a science we can quickly dispose of this question. Indeed, from an intellectual point of view, history has scant connections with Dutch architecture. We are posing this question here, however, out of an interest in the history that is concretized in the old building and in dealing with this history when that building once again is the subject of an architectural design: when it is converted, extended, facelifted or revamped. Such architectural tasks we would like to term Re-Architecture, *Re-Arch* for short.

What attitude do Dutch architects adopt when making a new design for an old building? 'Individuality plus respect for the original state' is the standard wish of clients and the standard design statement among architects. Old and new must be 'in equilibrium', one works to achieve 'harmony without pastiche', a 'dialogue with the historical state' or an image that is 'historical though not back-to-the-classics'.

This essay (and the book from which it comes) sets out to put the zip back into these euphemisms and clichés and inject habitual concepts with a new lease of life.

The fact is, the real content of the projects for old buildings resides less in the polite phrases used to explain them than in the architecture as a physical intervention in the existing. The intense one-to-one relationship that a new design enters into with history, and all the paradoxes and ambiguity this brings, is, for that reason, the subject of the book *Re-Arch.*

--- For the present we must conclude that there is no consistent approach to *Re-Arch*. Historical architecture is just too multifaceted in nature, status and meaning. An additional factor is that the relationship between old and new architecture is subject to changing cultural ideas about the significance of listed buildings and that of new-build. A 'scholarly definition' of architectural intervention would consist merely of frictions and paradoxes. But this is precisely where its essence lies. By analysing in every individual case the idea contained in a new design, it is possible to discover which characteristics inform the relationship between old and new at a given moment.

Use and abuse

Now the multiformity of Re-Arch issues on the one hand from the multiformity of present-day architectural culture, and on the other from a shift in attitude that we, along with the Spanish architectural historian Ignasi de Solà-Morales, can describe as 'from contrast to analogy'.-1- In the attitude of *contrast*, emphasis is on the singularity and contemporariness of the design; on its own identity with regard to the former state. This attitude derives from the presupposition that contrast intensifies and visualizes the meaning of old and new. In that of *analogy*, the design springs from the oscillation between old and new, whereby the interference between the two generates a new thing. Accordingly, the identity of the new is *connected* with history rather than being confronted with it.

--- The distinction between contrast and analogy thus exists in a formal architectural sense, but also occurs as a concept in more general texts on the dialectics between old and new. Of these the most probing is Friedrich Nietzsche's *On the Use and Abuse of History for Life*. Here he describes in ruthless terms the dilemmas and paradoxes, the dos and don'ts of dealing with history. This book was published in 1874, just as historic preservation in the Netherlands as advocated by the likes of Victor de Stuers and Alberdingk Thijm was beginning to gain a foothold. Nietzsche points to the dangers of history: too much can have a numbing effect and prevents a culture from managing to convert its creative powers into deeds: 'There is a degree of insomnia, of rumination, of the historical sense, through which living comes to harm and finally is destroyed, whether it is a person or a people or a culture.' He calls for 'forgetting', for 'the capacity to sense things unhistorically', and for an artistic, operative history that 'stands in the service of life'.-2-

Friedrich Nietzsche in uniform as a bombardier in 1868

Nietzsche formulated the thought, still relevant today, that in most cases history only requires renewing or rejecting. But he leaves us with more questions than answers: where exactly is the border between man the memory-less animal and a numbed being with a stomachful of undigested historical rocks; in other words, what is too much history and what too little? How can we equate history, placed in independence by the historian, with the ability of that history to produce effects?

Contrast

De Solà-Morales explains the complexity of the attitude of contrast using canonical designs by Mies van der Rohe, Hilberseimer and Le Corbusier. The skyscrapers on Friedrichstrasse (1921) and the Plan Voisin

-1- Ignasi de Solà-Morales, 'From contrast to analogy. Developments in the concept of architectural intervention', *Lotus* no. 46 (Interpretation of the past), 37-45 -2- Friedrich Nietzsche, *On the Use and Abuse of History for Life*, 1873, transl. Ian C. Johnston, Nanaimo, 1998

Design for a glass skyscraper in Berlin by Mies van der Rohe, 1921

for Paris (1925) have been interpreted by other historians as the death knell for the existing city. But according to De Solà-Morales even this architecture could do nothing other than give its own reading of the material presented to it by the city and by history, defining along paradigmatic lines a relationship marked by the emphasis on the effect of contrast above every other type of formal category.-3- He sees contrast and presenting projects as photomontages merely as a way of dealing with the existing and not necessarily as destructive acts.

--- In 1931, two years before CIAM, the Dutch professional organizations for historical preservation themselves published a document entitled 'The Athens Charter'. They propagated that all restoration should exhibit a visible contrast between old and new. This faction, traditionally regarded as hostile to designers, therefore contributed to the unchecked rise of contrast. Contrast was seen as a didactic principle and a striving to achieve clarity, not as a Marinetti-style exhortation to burn down the museums and churches.

--- For those who wish to see the 20th century not just in terms of an overhaul (dialectic or otherwise) of the history of architecture, modern architecture does prove to carry within itself the stance of analogy. Indeed, this holds particularly for a handful of pre-eminently modern architects, whose designs are geared to creating formal and semantic complexity instead of distinction and certainty. The extension J.B. van Loghem (modernist of the first generation and hardcore communist) made in 1928 for an ironmongery in Amsterdam - 'the palimpsest of the century' according to Joseph Buch - is characteristic of the search to find a way of making distinctions without polarity, of showing difference and similarity simultaneously. In Van Loghem's first version the warehouse and office are fronted by a taut concrete facade with narrow vertical strips of fenestration. After this design was rejected by the beauty commission he made a second version. Van Loghem designed - in concrete - a window 'order' that mediated between ribbon windows and those of an Amsterdam canal house. On the office level the full-width window betrays the non-loadbearing function of the facade, a theme known to us as much from the Golden Age as from Le Corbusier's Oeuvre Complète. With its 'modified' facade and slanting roof supporting three enormous dormer windows the new-build leans as a colossal volume on, alongside and behind the old building. The old warehouse has been unceremoniously tucked into the new volume with not a shred of respect.

Post-war modernism

In the decades after the war most architects of modern signature and their clients took a hard and unequivocal line: the contemporariness of new-build was of such importance that the historicity of the old

-3- Ignasi de Solà-Morales, op. cit., 39

building has no initiating role to play in creating the new design. The strategy of contrast was endowed with a cartoonesque banality it did not have in pre-war modernism. The architect Vegter designed the extension to the neo-classical town hall in Groningen (1949-1962), with old and new strictly distinguishable in terms of volume, material, building method and style. The reason in this case was that Vegter was searching for a modern equivalent of the 18th century town hall. His marble geometry represented a new monumentality and a new dignity. The Goudkantoor - a 17th century listed building - was drawn as a third object into the new order by linking it to an elevated glass walkway. This loose configuration issued from the Department of Preservation's resistance to extending the old town hall. Even so, the point of contact was later read as a deliberate and unfortunate break with history. The building, with all its aspirations as a hopeful and proud contemporary architecture, was demolished in 1994.

--- Around 1960 a new wind blew through international architectural theory that left its traces in Dutch architectural practice. In 1959 the new generation of modernists united in Team X pitted its version of modernism against the 'old' brand. Their seminal contribution on the Re-Arch front was to counter the generalizing concepts adhered to by the 'generation of 1930' with the notion of 'unicity'. Whereas in the Heroic Period existing buildings and cities were replaced by universal concepts, Team X chose the 'time-conscious techniques of renewal and extension derived from the recognition of the positive ecological trends to be found in every particular situation'.-4- This 'metabolic' conception of history as a process of growth became a window opened to the site's specificity as the foodstuffs of the design.

Herman Hertzberger's unrealized 1975 proposal to convert a 19th-century church (Broerkerk) in Groningen into a university library is emblematic of the ideas on the existing city as upheld by the 'Team X subsidiary' Forum, most particularly of the influence psychology and sociology had on those ideas. This design was the logical sequel to a 1972 policy document on government objectives (Doelstellingennota), which drew attention to the value of a fine-meshed, small-scale urban morphology. Clearly, preserving the historic Broerkerk was not the prime objective of this scheme; the building is used as an on-site container for a humming throng which can give full rein to its urge to create and digest literature. The building dissolves in the 'urban fabric': it disappears below ground to emerge in a wash of semicircular roofs. In secularizing the 19th-century church, the Neo-Gothic chancel would have become little more than an element of mystery in an otherwise 'open and inviting' library.

--- The site-specific, the concern with transformation and growth espoused by Team X on the one hand, and the historical research by the Italians (Aldo Rossi, Giorgio Grassi, Saverio Muratori) and later by French architects and historians (Bruno Fortier, André Chastel) on the other, paved the way in architectural thinking for a complex and layered - analogous - attitude towards Re-Arch, in which history is conceived of as a storehouse of form and knowledge. Dutch theory first encountered this foreign train of thought via Ungers's design for the TU Twente (1967) and Rossi's proposals for Kop van Zuid and the attendant research done by Donald van Dansik, Jan de Graaf and Wim Nijenhuis (1983). There were, additionally, the unremitting arguments of the architectural historian Ed Taverne for giving a serious role to historical research in architecture.

-4- John Voelker, quoted in Joan Ockman (ed.), *Architecture Culture, 1943-1968. A Documentary Anthology*, New York: Columbia Books of Architecture/Rizzoli, 1993, 19

Van Loghem's extension to an ironmongery in Amsterdam, 1928

The white Town Hall in Groningen (J.J.M. Vegter, 1949-1962) next to the Goudkantoor (17 th century) and the former town hall (18th century)

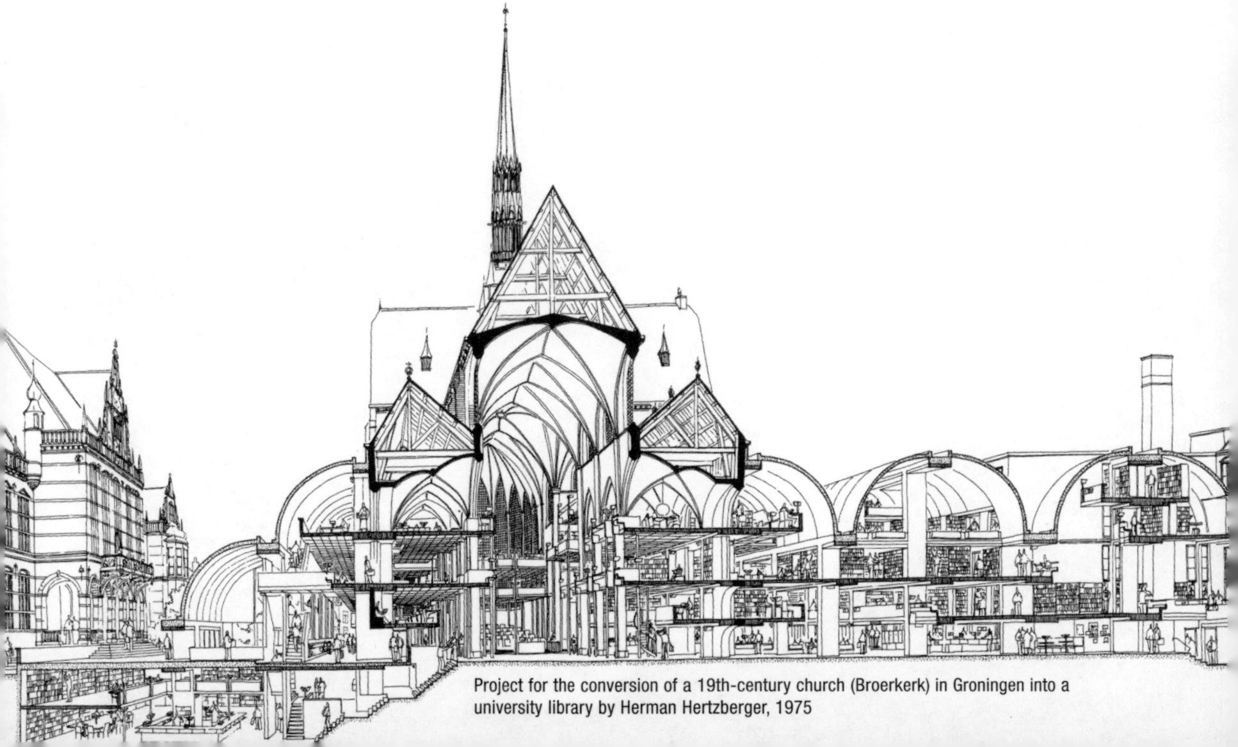

Project for the conversion of a 19th-century church (Broerkerk) in Groningen into a university library by Herman Hertzberger, 1975

1

2

Renovation and extension project for the Koepel Prison in Arnhem by O.M.A., 1980

3

4

1 J.J.P. Oud's Witte Dorp housing, torn down in 1989
2 The reconstructed works office building of J.J.P. Oud's Witte Dorp housing in Rotterdam, now in use as a barber's shop and museum
3 The second copy of Oud's works office building in Sassenheim in the grounds of Akzo/Nobel, main sponsor of the reconstruction project
4 The Kiefhoek housing quarters in Rotterdam, torn down and completely rebuilt, 1989-1995

A

B

A+B Extension of the Limburg Public Records Office by Marc van Roosmalen (1989-1996) including the foundations of a Gothic church and part of the mediaeval town walls

The ruinous state in 1999 of Sanatorium Zonnestraal in Hilversum (J. Duiker, 1926-1931)

An authentic Dutch contribution to the debates on historical context made its entrance with urban renewal. Aldo van Eyck and Theo Bosch reintroduced a small-scale urban morphology in Amsterdam in the Nieuwmarkt area; a redevelopment strategy which became the icon of seventies architecture and planning. The heroic deeds of 1970 - reasserting architecture's socio-critical position - have since fallen into disrepute due to the disappointing architectural offerings it went on to spawn. Concern for the built history of cities remained skin-deep. 'Building for the neighbourhood' and the allied 'contextualism' did, however, mean a turning point for the public at large, the authorities and the institutional clients and drove home the fact that preserving the historical city was worthy of respect and contributed to providing 'approved living conditions'. Housing associations, municipal bodies and architects adapted their ideas, working methods and organization to the new 'culture', which made a world of difference with the housing output in the sixties. The many recycling projects of the eighties and nineties were able to profit from the expertise gained in the seventies.

1980

In retrospect, two projects mark a major hitch in the relationship between history and architecture: the fault line lies somewhere around 1980 and the projects are the Lower House competition and the design for the Koepel Prison by OMA. The design for extensions to Parliament was an issue of national interest, full of drama and chaos. The prime meat of the matter was the relationship between old and new, in this case between the existing Binnenhof complex and the new addition.

The proposal submitted by OMA was rejected because of the incursion it made on the Binnenhof (Inner Court) with a volume that penetrated the complex from the side. Issuing from a paranoid-critical analysis of Dutch society, it gave our democratic system the same treatment as Rem Koolhaas's book *Delirious New York* had done for the Manhattan of the twenties. The scheme was a montage of the attributes and excesses of the Dutch democracy, including a 'smoke-filled room' and a sunken sitting area for discussions with the public.

--- Many ideas seem to have been buried along with the Lower House competition: the small-scale as symbolic of adapting to history, 'building for the neighbourhood' as a social foundation for architecture and lastly contrast as the exclusive means of dealing with the existing.

--- OMA's design of 1980 for the Koepel Prison in Arnhem marked less an end than the onset of a new concept. The relationship with the historical state was no longer described exclusively as a formal problem; the design attaches to the meaning and idea of the old building. This prompted the critic Hans van Dijk to describe the project as a kind of conceptual conservation: 'a strategy of respecting the existing not so much to the letter as in spirit'.-5-

The original panopticon designed by J.F. and W.C. Metzelaar in 1880 was an interior world controlled

-5- Hans van Dijk, 'Het bezwijken van tegenstellingen', *Wonen TA/BK*, 1982, no. 13/14, 12-49

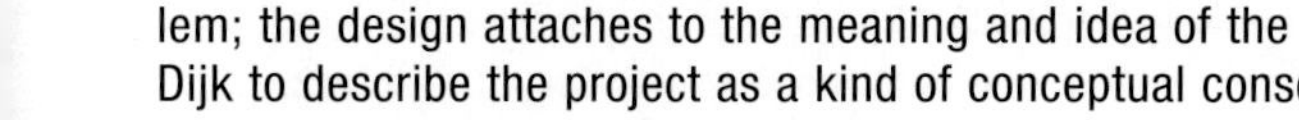

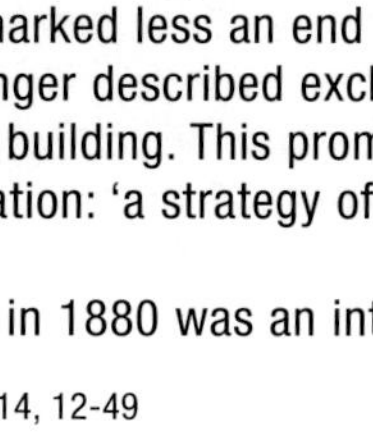

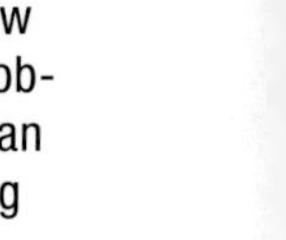

(and its occupants spiritually administered) from a central 'eye'. In the course of a century its panoptic principle had been turned inside-out: lack of space had meant housing numerous functions in sheds in the prison grounds, and the guards had been dispersed from their original central position. OMA accommodated the new use of this 'purely theoretical building' by totally overhauling the grounds within the prison walls. The rigid configuration of the old building prompted them to draw a cross of two sunken streets off which are new spaces for facilities. This Suprematist composition leaves the panopticon largely intact along with its principle of imprisonment and surveillance, 'saving the new the embarrassment of having either to ignore or express the idea of incarceration, which is incompatible with its aspirations. After the intervention, the dome represents the dismantled past, its former center crossed out, resting on a podium of modernity, which is concerned only with improving the prisoners' conditions'.-6- Proceeding from the required programmatic improvements, the image of the panopticon is used as an object alienated from the present, towering above the programmatic platform. The unrelenting geometrical and inward-looking form has been undermined by a not quite symmetrical cross, sweeping the core from the old building and taking it over formally and programmatically.

The recent past

A question that sets the heart of Dutch architecture culture all aflutter, is that of modern monuments. The old age of Modern Movement buildings now makes even young architects, given their almost paranormal affinity with the famous modern exemplars, set to work as restoration architects. Thus, the twin poles of invention and conservation are suddenly in hair-raisingly close proximity. This gives rise to the philosophical problem of how to preserve for eternity along honest lines, buildings whose designers certainly did not build them to last for ever, such as Sanatorium Zonnestraal and the Kiefhoek and Witte Dorp housing. Strictly speaking, respect for the ideas underlying this architecture sits uncomfortably with the need to protect it. However, we seem to have managed to leave our fear of a fetishistic response to these buildings behind and let the desire to preserve them prevail. The upshot is that it is in precisely these monuments of modernism that we now encounter the most extreme form of historic preservation, namely reconstruction. The 'white' work of J.J.P. Oud would seem to exert a particular attraction in this respect: Café de Unie and the Witte Dorp works office building were rebuilt (not at the original sites; there are even two examples of the works hut these days) as was the entire Kiefhoek housing estate, also in Rotterdam. That these icons of modernism have been resurrected is entirely thanks to their visual quality. A monument, it transpires, can simply be made anew. We express disdain when it comes to historical illusion of the likes of the Dutch Village in Nagasaki, yet the reconstruction of Kiefhoek itself amounts to an attraction for architectural tourists. We can only conclude that simulation is sometimes more fun than the real thing, the way Rotterdam's Tropicana 'swimming paradise' with all its features and without salt is more fun than the sea.

-6- Rem Koolhaas. 'Project for the renovation of a panopticon prison', *Art Forum*, Sept. 1981, 41

The historical experience

In the preceding pages we have seen that today the notion of contrast is losing ground; architects and clients regard adding a new portion to an old building more as an analogous operation exhibiting continuity with the past. Seen thus, experience of the proximity of history is a quality that is aspired to. Accordingly, old and new are not set in dialectic opposition, but are brought into alignment, in time and value as well as place.

The historical material at once becomes the backdrop against which the new architecture is enacted; a strategy taken to extremes by Aldo Rossi and Ignazio Gardella in their reconstruction of the theatre at Genoa (1982-1990), where new 'old' facades act as an 'urban' stage set in the main auditorium.

We see this displaying of history again, though now eschewing theatricalities, in Giorgio Grassi's project for the ruins of a Roman theatre in the Spanish town of Sagunto. Grassi reconstructed the architectural space, turning it into a theatre in modern working order. In the project there is no attempt made to imitate a historical unity, so that the outcome resembles the method of restoring sculptures and paintings where missing pieces or areas are filled in with 'blank' patches. Archaeological finds on site, parts of a frieze, columns, before then carted off to a museum, now have a place in the wall at the back of the stage. Here they are put on show rather than serving as decor. Thus the new building has become the museum of the old one.

--- This idea of exhibiting is present in a pedagogic sense in the Limburg Public Records Office in Maastricht, converted and expanded by Marc van Roosmalen in 1989-1996, where the foundations of a Gothic church have been excavated and can be viewed from the new promenade. The old town walls dug up in the courtyard, are back in view and a hole in the facade shows - also to passers-by - how the wall resumes its course across the street. In the chancel of the church, meetings are held underground beneath a glass roof bearing a bizarre exhibition of mediaeval tombstones.

--- These modes of displaying, of the mise-en-scène of old and new, result in an unpredictable moment of intimacy with the past, which the historian Frank Ankersmit calls 'the historical experience'; an uncontrollable moment in which history is sensed and undergone.-7- The value of this idea for Re-Arch lies in the call to conserve the paradox; in allowing buildings, building parts and ideas that clash, to coexist. There is no overarching principle that covers this; indeed a generalizing concept has a contrary effect. Letting contradictory ideas act upon one another can contribute to the unpredictable emergence of something truly new.

- 7- Frank Ankersmit, *De historische ervaring*, Groningen: Historische Uitgeverij, 1993

Today

Apart from being an intellectual issue Re-Arch is also a question of technique and material. There is a tendency to drop universal theories in the case of Re-Arch and seek out a unique and particular stepping-off point in the old building: at times colour, detailing or material, at others the surroundings or the landscape. Designers scour the old building for latent architectural qualities. In such cases the new design does not begin with an overarching concept but perhaps with the smallest detail. Nietzsche hoped that history would seek its significance not in universal laws, but that 'its worth is directly one which indicates a known, perhaps a habitual theme, a daily melody, in an elegant way, elevates it, intensifies it to an inclusive symbol, and thus allows one to make out in the original theme an entire world of profundity, power and beauty'.-8- This sounds like a manifesto for a design stance which we might term hyper-empirical.

--- What can recycling mean in an age where temporary, unstable aspects of architecture are central to the avant-garde and the economic lifespan of buildings is decreasing? The Dutch government however, now in the throes of calculating environmental expenses so that replacing buildings will become less lucrative, is pointing things in exactly the opposite direction. Reversibility - the new magic word in the marketplace - sounds like temporariness translated to the task of interventions: the new intervention can always be reversed because it does not essentially alter the old building. However, this argument seems to have been drummed up more to soften extreme proposals than to actually address their temporary quality.

--- The connection with recent developments in architecture is sooner found in the idea of layeredness, multiformity and the demise of generalistic and normative design principles. Layeredness and juxtaposition can surely be linked to the notion of historical experience. By placing objects in unmediated adjacency or wrapping them in translucent materials unpredictable frictions and paradoxes can arise. These do not necessarily need to be resolved and brought to synthesis, but proffer as they are a new definition of harmony. Re-Arch's aim, then, is to make something new at all costs, something that rises above what it was that was there first. When history is not restricted by a logic of politeness it can present itself unexpectedly, the way the historical experience does: as a thing that is new.

-8- Friedrich Nietzsche, op. cit.

Free at last!

Noordsingel Prison Rotterdam

In 1998 Crimson was asked to study the possibilities for the restoration and re-use of a 19th-century panopticon prison standing in the middle of the popular Rotterdam neighbourhood Het Oude Noorden. The people living in Het Oude Noorden had been promised that the prison would close and the building would be demolished, freeing the area for a beautiful neighbourhood park. Instead, however, the prison was to be closed gradually and the panopticon classified as a landmark. We chose to try and convince the people to learn to accept the prison as something they could use as a park. The technique we used was taken from modern Dutch rehabilitation policy. We resocialized the prison building, in the same way criminals are resocialized: by letting them go to work during the day and locking them in at night. We proposed a time-line along which certain portions of the grounds around and in the prison would be used by citizens and prisoners in separate time blocks, gradually phasing out the prisoners. In the end the prison would pass entirely to the neighbourhood, but as a three-dimensional, multifunctional park-building. Along the way it would have been restored to its historical architectural form, but turned completely inside-out in its social function.

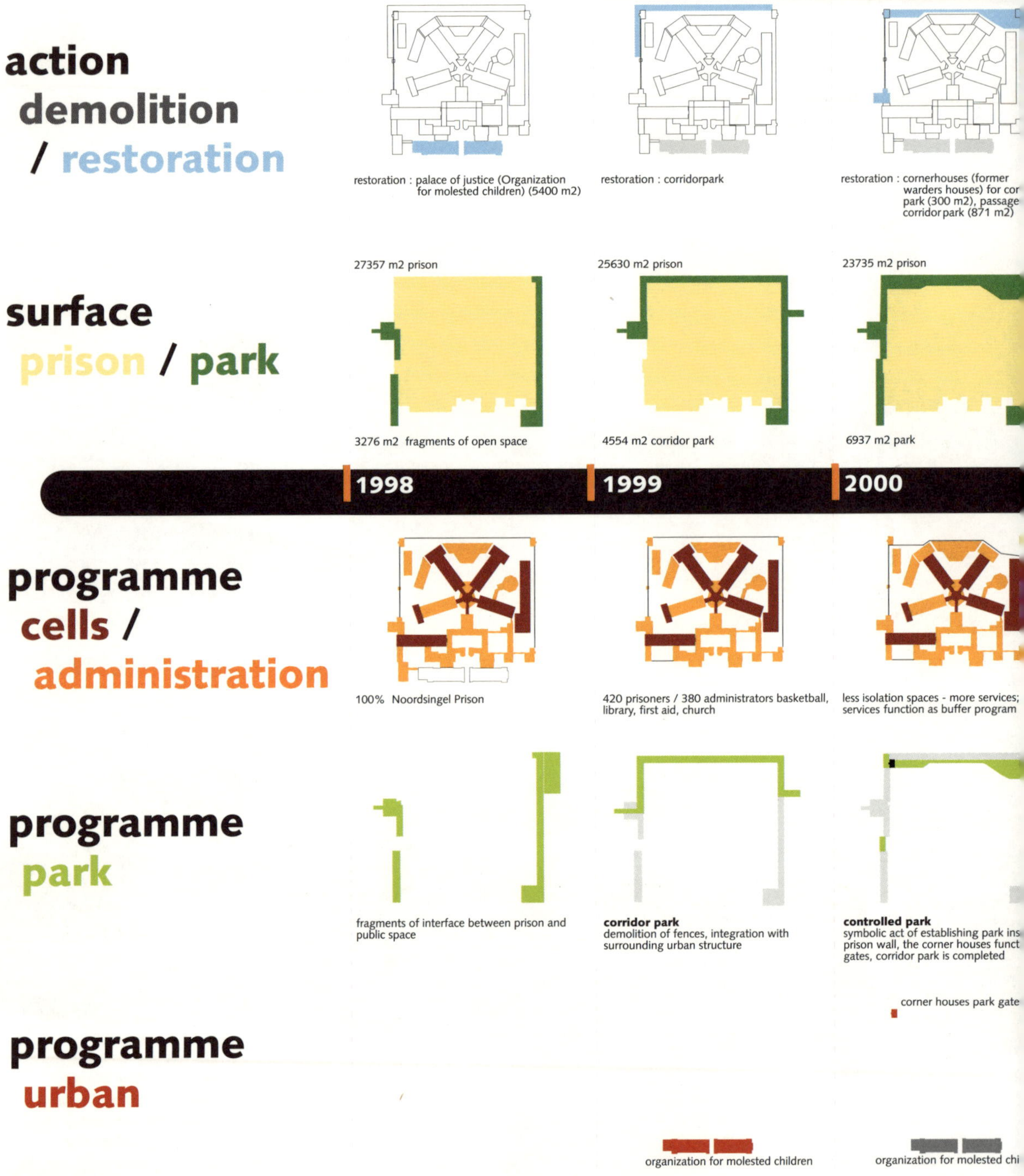

Proposed time-line of restoration and resocialization

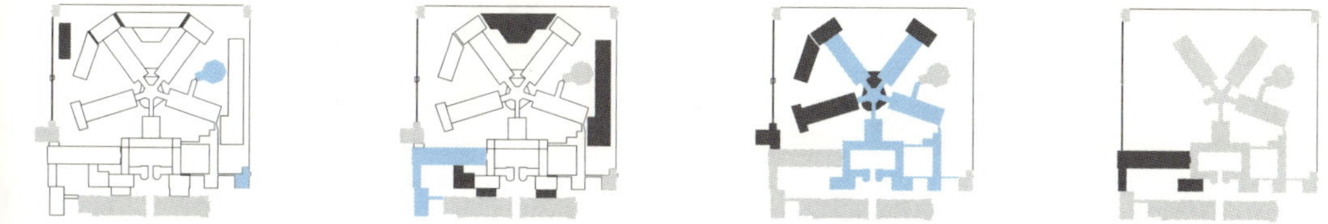

restoration : church (358 m2), kindergarten (546 m2); adaptation for shared use: library (120 m2), workspace (946 m2), basketball (425 m2)
demolition : storage (300 m2)

restoration : archives (1000 m2), conversion wing A (2576 m2) 120 cells
demolition : wings E and F (1979.6 m2 for 1248 m2 park), work space (946 m2), administration (492 m2)

restoration : wings B,C,D (6750 m2 / 336 cells), rest (3443 m2)
demolition : bombed wing (868 m2), gates (871 m2), panopticon distortions (194 m2), basketball (421 m2), isolation (596 m2)

demolition : wing A (2576 m2), administration (226 m2 and 387 m2)

…72 m2 prison | 16717 m2 prison | 0 m2 prison | 10578 m2 building

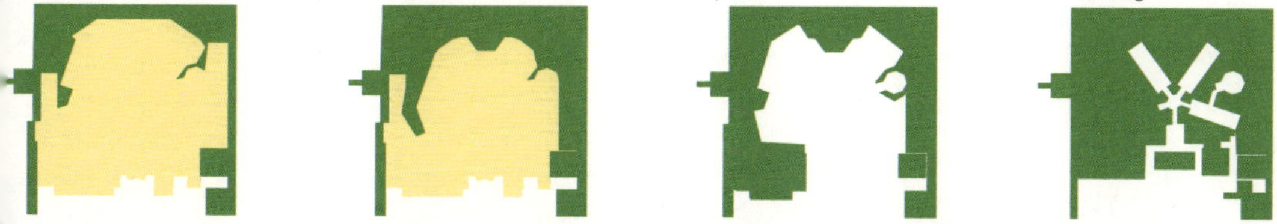

…4 m2 park | 13864 m2 park | 15796 m2 park | 23751 m2 park

004 | **2006** | **2010** | **2012**

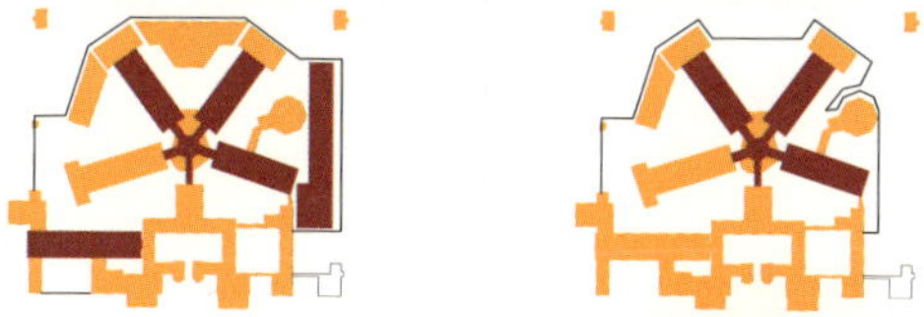

…s dangerous criminals (-48), services …ction as hinge program

services function as interface programme, day detention prisoners work as guards in the detention park, wing A hosts artists doing art therapy with the prisoners

…ogrammatic contamination
…adual conversion to a lighter form of …tention; interface of prison and …ighbourhood by sharing public facilities

programmatic contamination / detention park

prison archive park
expansion park into former A-wing

increased usage of park
amputation of the bombarded wing in 1943, Hortus Conclusus Conclusus

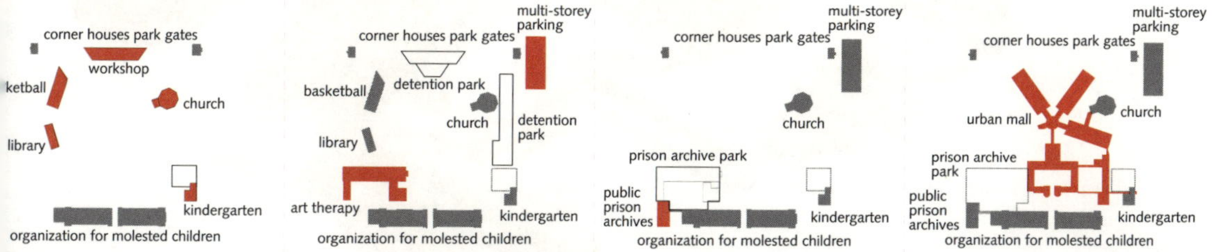

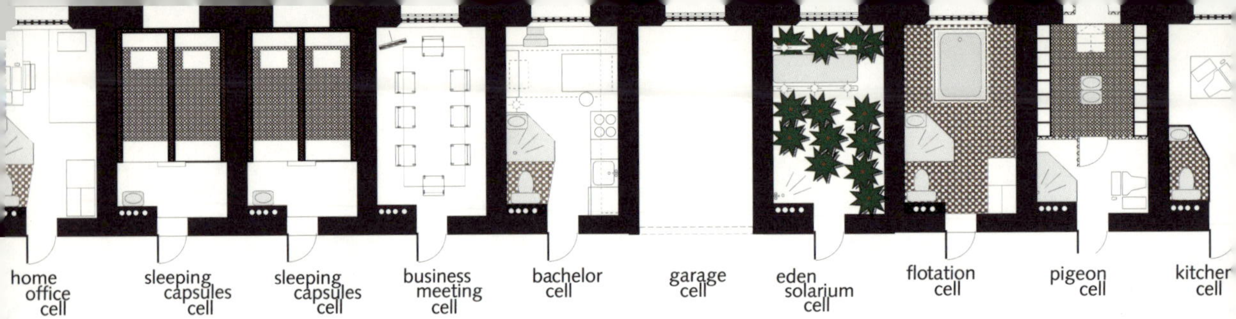

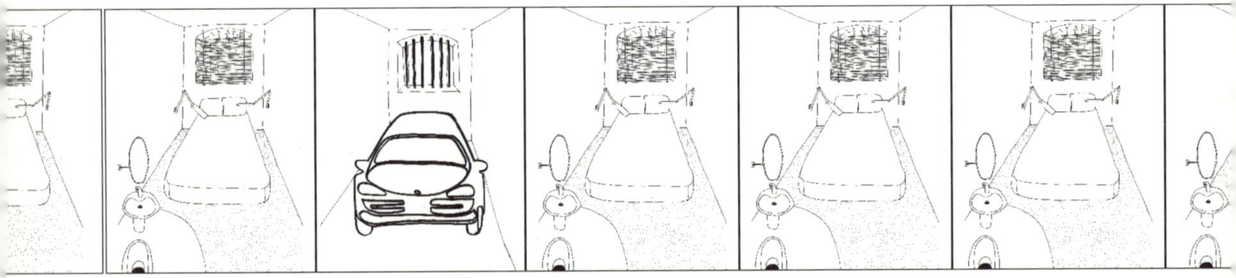

Possible uses for the cells in the former prison

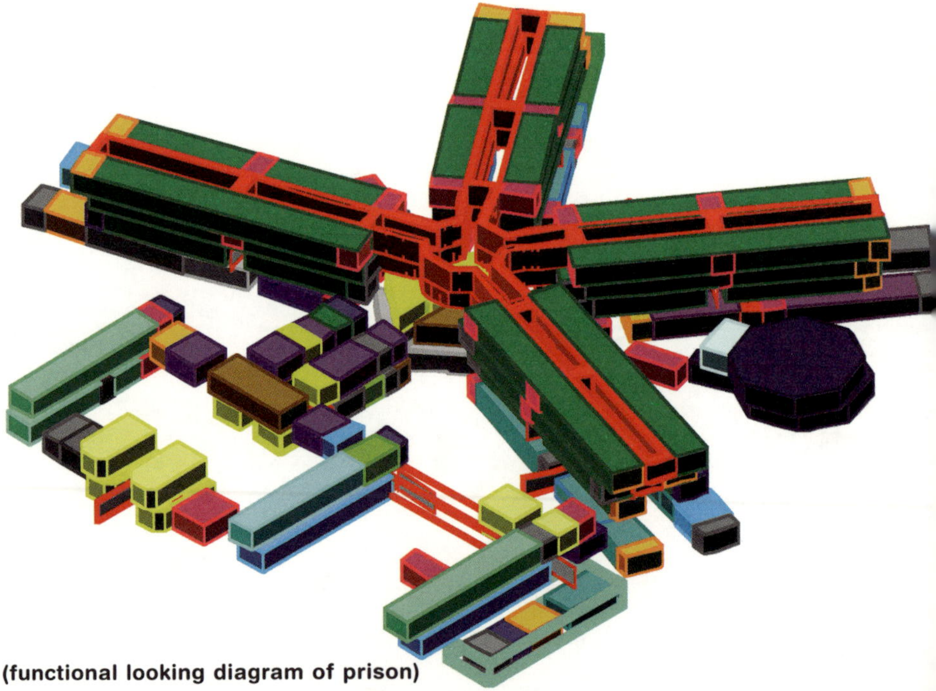

Flower of detention (functional looking diagram of prison)

OLD AND IMPROVED Delfshaven Rotterdam

What do we have?

The emergence of Delfshaven and its development into the 19th century is indelibly linked up with the ancient town of Delft. In the 14th century, Delft succeeded in carving a niche as a central market town on the basis of the trade in agricultural products and the craft industries deriving from it. In exporting its articles, which included the still celebrated Delft blue crockery, Delft stayed independent of towns like Schiedam and Rotterdam with an open sea link from the river Maas. To avoid paying the sky-high transshipment costs to these towns Delft decided to construct its own harbour beyond its territory. This it did in 1389 by digging the Schie canal and building Delfshaven, historically a 'second-category town'.

> Historic Delfshaven is special and well-loved for the reason that it presents a pleasantly surprising fragment of the kind of historic town that has almost completely disappeared from Rotterdam. It possesses a relatively great density of impressive architecture such as the late-Gothic Reformed Church, the warehouse 'De Dubbelde Palmboom', the Zakkendragershuisje (a porter's guild hall dating from 1653), a 19th-century statue of the Rotterdam naval hero Piet Heijn, 'De Ooyevaar', the Renaissance premises of the former Henkes distillery of Dutch gin (jenever) and, close by, the Delft Chamber of the Dutch East India Company.

Delfshaven is a rudiment, therefore enticing yet solitary. It represents history in a city that has made the very absence of history its theme. For that reason Delfshaven is completely cut off from the city surrounding it on all sides. It is likewise alienated from the sub-municipality Delfshaven, the multi-cultural working-class district under whose jurisdiction it falls.

If historic Delfshaven is the centre of that sub-municipality geographically speaking, it is also, largely in terms of the water, a cul-de-sac, a dead-end tailpiece of a now defunct body. Once the water was engaged with the Maas via a sluice, but these days it is arrested by the hard barrier of Westzeedijk, the principal dyke in Rotterdam. Now that it is no longer navigable and has lost the companies that depended on that capacity, the water has forfeited its logic. The aftermath being that Buizenwaal and Middenkous, once thriving harbour basins, are now extinct. Closing off the connection with the Maas is one of the main reasons why Delfshaven has increasingly become a *fremdkörper*, an alien body giving the cold shoulder to the surrounding districts.

Nolli Revisited

Although we can regard Historic Delfshaven as a fragment of an isolated stump, it does possess an urban fabric that attaches to the areas around. Delfshaven is laid out in narrow plots strung together in series and pointing at the harbour. The elongated perimeter blocks thus created are sporadically shot through with tight alleyways. Occasionally one of these blocks is opened up by including a building that is accessible from both ends, such as the engineering works between Voorhaven and Schansstraat.

All buildings give directly onto the quay, street or alley. The sparse gardens and yards are enclosed in the blocks. The one deviation is in the spatial build-up of the southern portion of Delfshaven with its blocks of social housing built in recent decades. If Delfshaven is to be regarded as an urban quarter of significance for visitors and tourists, for people who don't live there, then we have to know which parts are public and in what way.

> In the 18th century the architect Giambattista Nolli constructed a map of Rome in which he made a distinction between two types of spaces, private and public. This last-named category not only contains streets and squares but also the interiors of public buildings such as churches and government offices. In fixing the public realm his definition derived from the use of the space and not from how it was administered. What he did was to illustrate a spatial continuum that every citizen has at his disposal, where he is free to enter and leave, simply because he wishes it. Today we could add shops, cafés, museums, galleries and the like. By drawing a Nolli map of Delfshaven now, we can see a porous fabric of public space penetrating deep into the buildings, yet whose potential has hardly begun to be exploited.

If the public nature and accessibility of the public realm in Delfshaven is to be enhanced, the Nolli fabric will have to be made more porous still. This process is best demonstrated at the spit of land between Voorhaven and Achterhaven. To link up the two sides directly, each shop and café space must continue uninterrupted from one side of the perimeter block to the other. Then you have a permeable fabric. This will strengthen the internal cohesion of historic Delfshaven and extend its radius of exploitation, simply because the retail space will be more exposed to the public open space at large.

In the west of Delfshaven too the urbanistic structure can be made better use of by forging a link with the surrounding districts. A few tens of metres away lies Spanjaardstraat, which is slowly but surely evolving into the street it could be: now with mainly cycle shops and the odd cocktail bar, later perhaps a major urban artery for the Bospolder area to the west. Here too the fabric itself provides the solution. Making it more porous to the west as well will encourage links between Delfshaven and Spanjaardstraat in Bospolder. The inequality between the characters and progress made by the two areas can be bridged by certain shops or restaurants and suchlike, which extend via the courtyards of the blocks from one area to the other.

An important condition at this location is to make full use of the existing side streets (1e, 2e and 3e Schansstraat), where the many abandoned shops and business premises can soak up the overflow of artist's studios, galleries and small shops from historic Delfshaven.

Instead of Historic Delfshaven:
New Historic Delfshaven!

If Delfshaven is to be more than a scarcely justifiable cluster of windmill bodies, antique shops, cafés and restaurants, small galleries, museums and a church, it will have to make its presence felt in the city and expand upon its otherness with vigour. This in no way means that it has to abandon its identity as Historic Delfshaven; what it does mean is that the term historic will gain a richer, more positive connotation. So first of all Delfshaven must tune in better to its own past. For it is in the history of Delfshaven that we find the principal causes for letting it become part of the present-day city it unwillingly belongs to. History has been seen too long as something static and passive, that needs defending against the incursions of the present-day. We now know that history can be variously deployed to transform the present. If Delfshaven is to break out and become a network of tourism, recreation and consumerism, then it will have to wheel into position its key weapon: history.

VOC/Biotexplein

Researchers working in the fifties in what today is the Akzo complex, discovered the 'safe washing efficiency of biological enzymes' and they called the miracle substance Biotex. They made their discovery in and around the nautical warehouse of the Delft branch of the East India Company or VOC, from where the voyages to and from the Dutch East Indies were once coordinated, where the spices were unloaded and sold - in other words, where untold quantities of wealth and power were distributed. All that is left today of the industries once domiciled here is a handful of factory sheds.

This is where the new urban plaza will be: VOC/Biotexplein, the radiant centre of our scheme. First the site will need stripping of both the obscuring green fuzz and the industrial ruins so that the fully restored 'VOC house' can stand proud on this spotless if colourful 'Biotex Square'. The site can be revamped as a multifunctional complex with a shopping mall, a transferium and an events space, with the monumental VOC warehouse standing there discretely after being thoughtfully restored to its original splendour.

> Programmed as a shopping mall, Biotexplein is one of the planning elements that are to integrate Delfshaven and the districts around. Visitors to the plaza will come not just from Delfshaven but also from the up-market houses to be developed on the Müller Pier and at Schiehaven. It will transform this lifeless part of Delfshaven into a much-used core amidst the surrounding districts. With its metaphorical roots in the American mall, our shopping mall will seek to combine consumerism and tourism. But whereas the traditional mall sits in a sealed box, the Biotex mall is largely left in the public eye: an open-air mall.

The analogy with the American type mainly resides in the fact that the plaza as a whole is conceived of as a single building reachable by car and that you can drive into. However, unlike the traditional introverted model of the mall, the principal programme here is on the exterior, at the places where the sinewy roof folds upwards to make room for shops, offices, galleries etc. The rolling, undulating roof itself is in effect the most important 'facade' in the design. On the north and east sides of the site the roof curls skyward to reveal ground-floor shops; on the south side we have a view through the opened-up facade, and out across the harbour, of shops and parked cars.

Beneath the plaza are the foundations, in every sense, of the plaza project: a sumptuous parking garage. Shops, cafés and restaurants can only function if there is good accessibility. This applies to all investors in Delfshaven. Once the site is excavated to dispose of the polluted ground it will be possible to meet the entire parking needs of Delfshaven. By sweeping all the planned parking spaces into a single 'building' so as to create a new positive urban choreography, usefulness can be combined with pleasure. Here you can park your car and hire skates to get you to Schiedam along the water, or board a pleasure boat for a cruise to Delft and back. By radically scraping the plaza clean, it all at once becomes clear just how unique this urban space is: a monumental plaza with a hard edge of tall quays. From here you have a generous view out across the historic skyline of Delfshaven, with its prize exhibits lined up neatly as if in a portrait gallery or a museum. The expanse of plaza makes it suitable for an events space for every imaginable use, for markets, demonstrations, concerts, festivals. The unusually-shaped roof can act literally as a stepping-off point for the American-style culture flourishing among Rotterdam's young people. This is the place for stunts and extreme sports of all kinds. The many ramps make an ideal skills area for skating while the open plaza encourages plenty of wind for flying kites. One of the spaces below the plaza might accommodate a skate shop where you should also be able to hire roller blades, skateboards and bikes.

V. Bing (designer), J.F.C. Reckleben (engraver), The departure of the Pilgrim Fathers from Delfshaven to America, 1688

Akzo, Biotex enzyme-based detergent

Aerial photograph of Delfshaven before the demolition of the Akzo chemical plant, ca. 1980

'Nolli' map of Delfshaven, existing situation

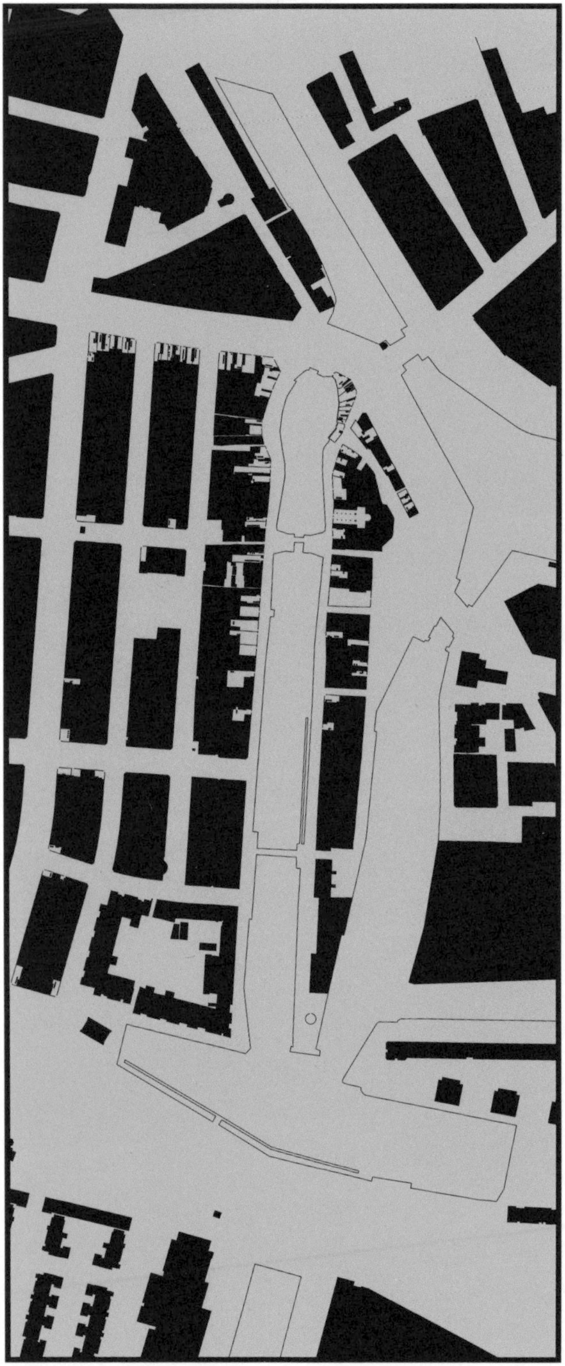

'Nolli' map of Delfshaven, Crimson proposal

Delfshaven with Biotex-square around VOC house

Mont des Arts Brussels
One Nation Underground

in collaboration with Maxwan

The Mont des Arts in the centre of Brussels consists of a number of high-culture institutions gathered around a monumental urbanistic ensemble of squares and stairs. Financially, politically and symbolically it was created by the Royal Family of Saxe-Coburg over a period of 125 years for their people: the Belgians.

The Mont des Arts, like a lot of other Belgian institutions, has been relentlessly criticized for its ugliness, emptiness, lack of identity and for its complete failure as a national monument or even as a public space. The Mont des Arts lacks luxurious connections to the city and its institutions are like crystal growths inside rock: hidden, isolated and autistic.

The result is a collection of institutions that lead a secret life inside a flawed monument in full sight of the entire nation. Behind the stone walls and beneath the empty streets and squares people study books, practice symphonies, look at art, restore paintings, speak at conventions and listen to recitals.

At the same time tens of thousands of Belgians arrive in the city, after a trainride from their suburbs and parental villages, at a subterranean station inside the Mont des Arts. From here they scurry through tunnels to their offices. At the end of the day they scurry back and are relieved when their train re-emerges from the ground to take them back home.

We do not want to make the Mont des Arts less empty. We do not want to make it into the kind of success associated with large-scale cultural and architectural interventions. We want to make it work on its own terms, but make it work better, much better.

By a limited number of discreet and inexpensive interventions we propose to short-circuit the subterranean routes and spaces of the Royal Library, the Palais des Beaux Arts, the museum, the convention centre and the train station and merge them into one sponge-like urban structure beneath the city. One opening punched in a concrete wall means that the convention centre might bleed into the corridors and auditoria of the Royal Library. One pathway between the station and the Palais des Beaux Arts, might syphon off the commuters through the Joseph Beuys exhibition. Etc. Etc. Without the need for a grand architectural gesture, the institutions will increase their surface area, attendance figures, accessibility, funds and a new synergy will be created.
We want to preserve the mountain-like crust of emptiness, ugliness and impenetrable boredom. This is the protective layer that is needed to make cultural and urban institutions thrive. In contemporary Belgium culture and economy come to fruition in the shadows, the cellars, tunnels, holes and pits.

Not only cultural projects like reading, writing, talking, listening, playing and studying happen outside the city's gaze; the national memory itself seems to shy away from too much attention and daylight. There exists a secret consensus that the Royal Family is what keeps this country together. In Belgium, underneath a thick crust of general apathy towards the royal family lies a deep and serious sense of need. Sometimes, as with the death of Baudouin, it breaks out and spills into the streets. The Royal Family is the secret connector, the secret glue.

This is why for us the only way to rejuvenate the Mont des Arts as the symbolic centre of the relationship between the Royal Family and the Belgian nation is to put it underground. Beneath the Boulevard de l'Imperatrice but on top of the underground railway tracks lies a secret space filled with concrete columns and strange crevices leading to the car park, the street or the train platforms. This space we have declared to be the counter-space, a mirror as it were, of the flawed monumentality of the Mont des Arts in the open air. In this space we propose placing sad and beautiful subterranean monuments to the ambiguous memories the Belgians have of their Royals, monuments to the cohesive power of collective shame and loss.

Just like its flawed counterpart on top, Albertina Square, this space organizes the different institutions of the Mont des Arts surrounding it. We propose to turn it into a subterranean and monumental urban lobby, that gives access to all the subterranean entrances and routes of the institutions and at the same time to Central Station and the old centre of the city, like a membrane: the Royal Membrane. The Membrane is the monumental form that introduces the larger but more discreet project of punctures and connections through the stony walls and thick floorboards of the institutions around Albertina Square. The Royal Membrane and its monuments give this new web of physical, organizational, visual and mental connections the focal point and visibility the Mont des Arts lacks today.

Reverend William Sheppard, one of the first to document the brutality of the Congo State of Leopold II

2 **If a village refused to submit to the rubber regime, state or company troops or their allies sometimes shot everyone in sight, so that nearby villages would get the message. But ... some European officers were mistrustful. For each cartridge issued to their soldiers they demanded proof that the bullet had been used to kill someone, not 'wasted' in hunting or, worse yet, saved for possible use in a mutiny. The standard proof was the right hand from a corpse. Or occasionally not from a corpse. 'Sometimes,' said one officer to a missionary, soldiers 'shot a cartridge at an animal in hunting; they then cut off a hand from a living man.' In some military units there was even a 'keeper of the hands'; his job was the smoking. ... The smoking preserved the hands in the hot, moist climate, for it might be days or weeks before the chief could display them to the proper official and receive credits for his kills.** From Adam Hochschild, *King Leopold's Ghost: A Story of Greed, Terror, and Heroism in Colonial Africa,* Boston/New York, 1998, and 165 respectively.

Bust of Leopold II, Army Museum, Brussels

1 **Rubber is coagulated sap; the French word for it, caoutchouc, comes from a South American Indian word meaning 'the wood that weeps.' ... As the lengths of vine within reach of the ground were tapped dry, workers climbed high into the trees to reach sap. ... No payment of trinkets or brass wire were enough to make people stay in the flooded forest for days at a time to do work that was so arduous – and physically painful. A gatherer had to dry the syrup-like rubber so that it would coagulate, and often the only way to do so was to spread the substance on his arms, thighs, and chest. 'The first few times it is not without pain that the man pulls it off the hairy parts of his body,' Louis Chaltin, a Force Publique officcr, confided to his journal in 1892. 'The native doesn't like making rubber. He must be compelled to do it.'** From Adam Hochschild, *King Leopold's Ghost: A Story of Greed, Terror, and Heroism in Colonial Africa*, Boston/New York, 1998, 160-161

As an evocation of the rubber harvesting techniques forced upon the Congolese by Leopold II, we proposed to cover the columns in the underground space between the boulevard and the train tunnel with rubber imprinted with human bodies

'Let us all now pray with a special intention for His Majesty King Leopold, who is having to make difficult decisions in these difficult times, although his heart is not really in it because he has not yet recovered from the death of Queen Astrid. 'They prayed. King Leopold was sitting all alone in front of his grate in which the fire had gone out, although he hadn't noticed. His Lord Chamberlain, not daring to disturb the mourner's reverie, kept careful watch over his sovereign. 'Goodnight, Astrid,' murmured King Leopold. 'Adieu, ma belle reine-claude.' From: Hugo Claus, *The Sorrow of Belgium*, Pantheon Books, New York 1990,58-59

Stained-glass ceiling depicting Queen Astrid in the roof of the underground railway station

Postcard 1935. 'The tragic death of young queen Astrid of the Belgians', 'The tree against which her royal head was smashed'

'William Tell takes refuge in Küssnacht.' 'That was where the queen died,' whispered Louis. 'Where?' 'In Küssnacht.' (Küss, kiss, Nacht, night, Vlieghe.) 'I didn't see any queen,' said Vlieghe. 'Queen Astrid, dummy.' Louis laid the tress on the 'strid,' just like aunt Violet who kept a musty suitcase full of clippings and magazines about the life and death of the Swedish Swan who had come from the North to marry King Leopold and who had died of it. From: Hugo Claus, *The Sorrow of Belgium*, Pantheon Books, New York 1990, 60-61

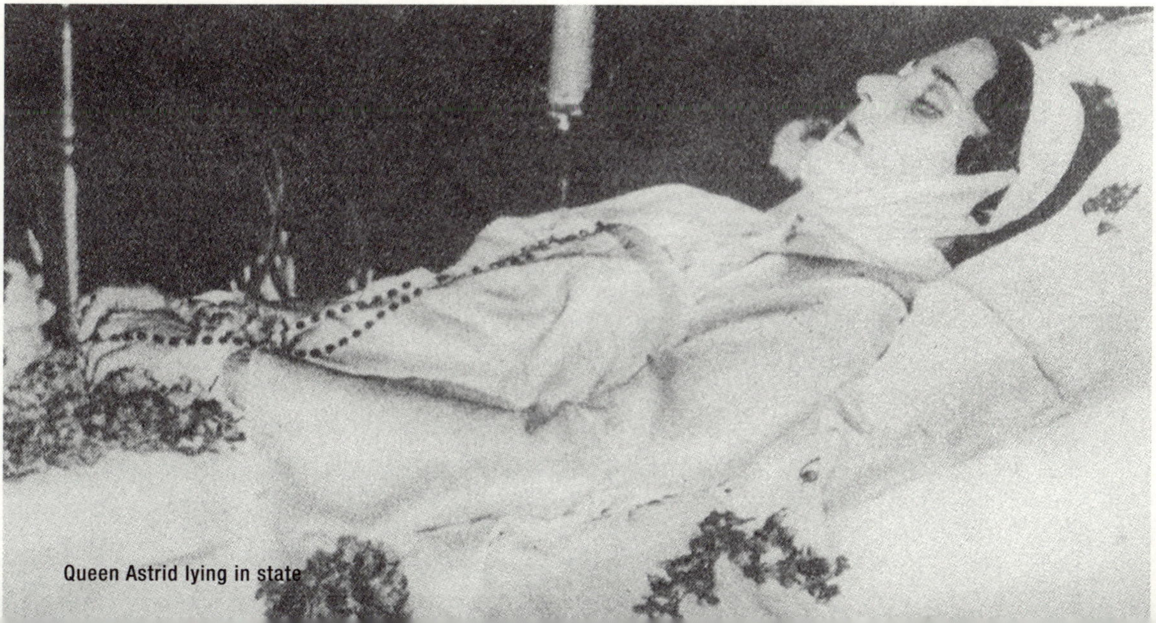

Queen Astrid lying in state

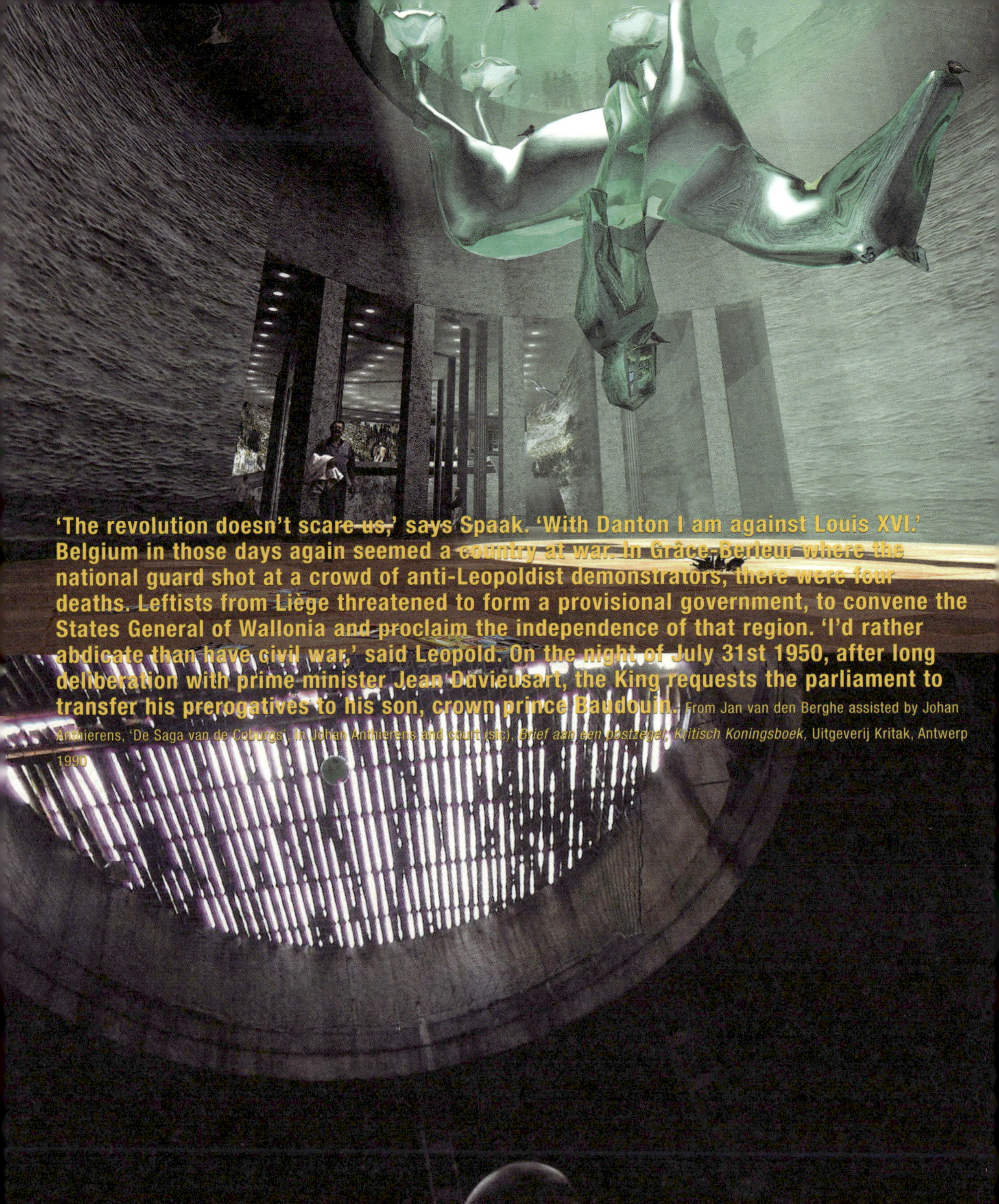

'The revolution doesn't scare us,' says Spaak. 'With Danton I am against Louis XVI.' Belgium in those days again seemed a country at war. In Grâce-Berleur where the national guard shot at a crowd of anti-Leopoldist demonstrators, there were four deaths. Leftists from Liège threatened to form a provisional government, to convene the States General of Wallonia and proclaim the independence of that region. 'I'd rather abdicate than have civil war,' said Leopold. On the night of July 31st 1950, after long deliberation with prime minister Jean Duvieusart, the King requests the parliament to transfer his prerogatives to his son, crown prince Baudouin. From Jan van den Berghe assisted by Johan Anthierens, 'De Saga van de Coburgs', in Johan Anthierens and court (sic), *Brief aan een postzegel, Kritisch Koningsboek*, Uitgeverij Kritak, Antwerp 1990

Leopold III is the only Belgian king without a statue in the capital. We proposed an equestrian statue made of glass, to be hung upside-down in the underground dome designed by Victor Horta as part of his unfinished Central Stati[illegible] design

For another good ten years Leopold would cast his shadow over the royal palace of Laken. Baudouin I is king, but in fact Leopold III still rules. In the young monarch's study is a photo of his father with the dedication: 'Baudouin, I am proud of you.'

From Jan van den Berghe assisted by Johan Anthierens, 'De Saga van de Coburgs', in Johan Anthierens and court (sic), *Brief aan een postzegel, Kritisch Koningsboek*, Uitgeverij Kritak, Antwerp 1990

Leopold III signing his abdication and ceding the throne to his son Baudouin, 1950

Baudouin on June 30 1960 at the independence of the Congo

'The independence of the Congo is the crown on the work that was designed by the genius of Leopold II, undertaken by him with hardheaded courage and continued by Belgium with perseverence. It signifies a decisive moment in the existence, not only of the Congo itself, but also – and I don't hesitate to say it – of the whole of Africa. When Leopold II undertook the greatest project that is being crowned today, he did not announce himself to you as a conqueror, but as a civilizer. 'The great independence movement that drives the whole of Africa has received the broadest understanding from the Belgian Government. In consideration of the unanimous longing of your people we have not hesitated to grant you this independence from the very start. Gentlemen, yours is now the task to prove that we were right to trust you. The world is watching. My country and I recognize with joy and emotion that on this day, June 30th 1960, the Congo acquires independence and international sovereignty in full accordance and friendship with Belgium. God protect the Congo!'

Answering speech by Patrice Lumumba:

'Our wounds are still too fresh and too painful to forget what our fate has been during 80 years of colonial government. We have experienced that work was demanded of us in exchange for wages that were insufficient to cloth or house us, or to raise our children the way we wished. ...We have endured humiliations, insults and beatings, from morning into the evening, because we were Negroes. We shall never forget that a black man was addressed familiarly, not as a friend, but because only the white man was entitled to be spoken to with respect. We have seen how our country was plundered, we have experienced that the law was never the same for a white man as for a black man. For the one the law was accommodating, for the other inhuman. We have seen the gruesome suffering of those who were persecuted for political or religious convictions: as exiles in their own country their fate was worse than death. We have seen that in the cities beautiful villas were erected for the whites, and ramshackle huts for the blacks; that a black had no access to the cinema, the restaurant or a store because they were reserved for the Europeans. We will not forget that a black man travelled in the lowermost hold of the ships, beneath the feet of the whites in their luxurious huts. ... Our independence is proclaimed today in the presence of a friendly nation. Nobody can forget though that this independence is the result of a war in which we have not spared our blood. A hellish struggle of arms, fire and blood. We are proud that we have fought this battle to end the humiliating slavery that was forced upon us.'

The opposing speeches by Patrice Lumumba and King Baudouin at the Congolese independence ceremony. We proposed printing them on the opposite sides of the lightboxes in the ceiling of the commuter tunnel between the metro and the railway station. Coming into the city you would read Baudouin's version, going home you would read Lumumba's.

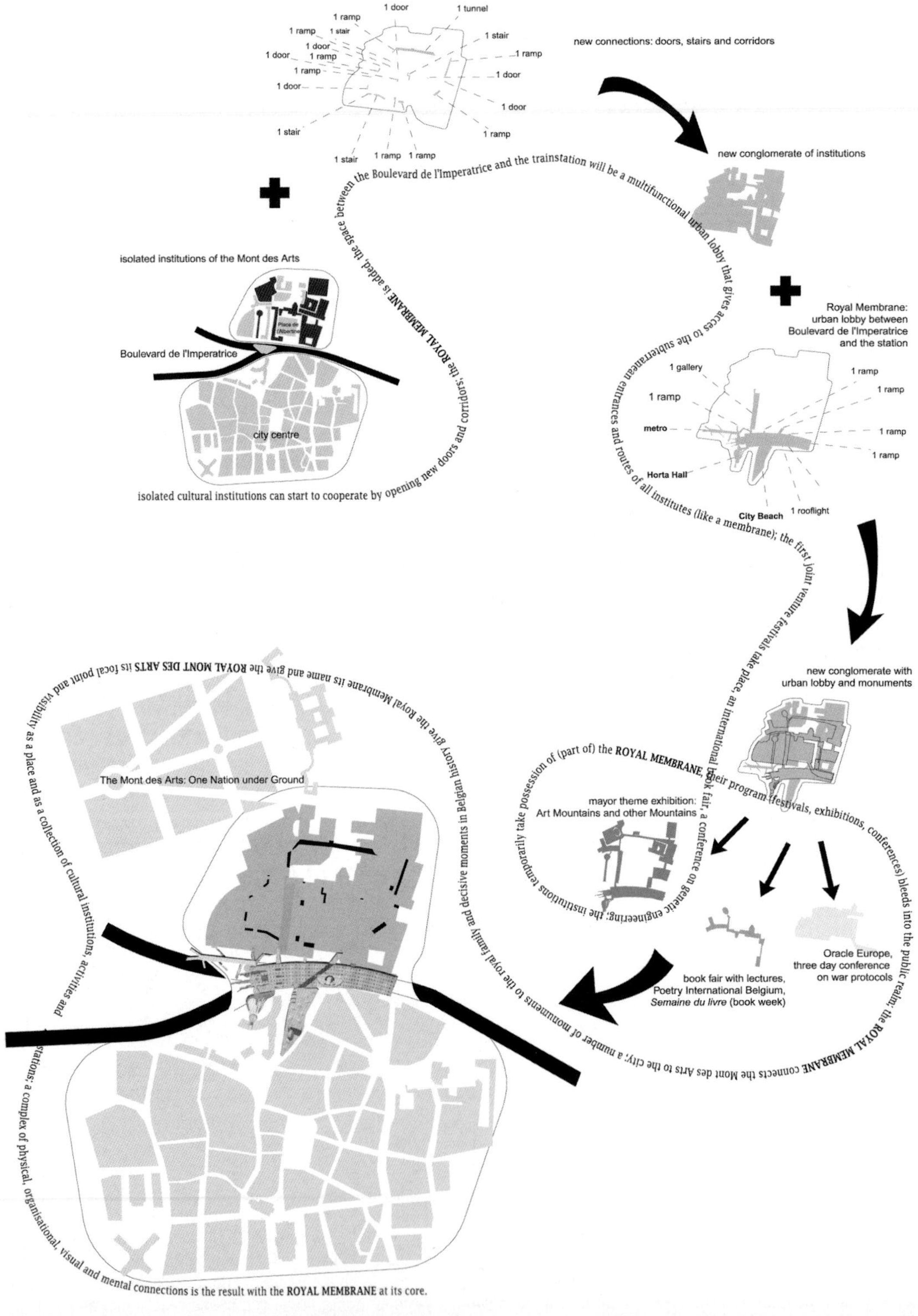

1 door
1 tunnel
1 ramp
1 ramp
1 stair
1 stair
1 door
1 ramp
1 door
1 ramp
1 ramp
1 door
1 door
1 door
1 stair
1 ramp
1 stair
1 ramp
1 ramp
new connections: doors, stairs and corridors
new conglomerate of institutions
isolated institutions of the Mont des Arts
Boulevard de l'Imperatrice
city centre
Royal Membrane: urban lobby between Boulevard de l'Imperatrice and the station
1 gallery
1 ramp
1 ramp
1 ramp
metro
1 ramp
1 ramp
Horta Hall
City Beach
1 rooflight
new conglomerate with urban lobby and monuments
mayor theme exhibition: Art Mountains and other Mountains
book fair with lectures, Poetry International Belgium, *Semaine du livre* (book week)
Oracle Europe, three day conference on war protocols
The Mont des Arts: One Nation under Ground
isolated cultural institutions can start to cooperate by opening new doors and corridors; the ROYAL MEMBRANE is added, the space between the Boulevard de l'Imperatrice and the trainstation will be a multifunctional urban lobby that gives acces to the subterranean entrances and routes of all institutes (like a membrane); the first joint venture festivals take place, an international book fair, a conference on genetic engineering; the institutions temporarily take possession of (part of) the ROYAL MEMBRANE, their program (festivals, exhibitions, conferences) bleeds into the public realm; the ROYAL MEMBRANE connects the Mont des Arts to the city; a number of monuments to the royal family and decisive moments in Belgian history give the Royal Membrane its name and give the ROYAL MONT DES ARTS its focal point and visibility as a place and as a collection of cultural institutions, activities and stations; a complex of physical, organisational, visual and mental connections is the result with the ROYAL MEMBRANE at its core.

LIVE LIFE
MOBILE LIBRARY

Phil
dy rotten

OBSESSION

Rabbits make us think of Alison Smithson; the electric whirring of household appliances makes us think of Huig Maaskant, Brompton bicycles of Reyner Banham, wrecks on the highway: Rem Koolhaas, fireplaces and snow of Philip Johnson, lakes of Alvar Aalto and Jon Jerde makes us think we're all living in a fantasy movie.

Crimson has been sitting around linking up their heroes in a chain, attaching them to each other at the extremities of their work. All of them have one tiny little thing in common with one or maybe two of the others. Alison Smithson, Beatrix Potter and Rem Koolhaas share the desire to burrow their dwellings into the hill. Philip Johnson and Koolhaas share the netherworld of autobiographical shame and pain hidden within the glamorous glass house. Huig Maaskant and Reyner Banham share their wide-eyed belief in the convention-shattering powers of technological gadgetry, and in the new world that it offers us. Banham shares with Jon Jerde the fact that he has let himself be born again a son of the desert: the desert of Southern California and Nevada where out of the absence of density and history 'city' can be made to appear and disappear like a dream.

Even more wilful than the selection of subjects to write about, is the selection of attributes from their work. When writing about Alison Smithson: why write about her writing about Beatrix Potter? When writing about Maaskant, why focus on his technophilia? When writing about Reyner Banham, why bring up Non-Plan again? When writing about Rem Koolhaas, why even mention the embarrassment felt while visiting Rem Koolhaas's villa for a paraplegic publisher? And when writing about Alvar Aalto, why let the homesickness creep up and eulogize a Norwegian sunset?

The pieces in this chapter are heterogeneous: book reviews, commissioned essays and a microhistory of one particular building. They all obsess over one obsession that seems to inform the work of these people. Often the chosen obsessions are attempts to connect with some aspects of the outside world, sometimes they are inward-looking, sometimes personal, sometimes professional. There is an unavoidable element of autobiography to selecting themes along these lines. It shows the soft underbelly of Crimson; it reveals our sources and at the same time our innermost doubts, fears and desires etc. But it never was that innocent. It was always about constructing our own critical/architectural attitude towards the world because we weren't happy with the dominant one.

Critics, like architects, have over the years created a rationalist ritual in approaching the outside world and all its contradictory demands. Lapidary statements are made about globalization, virtual reality, the death of distance, the demise of the book, the disappearance of public space. These simple but heavy statements permit the architect/historian to focus like a laser beam on a given commission or subject and at least produce a coherent design/text within a given time frame. Most of all they give the impression that at least he can make simple sense of the world we are living in. Behind this tough, confident, stern attitude towards the world lies fear for the staggering, often hilarious contradictions that govern and have always governed contemporary life. One example: our hero has designed a Public Library for the city of Seattle, and explains it by saying that 'its unquestioned loyalty to the book will undermine the Library's plausibility at the moment of its potential apotheosis' and; 'The Library stands exposed at its most outdated and moralistic at the moment that it has become the last repository of the free and the Public.' Why this bullying, negative, generic archispeak? Why if you reserve the right to be vague, be boring? There is an image that somehow through its mere existence and truth brings the reasoning behind the Seattle library concept crashing down: an enormous leatherclad biker, sitting at a wooden table, reading a

book with his eight year old, in the reading room of the Los Angeles Public Library, crash helmet on the table. Call us sentimental, but this is what we would have obsessed over if we were Rem Koolhaas.

In bringing together the obsessions of our favourite architects/ critics we try to find out what makes them tick. In aligning our own obsessions with theirs, we look for the reasons why we like them so much and we try to find out what we ourselves want. In chaining them all together we construct our ideal architect/critic. Therefore this chapter is a gallery of greats, a diary of our education, a psychoanalytical self portrait but most of all a design for what we think would be the best architect/critic in the world ever. The most important characteristic of this figure, is that he or she would be able to tackle the contradictory demands of the outside world not by simplification, but by throwing his or her own contradictions straight back at it.

Put differently: Crimson has spent many a night in the graveyard, digging up the corpses of dead oeuvres, sawing off a leg here, cutting off a tongue there, trepanning a skull, filling a bucket with entrails, popping out a set of eyes. Then, using the needle and thread of their historical profession, they have deftly sewn together all these limbs and organs into a new being and given it a soul of its own. The monster can be described as twisted and mixed up to say the least. It wants to be modern and practical and optimistic and recreate the world in its own image but at the same time stay home, roast a chicken and cuddle up. It wants the world to look like the set of a science fiction movie, but feel like the happiest memory of its youth, or vice versa.

A COMPULSION TOWARDS THE REAL

THINKING ABOUT THE BODY OF WORK THE SMITHSONS HAVE LEFT US AND PETER SMITHSON IS STILL WORKING ON, ONE IS CONFRONTED WITH TWO SEEMINGLY DISPARATE QUALITIES IN THEIR THINKING. ON THE ONE HAND THE SMITHSONS HAVE AN ABSOLUTE POWER OF ABSTRACTION, ON THE OTHER THEY APPROACH THEIR OBJECTS OF STUDY EMPIRICALLY AND IN THIS WAY DISCOVER WHAT THE BUILT ENVIRONMENT CONVEYS TO US AND HOW IT IMPACTS ON US. IN DOING SO, THEIR SENSITIVE EYE FOR THE SIMPLE AND QUIET MANIFESTATIONS OF ARCHITECTURE AND URBAN DESIGN IS SHOWN TO BE OF THE UTMOST IMPORTANCE. THE SMITHSONS' ONGOING INTEREST IN THE SIMPLE, THE ORDINARY, THE ANONYMOUS, THE AS-FOUND, FOUND ITS VOICE IN THE FIFTIES WHEN THEY WERE PART OF THE INDEPENDENT GROUP, STUDYING POPULAR CULTURE IN THE FORM OF ADS, HOLLYWOOD FILMS AND PULP FICTION. IN CONTRAST TO THE LATER - AMERICAN - POP ART THEIR RESEARCH WAS NON-IRONICAL AND GENUINELY TRIED TO DEFINE THE QUALITIES THAT EVERYDAY CULTURE POSSESSED.

THE EMPIRICAL AND REALISTIC APPROACH IN FACT SEEKS TO FIND THE ABSTRACT OR - AS ALISON AND PETER SMITHSON CALLED IT - THE POETIC IN THE SIMPLE AND THE ANONYMOUS. IT WAS IN THIS VEIN THAT ALISON SMITHSON WROTE THE ARTICLE REPRINTED ON THE NEXT PAGE. THE TEXT EXPLORES ONE OF THE SMITHSONS' MAIN THEMES: INHABITATION. THE CONTAINER-SPACES THAT ARE FOUND IN DRAWINGS ACCOMPANYING BEATRIX POTTER'S NURSERY RHYMES ARE THE OBJECT OF RESEARCH. IN THESE INTERIORS ALISON SMITHSON FINDS THE QUALITIES SHE AND PETER SMITHSON SO ADMIRED IN POST-WAR MODERNIST PROJECTS SUCH AS LE CORBUSIER'S MAISON JAOUL OR MIES VAN DER ROHE'S LAFAYETTE PARK HOUSING DEVELOPMENT. THESE SPACES CONTAIN EVERYTHING THE INHABITANT NEEDS, NOTHING MORE, NOTHING LESS. OBJECTS USED DAILY EACH HAVE THEIR OWN PLACE WITHIN EASY REACH AND ARE THEREFORE OFTEN DISPLAYED IN THE OPEN. '[THEY] ARE ALL THE "DECORATION" THE "SIMPLE" SPACES NEED, OR IN FACT CAN TAKE.' NOT ONLY DOES EVERY FUNCTION AND OBJECT HAVE ITS CONVENIENT PLACE, THE CONTAINER (GLASS HOUSE OR RABBIT HOLE) PROVIDES THE NECESSARY COMFORT, RESPONSE AND PROTECTION. THESE SPACES ARE TAILORED TO MEET THE NEEDS OF THE INDIVIDUAL AND EACH ROOM IS TAILORED TO ITS FUNCTION. EVEN THOUGH - AS ALISON SMITHSON STRESSES - THESE CONTAINER SPACES ACCOMMODATE THE BASIC NECESSITIES, THEY ARE NOT AUSTERE CELLS. THE SMITHSONS ALSO INCLUDE OTHER HUMAN NEEDS AND TREAT THEM AS IMPORTANT FUNCTIONS A HOUSE SHOULD BE ABLE TO ACCOMMODATE. FOR EXAMPLE: 'TO SIT COMFORTABLY AND READ OR TALK OF AN EVENING'.[1]

1

2

3

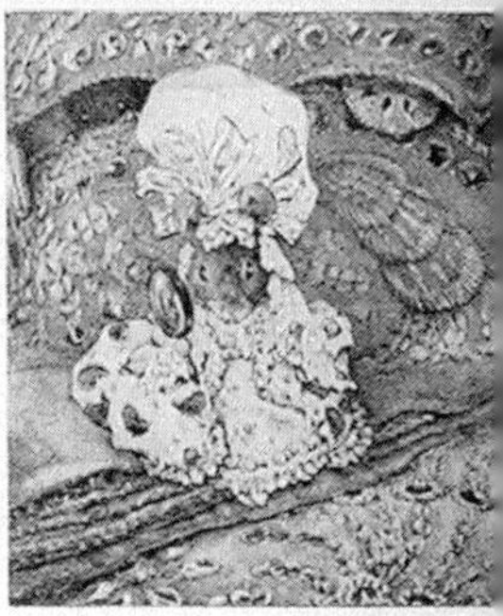

4

Beatrix Potter's places

Alison Smithson

There is a set of small books that are English nursery classics. Their interest for architects is in their detailed and imaginative exposition of a way of life. However, architects might be surprised at any suggestion that there was a connection between the houses of Beatrix Potter and those in the post-war style of Aalto (himself) and Le Corbusier: between the house of Mrs Tittlemouse and that for Mr Shodhan in Ahmedabad. Yet the same sort of striving towards good container-spaces, even the same sort of forms can be found in both the books and in the post-war works of the architects. A similarity of intention is also evident in the attitude to objects and possessions. In Beatrix Potter's interiors, objects and utensils in daily use are conveniently located, often on individual hooks or nails, 1 and are all the 'decoration' the 'simple' spaces need, or in fact can take. Those things in secondary use or needing long term storage are in special storage cubicles whose forms define the house space proper—as well as being pleasant spaces in themselves. 2 Here then, we find basic necessities raised to a poetic level: the simple life, well done. This is in essence the precept of the whole Modern Movement in architecture, but it is only in the immediate post-war period that there have been architects, perhaps old enough, to stand off from theories sufficiently to be relaxed—and sophisticated about them in practice. Beatrix Potter's interiors are tailored to meet the need of the individual and the individual room is tailored to its function 3: the group of rooms directly responding to their context in the environment. Nearly all cave-like in feeling, if not actually so in their moulded surfaces.* In their direct handling of materials, Beatrix Potter's spaces again touch something of the magic of our masters 4, 7.

This is not to say Beatrix Potter was mysteriously in advance of her times—animals were common on greeting cards; boys sold such *objets trouvés* from the country, still within an early morning's walk of the London slums, as birds' nests containing eggs; the natural environment of the Boltons had not been depressed to bare bird subsistence level by infill development, domesticated mews, flatted houses. Miss Potter in her odd way fitted into the spirit of what was afoot generally in the arts (her brother was trying to be an artist). What she instinctively felt about spaces—that they should be comforting, responsive and protective—was part of a general realization about spaces common to artists (cf. Whistler's comments on his own interiors and the exhibition gallery he decorated); poets (many of whom left the cities—Wordsworth actually choosing the Lake District itself); architects (Norman Shaw always included the 'small space'—the ingle nook, the minstrel's gallery). In Norman Shaw there was a deliberate attempt to break through the tradition of classical ranges of rooms of identical height to provide instead the particular shape and mood for an individual function. Shaw borrowed historical forms for his purposes. Morris tried to be more direct, but by using antiquated craft techniques merely instigated the uncomfortable Peasant Revival. (Which is just being reinterred.) Where architects failed in their imagination, Beatrix Potter succeeded in making forms entirely suitable for their purpose, forms of continuing interest in their sympathetic inventiveness for successive generations.

*A small boy, speaking of Johansen's house, 'It is a rabbit's house'.

It is perhaps interesting to compare the revolu tion in gardening (to make it typically English a we now understand it) brought about by Gertrud Jekyll. Lutyens bicycled over with his fiancée t see her. His fiancée wrote of the visit, 'the mos enchanting person in the loveliest little cottag Mr Lutyens calls her Bumps. . . . After dinner w sat in the chimney corner. A real old chimne with a huge wood fire, and there we sat, and at almonds and drank hot elderberry wine.' It evoke Peter Rabbit's mother stooping to make camo mile tea: or the frontispiece of *Cicely Parsley' Nursery Rhymes*. It seems architecture has bee involved in a gigantic detour. Norman Sha de-classifying, Baillie Scott cottageizing, Unwi canonizing, bureaucracy standardizing. In th face of this final degeneration of values, th spaces drawn by Beatrix Potter might appear mere dream and the Maison Jaoul an old man' sentimentality. But the strivings of the Moder Movement in architecture cannot be brushed of however far-fetched it might seem to brin nursery books into the fore of it. Their inclusio might be totally laughed off as fancy were thes books not in themselves such 'total man festations'.

It would still be a brave architect who woul submit a white house to a County Plannin Authority, even though it was suspected th the officers and the lay committee in questio read Jemima Puddleduck and Mrs Tigg Winkle 5 more often than a text book on, sa motorways. Beatrix Potter, in her concept town building was close—in Gloucester (par cularly under snow) and in the indigenou architecture of the fells—to an environment nowadays vital calmness. The dwellings of h people fit the landscape with that sort of anon mity that is only achieved through building in personally consistent language—or an internal consistent imagination 6, 8.

5

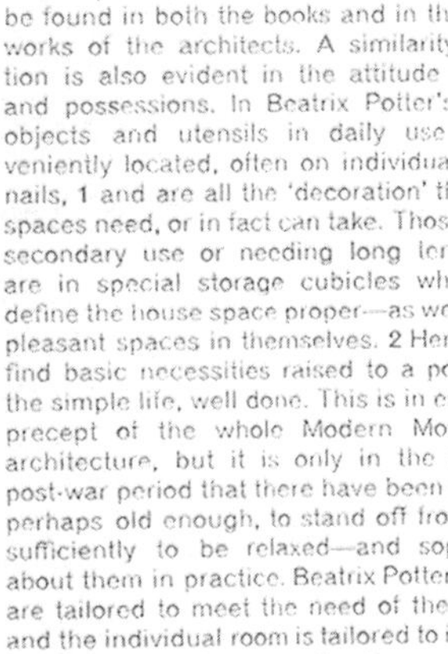

6

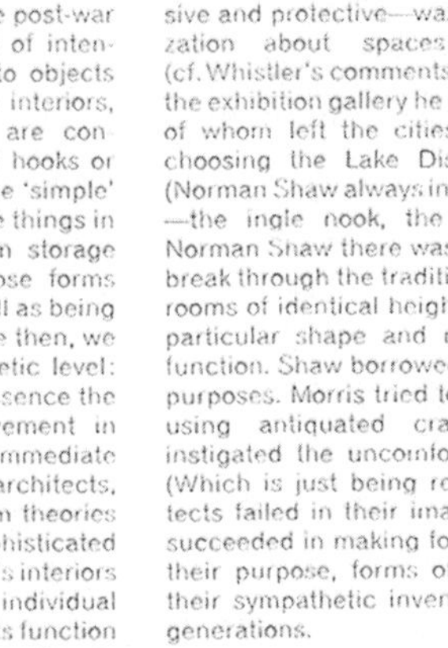

7

8

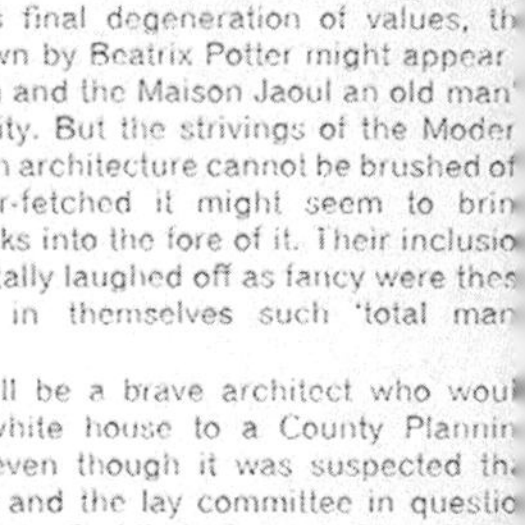

Illustrations: 1, 5 *The Tale of Mrs. Tigg Winkle*, 2 *The Tale of Mrs. Tittlemous* 3, 4 *The Tailor of Gloucester*, 6 *The T of Squirrel Nutkin*, 7 *The Tale of Samu Whiskers*, 8 *Cecily Parsley's Nurse Rhymes* all by Beatrix Potter, publishe by F. Warne & Co. Ltd.

OR THE STORY THAT ALISON SMITHSON QUOTES IN HER ARTICLE ABOUT EDWIN LUTYENS AND HIS FIANCEE DRINKING HOT ELDERBERRY WINE AND EATING ALMONDS IN THE CHIMNEY CORNER OF GERTRUDE JEKYLL'S COTTAGE. THIS TINY ANECDOTAL REMARK REFLECTS A SENSIBILITY IN WHICH THE HOMEY AND THE UTILITARIAN ARE INDISTINGUISHABLE. ONE WONDERS IF BY INCLUDING IT IN THE TEXT ON BEATRIX POTTER AN INDIRECT REFERENCE IS MADE TO THE ARCHITECTURE OF LUTYENS. A SCARCELY KNOWN SIDE OF HIS WORK IS HIS INTEREST IN THE 'SIMPLE LIFE' AND ALSO IN THE PARAPHERNALIA OF POPULAR CULTURE. BEHIND THE SEVERE GEORGIAN FACADE OF THE HOUSE HE DESIGNED IN CHEYNE WALK, CHELSEA (1930), A COTTAGE-LIKE WING PROJECTS ON THE GARDEN SIDE. THE INTERIOR IS DESIGNED WITH A SIMPLE FUNCTIONALITY WHILE NEW AND VERY UNEXPECTEDLY AS-FOUND MATERIALS ARE USED TO FINISH THE WALLS: PAGES FROM THE TIMES IN THE SERVICE CORRIDOR, TRAVEL POSTERS IN THE SERVANT HALL AND A PANORAMIC REPRINT OF A FRENCH LANDSCAPE PAINTING IN THE DAY NURSERY.

ALISON SMITHSON RIGHTLY WARNS US NOT TO DISMISS POTTER'S SPACES AS MERE DREAMS. AS AN ARCHITECTURAL CONCEPT THESE SPACES EXIST AND CAN BE MADE. THE SMITHSONS FOUND SUCH SPACES IN THE EAMESES' HOUSE (SANTA MONICA, 1949), THE ULTIMATE DESIGN ATTUNED TO THE NEEDS OF THE INDIVIDUAL IN THE SENSE THAT IT WAS BUILT IN DIRECT WORKING ASSEMBLY AND THUS FORMS AN EXACT RECORDING OF THE INSIGHTS OF THE EAMESES. THEIR 'LIGHT-HEARTED THINKING IN FEATHERWEIGHT CLIMATE-BITS-AND-PIECES SEEMING OFF-THE-PEG-ARCHITECTURE ... [THEIR] DO-IT-YOURSELF OUT OF GORGEOUS CATALOGUES, THE SEARS-ROEBUCK THINKING... THEIR WHOLE BLOW-UP, PLUG-IN, CAMP-OUT, DUMP-DIGGING TYPE OF THINKING AND LIVING', COULD BE SEEN TO BE THE MODERN-DAY EMBODIMENT OF POTTER'S SPACES.[2] THE SMITHSONS SOUGHT TO DESIGN SIMILAR SPACES THEMSELVES IN THE APPLIANCE HOUSE (1958) AND THE HOUSE OF THE FUTURE (1955-56) AND TRIED TO BUILD THEM IN THEIR OWN HOUSE IN UPPER-LAWN, WILTSHIRE IN 1963. WRITING OF THE EAMESES' CHAIRS PETER SMITHSON REMARKS: 'THE CHAIRS BELONG TO THE OCCUPANTS, NOT TO THE BUILDING.'[3] THEIR CONCEPT OF THE CONTAINER CALLED HOUSE IS BASED ON THE IDEA THAT THE HOUSE SHOULD BELONG TO THE OCCUPANT, NOT THE OTHER WAY AROUND.

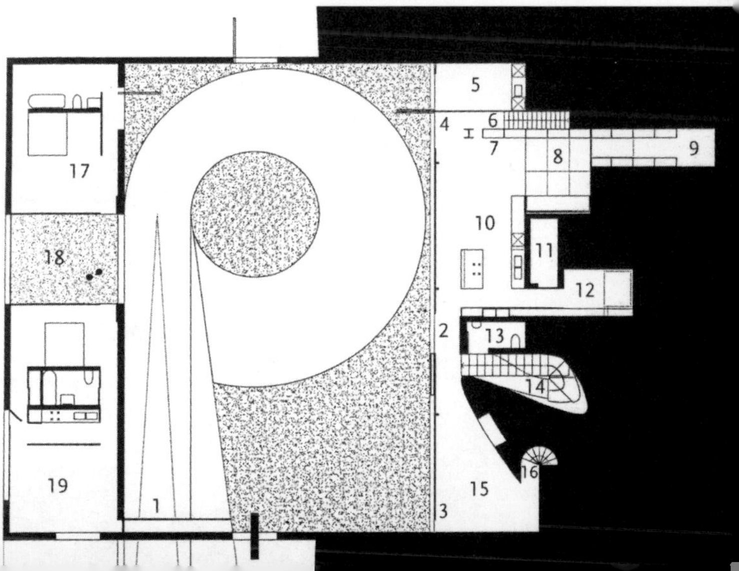

OMA, VILLA IN BORDEAUX, 1998

WOULDN'T EVERYONE WANT TO LIVE IN A HOUSE EXACTLY TAILORED TO THEIR NEEDS WITH OBJECTS BELONGING TO THEM, THE OCCUPANTS? ISN'T IT JUST BLISSFUL NOT TO LIVE AT ODDS WITH A HOUSE AND SHOULDN'T EVERY ARCHITECT DREAM OF DESIGNING SUCH A HOUSE: TOTALLY INDIVIDUAL AND TOTALLY SPECIFIC. REM KOOLHAAS IS IMPLEMENTING SUCH A DREAM AT THIS VERY MOMENT, DESIGNING A HOUSE TO MEET THE NEEDS OF HIS PARAPLEGIC CLIENT. IN THIS CASE IT IS A MACHINE - AN ELEVATOR MOVING A WHOLE ROOM THROUGH THE HOUSE - THAT IS THE MOST IMPORTANT AND ALL PERVADING ACCOMMODATING FEATURE. JUST AS THE SMITHSONS HAVE ALWAYS BEEN SEARCHING FOR AND POINTING OUT THE RICHNESS TO BE FOUND IN THE SIMPLE AND THE ORDINARY, THE ANONYMOUS AND THE AS-FOUND. LIKE THE WAY IN WHICH THEY FIND LUXURY IN MIES VAN DER ROHE'S FEELING FOR SIMPLE MATERIALS: 'THE LUXURY RESTS IN THE FACT THAT ONE IS AWARE OF THE ESSENTIAL THINGNESS OF BRICK AND THIS PARTICULAR FACADE IS SAYING "AND THAT IS ALL YOU'RE GETTING".'[4]

THE QUOTE EVOKES THE SAME NEARNESS, SENSUALITY AND REALNESS OF MATERIALS AND OBJECTS THAT PERMEATES THE SMITHSONS' OWN DESIGNS AND WRITINGS. THINGS ARE WHAT THEY ARE. THEY SIMPLY TELL US ABOUT THEIR USE, THEY DON'T PROCLAIM A REDUCTIONIST IDEOLOGY OF FUNCTIONALISM. THE SMITHSONS' ATTITUDE TOWARDS FUNCTION IS INCLUSIVE AND NON-HIERARCHIC AS OPPOSED TO THAT OF THEIR HIGH-MODERNIST FATHERS. THE WAY INHABITATION IS MADE EMPIRICAL AND DISINTERMEDIATED SETS THE SMITHSONS' WORK APART FROM THE BUILT SERMONS OF THEIR STRUCTURALIST PEERS. IT IS ULTIMATELY THE COMPULSION TOWARDS THE REAL AND THE INDIVIDUAL THAT FORMS THE BASIS OF AN AESTHETICS WHICH ASPIRES TO SEE AND MAKE WITH AN INNOCENT EYE.

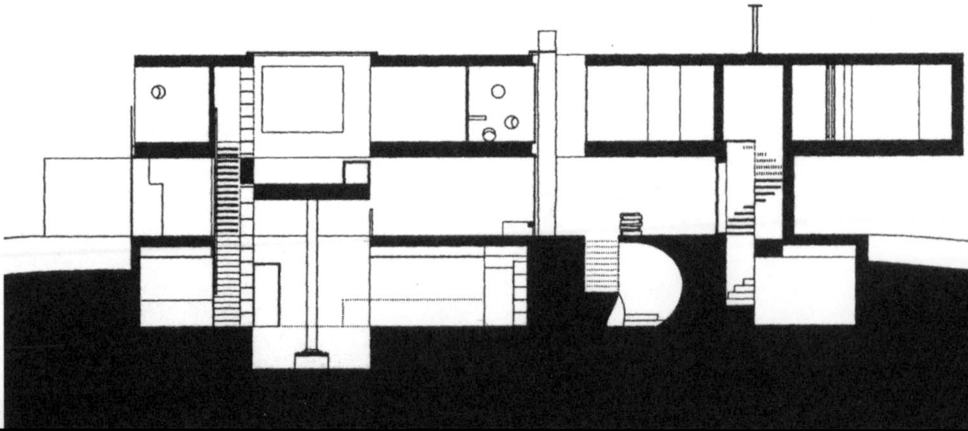

NOTES 1 ALISON AND PETER SMITHSON, **Changing The Art of Inhabitation. Mies' Pieces. Aames' Dreams.**, LONDON 1994, 112 2 IBID., 81 3 IBID., 74 4 IBID., 17

ROCKBOTTOM

OMA BUILDS HOUSE IN BORDEAUX

'... une condition très.....ahunh, ahunh, ahunh..... intéressante...', the voice booms in a great big old brick warehouse, between broken bodies swinging suspended from the rafters and immense steel spiders loitering around children's bedrooms. Above in the galleries surrounding the big space are tight phalanges of youth concentrating on television sets, themselves being watched over by severely dressed art femmes. This is not *the new Metallica video. Rem Koolhaas is giving a lecture at the opening of the OMA exhibition 'Living', in the Centre d'Architecture Arc en Rêve. The centre shares a building with the Musée d'Art Contemporain de Bordeaux, which is currently running a show by Louise Bourgeois, the French artist living in New York responsible for some of the most unsettling images in contemporary art. A thousand people have shown up. A hundred are sitting in the actual lecture hall, the rest have to make do with televised Koolhaas. The exhibition features four villas and an apartment project, all of which have been built and are lived in. The main feature, the reason that the place is teeming with foreign critics and curators and French politicians, is to be found somewhere else. For that you have to leave the building, take a left, follow the heavy traffic to the north over the quay, where the cars, trucks, gas stations and discotheques are incoherently juxtaposed against the elegant Louis XV sandstone riverfront. Then take the bridge over the river; follow it for a couple of kilometres, drive inland through a sprawl of identical suburban houses and industrial buildings; take a writhing road up the leafy hill until you reach a private dirt road which brings you further up. To your left lies a pasture with a ruin of an 18th-century tempietto, behind it an elegant neoclassical mansion, and in front of you the top of the hill, with a reddish-brown box punctured with holes hovering just above it. On top of the box lies an I-beam that sticks out on one side and is connected to the hill by a spidery steel rod. What can this be except a measure to keep the box from drifting away on the wind? As you come closer, the box appears to hover over a cut stone perimeter wall. The dirt road is carved into the hill and burrows its way* underneath *the wall into the courtyard.*

The house has been built for a wealthy publisher, his family, their guests, and some cars. The publisher was paralysed from the waist down after a car crash: a rubber-burning, steel-twisting, bone-splintering, marrow-leaking, nerve-splitting car crash. The design is, among other things a monumental accommodation to this fact. In no way does the architecture attempt to glaze over the minutiae of everyday life with architectural elegance and solemnity, as so often happens in villa-design. What actually happened is that Rem Koolhaas feverishly imagined architectural potential in this particular family life. He saw the limp lower body of the husband, being supported by a whole arsenal of trusses, carts, belts, diapers as architecture. He extrapolated this in a single huge heavy-duty contraption that provides the man with a way of moving through the house. Subsequently this contraption was made into the house's organizational core ('A machine was its heart')[1]: going up, going down, going up, down, up. As a counterpoint to this hydraulic simplicity, the beautiful and lithe wife moves through the house at will, negotiating her way between the armpits and crotches of the house and its dematerialized, entropic, smooth, modernistic planes. Koolhaas also saw architectural potential in his constructionally counter-intuitive decision to place the chromium tube on which the box-house lies off centre, so that a huge beam had to be placed and then anchored in the ground with a big rock, to stop the house from toppling over.

Visitors cannot look at the house as an architectural model that can be separated from its specific usage. The gaze of historians, critics or architects is just a mask. In fact you are investigating the most intimate and personal details of this specific family-life; the gaze is that of the babysitter wandering through the rooms, opening the drawers and looking in the medicine cupboard. At the same time, because in a way the family life has become architecture, it becomes strangely inclusive: a design equivalent of MTV's soap verité The Real World. Lastly, the specific demands and wishes of this family are dealt with on a planning and engineering level rather than on an architectural one: infrastructure and other technical facilities, zoning, and routeing. The family-life has been treated as an urban programme, making the house into a 'New Town' and making visiting it an unexpectedly civic experience. The mode of description that this house seems to ask for is therefore a combination of abject speculations by a voyeur about the private lives of his desired objects, and the urbanistic scenario where the different propositions are linked together by a hypothetical sequence or route. A day in the life: Early in the morning; after he has been lifted out of the car, and placed in his wheelchair, the glass wall slides open and he moves into the kitchen, passes the monolithic concrete stove and slips behind his desk set in a lofty skylit space.

Behind him a sea-green resin bookcase goes up three storeys. A knobless door opens into a dark cavern containing the bottles of claret. On the desk lies an industrial

1 OFFICE FOR METROPOLITAN ARCHITECTURE/REM KOOLHAAS, **Maison à Bordeaux**, OMA, ROTTERDAM 1997

remote control device, a telephone, a newspaper and a workbook for learning Mandarin. He takes the remote control and the room moves up; he slides past the bookcase. It is possible to stop at each given point and to leisurely take out - for instance - S,M,L,XL. *After a couple of metres, the room locks into the floor of a stunningly glassy glass house, the metallic floor flush with the hill. He looks down into the parking space in between the perimeter wall; he looks the other way over Bordeaux and the river; he looks around and sees some furniture, and also a huge chromium cylinder and a thin rod both connected to the big box floating above the living room. He drives off the platform towards the view, goes into the garden where the path burrows into the ground and looks inside a flower. He drives back in, manoeuvres himself behind his desk and makes his room go further up. He locks into the third floor; through the bookshelves he sees the terrace; next to him Gilbert & George's* Lifehead *looks apotheotically to the sky. He moves away again and passes a number of physiotherapy contraptions, crosses the terrace, and goes into the master bedroom. His wife is still sleeping. He quietly passes the bathtub, goes past the white resin washing slab: a face floating by in the mirror. Back in his study he sits a while behind his desk. One porthole in the wall is precisely positioned to give him a view of the horizon, another is aimed downward and gives him a view of the hill. The therapist arrives and gives him a workout. His wife helps him get into a different wheelchair for his shower. The water disappears in the cracks between the floorboards. From where he sits with water running over him, he looks in the split separating the adult half of the top house from the children's part and sees himself reflected twice in the glass. Then his wife dries him off and helps him into the hospital bed for a nap.*

She takes a bath, gets dressed and crosses the metal grate bridge between the two parts of the top house, into the children's quarters. This half of the box is divided by diagonally placed walls that strangely remind you of the folded doorwalls around Louise Bourgeois children's bedrooms and like these seem saturated with memories and nightmares. She wakes some kids, springs open some of the glass plates covering the portholes and takes a mediaevally tight and dark spiral staircase - hidden in the chromium tube - down two storeys into the TV room. She follows the curve of the wall into the kitchen, makes herself some coffee and a croissant, takes it back in front of the TV, and watches the Breakfast Show. She then gets up and enters a strange uterus-like staircase that takes her to the living room. Now that she is surrounded only by huge glass walls she slides away some of them and walks over to the end of the metallic floor where she looks out over smog-covered Bordeaux. In the middle of the living room is a big square hole with a hydraulic steel shaft supporting the platform, which is now locked into the top house. Through the hole she peers into the kitchen. She walks back behind the bookcase where her desk stands. She settles down to look at her e-mail; the wires of her PowerMac sway gently in the wind. After a while, when the children are all ready, she rushes up the concrete stairs glued to the bookcase and wakes her husband. He and the children will leave for the afternoon; she will receive the architect and a group of guests who are extremely impatient to inspect every nook and cranny of her home.

The house demonstrates the Paranoid Critical Method as a radical way of deploying the heat oppressed brain *in architecture. Explained in (pop)Kantian terms, the P.C.M. can be understood as a psychologically charged relationship between the world as it exists by itself, regardless of whether there is a human observer to interact with it - nouomena - and the world as it appears to us humans - phenomena. Koolhaas's Paranoid Critical glare makes the nouomena acquire such an obsessive intensity in the way they manifest themselves in the brain of the beholder - as phenomena - that they can be turned into architectural facts and returned to the world as new nouomena loaded with psychology, analysis, fear, love, disgust, angst, ennui or lust. The reality of this family has become hyperreal in architecture. The product is what we might call a concentration of phenomenally nouomenal phenomena, or nouomenally phenomenal nouomena.*

What makes *the house is that it is a bit of world in your face; the world is neither denoted or broken down into data and fed into an interiorized process of formal manipulations, as is common practice in contemporary avant-garde architecture. The world has become architecture, not by abstraction but by inclusion, or rather by intrusion. Gary Bates, architect at Koolhaas's office, confessed that when he saw the house for the first time, he was 'fucking scared because it raises the stakes even higher'. It does. It raises the stakes of how far architecture dares to let the real in. After this house the world can no longer be censored before being let into the architecture: no more radical-chic caricatures of life to be translated into formally inventive masterpieces. It is one thing to present innovative architectural ideas against the backdrop of Far Eastern statistics and an ever-expanding, ever-progressing generic metropolis as Koolhaas often does. Engaging the small, the personal, the painful and the sad and doing it beautifully is another thing. Here is an architecture that has more to do with for example steel spiders, broken bodies and children's bedrooms than with its own vocabulary of form or with a parallel universe of imminent hypermodernization. We eagerly ask Rem Koolhaas:*

'Are you a humanist?'

LIFE—HEAD

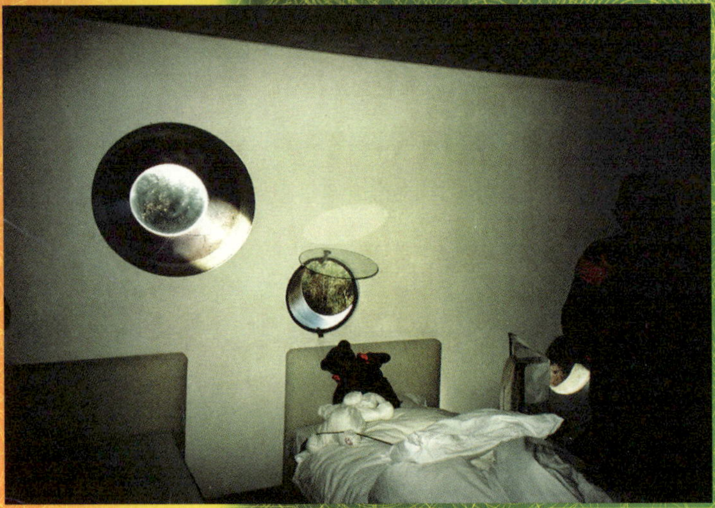

Northern Soul

REVIEW OF *Göran Schildt, 'Alvar Aalto: the Complete Works, The complete Catalogue of Architecture, Art and Designs'*

London: Academy Editions, 1994

This catalogue of the complete works brings to a monumental close the biographical series on the life and work of Alvar Aalto by art historian Göran Schildt. In his award-winning trilogy of the eighties - The Early Years (1984), The Decisive Years (1986) and The Mature Years (1989) - Schildt (Helsinki 1917) enlists the aid of magnificent illustrations to relate the saga of Finland's greatest architectural hero, Alvar Aalto (1898-1976). The treated works are illustrative of varying angles of approach (husband, colleague, friend, designer of public housing, capitalist, idealist). In many cases they serve to shed light on conceptual links in his body of work. However, a whole host of unrealized and lesser-known (because never publicly presented) projects and competition designs were missing in the trilogy. This has now been set right with the publication of the fourth monographic volume. It shows not only Aalto's wide-ranging oeuvre as a planner, urban designer, architect and furniture designer but also provides full documentation of his lesser-known work as an artist and a designer of interiors, vases, fabrics and jewellery. The catalogue attests to exceedingly conscientious work by Schildt who is justified in describing it as 'the complete catalogue of Alvar Aalto's architecture, art and designs'. Aided for the duration of the catalogue research by Joakim Hansson, the author has succeeded in rectifying the omissions in the string of previous publications on Aalto. Here they are in this book: all those previously unpublished projects and lesser-known competition designs (amongst which his design of 1956 for the Lincoln Center in New York). But Schildt's greatest service is his success in taking Aalto's immense oeuvre and casting it in a form that meets his cataloguing principle and still leaves the book an enjoyable read. The surprisingly poor quality of some drawings is compensated for with beautiful and adequate project descriptions which nowhere prove to be aridly objective (Schildt was a close friend of Aalto's). A thematic arrangement informs the presentation, with projects arranged chronologically by theme with a description of their whereabouts. A logical format for a catalogue, one would think. Yet for Aalto's work it is a curious choice since there must be few architect's oeuvres that are so clearly the result of interdisciplinary cross-pollination.

His furniture designs are indelibly bound up with his architecture, his architecture is a reflection of nature, and so on. This is something the author is obviously aware of, to judge from his lightly apologetic foreword. He warns the reader of the numbing dangers of such a rigid arrangement. Splitting up the work into categories does indeed fail to do full justice to the hybrid character of the work of this artist-architect-designer-urbanist. This 'artificially' sectarian format is therefore only justified by the three volumes published earlier and the introductory essays which reintegrate the different themes. There remains the question of why such importance is attached to the overall picture. In the introduction Schildt mentions the completeness crucial to gaining an understanding of Aalto's 'visionary impact on modern architecture, art and design'. Yet there is one thing alone that would have offered a real way out of this dilemma, namely Aalto's many writings and essays, and it is these that are lacking here. Now only a fifth volume, entirely devoted to Aalto's literary work, can bring the Aalto epic to a worthy conclusion. The catalogue fails to shed any real new light on an architect whose name, not entirely unjustifiably, is forever synonymous with bent plywood furniture for serial production: even today his pieces set a standard for the Scandinavian interiors gracing many a waiting room, assembly hall and office landscape. What this catalogue does teach us is that Aalto, besides being a creditable painter and talented designer, was an unbelievably multi-faceted architect. He designed literally at every scale (from chair to city) and at every level (buildings and complexes) for the widest range of clients (manufacturers, government, private individuals) and in the most varied circumstances (culture, health care, public housing, industry). His designs have made their mark outside Finland too, witness the impressive roster of international commissions including such bowers of bliss as Mount Angel (Oregon, USA) and Le Moyne Terraces (California, USA). Aalto's designs were still being translated into buildings long after his death - there was a veritable Aalto boom in the eighties - not to mention the many rip-offs sprouting up everywhere in the past decade. The popularity of Aalto's architecture, particularly within postmodernism, can partly be explained by a number of swerves in his career. Aalto's international breakthrough was preceded by a brief period of great rhetorical diversity. On the one hand this was catalysed by Gunnar Asplund's Public Library in Stockholm (1920-

1928), on the other it was influenced by the sober lines of the Wagnerschule via Aalto's teacher Carl Gustav Nyström. Aalto's early work in Jyväskylä between 1923 and 1927, a wide array of workers' apartments and a great many churches and church renovations, are all executed in the typical Doricist Classicism characterizing this formal syntax. Aalto debuted on the international platform at the fourth CIAM Congress in 1933 with his competition-winning design of 1929 for the Paimio Sanatorium. This fairly literal Nordic counterpart of Duiker's Zonnestraal aftercare colony (1926-1928) would long sustain him in the upper echelons of international functionalism. After first briefly dabbling in Russian Constructivism, in 1929 he moved towards the exclusively economics-based position of the Existenzminimum proclaimed by the German Neue Sachlichkeit architects at the second CIAM Congress in Frankfurt. The work that would bring Aalto lasting worldwide status was his winning entry of 1927 in the competition for the new Viipuri Library - 'the world's most advanced library', according to the competition brief. It was eventually built in 1935 in a radically altered form at another site. Fired by international recognition and the self-confidence this gave him, he decided in 1934, before the library was even on site, to exultantly and permanently break with 'the mechanistic functionalism of CIAM orthodoxy'. The different designs for the library, which Academy Editions presented together last year in a small publication devoted entirely to this 'key work', consolidate the various stages of this move away: how he managed to shake off Asplund's Classicism and, fuelled by his friend Moholy-Nagy and probably also Duiker, took a more Expressionist and clearly more organic approach to modernism that would place him in the same line as the 'first masters', Le Corbusier and Gropius. But over all else this prestigious building shows that faith in the New Age was as firmly anchored in Finland as anywhere else - hence its great historical importance. And yet it was his contact with the timber industry - a few successful industrial furniture designs had paved the way to the mass production of his pieces - that would remind him of his roots in Finnish National Romanticism. This movement was structured round the Finnish folk epic, the Kalevala, by its spiritual leaders Eliel Saarinen, Akseli Gallén-Kallela and Lars Sonck following Finland's independence in the early 20th century. That his vocation lay here is evident from his prizewinning entry design for the

Finnish Pavilion for the 1937 World Exhibition in Paris. Given the unequivocal code name 'Le bois est en marche', it was a rhetorical display of the structural properties of wood: the battened timber walls of the main space and the timber frame structure of the exhibition space surrounding it gave a virtuoso demonstration of various techniques for timber jointing. The design goes on to address the problem of shaping the building's surroundings. 'In modern architecture', Aalto would write, 'where the rationality of the structural frame and the building masses threaten to dominate, there is often an architectural vacuum in the left-over portions of the site'. In later years Aalto came to see the move from functionalist work in reinforced concrete to timber and natural materials as the turning-point in the evolution of his architecture. He regarded his laminated furniture as examples of what Kenneth Frampton calls 'an intuitive, indirect and more critical approach to design, which was capable of achieving a more responsive and inflected environment than that usually achieved by linear logic'. This organic response combined with the principles of 'plan libre' brought him, as Frampton points out, conceptually close to the group of Northern European architects centred around Bruno Taut's Glass Chain project. Like Hans Scharoun, Hugo Häring and others he had left behind 'the latent tyranny of the normative orthogonal grid' or inflected it where on-site or programmatic vagaries demanded it. This flexible rationalism, as he himself once described it, allowed him to focus on the overall ambience of a space and the way it changes through the filtering of heat, light and sound. This intense reciprocity between building and surroundings, light and space, gave his work a unique sense of continuity, from his functionalist period in the twenties to the more expressive phase embarked on in the early fifties. The uniqueness of his work lies in his intuitive sense of genius loci combined with an almost glamorous feeling for image. This gave him the opportunity to grasp on each new occasion the intrinsic values of place and brief. His gift, ultimately, was to fix the characteristics of the site so strongly in his buildings as to render them topographical metaphors in themselves. That he succeeded in this has everything to do with the enchanting light of a fragrant midsummer evening reflecting on the dark surface of a forest lake, contemplated from the verandah of a country house.

Paimio Sanatorium, built in 1930-1932

Scandinavian summer pleasures

Famous glass vases

Typical Finnish lake landscape

Aalto with the family boat Nemo Propheta in Patria, which he designed himself

Sauna belonging to Aalto's experimental summer house in Muuratsalo, 1953

OH HEAVENS

The architecture of Philip Johnson

Berlin 1996: Asked to build a huge edifice on Friedrichstrasse, the ninety year old architect Philip Johnson found himself restricted by the preconditions of the urban plan by which the city wanted to recreate the 18th century urban tissue that had been destroyed during the war. Johnson designed a contextualist monstrosity but at the same time he designed a fantasy version, a building for an imaginary Berlin, in which each architect is free and nobody talks about the 18th century urban grid 'which was bor ing anyway'. During lectures he would show it saying: 'In the meantime I would have liked to build this'. The design is absolutely fairytale-like, like a cross between early Walt Disney and late Frank Stella. Only the tiny figure standing next to the model says anything about its scale, or does it? The building might as well be ten feet tall or three hundred; it doesn't matter.

Johnson explains it as referring to Finsterlin. By being free, the design is cheerful; it profits maximally from the emptiness it stands in by being as beautiful as it possibly can. The attitude that has produced this design presents to us a possibility to defuse the urbanist debate going on in Berlin at this moment, between one group (the one in power) that wants Berlin to look as if there has never been a war, and another (the one not in power) that wants it to look as if the war is still raging. Johnson has made the first major design for Berlin since Mies's Nationalgalerie that does not insult the Berliners by rubbing something in they know already. In other words Johnson has made the first life-enhancing design for Berlin in thirty years.

In 1932 Philip Johnson (Cleveland Ohio, 1906) had his green-leather-upholstered sports car hoisted onto an ocean liner to Europe to go and see modern architecture in Rotterdam, Paris and Berlin.[1]

With a particular cheerfulness he travelled through the *abendland*, let Mies van der Rohe and J.J.P. Oud design apartments and houses for himself and his family, stayed ostentatiously unconcerned about all the social discourse but lifted modernism *out* of history and showed it to the world as a full-grown architectural style. Philip Johnson is a historian, but one of the perverse school. His cardinal work in architectural history is the Glass House of 1949. Mies van der Rohe entered the house once; but after the famous liquor-clogged evening he left, swearing he would never return. In hindsight it is understandable; about the same time Mies was working on the Farnsworth House. In this project the Glass House concept is placed explicitly in the advancing historical development of modern architecture. The house is programmatic; it hovers above the ground; the supports are placed outside the glass walls, the interior is defined by partitions in the open floorspace and the fire place is abstracted to the level of invisibility. The design is to be understood as the final consequence of a research into clarification and dematerialization and is therefore a radical design. It has a lot to do with Mies's incantation 'with infinite slowness arises the great form'.

Compared to the Farnsworth House Johnson's Glass House is ambiguous and therefore radical; it is made entirely of glass but is set firmly on the ground. It is immaterial but has as a core a brick cylinder that at the same time contains the bathroom and serves as a fireplace. The supports are not divorced from the wall but are integrated in it. The furniture comes from Mies's Barcelona Pavilion but the oil painting is by Poussin. In the Glass House Johnson stripped Mies's architecture of its Hegelian and Platonic indisputability and gave it a Nietzschean hybridity.

The second stage in a carefully designed process of perversion consists of Johnson's explanatory notes in *The Architectural Review* of 1950. The Glass House is not explained by an essay but by a legend to the historical references by use of which the architect made the design: Corbu, Mies, Van Doesburg, the Acropolis par Auguste Choisy, Schinkel, Ledoux and Malevich. Underneath Le Corbusier's plan of 1933 for a farmer's village Johnson notes: 'The footpath pattern I copied from the spider-web-like forms of Le Corbusier, who delicately runs his communications without regard for the axis of his buildings or seemingly for any kind of pattern'.[2] Underneath a picture of Schinkel's casino in Glienicke Park he tells us: 'The site relation of my house is pure Neo-Classic Romantic - more specifically, Schinkelesque. Like his Casino, my house is approached on dead-level and, like his, faces its principal (rear) facade toward a sharp bluff.' And under Malevich's *Black Circle* of 1913: 'Although I had forgotten the Malevich picture, it is obviously the inspiration for the plan of the Glass House. Malevich proved what interesting surrounding areas could be created by correctly placing a circle in a rectangle'.

It turns out Johnson also manipulated an apocryphal genealogy of the Glass House and to this day keeps doing so. It consists mainly of non-architectural references.[3] The house is compared to a dislodged glass elevator: 'then the snow comes down at night and the building floats. If the snow comes down at an angle, then it's as if you're in an elevator going up that way'. It is linked to the pioneer-feeling or just to the family camping trip by describing it in terms of coming together around the fireplace: 'When it is cold outside, I have to move closer to the fire.' (In fact the entire house has floor-heating.) Also sex has its place in the genealogy; the total transparency has been interpreted as referring to exhibitionism and to the secret desire of being caught red-handed while masturbating. According to Johnson the relation exists but is less straightforward: 'Much more important than exhibitionism is the interface of architecture and the desire for all kinds of sexual experiments. Whether you want to close yourself in is Freudian in one way, but exposing yourself is Freudian in another way'. The most famous reference is the one of the burned-out village in Poland with the charred hearths as the only reminders of the wooden dwellings, supplying Johnson, travelling through Europe immediately after the war, with the image of a transparent house with a brick core. Now he has this to say about it: 'Yes, I regret having said that. Because the burned-out village was in the Second World War, and I was on the wrong side. So we don't talk about that anymore. My enemies do. Of course. That's a part of my life I'd rather forget. But it was a horrifying sight. And yet, it's so symbolic, that you've got the hearth, the one thing that was left. And it was so beautiful. That's a horrible thing to say, but ruins are beautiful. You can't help it. Fascination with ruins, it's endless.'

It takes your breath away, the way Johnson volunteers to bring into the conversation the most unspeakable part of his life and proceeds to load the Glass House with even more meaning and drama. Until the beginning of the war Johnson was an active sympathizer of the Nazi regime and wrote agitated articles for American magazines about the possibilities for monumental architecture now that a regime had risen to power committed to leaving physical traces of its greatness. After the critics had been hesitating for years in front of an empty goal, Charles Jencks finally kicked the ball in by pointing out at the beginning of the 1970s the similarities between Nazi architecture and Johnson's monumental Neo-classicism of Lincoln Center. Thanks to Franz Schulze's recent biography we now know that the architectural dreams accompanying Johnson's infatuation with Hitler were Miesian more than Neo-classical. We already knew about Mies's, Corbu's and Gropius's intense flirtations with the Nazis, and we have long ago reached the conclusion that there is no unambiguous contract between totalitarian regimes and classical architecture. In other words Jencks's goal has to be disallowed. But at the same time Schulze, having had the opportunity to browse through the giant FBI file on Johnson and to talk extensively and intimately to Uncle Philip, has put to us again, and with even more ugly details than before, Johnson's past on the wrong side. This time Johnson himself takes the initiative in the unavoidable process of *hinein-interpretierung*, he connects his shame to a personalized image of destroyed homeliness and in this way saves his oeuvre from a rigged conviction of political abjectness. With an impressive agility he succeeds in securing the innocence of the art of architecture and implies the following statement: an architect can be guilty, a building can not. Jencks wrote something else in 1971: 'This honest a-morality is exactly what gives Philip Johnson his integrity.'[4] Philip Johnson has become famous with an eloquent a-morality on the subject of the architect's social position: 'I am a whore and I am very well paid for building high-rise buildings'. In this famous acerbicism we should not see the core of his work but the defence mechanism with which he keeps architecture free from all kinds of excuses, disclaimers, frustrations and false promises. To paraphrase Jencks: this honest a-morality is exactly what Johnson uses to save *architecture's* integrity.

Johnson sees architecture as art and takes his art extremely seriously. What distinguishes Johnson from his examples in philosophy (Nietzsche) and architecture (Mies, Corbu, Van Doesburg, Schinkel and others) is his feeling for liteness, the attitude that says that the quality of a work is not entirely dependent on the existential world-weariness with which it is carried out. In that respect Johnson is more related to Oscar Wilde who said: 'Many a young man starts in life with a natural gift for exaggeration which, if nurtured in congenial and sympathetic surroundings, or by the imitation of the best models, might grow into something really great and wonderful. But, as a rule he comes to nothing. He either falls into careless habits of accuracy or takes to frequenting the society of the aged and the well-informed.'[5]

Johnson has always been able to find the 'congenial and sympathetic surroundings' and has of course always copied the best models. One of the reasons we have to take his work so seriously is because he is one of the very few architects who have been able to do what they really wanted, and to such an extent. Take for instance Mildred Bliss, who in 1963 gave him the job of designing a museum for the collection of pre-Columbian art she

Philip Johnson's keeshond dog on the doorstep of the Glass House, New Canaan, 1998

Philip Johnson in the Glass House, New Canaan, 1950

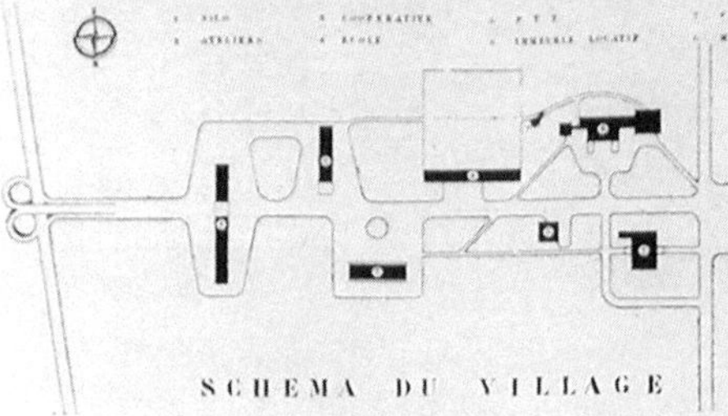

1 Le Corbusier: Farm Village Plan—1933.

The approach to the house through meadow and copse is derived from English Eighteenth Century precedent. The actual model is Count Pückler's estate at Muskau in Silesia. The driveway is straight, however, like the pathways in the plan above. The footpath pattern between the two houses I copied from the spiderweb-like forms of Le Corbusier, who delicately runs his communications without regard for the axis of his buildings or seemingly for any kind of pattern.

2 Mies van der Rohe: Ideal arrangement of Illinois Institute of Technology Buildings, 1939.

The arrangement of the two buildings and the statue group is influenced by Mies' theory of organizing buildings in a group. The arrangement is rectilinear but the shapes tend to overlap and slide by each other in an asymmetric manner.

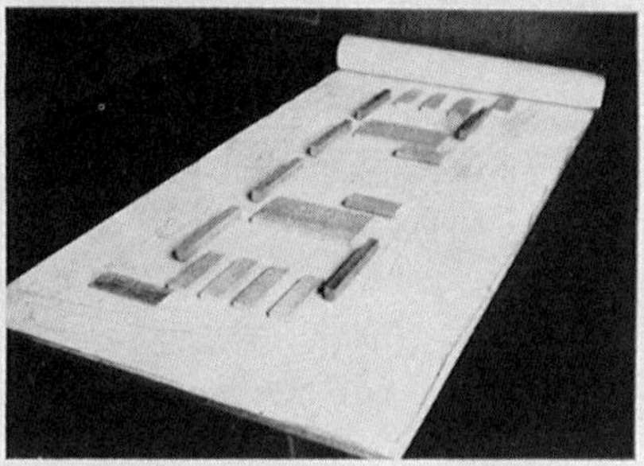

3 Theo Van Doesburg: The Basso Continuo of Painting. (Published in "G" an *avant garde* magazine by Mies van der Rohe in 1922).

The idea of asymmetric sliding rectangles was furthest developed in the De Stijl aesthetics of war-time Holland. These shapes, best known to posterity through the painting of the late Piet Mondrian, still have an enormous influence on many other architects besides myself.

4 Plan and Perspective of the Acropolis at Athens from Choisy *L'Histoire de l'Art Grecqu*

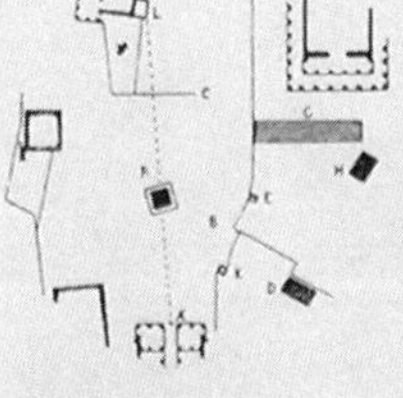

Choisy proved that the Greeks restrict the angle of approach to their buildin to the oblique; also that they plac their monuments so that only one maj building dominated the field of visi from any given point.
The grouping of my buildings follo Choisy: from the focal point at t beginning of the footpath near the par ing lot, the brick house (Propylaea) passed and forms a wall on the rig hand. The statue group (Athene Pr machos) is in full view slightly to th right. The glass house comes into vie (from an oblique angle) only after th pine tree at the angle of the promonto is circumnavigated.

5 Karl Friedrich Schinkel: Casino in Glienicke Park near Potsdam c. 1830. Entrance façade.

The site relation of my house is pure Neo-Classic Romantic—more specifically, Schinkelesque. Like his Casino my house is approached on dead-level and, like his, faces its principal (rear) façade toward a sharp bluff.

6 Karl Friedrich Schinkel: Casino in Glienicke Park near Potsdam c. 183[illegible] Terrace overlooking the Have[illegible]

The Eighteenth Century preferred more regular sites than th[illegible] and the Post-Romantic Revivalists preferred hill tops to th[illegible] cliff edges or shelves of the Romantics (Frank Lloyd Wrigh[illegible] that great Romantic, prefers shelves or hillsides).

7 Claude Nicholas Ledoux: Maison des Gardes Agricoles, at Maupertuis c. 1780.

The cubic, "absolute" form of my glass house, and the separation of functional units into two absolute shapes rather than a major and minor massing of parts comes directly from Ledoux, the Eighteenth Century father of modern architecture. (See Emil Kaufmann's excellent study Von Ledoux bis Le Corbusier.) *The cube and the sphere, the pure mathematical shapes, were dear to the hearts of those intellectual revolutionaries from the Baroque, and we are their descendants.*

8 Mies van der Rohe: Farnsworth House, 1947. (Now under constructio[illegible] near Chicago)

The idea of a glass house comes from Mies van der Rohe. Mie[illegible] had mentioned to me as early as 1945 how easy it would be t[illegible] build a house entirely of large sheets of glass. I was sceptical at the time, and it was not until I had seen the sketches of the Farnsworth House that I started the three-year work of designing my glass house. My debt is therefore clear, in spite of obvious difference in composition and relation to the ground.

18 Johnson House: Interior looking south.

Mies van der Rohe has not only influenced the concept of the house. He has designed all of the furniture—some of it a quarter century ago, none of it later than 1930.

19 Johnson House: Sculpture Group.

The papier-mache sculpture by Nadelman provides the type of foil which this kind of building needs (Mies again established the precedent in his Barcelona Pavilion).

20 Johnson House: Interior looking west.

The view of the valley, with its repoussoir of giant trees, is contrived with th aid of many Baroque landscapes. A view without a frame seems impossible afte the Seventeenth Century.

21 Johnson House: Cooking Unit.

The kitchen I reduced to a simple bar so that it would not close off any space. I have no idea what precedent I followed on that.

22 Johnson House: Ir rior, north-east corr

Bed and writing de with strips of panda cloth hanging from ceiling—the only scre ing I felt to be necess and her husband had donated to Harvard twenty years earlier. Money was no problem to Mrs. Bliss, according to Johnson: 'Very few times you get a client with a perfect program and with all the money in the world'. Johnson says he was inspired by the madrasa of Sinan's Great Mosque in Istanbul. The result was a system of octagonal pavilions with spherical vaults, so closely surrounded by trees that it does not have an exterior. The building was - according to a critic who took the pains of calculating it - probably per square metre the most expensive ever built. The window frames are made of copper, the floors of teakwood and marble, the columns of travertine and the walls of rounded double glazing. The vaults make every whisper boom through the entire building as if transmitted by an intercom, but then Johnson finds that: 'You should look at the art, be quiet and listen to the fountain'. With its modular classicism the building makes you think of Aldo van Eyck's orphanage in Amsterdam; but instead of unfortunate children it is used by fortunate adults.

The next maecenas was Nelson Rockefeller, billionaire, director of a museum and governor of the State of New York. He helped Johnson to the job of designing the urban plan for the Lincoln Center and to design the State Theater. The ceiling is covered with gold, the stairs look like travertine bavarois, the ceiling of the auditorium is an immense flower and the lighting attached to the lodges forms a giant diamond necklace. The lobby however is dominated by sumptuous wrought iron galleries derived from North American jails. This space is 'really great and wonderful' and proves that honest amorality works. Johnson has not attempted to blur the jail-reference (as Herman Hertzberger would do); nor has he tried to dramatize it (as Jean Nouvel would do). The 'clearly stated need' - to use the dictum of Johnson's great friend and mentor Oud - of a theatre lobby is to permit seeing and being seen; the 'clearly stated solution' then is using a typology that has proven its worth in doing exactly this. Foucauldian and Tafurian analysis misfire on Johnson's purely architectural interpretation of panopticism: 'If you visit a good jail, it would look like this. They're usually much narrower, but the little cells are on the balconies. You can always watch where everybody is, you see. There are some charming interiors of jails'.

Helen Searing, in her article 'The Crimson Connection' has pointed out the seminal role Harvard University has played in dispersing modernism as an architectural style and not as an ideological movement.[6] The three protagonists of the 'International Style' exhibition in last book *The Architecture of Good Intentions* written an essay on modern architecture on the basis of its deeply rooted desire of salvation from all evil. Rowe puts it to us that Modern architecture, by disposing of all cultural memory, wants to win back her nakedness and thus wants to gain entry to the earthly paradise. He himself underwrites this desire but suggests, since true nakedness is impossible to regain and the front door of paradise will probably stay shut forever, that we present ourselves at the back door, clad in the rags and tatters of our history. Rowe is sure that 'somehow, we and the world alike will be received into the all-consuming bliss of total redemption'.[11] To our young ears Rowe's ante-apocalyptic humility sounds terribly old-world; with his belief in the all-consuming bliss of total redemption he does however touch a tender spot. Redemption and Bliss are once again important subjects in contemporary culture. In a recent column in *The New York Times*, the art critic Hal Foster attacks what he calls The Cult of Despair, the tendency to overly identify with the victim, because this attitude offers a small chance of redemption. Johnson's oeuvre has been teaching us for years that Redemption should no longer mean identifying with man's suffering, but offering him something that is really new, showing him that not all is fixed in advance, that not all is the same, that not all is lost.

NOTES

1 Annie Oud-Dinaux, Wassenaar, letter to Ernst van der Hoeven, March 13, 1990 (Rotterdam: Ernst van der Hoeven Archives).
2 Philip Johnson, 'House at New Canaan Connecticut', *Architectural Review*, September 1950, pp. 152-159.
3 Hilary Lewis and John O'Connor, *Philip Johnson, The Architect in His Own Words,* Rizzoli, New York 1994. All non-annotated quotes in this article are taken from this book.
4 Charles Jencks, *Modern Movements in Architecture*, Penguin Books, Harmondsworth Middlesex 1973, pp. 204-210.
5 Oscar Wilde, 'The Decay of Lying', *De Profundis and Other Writings*, edited by H. Pearson, Penguin Books, London 1986, p. 61.
6 Helen Searing, 'International Style: the Crimson Connection', *Progressive Architecture,* no. 2, 1982, pp. 88-91.
7 Searing.
8 Cees Boekraad and Hans van Dijk, 'Autonomie en Autarkie: een vraaggesprek met Kenneth Frampton', *Archis,* March 1988, no. 3, pp. 8-11.
9 Rudolf Wittkower, *Architectural Principles in the Age of Humanism,* Academy Editions, London 1973.
10 Colin Rowe, 'The Mathematics of the Ideal Villa', *The Mathematics of the Ideal Villa and Other Essays,* The MIT Press, Cambridge Mass. 1976.
11 Colin Rowe, *The Architecture of Good Intentions: Towards a Possible Retrospect,* Academy Editions, London 1994, p. 43.

Philip Johnson's study pavilion and architect Matthijs Bouw, New Canaan 1998

The Glass House, New Canaan, 1998

Fireplace in the Glass House

^ Lincoln Center, State Theater New York

< Lobby, State Theater, New York

'In the meantime I would have liked to build this...' Alternative design for Friedrichstrasse, Berlin, 1996

Philip Johnson next to the visitors' pavilion, New Canaan, 1998

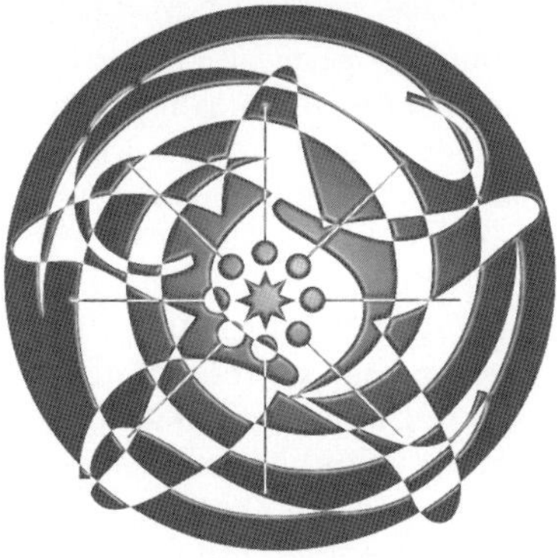

THE

TOMADO

HOUSE

BRAVE NEW OFFICE BUILDING

BY HUIG MAASKANT

The building rears up like a state-of-the-art dragon on the edge of the old inner city of Dordrecht, with a hard minimalistic design that pays no heed to its surroundings. Comprised of strips of concrete and glass clenched into a cube, its only relief is a gentle concrete bulge and a colourful artwork. Yet even these elements are disturbingly large and heavy, abstract and arresting. Designed in 1958, this office building called the Tomadohuis is organized along the lines of a 'self-bearing car body'. Its construction was to act like the tin body of a car, an independent entity without intermediate supports that is then placed over the chassis and wheels.

THE TOMADO CONCERN

The building's progressive design and high level of functionality were emblematic of the modernity of the Tomado concern, which owed its success to the great appeal of the 'wire sculptures' it produced. At a time when marble mantelpieces were being broken open en masse, lowered ceilings hid ornamental plasterwork from view and solid oak lounge suites were considered antediluvian, the airy wire-work of Tomado symbolized the modern age. The Tomado rack, perhaps the firm's best-known product, was a permanent fixture in every modern living room along with wicker chairs, three-legged tables and all the other fifties-sixties design ephemera. The construction kits of metal hangers and tin shelves could be extended with an almost infinite variety of systems elements into a veritable wall of shelves, doors, desktops, hatpegs and book rests. This could give you the most lightweight cupboard imaginable, hung on just a few nails; transparent and adjustable, it was a modular system whose components fitted together like a dream. The colours were mostly red, blue and yellow with black metal hangers creating a three-dimensional 'Mondrian' on your wall, exemplifying the ease with which the De Stijl vocabulary was popularized after the war.

¬ In the kitchen, Tomado was to the Netherlands what Tupperware is to the States. The catalogue offered an endless assortment of wire gadgets, handy racks and storage equipment. Tomado turned out all manner of now-obsolete kitchenware such as bottle scrapers, three-storey plate racks, potato baskets, sponge squeezers, oven hooks, mashers and trivets.

Tomado began with industrial mass production of the most ordinary domestic products at a time when people were earning more money to devote to housekeeping. Given the fashionable status of light wirework in the age of the Atomic Style, Tomado became tremendously popular and in the fifties the concern grew hand over fist. 'What we want these days, now that we have air travel, is to combine sturdiness and lightness in things. Tomado has managed to do this.'[1] The secret of Tomado's success lay not in inventing new articles, for in general Tomado produced existing household attributes. These were handy bits and bobs that were not just functional and of good sound quality but also had an attractive form. They might have been produced industrially, but they still looked elegant; they were good at getting those boring household chores done, but at the same time they seemed to be saying that housewives 'could get some pleasure out of them, their usefulness aside'.[2] Tomado was quite as practical as the Frankfurter Küche, the international figurehead of practical housekeeping of pre-war modernism, but this time made to look nice. 'It's odd, but the soft spot the housewife has for Tomado ignores or chooses to ignore the fact that this company is making millions, with an international reputation and exporting to many countries on a massive scale. For her it is and will remain the cosy store with a workroom at the back. No amount of efficiency can extinguish the pleasure and delight bound up with the name of Tomado.'[3]

The concern was led by the Van der Togt brothers, who in the twenties had set up *'Van der TOgt's MAssa-artikelen DOrdrecht'*, a well-nigh megalomanic name for an upstairs workshop that started off making copper-wire hooks for hanging photographs on wallpaper. When the company began to take off it opened a factory producing articles for industry and the home. In 1953 space ran out again and it was decided to erect a new factory exclusively for the production of domestic articles - Tomado's big successes - such as dish racks, sieves, drying racks, french fry cutters and sink refuse trays. A site was found in Etten-Leur due south of Dordrecht, and the Rotterdam architect Huig Maaskant was invited to design the factory, an act that established the latter's worldwide reputation as an architect of industrial buildings.

Jan van der Togt, Maaskant's client, played what the architect termed an 'inspiring' role in bringing about the Tomado factory and two further projects entrusted to Maaskant not long after, the Tozindo factory (1959-1961) and the Tomado head office, both in Dordrecht. Van der Togt was a self-made man with a working-class background and an American-style career; he had learnt from experience that 'those who don't work, won't eat'. Maaskant described him as 'a perfectionist with an unshakeable faith in modern technology and modern materials. Having an office building in, say, painted concrete would have been as unthinkable for him as having a surgeon in painted clogs.'[4] Van der Togt was the same age as Maaskant and the two were firm friends. So it was that the Tomado office building ensued from a common view of architecture and society, in which the architect gave an architectonic reading of the principal's insights into the corporate and social structure. Maaskant had nothing but praise for Van der Togt, for the freedom he gave his architect as well as for his own enlightening role. He regarded him as the ideal client.

¬ Maaskant's 'self-bearing car body' of a building was a far cry from the standard method of erecting offices in those days, namely a concrete frame wrapped in a curtain wall. The American offices, which inspired Dutch architects en masse, followed almost without exception the curtain-wall ideal of the moderns. The Tomadohuis is the very opposite of a transparent volume; it has great mass and great weight, giving it what Maaskant called 'accumulation capacity', that is, a critical mass. The forces and weight of the building are concentrated in the solid facade beams that dictate the look of its architecture. There is no distinction made between facade and construction: the facade *is* the construction. The accumulated mass of the office floors takes its place atop the 'chassis and wheels', in this instance just two gigantic piers. Maaskant described the curtain wall as being out of place in the Netherlands: 'We are suggesting with our modern glass palaces, however compelling and forceful their design, a contact with nature that simply isn't there. To make these buildings inhabitable we give them hefty air-conditioning plants and then keep the windows closed. What an office building needs in this climate is not a place in nature but protection against it, and good visual contact with the outside world.'[5]

¬ The principle of the self-bearing body seems a simple idea, but it was experimental nonetheless and extremely complicated to implement. Two slab-shaped columns a full twelve metres across thrust up through the building from the forecourt to the canteen on the top floor. They support the beams, which terminate at the facade elements, and the floor slabs. The entire structure is a single monolithic entity without intervening supports, resulting in the most freely subdivisible office floors with a six-metre cantilever on two sides of the columns.

Just how exacting the consequences of a simple idea can be is demonstrated on the upper floors, where the columns divide into two parts of six metres each. So as not to interrupt the continuous window bands it was necessary to incise these columns at the windows, with the resulting gaps kitted out with plant boxes.

So as to get as close as possible to the overall design concept – a cube with alternating bands of concrete and glass - the windows were put in place without frames. The risk that the forces acting upon the facade components would crack the glass was countered with a specially developed system of springs that held the upper and lower edges of the panes clear of the concrete. Naturally the vertical posts were made as slender as possible so as not to disrupt the horizontal line of the glass.

¬ The contrast between the great mass of the building and the void of the forecourt is dramatized at the glass entrance hall (inspired by Mies's Seagram Building and Staatsgalerie Berlin) set between the two black-marble piers. The forecourt continues on beneath the building, a condition emphasized by the materiality (glass walls, stone floor) and the module of three square metres strictly adhered to inside and outside. The entrance hall is in fact part of the outdoor space, being nothing more than a glorified air-lock entry which was permanently unmanned but carefully guarded by the spying eye of the company's close-circuit television. Maximum transparency was achieved here by hanging in place mullionless expanses of glass 5.80 metres tall. By contrast, the narrow strips of fenestration in the office volume above give that part a sense of great weight. The result, as intended, is the image of a colossal mass hovering in space.

CENTRAL BUSINESS DISTRICT

Exceedingly radical in its modern design, the Tomadohuis served as an example for the future countenance of Dordrecht. The basis for that development was laid in 1949, with the municipal council's decision to redevelop the town. They invited the office of Van Tijen and Maaskant to draw up a redevelopment plan for 'Greater Dordrecht', a city housing 100,000 inhabitants in 1970 instead of the 70,000 it had at the time. In its final form the plan was typical in every respect of the way this issue was handled in those years. To retain the historical character of the town centre, according to the paradoxical line of reasoning adopted, this had to be made accessible to traffic which would inevitably mean sacrificing monuments and streets. The centre was reprogrammed as a central business district with concentrations of offices, government buildings and shops, to be reached from a ring road laid out on an old filled-in dock basin. A broad, distinguished boulevard was to lead from the station to the centre.

That the Tomadohuis was free-standing ensued from the new planning aesthetic espoused by the development plan, as Maaskant explained: 'In view of the development of Dordrecht and the new link-up with the above-named boulevard, the existing station forecourt proves to be too small-scale and calls for a grander spatial impact.'[6]

With its autonomous position and dazzling white architectural resonance the Tomadohuis was clearly not of the present but belonged to a world that had still to come. It literally held the existing development at arm's length with a narrow strip which contained the cycle shelter, boiler house and porter's lodge. This thick wall gave the Tomadohuis its own concourse and its own backdrop, an effect that would be strengthened with the planned extension of the complex with a corner building on the north side. The building contrasted so strongly with its surroundings 'that it was neither a question of disturbing (negative) nor one of overwhelming (positive): here two styles stand together in the way that two people speaking different languages may stand together', according to the architectural critic Albert Buffinga.[7] There was a sudden display of tenderness in the decision to spare a 'magnificent tree' occupying a corner of the grounds and incorporate it in a new design for the building's outdoor space.

GLASS SCULPTURE AND INTERIOR DESIGN

The building sought to make a key 'cultural contribution' to the urban surroundings in the form of a glass sculpture on the front facade courtesy of Maaskant's regular glass artist Joop van den Broek. Weighing 15,000 kilos, it was held in place by a quartet of two-centimetre-thick bolts. As in the Tomado factory in Etten-Leur, where a large Zadkine sculpture hung above the entrance awning, it expressed Maaskant's idea that architecture and art should function together as a unit, without art being merely a way of decorating a building. So rather than place the artwork in a left-over space, Maaskant housed it in

a volume of its own issuing in a refined gesture from the main mass, and giving a wonderfully voluptuous swell to what otherwise is the tautest of rectangular blocks.
Van den Broek was requested to provide an image that would be visible from the outside in daylight, which is not normally the case with stained-glass works. The window had to be illuminated from inside at night and let in natural light during the day. To resolve this paradox Van den Broek applied an infinitely thinly rolled layer of gold and silver, so thin that it reflected light during the day and let it through after dark.
¬ The interior was spectacular too. Maaskant's office had a major say in how the interior, on which they collaborated with interior designer Carel Wirtz, was to be fitted out. Just how successful and prosperous the Tomado company was in those days is clear from the fact that no expense was spared.
There was by then something of a standard in office interiors that in Maaskant's opinion leaned far too heavily on the use of plastics and synthetic materials. To compensate for this, in the Tomado offices he used natural materials with a precious resonance such as white marble and dark polished walnut. Gracing the entrance hall are the celebrated Barcelona chairs of Mies van der Rohe and a Czech glass sculpture in a glass case; 'Swan' chairs by Arne Jacobsen are ranged round the tables in the director's room and commissioner's room.[8] In the double-height reception hall the vague shapes of people can be made out behind sections of green glass, and seats by Mies line a wall of Japanese mosaic. Obviously there is no place for natural greenery in a setting as supremely artificial as this, only for cultivated exotic indoor plants in a designed box. In the office spaces themselves the overhead strip lighting in sunken trays and the slits of the windows together carve out spaces of an abstract perfection that made others of Maaskant's profession shudder. They found it 'too well-groomed and too impregnable',[9] 'an architectural thump in the head and a 1:1 model'.[10]

The elementary nature of the architectural composition contributed much to that impression: the horizontal white lines; the building's unassailable position in its clearing; the ease with which it sits on two piers; the module of three metres maintained throughout from floor to ceiling, and from the floor plan to the layout and detailing of the surrounding outdoor space.
Critics felt that Maaskant had refined the interior at the expense of creating a human environment and accused him of exploiting the architectural aesthetic to suppress the individuality of those working there.
Admittedly the building did require some adjustment on the part of the Tomado employees. The staff were asked to make the best of the limitations to their personal freedom in deference to the perfection aspired to by the architect, the artists and the client. For example, wearing high heels was forbidden because of the plastic floors. So was smoking whilst walking, as falling cigarette ash could damage the floor surface. Similarly, 'sticking postcards from holidaying colleagues on the walls is to be discouraged, and use of the cloakroom by the staff entrance has been made compulsory to prevent coats and hats from cluttering up the exquisite office areas.'[11]
Even so, the photographs clearly show female personnel sporting high heels, unavoidable as these were in those days.

ARTIFICIAL CLIMATE

Van der Togt came to the conclusion after a trip to America that his building needed the best that technology had to offer to make the office a fully automated, comfortable, efficient and decent environment to work in.
'Building is a complicated business these days,' Maaskant wrote in his design account. 'Besides ducting and piping for water, sewage etc and fire lines with the attendant spaces for transforming, distributing and the like, the building contains the following services:

'TOMADO WALL RACKS, ALL PARTS OBTAINABLE INDIVIDUALLY'

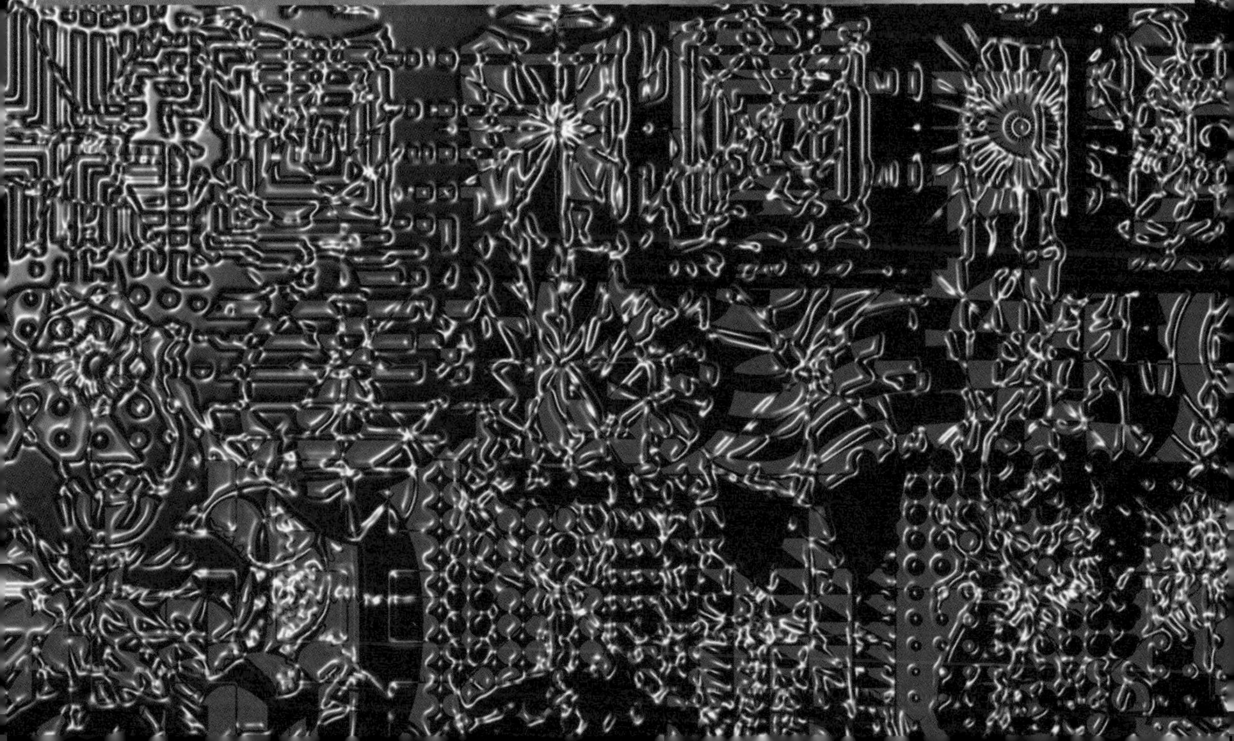

THE TOMADO COMPANY'S CHRISTMAS CARD FOR 1958

1 Heating and air-conditioning
2 Light and power
3 Passenger lift
4 Supplies lift (canteen) with external loading/unloading
5 Post lift, with external loading/unloading
6 Escalators with electric eye switch
7 Telephone and telex
8 Fully automated pneumatic dispatch
9 Electronic loudspeaker communication
10 Inductive paging system
11 Emergency power generating set
12 Radio and television. Central aerial system for radio and TV
13 Lightning conductor (earth electrode)
14 Window-cleaner's cabin
15 Venetian blinds, both horizontal and vertical, electrically operated
16 Meters
17 Dish-washer
18 Kitchen installation
19 'Compactus' archiving (elec.)
20 Refrigerators and freezers
21 Sanitary incinerators[12]
22 Drinking fountains with cooled water (elec.)
23 Rubbish chute'[13]

Maaskant himself was thoroughly aware of the discussion the technology in the Tomadohuis would provoke: 'We are aware of the fact that although this building may not hold revolutionary ideas, it does raise one issue. In Randstad Holland, which has the greatest population concentration in the world, culture is pushing nature aside. We cannot contain our swelling numbers by inflating all our small towns and villages. If we are to ensure that our country is not pinned in place by myriad small built structures, we are going to have to concentrate the lion's share of the population increase in our cities. Those who come to live there will adopt in large measure the typical city-dweller's culture. So in all probability our grandchildren will be able to tell the difference between two types of neon lighting as easily as between two species of tree. This is the price we have to pay to technique - that same technique we need to have in order to avoid starving.'[14] He added that the Tomadohuis was not just about technique, and certainly not about the predominance of mankind through technique, but it was about 'placing the people who work there in an environment that will cause them to have faith in the technical potentials possessed by our generation'.[15]

¬ Maaskant saw the assumed link between the growth of technology and the growth of urban culture as a necessary and unavoidable development; not positive or negative but just the way thing's were. His point about the lighting, an essential part of the architectural idea underpinning the Tomadohuis, demonstrates just how controversial the subject was, and that technological progress was still largely uncharted territory. In the first place because that idea was rooted in artificial light; the windows are only there for the view out. Buffinga wondered in this respect whether the lighting technique really was advanced enough: 'Having acquainted myself with the technical side of things, it seems today's tube lighting will eventually make you go bald'.[16]

Maaskant, himself without hair, responded thus: 'You can't expect me in my follically challenged state to know how to combat loss of hair. But I am convinced that the last resort for turning into curly-heads those of us who have gone bald unaided by "luminated [sic] ceilings", will be that much-maligned commodity, technology'.[17]

Now that technique provided a type of artificial lighting superior to the grey skies above Holland, architects had to draw their own conclusions. Maaskant's was that lighting and lighting technique were no longer an appendage to architecture but one of its essential components. This was evident from the role the unbroken row of fluorescent tubes in the windowsills played in the look of the building: during the day a white mass cut by narrow dark lines, at night the reverse image, with the built mass dissolving against the dark sky to leave only six dazzling lines of light.

INELUCTABLE TECHNOLOGY

Although the burgeoning role of technology in daily life was merely one part of a complex of changes shaping post-war society, technique was one of the most contested aspects of progress. Buffinga's criticism of the danger of technology dominating man, and the *unheimlich* feeling the building excited among colleagues, can be regarded as the after-effects of the discourse on automation. Such noises were amplified by the situation in America, where automation was at a far more advanced stage. There the working population fostered the very real fear that automation would usher in a second industrial revolution, bringing mass unemployment in its wake and rendering manpower superfluous, as had already happened at the Ford factories in Detroit. Automation was the second great fear following that of the outbreak of nuclear war with Russia.[18]

¬ The warning voices raised against inhuman technology were nurtured by the fact that after the war there was a growing interest in approaching the work environment from a psychotechnical angle. As far back as the inter-war years the new branches of management consultancy and psychotechnology arose in the wake of the growing and professionalizing office sector. There was research done into the 'psychotechnology of the typewriter' and the influence the layout of the workplace would have on the functioning of those working there. Psychotechnology militated against the 'scientific management' system popular between the wars, as that approach subordinated the psychological factors of work (people in other words) to the regime of the stopwatch.

The biggest cause of uneasiness towards the Tomadohuis seems to have been the fact that the building was not only efficient itself but manipulated its workers into efficient behaviour, even to the extent of transforming the office clerks into robots.

¬ It is striking just how quickly the chorus of apocalyptic utterances in the late fifties about the consequences of automation was silenced. The labour shortage suddenly elevated automation from a threat into a useful resource. More than that, the feeling grew among its critics that it was impossible to stop technological advances, and that any real criticism of this process might, given the pragmatic Dutch milieu, relegate these critics to the sidelines. Indeed, Buffinga in his description of the Tomadohuis limited himself to articulating a feeling of *unheimlichkeit*, while admitting that the employees had in fact adjusted to the situation within a few months with no appreciable influence on their 'essence'. In the end he was forced to admit that the Tomadohuis experiment was a 'noteworthy' endeavour.

Furthermore, it is here in the Tomadohuis that we see the ideas on human relations and psychotechnology making headway. The fitout of the interior and the communal spaces and the care lavished on the individual workplaces, articulated a sincere concern for the office personnel. And the many square metres provided per person (the Tomadohuis had a staff of just 145) was a reflection of the staff and management policy then in the ascendant. A decent work environment and working conditions were crucial factors in obtaining staff from a depleted labour market (in 1960 the Netherlands enjoyed almost 100 per cent employment). So Van der Togt could state: 'I believe that beauty and perfection in *joie de vivre* and stimulation pay back with interest what they cost in investment'.[19] And Maaskant: 'You can only really achieve a better performance in the workplace by having ideal working conditions'.[20]

FULLY AUTOMATIC MACHINE

In the history of technology the term 'regime shift' is used to indicate an important change in technique, defined there as the broad system of behavioural patterns, use, rules, techniques, institutions,

knowledge and production processes.[21] An example is the transition from punchcard to computer, from analogue to digital processes. In the Tomado design we can identify on several fronts a regime shift in the architectural discipline in the sense that the building signifies a clear break with pre-war modernism. Although the Tomadohuis was described as functionalist and modern, it threw overboard the principal tenet of modernism, that of light, air and hygiene and everything connected with these. Modernism stood for a certain attitude to life, an educational element in architecture, it was linked to principles of emancipation for workers, it subordinated form to function, and so forth. In the Tomadohuis there is no light save for the artificial variety; no air, just air-conditioning; no tap for washing-up but an electric dishwasher; the main contact with the outside world is by telephone and telex, not by looking through the window. Lastly, the building's functionality is captured in an all-embracing formal and aesthetic system. It is not an educational building that seeks to elevate employees to a higher level of development, but a building that assumes they have a higher development level to begin with. Instead of bringing emancipation like the Van Nelle factory in Rotterdam of 1929, it proclaims the new era.
Besides regarding it as a self-bearing car body we can see it as a fully automatic machine with all office functions automated and electrically operated wherever possible. It is not a Corbusian *machine à travailler*, but a self-functioning machine.

¬ Some regarded the Tomadohuis with astonishment tinged with suspicion, such as the journalist from the magazine *Goed Wonen* who reviewed the building and compared the porter on the first floor with Orwell's Big Brother: 'From there he observes through a barely perceptible television eye the gigantic entrance hall below, where a gadget hidden immediately behind the entry alerts him to all who enter. "Good afternoon, sir", says the eye in a woman's voice, with one barely inside the door and looking round in vain for a porter. "Would you like to ascend to the first floor?" This greeting, that seemed to emanate from thin air, threw me into such confusion that I started heading in the wrong direction until the eye informed me: "Other way, sir". And as if that were not enough, the lift doors opened of their own accord and the vehicle started moving when my right forefinger merely pointed at the button with a 1 on it. A light soon flashed on at the back to inform me that it was quite unnecessary to touch the button.'[22]

¬ Buffinga branded the building's artificial aspect as a form of cynicism targeted at the outside world and nature; in his eyes Maaskant's proposal would lead to the domination of humans by technique. And he had plenty of arguments to back him up: every floor had its own officer in charge of the tube lighting and the venetian blinds (these extended 32 metres from wall to wall). Their job was to decide whether the blinds should be raised or lowered and to regulate the amount of light these let in. The escalators for the staff started moving of their own accord when approached. The employees had buttons to press to inform the telephonist via an electrically operated tablet whether they were in or out. Critics of the Tomadohuis felt that the needs of employees were placed second to the rational functioning of the company as a whole.

¬ As is usual when moving over to a new technical regime, the Tomadohuis is not equally successful on all fronts, both in the application of new techniques and in the implementation of the design. Everything was being tried out in practice for the first time, everything was an experiment. It was still not clear exactly how the building was to be used. One just had to wait and see how the construction, the spring-mounted windows or the suspended sheets of glass would behave. And as to whether there were advantages to working in an artificial, climate-controlled and fully automated environment, only time would tell.
The transitional character of this building can also be read in the fact that here many specialisms that would later gain a life of their own are still the architect's responsibility, still part of the 'old' regime: for instance, the lighting and system ceilings were designed by the architect and his office.
Looking at the section through the ceiling and the facade we can see how the technical services were given shape in the design. The system ceiling is not comprised of standard panels but has a sleek finish of stretched imitation leather. The reflectors in the fluorescent light trays were fitted with a hinge

so that they could open upwards to allow access to the ducting above the ceiling. Air-conditioning, heating and blinds are worked into the section through the facade. All these elements, which would later become standardized and obtainable from the respective services engineering companies, had to be specially designed for the Tomadohuis. Only later would these items be added to the architecture as specialisms in their own right and a new 'regime' in office design would ensue. The use of air-conditioning and system ceilings, the simultaneous and integrated design of lighting, and the inclusion of all manner of appliances and electric operation have since become the norm, but now in a standardized office with a central corridor between two rows of rooms and a concrete frame construction plus curtain wall.

¬ The combination of experimental factors in office, design and equipment is unique to Tomado and was never repeated in this concentration. This is in fact a hallmark of various of Maaskant's pioneering buildings. It seems as though he and his firm sought to develop new standard types, yet the Wholesale Building, the Technicon school complex (both in Rotterdam), the Tomadohuis and the Tomado factory are so experimental as prototypes that there were to be no repeat performances. Each and every one was and is unique, in the way that designer cars like the Volkswagen Karman Gia or the Peugeot Pinin Farina were the swish exclusive versions of the standard mass-produced fare and were only ever made in a small batch. Instead of marking the onset of a typology, the Tomadohuis is a special case, a monument to Tomado.

NOTES

1 Newspaper article about the Tomado concern, unattributed and undated.

2 Idem.

3 Idem.

4 H.A. Maaskant, 'Het Tomadohuis te Dordrecht', *Bouwkundig Weekblad* 1962 no. 12, 254.

5 Ibid., 245. Maaskant would make sporadic use of the curtain wall principle in later works.

6 H.A. Maaskant, 'Tomadokantoor te Dordrecht', *Bouw* 1958 no. 36, 926.

7 A. Buffinga, 'Tomadohuis kritisch bezien', *Bouw* 1962 no. 24, 84.

8 The glass sculpture came from the Brussels World's Fair of 1958, where Maaskant had advised Van der Togt to acquire the thing on the principle of 'buy it, we can always use it' (*Bouw* 1962 no. 24, 848). Wim van der Weerd of Maaskant's office regrouped it for display in the hall of the Tomadohuis.

9 'Architecten over het Tomado-kantoor', *Bouw* 1962 no. 44, 1608.

10 F.E. Röntgen, 'Het Tomadohuis te Dordrecht', *Polytechnisch Tijdschrift* 7-9-1962, 706b.

11 Pol Kleijn, 'Het Tomadohuis in Dordrecht', *Goed Wonen* 1962 no. 7, 210-211.

12 These were intended for burning used sanitary towels!

13 H.A. Maaskant, 'Het Tomadohuis te Dordrecht', *Bouwkundig Weekblad* 1962 no. 12, 246.

14 H.A. Maaskant, 'Tomadokantoor te Dordrecht', *Bouw* 1958 no. 36, 928.

15 Idem.

16 'Kaal', *Bouw* 1958 no. 43, 1119.

17 Idem.

18 *Techniek in Nederland in de twintigste eeuw, kantoor en informatietechnologie*, Zutphen 1998 299.

19 Pol Kleijn, 'Wonen buiten de woning. Het Tomadohuis in Dordrecht', Goed Wonen 1962 no. 7, 210.

20 'Kaal', *Bouw* 1958 no. 43, 1119.

21 For this see *Techniek in Nederland in de twintigste eeuw, kantoor en informatietechnologie*, Zutphen 1998, 37-51.

22 Pol Kleijn, 'Wonen buiten de woning. Het Tomadohuis in Dordrecht', *Goed Wonen* 1962 no. 7, 210.

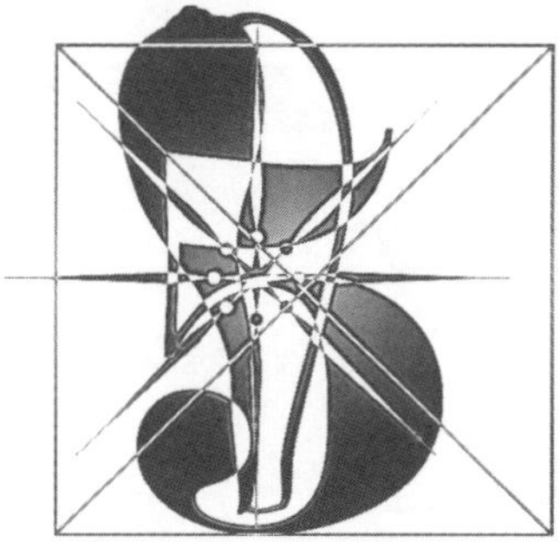

ENTRANCE HALL ON THE GROUND FLOOR

CANTEEN ON THE TOP FLOOR

ARTWORK BY GLASS ARTIST JOOP VAN DEN BROEK

ENTRANCE HALL ON THE FIRST FLOOR

ENTRANCE HALL

THE TOMADOHUIS JUST AFTER COMPLETION IN 1962

Gizmoism and Gadgetry

The world of Reyner Banham

Reyner Banham died on the job, admiring the intricate craftsmanship of the high-tech life-support system to which he was hooked up and writing his very last text, 'A Black Box,' which explored what, if anything, positively distinguishes architecture from other modes of design and manufacture.

Reyner Banham's distrust of architecture was legendary, as was his love for technology. But the image of the plugged-in, hippie engineer/historian has somehow blunted some of the potential effect of his writing. In an early essay, 'The New Brutalism' of 1955, he described such an effect: 'Introduce an observer into any field of forces, influences or communications and that field becomes distorted. It is common opinion that Das Kapital has played old harry with capitalism, so that Marxists can hardly recognize it when they see it, and the widespread diffusion of Freud's ideas has wrought such havoc with clinical psychology that any intelligent patient can make a nervous wreck of his analyst. What has been the influence of contemporary architectural historians on the history of contemporary architecture?' (p. 7).

This was, of course, aimed at those historians — the Pevsners, Giedions, Richardses — whose views regarding the straight path — the teleology — of Modernism had produced a lame style that was then, in the mid-1950s, being challenged by the New Brutalists, who looked not to the history books but to everyday life. Now, what was Banham himself looking at, and what did his observations produce? Well, he focused on clever gadgets, on car design, and on highways; he made technology groovy; he supported and promoted Archigram and high-tech Brit-arch. In a way, then, the success of Norman Foster, Richard Rogers and Renzo Piano, and the technodelica three-times-removed of some contemporary would-be avant-gardists, can be partly attributed to Banham, as can the ever-increasing quantity of books about Los Angeles sold in stores all over the world.

But this sense of his influence is misleading, really — you might say the landmine fizzled out. Banham might also have silenced the contemporary and future metaphysical warbling about architectural space, tectonics, human scale, representation, complexity, the public realm, undecidability, the interstitial, l'informe, etc. Just imagine if R.B. were still alive, talking about in-line skating, drum 'n bass music, and airport conurbations, with the ANY Corporation just a grease-stain on Peter Eisenman's glasses.

Why didn't Banham succeed in sufficiently distorting the field in which he played? Because, in the reception of his work, the techno thing, the beard and mini-cycle thing, and the history thing were all separated from their grounding: a rich, excitable and coherent view of an urbanizing society, a view that was beautifully constructed and that developed as a kind of basso continuo through four decades of writing. And it was not merely a view, but also a programme to be fought for; this becomes clear from the astonishing collection of writings brought together recently under the title A Critic Writes. From the admiration for the car designers of Detroit, to the analysis of ice-cream-cart art, the evocation of power stations, the execration of the Getty Museum, the historiography of the motel, the archaeology of the sheriff's star, the anthropology of the bolo tie, the survey of Frank Lloyd Wright, all the way to the celebration of air shows, Banham's critique of design was always founded in a strong commitment to the people who were using and adapting and living on the land.

Banham treats the technological gizmos and gadgets he loved to use and write about primarily as colonization devices: minicycles to colonize London, cars and caravans to colonize the landscape, air-conditioning machines to colonize the climate. The backdrop was always America. Thus he develops the theme of the Great Gizmo: 'The quintessential gadgetry of the pioneering frontiersman had to be carried across trackless country, set down in a wild place, and left to transform that hostile environment without skilled attention. Its function was to bring instant order or human comfort into a situation which had previously been an undifferentiated mess' (p. 110). The gizmo not only serves to colonize the wilderness but also to improve the nasty pre-industrial city: 'North America's cities of pre-industrial foundation — Montreal, Boston, New York, Philadelphia through to New Orleans — could be regarded as the archaeological remains of a culture that ought to have died when the gizmos came in. They represent the kind of enormously massive infrastructural deposits that are left behind by handicraft civilizations, for (in the absence of rapid communications and compact artificial power sources) the only way to get anything even half-way clever done was to pile men up in vast unhygienic heaps' (pp. 116-117). Being a historian and an observer, Banham presents his programme of urban dispersion by gadgetry not as something new and original — as did his architectural avant-garde contemporaries at Superstudio or Archigram — but as a valid historical tendency, as something real that has been going on for ages, that has a tradition, and that is happening at this moment somewhere near you. Banham shows that Frank Lloyd Wright saw it, too. 'The distributive civilization of gizmo culture is here already. . .,' Banham wrote in 'The Great Gizmo' of 1965, adding that that may not sound like 'a very original observation thirty years after Frank Lloyd Wright's injunction to "Watch the little gas station ['it is the agent of decentralization']". . . .' (p. 117).

In its references to Frank Lloyd Wright's Broadacre City, especially, Banham's 'distributive gizmo' can sound like some kind of anti-urban, techno-pastoralism. But I would argue that we must recognize it as urbanism, as the projection of new urban models that might look more like suburbia than urbia, but that are in fact, in their alignment with contemporary culture and everyday life, more urban than our contemporary cities. Nowadays, Banham seems to be saying, exurbia is more inclusive than urbia and therefore more urban. In '1960: Stocktaking', published in *The Architectural Review*, he put it this way: 'The idea of cities is an ineradicable part of the operational lore of civilization — a word which implies cities anyhow. The concepts we have of cities are as old as philosophy, and are so rooted in the language of cultured discourse that to say "Cities should be compact" is to commit a tautology — we cannot conceive of a diffuse city, and have invented other words, such as conurbation, subtopia, to underline our inability to conceive it' (p. 61). Helping us to conceive of a diffuse city is what Banham did, and he used all registers: the architectural-historical, the journalistic, the critical, the technical, the pedagogical, etc. Each of the pieces in this new anthology explores one aspect, one attribute, or one player in the contemporary, crystallizing urban globe. Pointing out how big things and little things are all connected was Banham's speciality, and he focused not on space and form, as his Team X peers did, but on the technologies, economics and aesthetics of the modern world. Thus 'Paleface Trash,' the 1973 piece about the bolo tie, becomes not just a campy exercise but a fascinating discussion of how pseudo-folklore is distributed through the interconnected spaces of North American airline terminals as talismans against the white man's burden of non-place angst. And the 1977 essay 'Grass Above, Glass Around', an otherwise classic piece of architectural critique on Norman Foster's Willis, Faber and Dumas headquarters in Ipswich, shows how the mutation of historical urban tissue by motorways and glass office boxes can provoke an entirely new set of townscape-like effects, such as 'fitting in' by faceted reflection, weak-form footprints, and violent visual discontinuity.

Making modern urban life conceivable within and without the city was one of Banham's main subjects; mostly he wrote about it, sometimes he proposed projects. In 1969 Banham was part of a gang of four — consisting of the professor of planning Peter Hall, the architect Cedric Price, and Paul Barker, the sociologist and editor of Banham's favourite periodical, New Society — that proposed a radical experiment called Non-plan. (In fact, although the anthology does not include writings about Non-plan, Hall, Price and Barker, together with Mary Banham and Sutherland Lyall, have put together this new anthology; it is almost like a late wake, a return to an adventure that, as Peter Hall writes in his foreword, 'conferred on a group of us — he, Paul Barker, Cedric Price, and me — a certain collective notoriety' (p. xv)). Non-plan was a reaction to the sophisticated and ubiquitous post-war British planning system which had stretched a blanket of restrictions over the entire landscape. According to the Non-plan four, this was based on a set of values inherited from a class-based, pre-war society and could no longer accommodate the real dynamics of everyday life in the 1960s and 70s: 'To impose rigid controls, in order to frustrate people in achieving the space standards they require, represents simply the revived personal or class judgments of the people who are making the decision.'[1] In the end this was an attack on overdetermination of space and a plea for the creative powers of unplanned urban processes. The gang proposed to get acquainted with these processes by creating Non-plan oases in the desert of planning, and seeing what would happen there. As Banham wrote, 'At the least, one would find out what people want; at the most, one might discover the hidden style of mid-20th century Britain.'[2]

Three areas in the south-east of Britain were hypothetically relieved of all planning restrictions; the Non-planners then described how they might be expected to develop, given contemporary demographics, economics, technology and especially consumer culture. For the area north of the new town of Harlow, called Constable country because of the bucolic landscape featured in John Constable's paintings, the gang hypothesized that strip urbanization might develop between the towns and villages connected by the A11 motorway. Precisely the type of development that most official planning was trying to stop was described by the fab four as positively delectable:

'Actually the close-textured, tree-grown, Constable-type country is supposed to be able to absorb practically anything that is not taller than a grown tree, and the buildings which free enterprise would put up in this planning-free situation would not be half that height... So this small scale, rather private landscape might barely reveal its new commercial buildings to the eye. But this would be very bad commercial practice, since an invisible building is no advertisement, and there would certainly have to be a compensatory efflorescence of large and conspicuous advertising signs. The overall result could thus be low commercial buildings set well back from the road behind adequate parking courts, backed by tall trees and fronted by tall signs, with a soft roly-poly countryside appearing behind.'[3]

Another scenario was for the Southampton/Isle of Wight area, in which the preservationist lobby permitted only 'posh leisure zones'. Non-plan now lets the sexually and automotively liberated working class create their own 'pleb leisure zones': 'Large retractable marinas would have sail-in movies and row-in bars. Beach buggies would drive through the heartland. Particular villages, especially on the Isle of Wight, would be got up as showpieces. Britain's first giant dome would rise on the Isle of Wight coast: the first all-weather, all-public Ile du Levant nudist scene in the country — thermostatically controlled and ten bob a head.'[4] For the region between Sheffield and Nottingham — called Lawrence country, because Lady Chatterley's Lover was set there — a scattering of suburban clusters was foreseen as developing between stretches of forest. To preserve the much-loved large parklands, the quartet proposed simply that interested parties should acquire them: 'Land for these parks would simply be bought in the market by a state Countryside Commission because the social benefits from recreation would outweigh those from development.'[5] They seem to be saying: 'if the state wants to forbid things, let 'em do it on their own property!'

Although Non-plan might have conferred 'a certain collective notoriety' on the four at the time, it certainly has not survived as one of the famous urban concepts of the 1960s and 70s. This is due probably to the fact that Non-plan could not be reduced to an architectural image; and also, of course, to the fact that it was not proposed as a design, but as an experimental project. Non-plan never projected an imagery upon cities (and, in any case, real cities always refuse to conform to these kind of expectations); instead, it stayed close to the 'minutiae of everyday life', using these, instead of the drawing board, as its point of departure. As urbanism, Non-plan was radical. Not only did it seem to possess a much greater potential to 'make a difference' than did restrictive planning laws, it also promised a new kind of bucolic landscape, car-fed and unashamedly populist. The 'designing' was found not in drawings, not even in the noting of functions, but in the selection of areas, the specifying of certain land-use tendencies and the subtraction of territorial claims. Non-plan was powered by a populist ideology, informed by a large imagination and a sharp aesthetic eye; it is indeed design.

Moreover, its unit of urbanistic manipulation was not the planning document, but the (Ur)Banhamian gizmo: the intelligently crafted, efficiently functioning, appropriately beautified object, for example, the filling station, houseboat, car, motel, airplane, telephone, Coke dispenser, the bungalow with all mod cons, the architectural masterpiece, country church, etc. While in America the gizmo served to transform the wilderness into an inhabitable space, in 'sensible' countries like England, or for that matter Holland, the gizmo can hack a path through the forest of planning restrictions, creating space for the 'style' of the period. And style pertains equally to the style of the object as to the style of life in which it plays its role.

Non-plan suggests a mode of urbanism that is still worthwhile. It recognized the unplanned dynamics of the 'second machine age,' but did not trap them in a dialectic system of 'order' versus 'chaos'; nor did it trap them in a form of complexity represented in form, as Banham's Team X peers did and as the current avant-garde still does. This 'newly new' urbanism would be object-oriented, not territorial; it would use techniques of extrapolation, exchange, prediction, dispersion, networking, and graphic and industrial design, and it would involve lots of driving, walking, flying and cycling around to see what's really going on. Its heart lies in the ambiguous territory between surveying and actual intervention; its design technique lies in the precise framing of a piece of reality.

Banham observes the attributes of urban society very hard and with great concentration, just as one should observe a church by Hawksmoor or an airplane engine. And today the list of Banham's urban gizmos might include the Powerbook, the condom dispenser, the mobile phone, the methadone van, the mobile sound system and the freight container. In these and other gizmos one sees contemporary life.

In the end, it would be reductive to equate Banham's thinking and writing with a single urbanist model. The only analogy that fits this oeuvre is the thing itself: a big, diffuse metropolis.

Review of A CRITIC WRITES, ESSAYS BY REYNER BANHAM

SELECTED BY MARY BANHAM, PAUL BARKER, SUTHERLAND LYALL AND CEDRIC PRICE

BERKELEY: UNIVERSITY OF CALIFORNIA PRESS, 1996

***Notes** 1. Reyner Banham, Paul Barker, Cedric Price and Peter Hall, 'Non-plan: An Experiment in Freedom,' in* New Society, *20 March 1969, no. 338, 435-443. 2. Ibid. 3. Ibid. 4. Ibid. 5. Ibid.*

Reyner Banham in London, 1964

Reyner Banham in Silurian Lake, California, 1978

Graham Percy

tionate) traffic load on the A11, which probably ought to have been let rip to develop as a thick local "midway", rather than being regarded, as at present, as an inefficient trunk route to remoter parts of East Anglia. The building of the M11 motorway (which an airport at Nuthampstead would certainly hasten) will lift the through-traffic load from the old A11 trunk, but will leave untouched the unacknowledged local pressures to which that road is increasingly subject in its role as a kind of diffuse, linear "downtown" for the whole area between Potter Street and the Chesterfords. These pressures are revealed not only by the eruption of more motels than their national average distribution would suggest (two at Epping, one at Harlow, others rumoured further north) but even more clearly by the constant widenings, re-alignments and general tinkering with the A11 to cope with the local traffic crossing or turning on and off it.

Of course, Harlow New Town is the major cause of hidden pressures on the whole area. Not in the way in which, for instance, Stevenage has become a focus for junkie activity in the northern home counties, but simply because the introduction of a large and unbalanced new population in any area brings with it many more demands and needs than can be accommodated by the building of homes, schools and community centres. Harlow has been parasitical on surrounding communities for entertainment, to take only one example, ever since it was founded—and Bishop's Stortford appeared to be profiting handsomely from the New Town's unsatisfied needs in its early days.

Pressures of this kind appear to be contained for the moment, but it will be physically impossible to contain them if Harlow grows much bigger. And, if the population target of about 100,000 is achieved, Harlow will be the largest settlement on the A11 between the Greater London boundary and Norwich, and must make dependent suburbs of all other roadside communities from Epping to the Chesterfords, including Stortford and Saffron Walden, and the Ware/Hertford bijou mini-conurbation. And then add to this the effect of an airport, with all the attraction that scheduled flights would have for factory owners—consequently for speculative house builders. (One ought to remember, too, that there's an airport at Stansted *already*—and, though small, not all that tranquil.)

The result of these pressures would not, probably, look like the prewar ribbon development (of evil fame). The lifting of planning restrictions would not simply connect all the A11 villages into a continuous

Reyner Banham, Paul Barker, Peter Hall and Cedric Price, 'Non-plan: An Experiment in Freedom', 1969

^ Irvine, California, 2001 v Elysian Valley, Los Angeles, 2001

Hancock Park, Los Angeles, 2001

Glow-in-the-Dark store, Irvine, California, 2001

Dr. Jerde's Urban Rejuvenation Center

REVIEW OF **Frances Anderton with Ray Bradbury, Margaret Crawford, Norman M. Klein & Craig Hodgetts**, *You Are Here. The Jerde Partnership International* LONDON: PHAIDON PRESS PIMITED, 1999

We were there; in Los Angeles I mean. In the middle of all the trashy splendour, one phenomenon stood out and made us realize how much work we would still have to do to become part of the urban culture spreading from this city. Everywhere we went we found flyers, magazine ads, billboards and radio jingles promoting Dr. Matlock's Laser Vaginal Rejuvenation Center for the Enhancement of Sexual Gratification on Sunset Boulevard. On Dr Matlock's web site, carefully rendered perspectives and plainly lucid diagrams explain the procedure that is aimed at women who through vaginal relaxation experience a loss of quality in their sex-life. Through laser-stimuli the muscles of the perineum are strengthened and the grip of the vulva is tightened. The effect is readable on the Masters & Johnson graph of the female orgasm, making the rise towards the plateau of excitement steeper, the duration of the plateau longer and the ripples and peaks that indicate the orgasm or orgasms higher and more frequent. (Yes it does look like a datascape.) Vaginally rejuvenated women have improved (sex)lives, they feel more secure, look more secure, become more beautiful and achieve more. Dr. Matlock is no charlatan, neither is he sleazy; he is a respected member of many venerable medical and gynaecological societies and institutions, and regularly lectures and publishes on his subject.

During that same trip we visited the office of the Jerde Partnership on Ocean Front Walk in Venice. We saw endless artist's impressions and photographs of building blocks all over the world whose insides billow and fold, are covered with a soft coat of greenery and have streams of water and people eddying through swirling canals and congregating in great big egg-like domes from where they watch a particularly engaging moment of urban collectivity happening on a lower level. Vertical elements like towers or slabs are either shrouded or hardly represented at all. The aerial views are always nocturnal and suggest that the giant malls, urban entertainment centres, mixed use projects, casinos and town centres are illuminated to dramatic effect by spotlights that are suspended from the sky. The insides of the building blocks seem to burst through the skin on one or two points, creating huge apertures radiating light and movement and drawing in everything in sight.

We were there too; we used to live in one of the vertical elements sprouting from a Jerde-designed multi-use development in the centre of Rotterdam. From our living room on the thirteenth floor we could see the shoppers flowing towards the retail canyon cut into the ground underneath; there the cut stone surfaces, slippery with water gushing from fountains, guided the people towards the mysterious cave in the middle where the shopping area is connected to the tube station. Even on Sundays, we couldn't leave our house without being swept up by the droves of shoppers guided by some strange collective impulse, like the zombies staggering around the mall in George Romero's **Dawn of the Dead**. And now there is the long awaited book on the Jerde Partnership, describing at length and beautifully illustrating 25 projects all over the world, one of which is the same Beursplein development in Rotterdam. 'Hired by developers and city managers around the world to transform sites inside and outside of urban environments, the Jerde Partnership International is brought in to analyse what could improve the life of a designated area, street, neighbourhood or city. The firm devises site-specific, large-scale strategies for 'place-making', weaving together 'objects' in the modern urban landscape, in order to stimulate social and economic regeneration, encouraging new vitality and interaction.' After leafing through the book and seeing all the folds, all the 'sensuous curves', 'slightly tilted mounds' opening up to reveal 'verdant canyons' and the eggs tucked away in the developments' deepest recesses, it was only when I read the blurb on the dust jacket that it hit me: Dr. Jerde's Urban Rejuvenation Center. Three quotes by the doctor: 'Our curves are not formal but perceptual; they are used to draw people in'; 'We are like psychoanalysts, uncovering the dreams of our clients and making them come true'; and 'We are trying to build the metaphor for the earth.' Jerde is the opposite of most International Architects whose projects are used to regenerate cities. While their paradigm is the free-standing object that by its size, its form or its skin attracts and impresses the people that swarm around it and in doing so jolts the city back into action, Jerde uses the insides, the viscera, the phantasmagorical interiors that let the people swarm through them and the city throbs with life again. So, to use the metaphor for the last time, it is a question of vaginal rejuvenation versus penis enlargement as forms of urban therapy.

Dr. Jerde's urban therapy however seems to have started out as cosmetics and accessorizing; so much becomes clear from the first project documented in **You Are Here**: the transformation of Los Angeles into a festive public arena for the 1984 Olympic Games. For the ludicrous amount of $10 million this cheapest of all Olympic Games gave Jerde the job to dress the city up using confetti, folded paper, cardboard, fabric and not one bit of brick and mortar. Working together with a team of graphic designers Jerde created a kit of parts with which they could create towers, tents, hang banners over streets, redecorate stadiums and swimming pools and create festival areas. The kit of parts was used in small and big interventions all over the city and functioned as a routeing system and decoration at the same time. The language was one of simple but gaudy colours, symbols, signs, lettering and flowers. There is no other project, except maybe the Groningen Museum built in the nineties to a design by Alessandro Mendini, that so perfectly captures the spirit of the eighties. Its most impressive quality, and the one that should be the most thought-provoking, is that this low budget, momentary intervention was an incredibly successful piece of urban planning, succeeding in the impossible task of making Los Angeles into a whole city for a couple of weeks. This was a one-off procedure though; it was never really followed up by Jerde himself, and more worryingly never really led to a school or a wave or even to a hype of momentary urbanism in the magazines or in Academia, let alone in practice. Using confetti and folded paper instead of brick and mortar to transform a city is such a beautiful move that it makes me feel sure that very soon we will come back to this project and copy it to death. Why? Because it's archaic, popular, global and cheap (go to wedding parties in India or Day of the Dead in Mexico and you will see coloured-paper urbanism in practice) and it challenges the ideas about urban planning that were handed down to us.

-One year after the Olympics another project by the Jerde Partnership was completed: Horton Plaza in San Diego. Since this development was the reason that Jerde quit his job at the retail architecture firm of Charles Kober and started his own firm in 1977, we should see it as his real debut. And a devastatingly assured debut it was, basically laying down the law for all Jerde projects to come, and reducing the LA Olympics project to an incident. The story of Horton Plaza reads like a screenplay for a corny television film based on real events. The mayor of the city persuaded the hard-nosed developer Ernest Hahn to build a shopping centre in the blighted downtown of San Diego. Hahn asked the semi-retired mall designer Jerde for 'one more mission' and realize the ideas that he had been unable to carry out in the last ten years. Jerde decided to create a total experience, where inside the six abandoned building blocks a wholly absorbing allegory of 'the urban experience' would be the carrier for the retail stores. To convince the developers Jerde staged a sort of Punch and Judy show. First a team of 'experience makers' drew and collaged a street scene out of fragments of fantasy Latin American, Italian, Moorish and Spanish town centres, theatre, fountains, sculpture etc. Then architects came and put up scaffolding to hold up the street scene, then came puppeteers in black turtlenecks and balaclavas against a black background that held spotlights and played out the street scene; the curtain was raised, the developers gasped, wiped away their tears and pulled out their chequebooks. The actual construction wasn't much different, the street-collages were made of cheap stuccoed constructions that created the inside decor of the canyon that runs through the six blocks in San Diego. The canyon is a configuration of straight and curved facades, circular domed spaces and triangular volumes jutting in. A total loss of orientation and a blissful feeling of immersion that keeps the people, and their money, flowing is the result. In the first year Horton Plaza attracted 25 million visitors and became a magnet that caused the reconstruction of the nearby waterfront and the historic district. In her introductory essay Frances Anderton efficiently wraps up the plot: 'San Diego's downtown had returned from the dead, and Jon Jerde and his office, the Jerde Partnership International, was launched.'

-The next project, New Port City, in New Jersey across from Wall Street on Manhattan, was never realized but showed that the seemingly site-specific project for Horton Plaza, was in fact just a fragment of an obsessively detailed fantasy world, a kind of autistic micro-universe consisting of spiralling roads and canals, tilted planes, collaged street scenes and a disorienting use of spotlights, mirrors, darkness and colours. In plan the 400 acre, 90 million square foot multi-use urban scheme looks like a coiled-up serpent with dangerous fangs ready to strike at the heart of the 'real' city on the other bank. In section it turns out to be 'a great tilted Disk City', tilting towards Manhattan and deflecting the sun on downtown using 'Egyptian sunlight manipulations'. The tidal Hudson River is fed into cisterns in the heart of the city, and flows back through the spiral canals, creating a gravity-based energy source. The wind is harnessed also; it would not only 'clean' the city, but propel urban sailboats through it. The heart of the city is the mysteriously named 'celebratory space': a huge block with Manhattan-like skyscraper tops from where anti-aircraft lights swing over New Jersey and Manhattan. In the middle is a giant upside-down dome where spectacles are to be played out to the people gathered in the stands. In one drawing the spectacle seems to involve a collapsing Chrysler Building. What are they celebrating? The feverish sketches and diagrams come accompanied by homely drawings of life in New Port City, making it completely convincing and reassuring. The project could be described as the relaxed tissue of the American small town being twisted into a spiral so that near the middle the urban energy reaches a point of unbearable intensity before being beamed at Manhattan to destroy it utterly.

-A little after New Port City Jerde went further with his project for a Satellite New Town near Paris, as an accompaniment to Eurodisney which was then being planned. Again the urban tissue is spread out on a disc and cut through with a spiral system of roads and canals; this time however the spiral does not end in a central climax but, like the axial systems of Louis XIV and of Haussmann, suggests an endless extension. The 6000 acre disc is not tilted but a 'spheroid plane', the top part of an imaginary sphere. 'We are trying to build the metaphor for the earth' as Jerde puts it. In plan the tissue seems to be a better version of Paris: boulevards, building blocks with differently formed interior courtyards, 'passages couvertes' running perpendicular to the boulevards. In section it appears that the tissue is not built up but cut into the mound, creating strange inversions of familiar archetypes: a pyramid of glass sunk into the built mass and penetrated by an aqueduct. What the drawings suggest is a planet entirely covered with Parisian urban tissue, and collective spaces excavated out of it. This planet is still buried in the earth for its biggest part, but will inevitably be completed, detach itself and float off into orbit, like a satellite. Projects like New Port City or the Satellite New Town, seem to be the motherlode - or sim-

Beursplein multi-use urban development, Rotterdam
Insert: George Romero (dir.), Dawn of the Dead, 1978

You won't believe how℠ *good sex can be*

LASER VAGINAL REJUVENATION℠

Our Board Certified gynecologist of

THE LASER VAGINAL REJUVENATION CENTER OF LOS ANGELES

can completely resculpt and rejuvenate the vagina in a 1 hour laser procedure

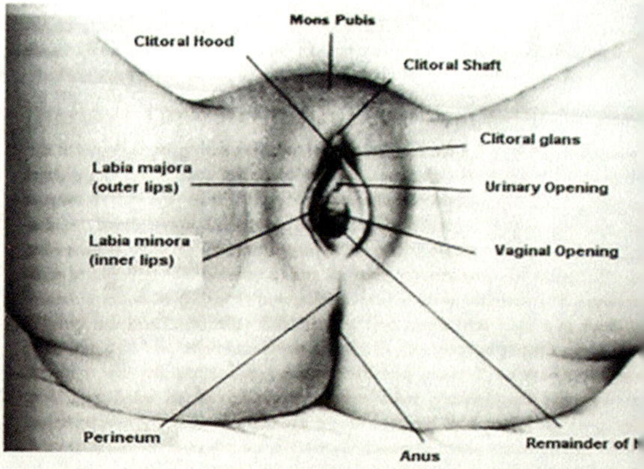

As a sexual biological organism Women are superior to men

Women are multiorgasmic. The female sexual response cycle is unimpeded by a refractory period which prevents successi orgasms in the male.

Laser vaginal rejuvenation was designed to enhance sexual gratification for women with vaginal relaxation. The procedure can also be effective for women who desire to surgically enhance their sexual experience.

Canal City Hakata mixed-use district, Fukuoka

19

VILLAGE
SQUARE
MAIN STREET

ply the mother - of a whole series of projects all around the world. In the heart of a development of incredible density, there lies a verdant but vertiginous canyon, consisting of layer after layer of celebratory public space, framed in cut stone and cut through with spiralling canals. From Rokko Island in Kobe, Canal City Hakata in Fukuoka to Santa Fe town centre or even Beursplein in Rotterdam, they all seem part of an emergent man-made, retail-based but nature infused, geo-eco-psycho-urbanological crust that the earth is breaking out into and that will gradually cover its entire surface.

-If you think my interpretation of the aim of these projects is too fanciful, here is an excerpt from SF writer Ray Bradbury's essay in which he describes his friendship and collaboration with Jerde: 'We threw conversational confetti to the air and ran under to see how much each of us caught. We blueprinted cities, malls and museums by the triple dozen, threw them on the floor, stepped on them, and birthed more with all three gabbing at once. I felt honoured to be allowed in as an amateur Palladio with my meagre experience but Futurist hopes.' And: 'I sat with Jon when the Baltimore Power Plant people asked him to reconceive their waterfront property. With John DeCuir Jr. we came up with some wild Jules Verne, H.G. Wells 21st cum 19th century concepts.'

When I was a young boy in the 1970s I could hardly wait for the moment when I would be an adult living in the year 2000. In a time when **Space 1999** was a science fiction show, I was sure that life in the year 2000 would look and feel like the future. The realization that through habituation the future will always feel like the present and that even trying to imagine it as something new **now** would just make it seem old then was and has always been a great source of disappointment and gloom. The general expectancy of the future as something in-between NASA and giant floating Eames furniture with people in hi-tech pyjamas was gradually replaced by an image of the future as an intensified version of the present combined with a hotchpotch of histories. Desert and jungle planets inhabited by people dressed like mediaeval monks and Chinese emperors, driving roman chariots and Ferrari spacecraft, building Mayan temples and huts from the Iraqi swamps, worshipping Egyptian gods while building androids, writing in Celtic runes and speaking in ultrasound Dolphin squeaks, became the new standard for the imagination of the future. Projecting the future was no longer about extrapolating the best of the present into an ideal, modernistic and progressive future, but a giant leap backwards into all the pasts and futures that have ever existed or have been imagined, taking them apart and reconfiguring the pieces into endless numbers of future worlds. The future will look like the future because it will look like all the pasts and all the presents mixed together in a giant salad bowl. Ray Bradbury describes the epiphany of this new history-soaked future to his friend Jon Jerde during a visit to the Disney studios: 'If Jon Jerde's hair did not stand on end, it bristled; if cold chills did not ripple his neck, I imagined them. He moved faster than I could in this sublime territory. Time does not have to die, it all said.

^ Horton Plaza, six-block mixed-use urban centre, San Diego
< Los Angeles Olympic Games, 1984, kit of parts

Fashions do not have to go out of fashion. Palladio only seems dead, sound his alarm clock. Goya and Klee gone? Still here! Sir John Soane's Museum in London, with its Piranesis and Hogarths still alive alive-o? Turn left, then right in Imagineering.'

-This approach becomes abundantly clear in the recently completed Steve Wynn Casino in Las Vegas: The Bellagio. It is a huge flat building, with an Italianate hotel slab rising from it. The Casino breaks out in a crust of Italian Lakeside Villas on a lake and looks out on Paris with its Eiffel Tower. The lakeside villa crust looks completely and utterly convincing; the fact that cabs drive through it, that the dome of the Pantheon has escalators in it, that you are wearing sneakers, that a villa on Lake Como has valet parking, that 19th century Paris is nearing completion, that you have a good view of the pyramid and the sphinx, that the French Impressionist paintings on the wall next to the Gucci Shop are real, makes for a close encounter with the future. Many times however Jerde does not go centuries back to other continents, but stays close, very, very close, which has an even more disorienting effect. For Universal Studios in the Hollywood Hills, Jerde designed Universal Citywalk, a Horton Plaza-like 'street' with retail, restaurants, streetlife within a collage of historical cityscapes that links the parking lots, the studios, the theme park, the amphitheatre and the cinema complex. The street is designed as a Hollywood version of Hollywood in Hollywood: a collage of thirties and fifties Hollywood architecture, with movie posters, King Kong models dangling from art-deco movie houses, palm trees, motels (in a pedestrian area), fifties hamburger restaurants etc. Even before the original Hollywood is entirely destroyed, there is already a themed version of it, just around the corner. The mix of real and fake, past and future, copy and original becomes even more dense in another project for Las Vegas: The Fremont Street Experience. The change-over of Las Vegas to a family-oriented entertainment and residential capital, with huge historically themed complexes like the Bellagio, means the gradual demise of the classic, sleazy, Venturian Las Vegas, of decorated sheds on the strip that look like hell during the day and heaven during the night. The disappearing Las Vegas of 'glitter gulch' is the theme of a 'linear, urban canopy of light, music and sound' that reactivates the very same glitter gulch. It runs through six blocks, is 600 metres long, and with its 'celestial vault' containing 2.1 million lights and its 540,000 watt sound system and its facades that are a collage of the typical 50s Las Vegas strip architecture, turns the experience of the street into a real multimedia show, a kind of pedestrian roller-coaster ride, with giant violins flying and astrological signs flying overhead and twenty sunsets a day. The theme is not only Vegas, but 'the street' in general. In that way Jerde not only pays homage to it like he does to Italian Lakeside Villa Architecture, but declares the original to be a thing of a distant and romantic past, so that in its remixed and amplified version it may become futuristic.

-Jon Jerde seems to us Europeans one of these typical American populist artist-inventor-businessmen:
H.P. Barnum, John Portman,

Cecil B. de Mille, Ron Hubbard, Buckminster Fuller, Howard Hughes, Walt Disney, Henry Ford, Andy Warhol. He belongs to a family of haunted showmen who combine idiosyncratic, nearly autistic personal belief-systems with an incredible gift for mass communication, and who combine the most esoteric and utopian motivations with a relentless opportunism and a near perfect success rate. Their total lack of irony, the intensity of their vision and their hyper-pragmatism have permitted them to create breakthroughs and paradigm shifts that changed their profession for ever and sometimes even the world. Jon Jerde's equivalent to Ford's Model T is an urban project that begins with the theme, then works to the theatrical experience, then builds the necessary stage set, then designs architecture that can support the sets and then searches for programmes and activities that can pay for and fill up the architectural substance that holds up the sets, that enhance the experience etc. The spatial inside-outness of his projects is no less than a metaphor for the inside-outness of the trajectory leading up to them. Therefore it is not his populism or his nostalgia that makes him a radical, but the break with centuries of rationalist thinking behind architecture that makes the authentic architectural experience the result of the transparency of either the tectonic consistency of the building or the analytical process used to form a building out of a given programme. Jerde has not only turned this logic inside out, he has made it work in the real world which, as opposed to the European way of proving paradigm shifts through experimental design and theoretical debate, is the haunted showman's way of getting his point across. The theoretical implications of Jerde's inversion are too great for current architectural discourse which still favours an aesthetic of production over an aesthetic of consumption, and of course is obsessed with good taste. Their importance however is proven by the fact that Jerde's work has sped innovations along in economic theory. In his recent publications on the experience economy, Joseph Pine II refers to the projects of Jerde to describe the shift from a service-based to an experience-based economy. Pine uses many examples of experience-based economic practices like the Rainforest Café, or the Geek Squad (computer repairmen that come to your door dressed in fictional special agents' uniforms), but uses Jerde's projects and the enormous investments they attract to show how experience has become an economic dominant, instead of an added value. Not the quality, the price or the efficiency of the services is the decisive factor for success, but the memorable event, with which they come to us.

-So Jerde is a radical innovator, a revolutionary, whose influence is too deep to be fathomed by the current architecture and urbanism scene just now. Then why is his book so shy? Why are the fantastic photographs, the Richard Scarry-like artist's impressions, the deeply disturbing sketches by Jerde himself, accompanied by three worthy essays by well-respected members of the progressive architectural discourse community? Why didn't they ask Ray Bradbury to keep on going for twenty more pages? Why is the one text that can be read as Jerde's manifesto not published in the book but in a German theory magazine called **Daidalos** (in a special issue about diagrams, for god's sake), accompanied by Jerde's most crazed metaphysical sketchings? Why is this text called 'the ten amendments of urban revitalization'? Is Jerde Moses? Then who is God, and more importantly: who is the golden calf we have started to worship while he was up on the mountain? Is it too much to suspect that a wicked game is being played on us by the Jerde Partnership International? A game aimed at giving Jerde the academic credibility he had been lacking for so long, but which he understands is a way to gain permanent entrance into the subconscious of the design community, as opposed to the incidental campy presence of, say, John Portman. Is this the reason for hiring the second-generation avant-garde firebrand Stephanie Smith fresh from Rem Koolhaas's Harvard Project of the City as a propagandist/stylist of the New? Her position in the office is precarious: a harbinger of nineties trashpop culture inside a design environment drenched in Disneyite nostalgia. The contamination shows in the blurry but garish photos of crowds of people moving through the garish urban interiors, looking more like vidcaps from MTV than stills from Hollywood films. The general impression the book makes is ambiguous however, at once contaminated by contemporary visual culture and academically respectable. A truly remarkable thing about the essays in the book is that they contain some severe criticisms of Jerde's work and especially of his ideas, even when the book is so clearly initiated and paid for by the office. Architectural historian Margaret Crawford for instance writes: 'On the margins of an architectural discourse that privileges theoretical understanding, Jerde is notably unsuccessful. Even his own attempts to codify the principles behind his work are unconvincing: a mixture of leftover post-modern rhetoric, marketing slogans and autobiographical insights.'

-It is as if Jerde knows that giving us his views, his images and pictures of his built work all at once would be too much for the architectural community which he is clearly trying to get a hold on; it would be too dense, too scary, reading the ten commandments and seeing that he actually gets them built and that his crazy sketches are not just expressions, but real working documents; it would alienate him from the current architectural discourse. So instead of dropping a bombshell à la **S,M, L,XL,** Jerde opts for a discrete campaign of silent diplomacy, undercover operations, public contrition and disguises. The seeds have been sown, the cordon sanitaire around bad, corporate architects that has separated Jerde from academia and the avant-garde, is leaking. This is the dawning of a new age; architecture and its discourse will be swept aside by a wave of experiential design coming from inside the institutions of 'progressive' architecture and urban planning. Jerde's crazed paradigms and the many proofs of their effectiveness will unleash the urban and aesthetic obsessions of thousands of still adolescent designers. In schools and offices all around the world they will forget about architectural and theoretical models and turn to their movies, their books, their music, their games, their private fantasies and to their religions to create new and futuristic urban experiences for the Enhancement of our Urban Gratification.

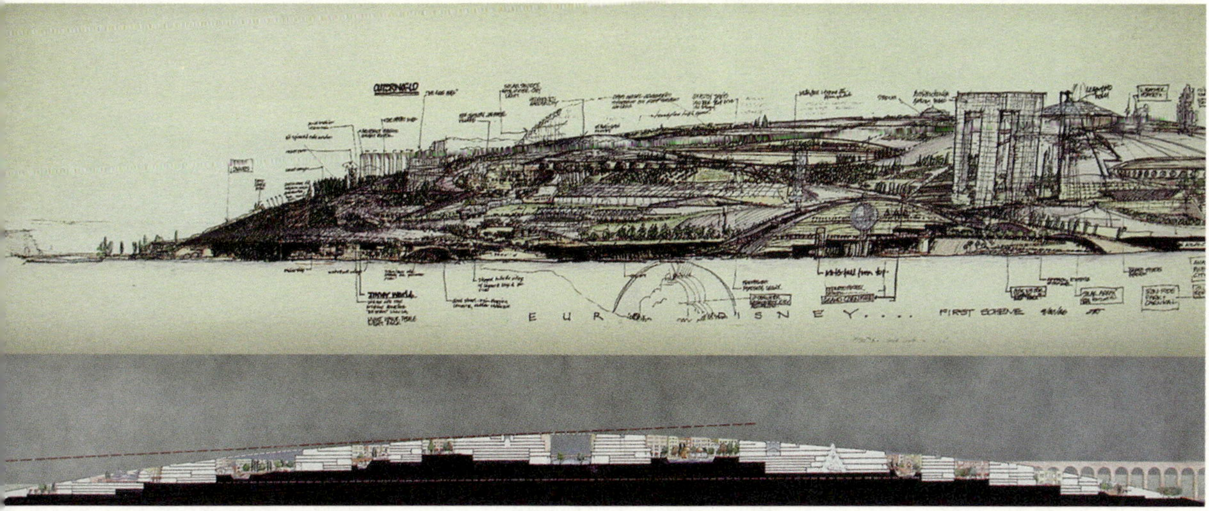

New Port City masterplan for Jersey City
Satellite New Town scheme for Eurodisney, Marne-la-Vallée

Urbanopolis, microcosmic city for the Disney Corporation, Anaheim

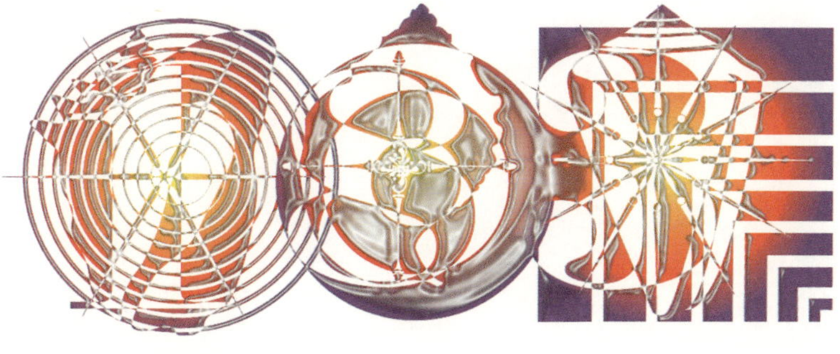

'The Bellagio', hotel and resort casino, Las Vegas

Project for a fantasy world commisioned by Diesel, planning & design: FAT (Fashion Architecture Taste) London

Urbanism as an act of deliverance

BAKEMA ON MONT BLANC

ED TAVERNE

In the library of Jacob Bakema is a copy of one of the most scholarly planning documents from the first half of the twentieth century: *Studi e proposte preliminari per il piano regolatore della Valle d'Aosta* (1943).[1] This beautifully turned out document of some substance (250 pages) is based for the main part on maps, statistics, photographs and montages shown six years earlier at a major exhibition in Rome. This provenance is what gives the book its demonstrative character; an impression strengthened by the way the document is organized. It is not a regional plan for the entire Aosta Valley as the title might have us suppose, but a straight montage of five case-studies of widely differing subjects and treatments. There is, for example, a scintillating geological and sociographic study of the Italian slope of Mont Blanc; a proposal for a new centre for mounting-climbing and winter sports in Breuil; a new masterplan for the ancient town of Aosta; another for a residential district in Ivrea and, lastly, a design for Pila, a complete new tourist centre high in the Alps. Compare the different studies and plans and you will find neither a uniform and methodical approach nor a recognizable architectural style. Pollini and Figini's scheme for Mont Blanc is, in our eyes, arguably the most orthodox: proceeding from a thorough analysis of the natural surroundings, it charts the conditions for local agriculture and stock-breeding, going on to sketch a picture of the social life of a material culture high in the mountains. But it also formulates a programme for the future development of tourism in this region and for laying out and improving road links. All this ends as if naturally with a proposal to revamp a small mountain village as a new local tourist centre. The proposals for Aosta by Banfi, Peressutti and Rogers are a good deal more radical. They concentrate mainly on aspects of climate and location, on demographic studies and on statistical data as regards public health and hygiene. Nor does it stop there. The panels on which the architects present their research show not just graphs and statistics but also photographs which quite deliberately and dramatically set out to underline the deplorable state of life, work and transportation in the former Roman settlement ('evidenza parlante'). The illustrations prepare the spectator, in a manner of speaking, for the far-reaching proposals for a new Aosta as envisaged by the designers: a town admittedly anchored in the existing Roman grid but stripped of all 'irrelevancies' in the ways of streets, houses and squares that had accumulated there since the year dot. The models and maps illustrating the scheme exude a freshness and optimism that could only be justified by being preceded by some hideous turn of events. But there was no such calamity, except perhaps in the minds or pipe dreams of the designers.

Is there life beyond CIAM?

How did this remarkable plan get to end up in Bakema's library? Is there some link between Bakema's contribution to the post-war rebuilding of Rotterdam in particular and the Netherlands in general, and the ideas about architecture and urban design as set down in the *Piano regolatore della Valle d'Aosta?* These are questions we today are scarcely able to answer. Bakema might have been personally presented with them by the likes of Ernesto Rogers or his business associate Belgiojoso, whom he met at one of the many post-war meetings of CIAM or at all events at a Team x gathering. Are there signs that for one or other reason the book's substance found its way into Bakema's intellectual storehouse, and if so, what might these signs be? More questions we have no meaningful answer for at present! The presence of this remarkable planning document in Bakema's library raises issues of which architectural historians were until now scarcely aware. What is needed, in fact, is an enquiry into the routes by which the average architect of the past century has been coming by his information; into the significance of congresses, exhibitions, symposia where architects met and into the value and purpose of the informal contact following thereupon. Granted, we are well informed about the various post-war CIAM and Team x congresses and about the discussions they had there; we know who took part and what their contributions were; there have been transcripts published of speeches and debates. But was there life beyond CIAM and Team x? We have virtually no information as to the purpose served by the official and the more informal meetings within the complex network of large groups of mostly nameless architects. Almost nothing has been published up until now about the impact that magazines, books and congresses had on the exchanging of ideas and designs, and of assistants, draughtsmen and students. Architectural history will have to tap some major sources if it is to get at such information. This should mean making a long-awaited start on systematically accessing the most important post-war architecture magazines; the private collections (letters, jottings, reports, articles) not just of a few 'key' architects but more especially the great mass of largely anonymous designers who despite being responsible for a major chunk of the post-war building stock, have not yet penetrated the top ten in post-war architecture.

Even if one suspects that Bakema did not understand a word of Italian, one must assume that he understood only too well the sheer scope of the *Piano regolatore della Valle d'Aosta* as a planning document. At a time when the results of the CIAM congress on the Functional City (1933) were not yet published and the Nieuwe Bouwen architects had yet to feast their eyes on the documents, maps and analyses of the individual cities presented in Athens and Marseilles, the regional plan introduced by Adriano Olivetti manifested itself as a new, social charter for planning and urban design. Not so much because of the systematic or scholarly set-up of that plan, or because of the way the disparate modes of research and design were roped together. The fascinating thing about the book - for Bakema as well - lies above all in the planning's successful endeavour not only to open up the glorious yet impenetrable mountain landscape but to 'modernize' it too, that is, prime it for contemporary mass culture. The scheme for the Aosta Valley is nothing less than a successful mountaineering expedition. More than seventy-five years after Eugène Viollet-le-Duc's equally successful venture resulted in the publication of a map, Le Massif du Mont-Blanc (1868-1879), this time there was not just a map to show for it but a detailed plan for the urban and rural redesign of a future paradise.[2] And precisely because the planning area was literally so far above the worldly tumult of those war years, the photographs, montages, statistics and pristine models of the *Piano Regolatore della Valle d'Aosta* radiate an urbanistic ideal in which all oppositions - economic, political, technical and social - evaporate into thin air. And it is conceivable that to publish a planning document such as this, and for architects, urbanists and planners to possess it, particularly in the many devastated countries and cities round the North Sea, must have amounted to the yearning for a very real Utopia.

Instrument for a social policy

There would be nothing special about happening across a unique document of this kind in Bakema's library were it not for the fact that it provides an unsuspected key to the ideas, ideals and attendant strategies of a small 'technical' elite with varying roles in the reconstruction of European society in the first postwar decades. Concepts central to these circles were society, plan and technique. A good illustration of the cohesion that existed between these concepts is the introduction to the plan for the Aosta Valley by Adriano Olivetti, initiator and linchpin of a sociocultural movement largely inspired by French personalism (Mounier; De Rougemenont; but in the journal *Comunità* we also regularly comes across the names Mumford and the Tennessee Valley Authority).[3] In his introduction Olivetti explains that the coming decades will have to usher in a new social economics as the expression of 'un tipo di civiltà', a type of civilization. And that plans would have to bring about the necessary link between individual development and social life. Planning, in short, should not be kept restricted to sub-areas defined by planners or economists alone. Nor is it sufficient to have at one's disposal a National Plan or a string of small sector plans. What is lacking, according to Olivetti, is an intermediate regional plan in which the relationships between State, region and city are described and regulated with much greater precision and efficiency. Planning Olivetti sees in the first instance as an instrument for a new social politics: 'The transformation of our way of living is intimately bound up with the launching and developing of such a planning technique as, in its absence, the chaos of our industrial, economic and metropolitan structures will get out of hand and in the long run threaten the harmony between individual and collective life. But that necessary transformation will only come about if the notion of "Humana Civitas" manages to penetrate to the design problematic and if architecture, conceived of as a social service, becomes the point of departure for renewal on all fronts.' The train of thought Olivetti is developing here, with a key role appointed to the sequence of planning, urbanism and architecture in a corporatively ordered society, is not specifically Italian but can be come across in many political and social reconstruction programmes involving architects in Europe during and after the war.

Another, less familiar initiative is that of the Swiss architect Alfred Roth. During the war he prepared a major series of publications on 'the human settlement' entitled Civitas-Sammelwerk: Die Menschliche Siedlung (1943-1950).[4] In 1943 he issued a manifesto and a programme for a great many books of which only two were to materialize: Hans Bernouilli's *Die Stadt und ihr Boden* (Towns and the Land) in 1946 and Roth's own Das Neue Schulhaus (The New School Building) in 1950. As with Olivetti, Roth's Civitas project was not so much concerned with the technical and economic reconstruction of European towns and cities and with the practical contribution architecture could make to the production of urban space. In the manifesto he is primarily mapping a sociocultural programme for a city without physical dimensions; for the 'human settlement' as a prototype of the harmonious society brought about by planning and architecture. Roth - just prior to the war the principal Swiss representative at CIAM - was led to his remarkable venture by the lectures the Finnish architect Aalto had given in Switzerland in the spring of 1943 about the reconstruction of his own country after the devastation of the initial war years. In 1944 Roth wrote: 'Meanwhile the explosion of violence and destruction has spread throughout all the countries caught up in the war. Countless villages and towns, industrial and agricultural areas have been devastated. And more destruction will follow. The real victims of this all-out war are the defenceless civilian population and its dwellings. And we see etched more starkly than

aosta vista da sud

12

la vita famigliare si svolge nelle stalle

D'inverno la stalla è molte volte l'unico ambiente caldo di cui la famiglia dispone e ivi vengono alla luce i figli.

stazione di pila: veduta invernale

CCXLI

La veduta invernale ripete il punto di vista della fotografia estiva a pag. 176. Le costruzioni sono rappresentate nelle loro linee schematiche; a sinistra i nuclei alloggi a piccoli appartamenti, a destra l'albergo turistico e più in fondo le costruzioni che si affacciano sulla piazza centrale. Sullo sfondo campi di sci a sinistra la punta della Valletta e a destra del Tzasetze e del Drink.

LXXIX

Panoramica della catena del Monte Bianco, dalla vetta del Monte Bianco (4810 s/m) alle Grandes Jorasses.

LXXX

ever the image of today's city with its tightly packed buildings, its chaotic jumble of residential and industrial areas, its unresolved issues in the province of infrastructure and land use. An image of utter absurdity [*Sinnwidrigkeit*]. Among the future efforts in post-war rebuilding a prominent place must and shall be accorded the reconstruction of the "human settlement". It is not so much a question of quickly satisfying the most pressing needs; that is, of finding the efficient solution to the housing shortage or combatting unemployment with economic measures. Nor does it concern the impending chaos in physical planning and material facilities. The essence of the "human settlement", of dwelling, is deeply embedded in our nature and inextricably bound up with mental and physical health: "Mit der Begriff der Heimstätte verbindet der Mensch von jeher die Vorstellung von Schutz und Geborgenheit, von Verbundenheit mit den Seinen und festem Stand auf der Erde".'[5]

The 'elites' of post-war reconstruction

It is not difficult to unearth texts like the above in the Netherlands too, say among architects, engineers and housing officials involved in rebuilding Rotterdam - in the library of an architect like Bakema, for instance. Remarkably, such texts draw attention to a discourse on reconstruction in terms of a new Utopia. This regards destruction *and* restoration as twin inducements to accelerate the modernization process. And it is remarkable that with the odd exception the historical backgrounds to these views, not held by architects alone, have yet to be researched. The history as written of the reconstruction of the towns and cities in the post-war Netherlands is still dominated by the stalemate between continuity and breaking with the past. The first strategy focuses principally on the reverberations of pre-war economic, political and social structures as well as on the impact made by corporative models of decision-making and planning largely subscribed to by the occupying forces. Against that, breaking with the past is invariably associated with the theme of Americanizing and the many forms this was able to take until the sixties.

To avoid the pitfalls of making too broad generalizations and to elude the ambush of false oppositions (between traditionalism and modernism, free-enterprise and state economics etc.) the historian Carlo Olmo proposes doing further research into the origins, ideas and strategies of the 'elites' variously involved in the post-war reconstruction, including those of architects, urbanists and planners. Not so much in the form of new biographies but more of intellectual prosopographies analysing the backgrounds, continuities and fault lines in their thinking and acting. Olmo himself has made an interesting first move in this respect with his *Urbanistica e Società Civile. Esperienze e Conoscenza 1945-1960* (1992) which tells of the adventures of Italian architects and urbanists post 1945; of their struggles for public acknowledgement of the intellectual and social status of their profession, of the strategies they deployed in confrontation with the wide variety of institutes for urban, regional and landscape planning. This is a history drawn from a stash of source material, congress reports, magazines and cultural events, all not just shedding light on the continuity, or lack of it, in the ideas of architects and urbanists, but placing the remarkable post-war 'correspondence' between the *forma urbis* and a new social order with great precision in an intellectual climate of politicians, scientists, scholars and architects in search of the fundamentals of a 'democratic urbanism' without having to hand the exact models for the purpose. This discussion was conducted in Italy - and why should it be otherwise in the Netherlands? - in magazines, institutions and movements where myriad factions with the most wide-ranging ideas (about social reality or urban developments) convened without these being immediately noticeable for a particular 'style' or party colour. There were, moreover, remarkable differences between the language, rhetoric and *exempla* architects wielded in the cautious skirmishes with official institutions for housing and spatial planning, and the programmes, manifestos and foreign models staged in their own professional journals. The essence, then, is that the spatial images projected by the 'elites' via all manner of channels are conflicting and interpretable in more than one way. We can identify a strong political moment of personalistic bent (Olivetti and the circle centred on the magazine *Comunità*, suspiciously sounding out the borders with related strands in planning, urbanism and architecture) as well as an urbanistic culture with a steadily growing self-awareness that seeks to fix its position by emulating foreign examples. And it is striking that the lack of a sense of reality, the incapacity to get a firm grasp of the existing legal, political and financial structures, is in inverse proportion to the orientation on experiences and techniques on the planning front in England and the United States. The principal focus is on concepts relating to an urbanism for a 'made-to-measure society', with the residential unit or 'cluster' an obvious favourite. In magazines like *Metron* or *Politecnico*, one issue after another (between 1945 and 1951) takes an in-depth look at almost every icon of reconstruction, from Lewis Mumford's regionalism to Clarence Perry's neighbourhood unit to Ernest Simon's twenty-year plan for rebuilding Britain. The 'organic' cities of Saarinen, Sharp and Abercrombie are not forgotten either. Bruno Zevi gets the opportunity to present Abercrombie's Greater London Plan (1944) as an example of an urbanism that not only makes good the damage inflicted but most importantly is to eradicate for all time the shortcomings of the Victorian town. Both *Comunità* and *Metron* display not just countless foreign urbanistic models as 'potential' new paradigms for an Italian 'urbanistica'; they also define the contours of a new social contract for the dwelling-house. Nor do they leave aside the experiments with standardization and normalization, and with technological innovation in the construction industry. But here again these are presented with a sense of reservation: industrial constructional systems only have meaning in a social programme brought about exclusively by a planning of 'arte di governo'. Through this editorial process of selecting and screening mainly British and American examples of planning, urbanism and housing there is a directly perceivable break with all foregoing 'idées reçues' of Italian urban design culture. Typical of this yearning for an 'urbanism of deliverance' is the inclusion of a contribution by Joseph Hudnut, a key figure in the Crimson Connection of Harvard University whose members also boasted Johnson and Hitchcock (*The International Style,* 1932).[6] In it Hudnut argues in recalcitrant tones for the American suburb so scorned by the Moderns, characterizing it as a preeminent example of a 'democratic urbanism'. In a remarkable parallel with the much better-known *The Castles on the Ground. The Anatomy of Suburbia* (1946) by the English architectural critic J.M. Richards, Hudnut expresses the following: 'I often think that the eclectic spirit that speaks from these suburbs comes much closer, both intuitively and intellectually, to the essence of architecture than to property development, with which it is usually associated. By this I mean the cool, calculating brains that understand nothing other than economics and construction technology.' Hudnut depicts the suburb as an example of an architecture (and urban design) that resolutely advertises itself as political and democratic inasmuch as its plan, its brickwork and construction encapsulate ideals expressed elsewhere by that same community at the polling booth. Yet in the end it was up to Martin Wagner and Walter Gropius, armed with American ideas on the civic centre and urban renewal, to ditch once and for all not just the paradigms of Das Neue Frankfurt, La Ville Radieuse or the Athens Charter, but more generally the existing models of functional zoning that had 'terrorized' the thinking on the city since Joseph Stübben and the Chicago School. Basing their argument in part on the organizing patterns of the Greenbelt Town, they called for the clustering of dwelling and work and for a reappraisal of infrastructure, years before Team x was the hub of such sentiments. Gropius and Wagner moreover enriched the Italian debate with examples of an urbanism that manages to rise to the challenge of quantity - upscaling, the 'new dimension' - aided by new legal, financial and administrative tools.[7]

Curiously enough, the experiences of post-war reconstruction in the Netherlands, and Rotterdam in particular, are seldom if ever held up as an example by *Metron* of *Politecnico.* The same can be said of the experiments made simultaneously in many German towns. This absence is as puzzling as the presence of the

Piano regolatore delle Valle d'Aosta in Bakema's library. An absence, moreover, that contrasts starkly with the well-nigh aggressive presence of the Dutch delegation (the Opbouw group) at the many post-war congresses of CIAM and Team X on whose basis a large part of the Dutch post-war history of planning, urbanism and architecture has been written. It must surely be time for the historians to redirect their gaze; time, simply, to enquire of Bakema what he was looking for on Mont Blanc. That is, to hold up to scrutiny themes such as those of a small 'elite' of architects and urbanists and their ideological contribution to launching new planning instruments for housing and spatial planning. Themes like the impact of new paradigms from the USA, Scandinavia, the UK and Germany on existing concepts in architecture and urbanism. And to ask questions about the part played by magazines, symposia, exhibitions, educational courses and the like in bringing to bear a new knowledge infrastructure for the 'average' architect. Maybe raising such issues and themes is in itself enough to arrive at the insight that the modernizing of society as this was enacted post 1945 in the Netherlands, was less clear-cut, and the links normally made between social reform and spatial transformation less clearly organized, than the non-committal architectural account of the rebuilding of the Netherlands would have us believe.

Notes

1 STUDI E PROPOSTE PRELIMINARI PER IL PIANO REGOLATORE DELLA VALLE D'AOSTA, IVREA 1943

2 P.A FREY, E. VIOLLET-LE-DUC ET LE MASSIF DU MONT-BLANC 1868-1879, LAUSANNE 1988

3 FOR AN ANALYSIS OF OLIVETTI'S IDEAS ABOUT PLANNING SEE M. TAFURI, 'ADRIANO OLIVETTI AND THE COMMUNITAS OF THE INTELLECT' IN: HISTORY OF ITALIAN ARCHITECTURE 1944-1985, CAMBRIDGE (MASS.) 1988, 35-40

4 ALFRED ROTH, ARCHITECT OF CONTINUITY/ARCHITEKT DER KONTINUITÄT, ZÜRICH 1985, 282FF.

5 ORIGINALLY PUBLISHED IN WERK (1, 1944) OF WHICH ROTH WAS EDITOR-IN-CHIEF. REPRINTED IN ALFRED ROTH, OP. CIT., 282

6 HELEN SEARING, 'INTERNATIONAL STYLE: THE CRIMSON CONNECTION' IN: PROGRESSIVE ARCHITECTURE, 2 (1982), 88-91

7 WALTER GROPIUS AND MARTIN WAGNER, 'UN PROGRAMMA PER LA RICOSTRUZIONE DELLE CITTÀ' IN: METRON 12 (1946), 57FF.; CARLO OLMO, URBANISTICA E SOCIETÀ CIVILE. ESPERIENZE E CONOSCENZA 1945-1960 (1992), 95-96

List of illustrations

IN MEMORY OF
OUR PATRIARCH
DEAR DEPARTED
Grandpa
Crimson

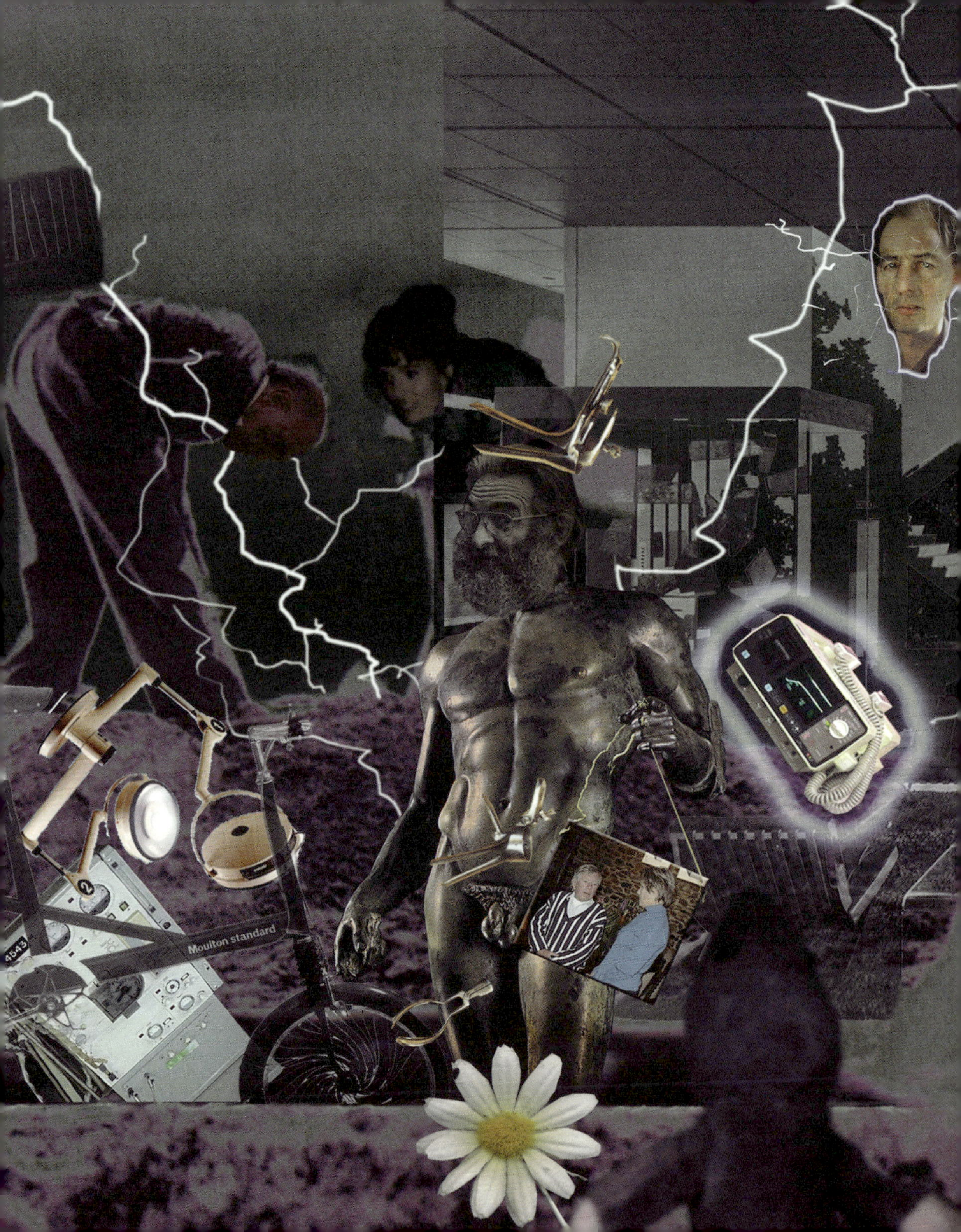
Moulton standard
4643

TOP DOWN

From a good city we expect that it possesses such a rich urban culture that it produces the seeds for its own transformation. The city becomes a giant historical personality that thrashes around and shapes its surroundings, or a highly evolved destination that acts according to its own script, disregarding the massive changes happening in the outside world.

— Then there are cities that are ripped apart, gutted, turned upside down, stretched out, held underwater, blown up and shrunk, left to rot and made over again, pushed to the edge and pulled to the centre. Their rudimentary urban culture never has and never will hold the clue for the next chapter. The great world outside does. These cities seem exposed to everything happening in the world outside. The citizen peers over the ramparts, listens to the latest despatches and looks in the tea leaves to predict what shape the city will have to take on next. The factors that shape it are not only alien to the city itself, they are often alien to anything we can imagine being 'social', 'cultural', 'urban', 'architectural', or even fit for any form of human occupancy. Each time, some kind of urbanity is able to fold itself around the new reality, adapt and continue, in a form incomparable to how it used to be. Yes the city we are talking about here is Rotterdam but it could also be Delhi, Berlin, Panama City, Hong Kong.

— Involuntarily connected to the world by a canal and a railway, expanded ten times over into an industrial city in the space of fifteen years, bombed to oblivion and then used as the testcase for modernist town planning, stretched out to breaking point as an archipelago of settlements around 'the largest port in the world' and relieved of its industrial environment the moment it started getting accustomed to it: Rotterdam has been a most enthusiastic Victim City of The Modern Age. And Crimson is proud to be part of it.

— Proud? Lucky! For historians Victim Cities are a dream. There is no need for deep analyses of the subtle changes in economy and political mentality or speculations on the motivations of planners and politicians. The events are real, big, noisy and come in from the outside. You describe them as if you're there and the story seems to write itself. The spaces and objects produced in the Victim City are equally advantageous to the writer-researcher. They are spectacular, strange and raw. Typical Victim CityScapes like a highway broken through what used to be a village, possess a quality of wonder and alienation that is hard to come by nowadays. Finally the polemical possibilities of these cities are also considerable. Since events just tumble down over the unsuspecting city, the rules change dramatically every couple of years or decades, and traditions, conventions, positions become useless instantaneously. Planners, architects and politicians can't really afford to just fall into a groove. The funny thing of course is that this is exactly what most of them do most of the time, but not all of them, at least not all of the time. Some retreat into the confines of their profession and declare the new wildernesses and deserts produced by for example - automobility or containerization - off limits for urban design. Others are able to change their notion of urbanity when the city is bombed, automated or immigrated into a completely different shape, and thereby reinvent their profession. Planning and architecture in the Victim City separates the 'boys' from the 'men'. You figure out who's who.

— But in the end, Crimson learnt something else, something far more valuable, from living and working in the Victim City. We have learned of an entirely different relationship between plan and result, cause and effect. We have learned how immense, misanthropically scaled infrastructural works have caused the coming together of landscapes and programmes, and the flourishing of new and unexpected strands of urban life. We have learned how incredibly optimistic schemes can completely fail in their intentions, but become huge successes when invaded and abused by parties and activities that had not been foreseen. We have seen forms of intimacy in the most barren peripheries and have experienced feelings of extreme desolation in the most 'humanely' planned centres.

— We have grown to understand the totally different relationship between Plan and Effect in the Victim City. And we have tried to put all of this to some practical use. Even the most courageous and brilliant urban designers and architects find themselves in a somewhat ridiculous position in the Victim City. They oversee the strange landscape produced by the unplanned effects of all the carefully planned schemes and come up with their own earth-moving solution, which - if carried out - is doomed to a success it never foresaw. Crimson has chosen to work with the very forces and figures that seem to colonize or dismantle the big schemes the moment they hit the ground. To us, urban design within an urban landscape that has been formed by elements alien to the human scale or urban culture can only be done by way of constant exploration. Crimson treks through the canyons, valleys, dried up streams, mangrove forests, deserts and cannibal villages of the Victim City and tries to set up camp using what it finds lying around. We find ourselves next to a huge highway, to the north lies a petrochemical factory, to the south a satellite town, in the middle a McDonald's drive-in. Where we stand we can't build because of the underground pipeline. The truckdrivers need a motel; the Scottish highland cattle need a place to graze. The kids in the town have nowhere to party. We know that in a faraway department of public works plans are being made to widen the highway. To put this to our advantage, we need to come up with an idea. Tick Tock Tick Tock Tick ...

Rotterdam 1960-1970

Panorama 2

->Rotterdam 1960-1970

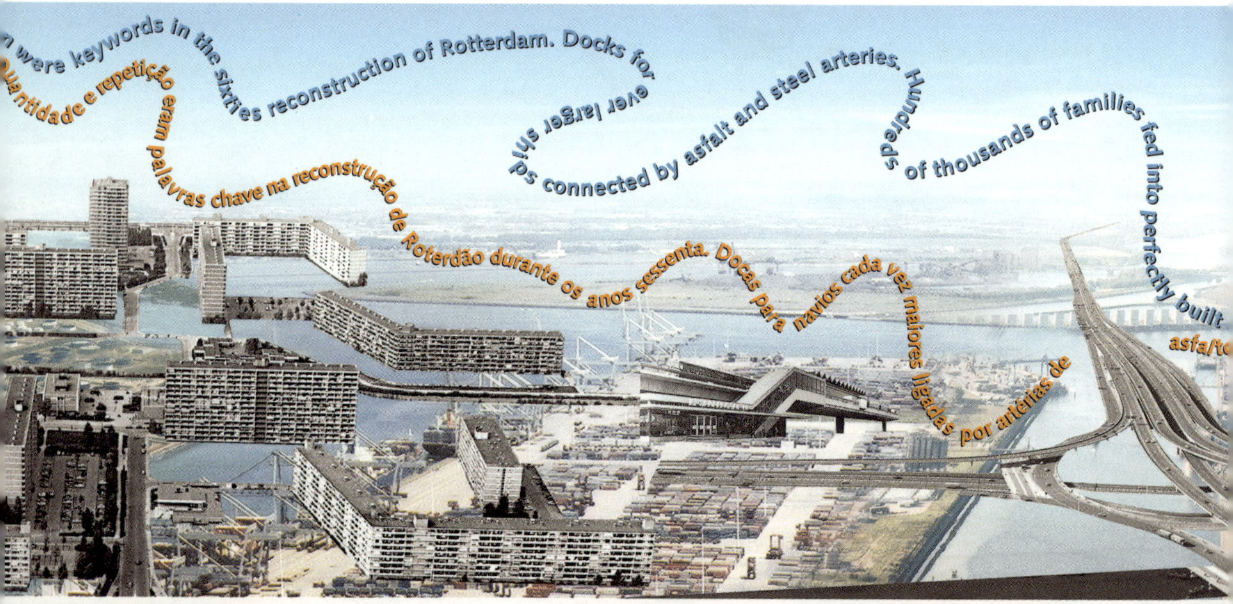

ord housing estate, Public Works Rotterdam, 1965

Metrostation Rijnhaven, Public Works Rotterdam, 1960

Traffic interchange Kleinpolder, Min

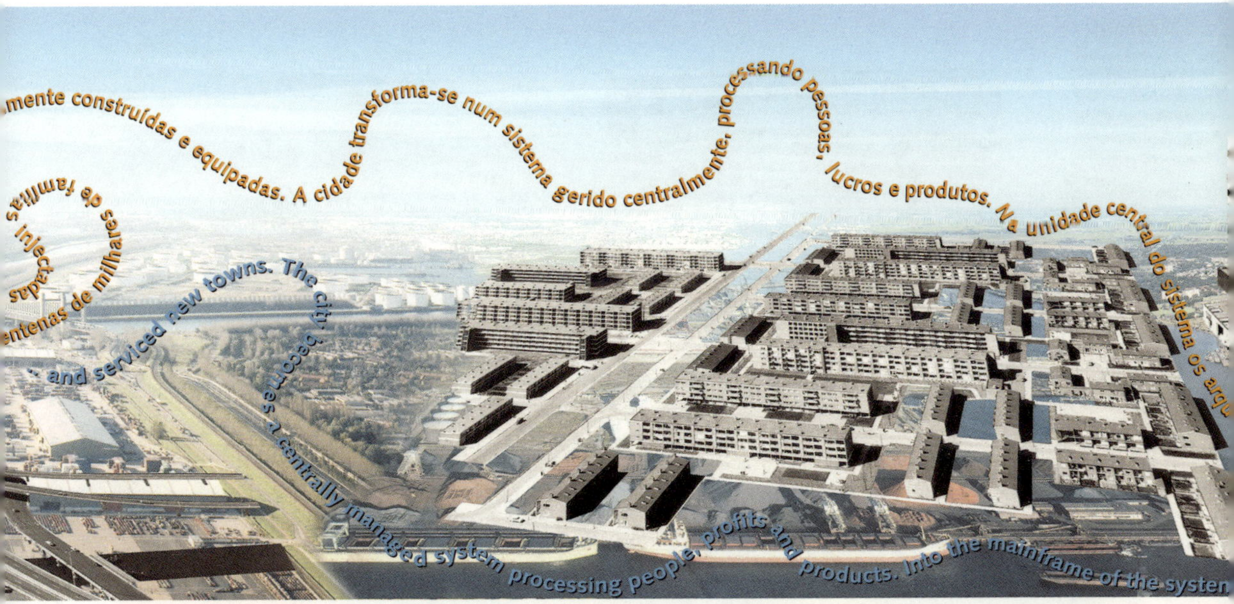

PENDRECHT HOUSING ESTATE, LOTTE STAM-BEESE, 1951-1965

-> Rotterdam 1960-1970

TECHNIKON SCHOOL, H.A. MAASKANT, 1955-1971

TRAFFIC INTERCHANGE KLEINPOLDER, MINISTRY OF TRANSPORT, 1967

With a direct water connection with the sea constructed in the years around 1870 (Nieuwe Waterweg) and a rail link with Belgium laid out five years later, Rotterdam had become a turntable in the flow of goods from north-west Europe. But the town was in no way up to the job either administratively or technologically. To profit the fullest from this new position in the world, between 1872 and 1879 a new 'town' was built on the opposite bank of the river Maas, from a single plan and in one fell swoop. It was geared exclusively to transferring goods between various modes of transportation: ocean-going vessels, inland craft, trains and horse-drawn carts. The area was called Feijenoord and would later be nicknamed Kop van Zuid (literally, southern headland), an area that Town Engineer Willem Nicolaas Rose had made plans for decades earlier. In a matter of years it grew into an infrastructural and industrial complex without parallel anywhere in Europe. In this the lead was taken not by some specially appointed officials but by an entrepreneur, Lodewijk Pincoffs. He would give Rotterdam its most important expansion since the construction of Waterstad, the area south of the old river dyke, in the early years of the 17th century.

Mechanization takes command The town council had itself been engaged in a planning procedure to build a new industrial area on the other side of the river since 1834. The Town Engineer and architectural mind W.N. Rose had already attempted to bring together the new docklands, the new residential districts and the existing town centre in a single lucid and balanced neo-classical town model. Pincoffs, who besides being an entrepreneur was also on the council, made his move. He founded the Rotterdam Trade Association (Rotterdamse Handelsvereniging or RHV), amassed 15 million guilders, took over the land, tasks and plans from the council and set to work. He had a port facility built on Kop van Zuid that was separated from the surrounding areas by a kilometres-long wall. Pincoffs' port was based not on an all-encompassing urbanistic whole but on a fiscal construct that specifically held town and docklands apart. This was the free customs zone or 'free warehouse' (*vrij entrepôt*), an enclave virtually closed off from Dutch territory (and therefore from Rotterdam) for holding goods not entering the country but waiting to be exported. At the end of the 1870s the need for such free zones was so great that it was decided to declare the entire RHV terrain a *vrij entrepôt*, and so seal it off from the rest of the town in terms of revenue too. Feijenoord showed that some parts of town might well belong to Rotterdam geographically but were of quite another order on all other fronts. The grounds at Feijenoord brought home two facts: that the council had lost out in its venture to transform the town, and that the project to design Rotterdam as a single urban entity was over.

Mechanization takes command The RHV 'fort' at Feijenoord consisted of a triple network of water, rails and quays. Buildings were attached to these networks: sheds, office buildings and warehouses. Rudiments of the plans Rose made for Feijenoord could still be discerned especially in the way the two harbour basins of Spoorweghaven and Koningshaven carved out a near-regular wedge, a pier and an island. But the original regularity and hierarchy of the ground plan was overrun by the flowing geometry of railway lines, marshalling yards, sheds and mooring bays. The link between arriving and departing trains, vessels and carts and the static buildings came care of a hydraulic system operating along the quays of the channel-like inner harbour, attached to which were various kinds of mobile cranes and elevators. The RHV was awarded a gold medal at the Paris Exhibition of 1878 for the way it had equipped industrial grounds of such size with the most advanced and experimental techniques.[1] Pincoffs' civil engineer, Thomas Stieltjes, added in his report that if the Rotterdam Trade Association and the State were stakeholders in the project, the town council had also been allocated a role.[2] In other words it was an example of a public-private partnership.

The State built the railway embankment, viaduct and bridge that sliced through Feijenoord and crossed the Maas river. In addition it dug in the western part of the peninsula the low narrow basin of Spoorweghaven which joined the river on the other side of the peninsula via a discharge channel. It also built a bridge over Spoorweghaven and laid out grounds containing customs facilities, sheds, train depots and a goods station.[3] The council dug out Koningshaven, thereby severing Noordereiland from Feijenoord, and built the quays along this island. It erected road bridges over Koningshaven and over the river. Lastly, it took upon itself the forthcoming task of paving the streets of Noordereiland, the square south of Koningshaven and the long narrow Spoorwegstraat and providing them with drains and street lighting. The Trade Association for its part dug out Binnenhaven, built a bridge over it and dug out the smaller Entrepothaven which joined Binnenhaven at an angle.

The complex on Entrepothaven was the fiscal hub of the complex as a whole. Its key components were the harbour basin, a warehouse building and a network of railways. This 'free warehouse' (De Vijf Werelddelen, or five continents) was built to a design by the engineer G.J. Morre along the entire 200 metres of Entrepothaven. It consisted of loadbearing brick facades with an internal supporting structure of cast-iron columns, and rested on a system of waterproof cellars. Three railways lines could reach the quay along ground-level trenches extending from the grounds at the rear and stabbing through the building. The loading balconies were attached to the building with the hydraulic cranes travelling alongside.[4] The long pier between Spoorweghaven and Binnenhaven was inlaid with a network of roads, rails and quays and covered with a long string of sheds alternately in brick and timber. Train rails and mobile cranes were installed along all the quay walls for a rapid transfer between train and ship. The most striking feature was the gateway building where Pincoffs and his RHV had their headquarters. Designed by J.S.C. van der Wal, it oversailed the bascule bridge with which Stieltjes had spanned the entrance to the inner harbour. According to the original design there were to be two identical gateway buildings on either side of the bridge. The underground vaults where the iron bascules turn doubled as the foundations of the gateway buildings.[5] Bridge and building joined forces as a mechanized town gateway for boats, trains, carriages and pedestrians, from where Pincoffs and Stieltjes could oversee and run the entire show.

Electricity and the modern port authority

After a spectacular financial nosedive by Pincoffs and his Rotterdam Trade Association, the port services came into the possession of the City of Rotterdam. It appointed as director of Public Works the engineering officer G.J. de Jongh, a man who united the qualities of a Ferdinand de Lesseps and a Baron Haussmann. De Jongh used the latest techniques to expand the port area of Rotterdam exponentially. Unlike Pincoffs he saw the entire town as a technical task and the construction of new residential districts, gas mains, telephone cables, abattoirs and railway lines followed in the wake of the newly dug harbour basins. After De Jongh's steam-driven dredges and dragheads, excavators, suction dredgers, floating cranes large and small and diving bells had done their work the harbours were fitted out for transsshipment. The RHV still used a hydraulic system for its cranes, winches and the like. But the sheer scale of the new area demanded an energy network that could extend over greater distances. In 1890 work began on laying out a many-tentacled electricity network and on developing port installations that were driven by electricity, an almost unique occurrence worldwide at the time. De Jongh had arrived at the idea of electrically powered installations at a trade and industry exhibition in Bremen (Nordwest-Deutsche Gewerbe und Industrie Ausstellung), where the chief engineer of the Port of Hamburg intimated that he was considering fully electrifying the port installations as had been done in Boston. After an extensive research trip taking in various European port and industrial zones, De Jongh and his staff made a detailed proposal for an electricity network that was to drive the transshipment installations in the Port of Rotterdam. Electricity would not only drive the port cranes but also power the lighting on the quays so that work could be done at night too. The port had to function day and night, everywhere and without cease. This would put them ahead of Hamburg. De Jongh proposed generating the electricity using steam in an electricity factory on Oostzeedijk. From there it would be conducted to two large accumulator substations on Westersingel and Wilhelminakade that would in turn disseminate the current further.[6] De Jongh wanted to use the same network to bring electric lighting to the streets and squares.

The council accepted the plan in 1891 and four years later produced, in a new electricity factory built by the German firm of Siemens, an electromotive force of 440 volts which was spread over the port via the substation on Wilhelminakade. At the same time the new energy was used to illuminate the town centre from the other substation on Westersingel. After 1905 the network was radically expanded with the construction of a new power station between Schiehaven and Parkhaven. The new station had to power the harbour basin of Waalhaven as well as the new harbour basins on the right bank and the port railway that was to stitch them together. In addition, the electricity produced by the power station drove the new electric trams.[7] With the laying of the electricity network, the modern port area took shape as a council-exploited structure of land, water, electricity, gas, railways, roads, buildings and devices. This structure was traversed at certain points by the networks of private companies, such as certain goods lines, pipelines, installations and so on. Of greater importance, however, is that laying out and extending networks such as that for electric power caused the modernizing of port and city to interlock.

Mechanization takes command The authority wielded by De Jongh would have been inconceivable without the integration enjoyed by the municipal services. What later would become the distinct divisions of Port Authority, Town Planning, Housing and Public Works all came under the one heading of Public Works between 1879 and 1917 and were led by one man, Gerrit Jan de Jongh.[8] In this system there was no question of a distinction between public administration and private interest; the two operated along one front from a single vantage-point: Rotterdam. Through the channels of the Port Authority, the council embarked on an area that basically was not theirs to enter, to wit, the competitive arena of trade and industry. By linking arms with private enterprise, the council was able to guide the town's development along much more effective lines than if it had kept a distance befitting its status. The town, the river and the polders had to be changed into a transshipment machine that would attract and make space for the greatest number of traffic movements.[9] With De Jongh at the helm, the town's centre of power shifted from the town hall to the Public Works building. In addition part of the executive power moved from the municipal authorities and councillors to the large private port companies.[10] That the responsibility for public management was divided between the large companies and Public Works, was a situation that arose for the first time under G.J. de Jongh but would later re-emerge with renewed vigour during the period of reconstruction after the Second World War. This did not mean, though, that public administration was weakened as a result. It meant that at the moment when the town became defined as a locus of transshipment and construction administrative powers passed to the Town Engineer who was then able to direct the private companies. The destruction and rebuilding of the city gave an impulse to its development comparable with the digging of the Nieuwe Waterweg and the arrival of the railway.

The port and its equipment

For a port, the most essential aspect besides accessibility is technical equipment. A vital component of De Jongh's project, accordingly, was the constant expansion and renewal of the immense machine park. This machine park was, moreover, one of the factors used to lure new companies to Rotterdam. The port equipment was

The railway bridge over the Maas, 1877

The railway through the centre of Rotterdam, ca. 1900

Free warehouse 'De Vijf Werelddelen' under construction, ca. 1875

Free warehouse 'De Vijf Werelddelen', ca. 1880

The gateway-building housing the headquarters of the RHV, ca. 1880

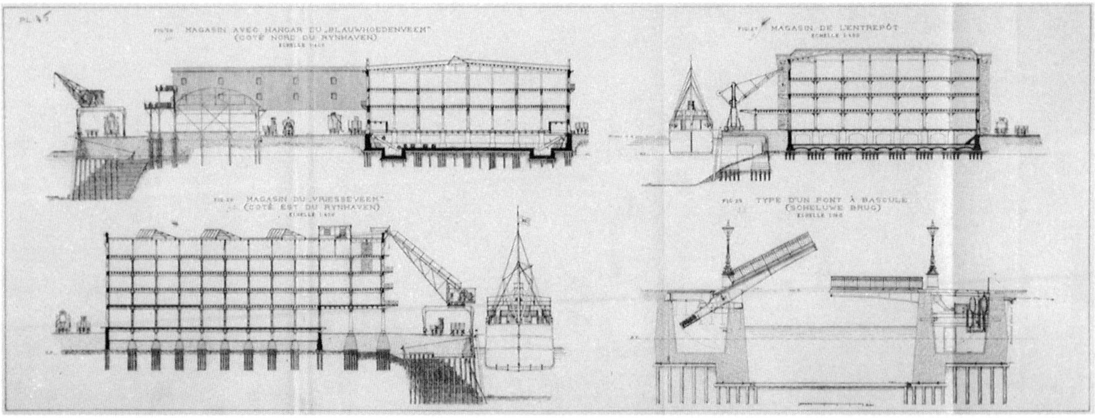

Sections through Blauwhoedenveem, Vrieseveem, free warehouse 'De Vijf Werelddelen' and bascule bridge, ca. 1901

Presentation of port equipment, 1911 >

ation peut, sans objection, être fixée plus haute.

Grue électrique de la «Basalt Stone Cy.» au 2e Katendrechtsche Haven.

Fig. 14.

t suivante:

par minute et à la portée de 26.50 m.
» » » » » » » 22.25 »
» » » » » » » 45.50 »
» » » » » » » 45.50 »

Comme con
fréquentant no
„Sir Ernest C
Bolaget Lutea
Ces deux ba

ort de blocs de béton.

(1.5 tonne).

d'un
rées.
efois
les
vite
nent
eurs
de
ent;
que
e.

Fig. 6.

nouvelles grues et qui saute immédiatement aux yeux,
es. Ces dispositifs assurent une
dant le mouvement de
ebalancement adopté, le

La «Girafe».
(25 tonnes).

Fig. 20.

vant à la fois fournir l'électricité tant pour
que pour actionner les appareils de levage
eaux bassins.
te station centrale fût achevée, on fit déjà,

e hydraulique du Binnenhaven.
(2.5 tonnes).

Fig. 3.

en 1892, grâce à une installation provisoire, des ess
une grue électrique fournie par la maison Haniel
de Dusseldorf. Cette grue (fig. 4) qui, bien que
existe encore, travaille au moyen d'un seul moteur
à la fois soulever la charge et faire tourner la cabi
grue à l'aide d'un deuxième jeu de transmissions.
A la suite de ces essais on commanda, en 1893
d'œu
Le
augi
je re
La
en a
1e
2e
qui
sanc
La
ayai
lesq
par
J'
A
Il
céré
eu
mais
pas
Je
visit
avec
A
(éch

Élévateur-transporteur, le «Holland» (420 tonnes par heure) et élévateur déversoir des charbons N

Fig. 32.

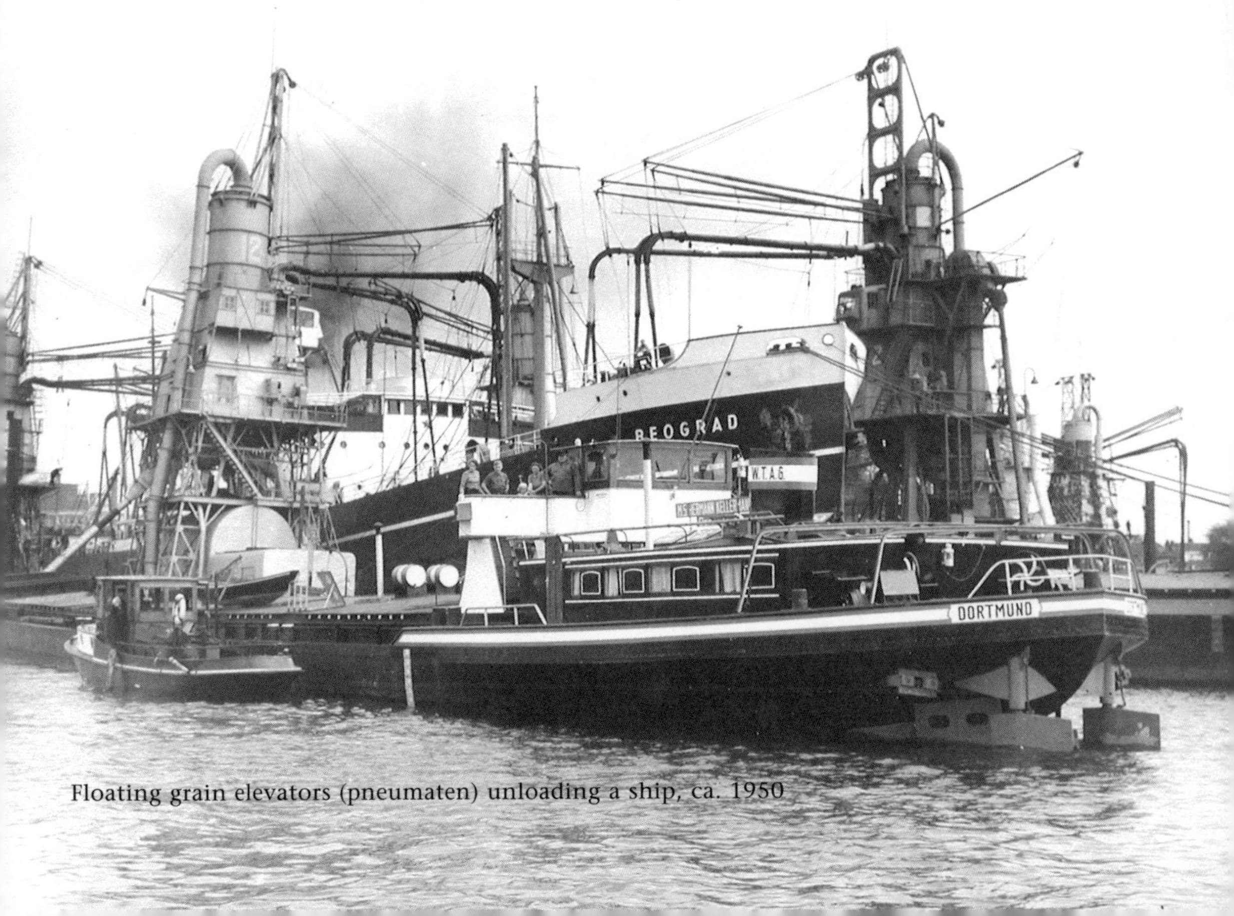

Floating grain elevators (pneumaten) unloading a ship, ca. 1950

invariably the subject of the international lecture tours undertaken by De Jongh and his engineers. Their aim was to use text and image to bring the workplace that was Rotterdam to the fullest international attention. Slides showing the harbours and installations in various stages of completion served as a carrot on a stick for international trade. From the lectures and international publications of G.J. De Jongh and his deputy directors H.A. Ysselsteyn and Wouter Cool in 1911 a picture emerges of a fantastic menagerie of pulsating iron and steel machines for transferring goods between boats, trains, ocean-going vessels and carriages, powered by a ramified network of electricity, compressed air and steam.

Mechanization takes command The most salient elements were the cranes; this machine type underwent furious diversification after the arrival of the first hydraulic and steam-driven cranes of the RHV, which at the start of the 20th century could lift something like 2 tonnes. Soon enough the cranes were mounted on moving undercarriages and the span of their jibs increased so that they could reach across several ships without disrupting the activities and traffic on the quay. The driver sat in a wooden cabin and turned with the movements the crane made at his instigation. Because the ships were getting ever broader and because their cargoes needed to be transferred from them to the river craft lying alongside directly from the quayside, the jibs became increasingly manoeuvrable. They became taller too and came to dominate the skyline more and more.[11] One offshoot of these mobile cranes were the overhead travelling cranes; these mobile horizontal behemoths could organize the transfer of goods between warehouses, trains, quays, sea-going vessels and river craft. With the development of bucket grabs, timber grabs, orange peel grabs and others it was possible to move all kinds of bulk goods from one place to another. The loading cranes of the firm of Thomsen had a reach of 40 metres from the quay and a total span of almost 100 metres. Built over the sheds, they could service five or six ships moored alongside each other. The control cabin moved with the grab to just above the ships' holds.[12] Around the harbour basins there grew a thick rind of immense port buildings which though immobile in themselves still played a key role in the process of exchange and distribution. In these objects architecture and machinery blended seamlessly together. Wires, tunnels, chains, cellars and cables linked these buildings with the layered structure of railways, electricity mains, foundations and drains comprising De Jongh's quays. The superstructure served to hold and process, to financial advantage, goods that the port was unable to immediately transfer to a subsequent mode of transport, before returning them to the flow of goods through the harbour. In De Jongh's electrified port the warehouse type would lose its clear-cut silhouette and thus its architectural integrity. Under De Jongh the boats and cranes kept on getter bigger so that the mechanical installations steadily gained in importance and the buildings gradually became lost from view behind their own equipment.[13] The sheds and storehouses of the Blauwhoedenveem company on the north side of Rijnhaven, work on which began in 1890, constituted the first electrified port complex specifically designed to attach to the new electricity network. Its architecture was informed not by an urban plan but by a network of ducting and piping.

The Blauwhoedenveem building was built close by the new accumulator substation on Wilhelminapier. This pier lies between Rijnhaven and the Maas and was divided lengthwise into seven strips: quay, building, road, building, road, building, quay.[14] Four of these strips, from the Rijnhaven quay up to and including the central building strip, were occupied by Blauwhoedenveem. The quay was given over to a number of electric cranes belonging to the Port Authority; these retrieved the goods from the boats and loaded them directly into the wagons travelling between their feet. They could also discharge the goods at the hangars built along the quay for loading shortly after onto the trains at the other side of the hangar. Again, the cranes could lower the goods onto the loading balconies at the head of the four double-height bridge-buildings straddling the quay. These hovering timber structures were built across the sheds on the quay but also bridged the road. The goods arrived at the topmost level of the shed, descending via a system of electric winches and goods lifts to the cellar. The building's cellar held an electric installation that collected barrels and drums at street level and rolled them down into the cellar where they were conveyed on electric trolleys and later brought back up to street level using a system of escalators, or transported throughout the entire building via one of the goods lifts. Aside from buildings like Blauwhoedenveem, the principal installations were not buildings but floating and rolling equipment populating the vast expanses of water and kilometres-long quays. But they were often as large as buildings. This was what the critic Rein Blijstra more than half a century later described as 'a strange brand of urbanism ... since the most striking elements, the ships and cranes, are continually changing position'.[15]

 A device conspicuous in both appearance and number was the floating grain elevator or *pneumaat*. These would prove indispensable for transferring grain from sea-going ships to river craft. Once a ship laden with grain had been piloted through the sheds of the Smit company into Maashaven, a cluster of four or five of these machines would steam alongside the vessel. The elevators were run by a company (N.V. Maatschappij tot Exploitatie van Drijvende Elevatoren) whose shareholders included ship brokers and stevedores. One such elevator consisted of a floating tray on which stood a steam engine, a steel frame containing a grain sluice and a drum kept at a constant vacuum. Various moving suction tubes poked out of the head. The mouths of the tubes were placed in the ship's hold and attached to the vacuum. The grain was sucked up into a funnel-shaped receiver; it then passed on to the horizontal revolving door of the grain sluice so that the vacuum would be retained, fell into the bunker, descended to the weighing room and was deposited in precisely weighed quantities by way of a lighter into a river vessel lying alongside. The grain elevators were operated by four men and could syphon 200 tonnes of grain per hour.[16] The 27 *pneumaten* operative in the port of Rotterdam around 1905 must have given the impression of being creatures from another planet that had landed on earth to drive us out. This at least was the reaction of the dockers when in 1907, out of fear of becoming redundant, they launched the so-called 'elevator strike' which was brutally suppressed.[17] In the shorter term their fears were unfounded. Rapid though the growth of the port capacity was, the absolute quantity of goods that passed through it annually always rose many times more quickly. At all events Rotterdam would keep on drawing in an average of 10,000 new employees a year until the outbreak of the First World War.

Plans to expand

From 1901 on, the Housing Act of that year obliged every local administrative council to draw up expansion schemes, meticulous urban designs which gave primacy to housing and street profiles - bona fide 20th-century town planning. The reason De Jongh had such a bad name throughout the 20th century as an urban planner may be because his expansion schemes were not presided over by dwelling and the public domain. Regarding the conditions a well-functioning port had to meet, De Jongh said: 'Bring water, make tracks', on port layout: 'the ships will follow the dredgers' and on urban expansion: 'the city follows the port'.[18] For him, City and Port were united within a single dynamic building process rather than within a town-planning composition. This process brought the strange urbanistic elements Blijstra saw moving across water and land, but also the unremitting expansion of the port area and with it the constant growth of the urban substance.

Mechanization takes command De Jongh's first expansion schemes for residential districts were made for the immediate vicinity of the new harbour basins. Dykes were pierced, millions of cubic metres of soil were dredged, villages were cut off from their hinterland and sometimes wiped off the map entirely, and houses were built.[19] The sludge accumulated from dredging the harbour was used to lay out new sea dykes and raise the polder land so as to be able to build houses on it. This explains why residential estates were placed up against the 'rind' of port companies. They were as much a side effect of the physical structure that was the port, as a necessary condition to keep it going as a workplace.[20] Like the utilitarian architecture on the quays the housing districts too were distorted by the proximity of the mechanized port. In the street layout that De Jongh designed in about 1880 for the grounds east of those of the RHV (Pincoffs' Rotterdam Trade Association) he gave a scrupulous account of a boulevard profile: a broad road with wide pavements to either aside and surrounded by trees. But his boulevard design distinguished itself from the familiar examples in Paris, Brussels or Vienna by the fact that they had goods trains crossing them. Rails had been sunk into the clinker brick so that the trains could travel from Spoorweghaven through the housing estate to reach Persoonshaven and Koningshaven in the north-east. De Jongh's street plan was defined by rolling lines; instead of intersecting, the main roads either split into two or merged one into the other. This principal structure was wrapped around enclaves laid out in accordance with the automatisms of speculative building and the grid of drainage ditches in the polder.

From the plan for Maashaven of 1895 it can be seen how the curving train boulevards, the orthogonal grids of smaller streets, the parks, the network of railway lines, the complexes on the quays, the expanse of water and the points grid of mooring buoys and piles could present a single cohesive urban composition.[21] Dwelling was taken up in the complex as one of the port's functions.[22] This was realized most explicitly in the triangular district on the south-east side of Maashaven which dated from the beginning of the 1890s. This area, Hillekop, consisted of four large building blocks, the largest two of which were chamfered by the train boulevard linking the area with the port railway and the quay complex. These plans, then, were based on the shape of the movement followed by the technological port. Boulevard and goods rail, housing and industry, brick and iron were meshed together without conventional planning formalities. The railway was the network that linked the housing blocks with the warehouses, quays and ships; living and working were strung together. The key planning element was the boulevard, shared as it was by cyclists, pedestrians, carriages, cars, trams and goods trains.

Mechanization takes command De Jongh's interventions at times made use of existing historical and landscape structures and at others simply erased them, depending on what worked out best. An example of encapsulation and partial consolidation is the mediaeval village of Charlois. The sloping streets, the water courses (*singels*) and block parcelling of the expansion plan were folded round the village centre, designating it the hub of a rapidly burgeoning working-class district. The bowl-shaped village centre with its houses built along the dyke and its church is still recognizable as such today. An example of encapsulation followed by liquidation is the village of Katendrecht. Katendrecht lived from the fishing industry and from the seemingly endless hinterland of polders. It lay directly opposite the western districts of North Rotterdam. When Maashaven was dug, the first basin was excavated right up against the dyke linking Katendrecht to its hinterland, with the goods boulevards, the *singels* and the field pattern of the polder marked out around it. By digging the basin of Rijnhaven the village found itself on a peninsula surrounded by the new docklands and companies. These attracted so many new workers that the old village buildings were demolished and replaced by city blocks. The original inhabitants of Katendrecht and surroundings and the new ones from the provinces of Brabant and Zeeland but later also from China, found work in the harbour and moved into the one-, two- and three-storey alcove houses. Katendrecht remained a village with its own special ambience and identity, isolated from the outside world not by polders and the river but by boats, cranes, silos, quays, trains, lorries, factories, machine halls, gantries and warehouses.

1
H. van der Cammen & L.A. de Klerk, *Van Ruimtelijke ordening van plannen komen plannen - de ontwikkelingsgang van de ruimtelijke ordening in Nederland,* Uitgeverij het Spectrum, Utrecht 1993 (1986), 30-31.

2
T.J. Stieltjes, 'Openbare werken in Nederland De Spoorweg - en Havenwerken te Rotterdam en Feijenoord', *De Ingenieur*, 1878, 358-360

3
Jan Willem van Borselen, *Sporen in Rotterdam, Stadsgeschiedenis rondom de trein,* Stichting Historische Publicaties Rotterodamum, Rotterdam 1993, 187-205

4
Remmert Daalder (ed.), *Werkstad, 30 industriële monumenten in Rotterdam,* Rotterdam 1985, 33-40

5
Peter de Winter et al. (eds), *Havenarchitectuur: een inventarisatie van industriële gebouwen in het Rotterdamse havengebied,* Rotterdam 1982, 31

6
Jan van den Noort, *Pion of Pionier Rotterdam - Gemeentelijke bedrijvigheid in de 19e eeuw*, Stichting Historische Publicaties Rotterodamum, Rotterdam 1993, 108-109

7
Ibid., 109-111

8
Herman Moscoviter, 'Een civieltechnische supermarkt van alle tijden', in: Moscoviter (ed.), *Op de groei gemaakt 'Gerieflijkheden voor een wel-ingerigte stad', Anderhalve eeuw Gemeentewerken Rotterdam*, Gemeentewerken Rotterdam, 1996, 83-103

9
Ferry De Goey, *Ruimte voor Industrie, Rotterdam en de vestiging van Industrie in de haven 1945-1975*, Historische Publicaties Roterodamum, Rotterdam 1990, 45-56

10
Paul van de Laar, *Bouwers in de natte*, in: Moscoviter, 153-173

11
Wouter Cool, 'Les Installations mécaniques du Port de Rotterdam, Conférence dans l'Assemblée extraordinaire du "Koninklijk Instituut van Ingenieurs" à l'occasion de la visite de l'Association design Ingénieurs sortis de l'Ecole de Liège. le 26 Juin 1911', *De Ingenieur*, no. 42, 1911, 930-946

12
N. T. Koomans, 'De Haven en haar outillage', in: J. Schraver (ed.) *Rotterdam, De Poort van Europa, De geschiedenis van haven en handel van Rotterdam,* Uitgeverij Ad Donker, Rotterdam/ Antwerpen, 1946, 37-46

13
Wouter Vanstiphout, 'How the twentieth century didn't pass our country by. Radical tendencies in modern Rotterdam', *Archis* 11, 1994, 60-80

14
Peter de Winter et al. (eds), op. cit., 8-9

15
Rein Blijstra, *Rotterdam stad in beweging*, Rotterdam 1965, 308

16
Cool, op. cit., 941

17
Cor van Asch, 'Van Baal tot Bulk', in: Jurr van Dalen et al. (eds), *Oud Werk. Overzicht van industrieel erfgoed in Rotterdam,* Stichting Industrieel Erfgoed Rijmond, Rotterdam 1983, 29-60, 38-41

18
Van de Laar, op. cit., 157

19
Frits Palmboom, 'Rotterdam-stad en delta, Rotterdam als verstedelijkt landschap', in: D'Laine Camp & Michelle Provoost (eds), *Stadstimmeren 650 Rotterdam Stad*, Phoenix & Den Oudsten Uitgevers, Rotterdam, 1990, 81-89.

20
Jan de Graaf, Wim Nijenhuis, Donald van Dansik, 'Een Schoone Stad. Rotterdam maakt de sprong naar Zuid', in: *De Kop van Zuid ontwerp en onderzoek,* Uitgeverij 010, Rotterdam 1982, 170-172

21
G.J. De Jongh, 'De Haven van Rotterdam', in: *Notulen der Vergaderingen van het Koninklijk Instituut van Ingenieurs 1890-1891*, Uitgeverij Gebr. J. H. van Langenhuynse, 's Gravenhage, 1891, 30-33

22
De Graaf et al., op. cit., 169-170

Hilledijk in Rotterdam-Feijenoord, ca. 1980

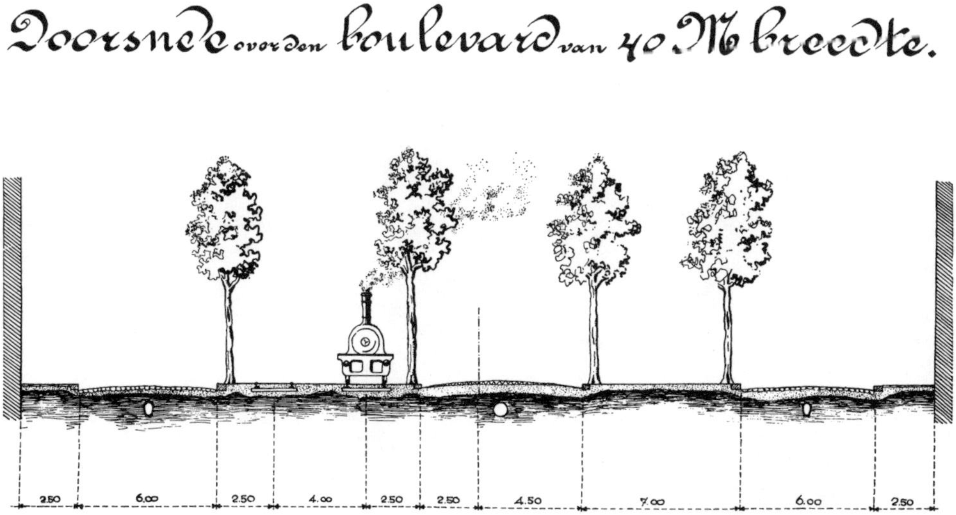

De Jongh, section through a boulevard with freight train, ca. 1880

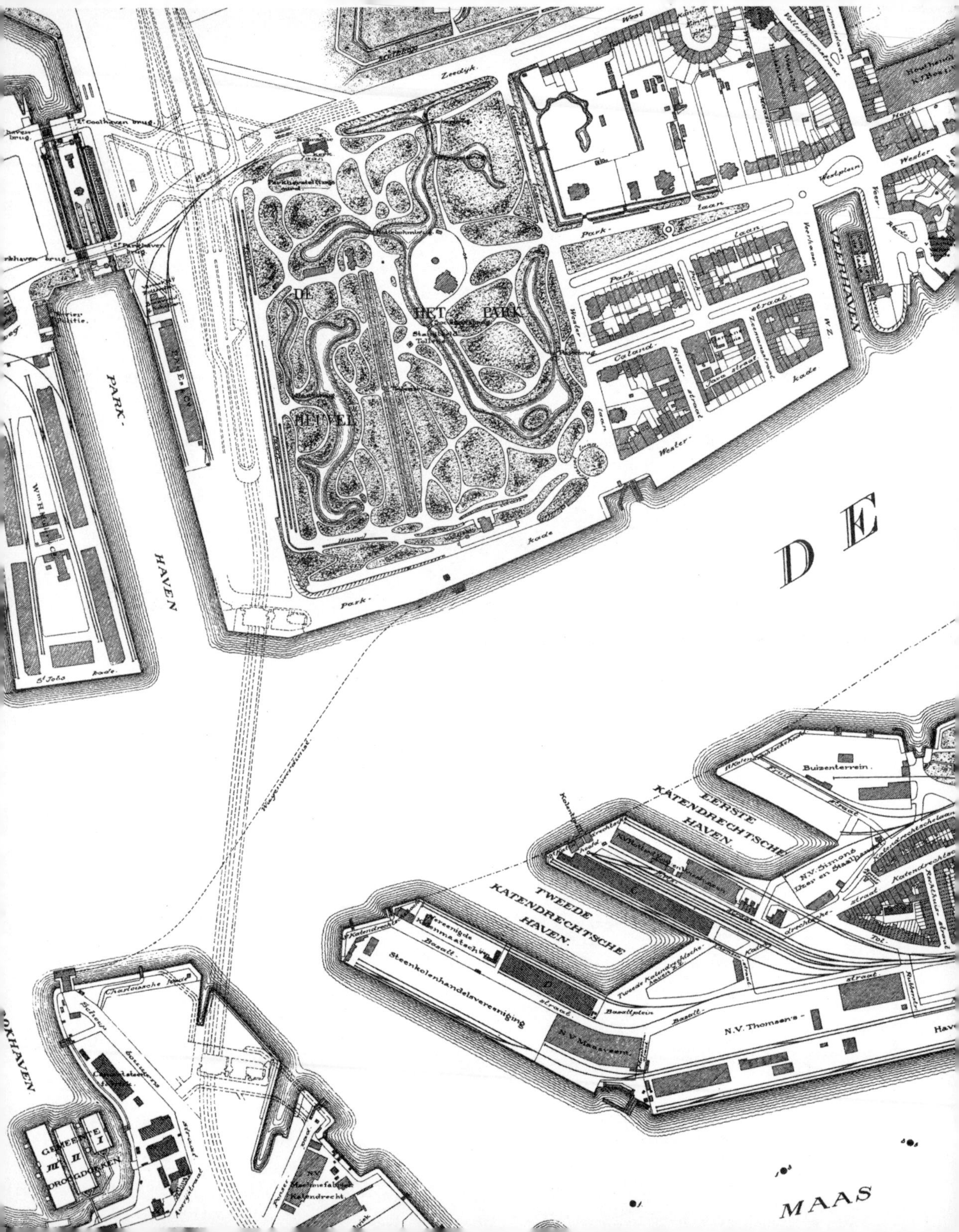

HET PARK
DE HEUVEL
PARK-HAVEN
VEERHAVEN
Zeedyk
Westplein
Park-laan
Park-straat
Caland
Java straat
Zeemanstraat
Park-kade
St Jobs kade
DE
MAAS
EERSTE KATENDRECHTSCHE HAVEN
TWEEDE KATENDRECHTSCHE HAVEN
Buizenterrein.
Steenkolenhandelsvereeniging
N.V. Maasveem.
N.V. Thomsen's
Basaltplein
Basalt-straat
GEMEENTE DROOGDOKKEN
Charloische hoofd

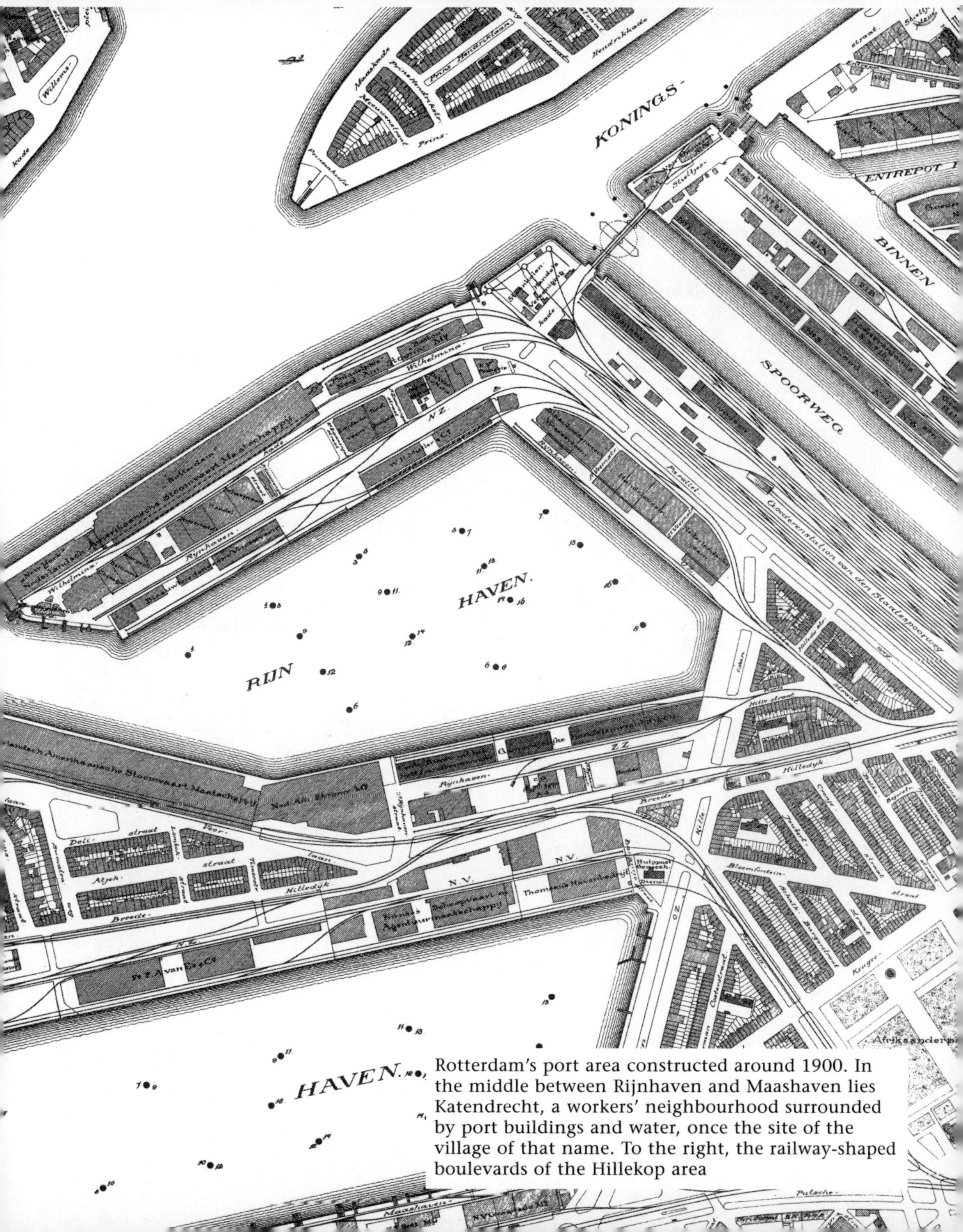

Rotterdam's port area constructed around 1900. In the middle between Rijnhaven and Maashaven lies Katendrecht, a workers' neighbourhood surrounded by port buildings and water, once the site of the village of that name. To the right, the railway-shaped boulevards of the Hillekop area

Katendrecht 2002

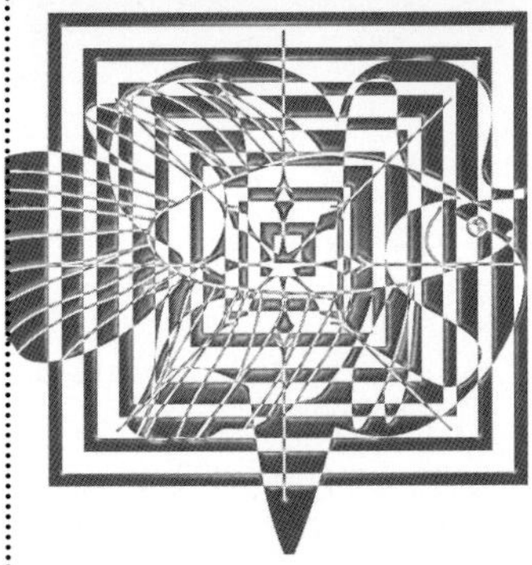

Rotterdam Port City

With all the thought being given to the transformations in the old port area of Rotterdam we might almost forget that there is a real port as well. There are even calls for the city to abandon the port altogether, and do away with Rotterdam's traditional identity as a port city. This is inadvisable, however, as this port could teach the city a thing or two.

The notion that port and city are preventing each other from functioning to the full was recently articulated by an occasional working alliance between the Office for Metropolitan Architecture and the Nyfer economic research institute. They were called in by an agitated business community to oppose the Central Planning Office who had suggested that the creation of Maasvlakte 2 (the second vast 'plain' of that name south of Rotterdam) would not make for economic progress. In the publication *Maa$vlakte*, Nyfer used all the statistics and arguments on hand to show that the second Maasvlakte could be of inestimable importance for the economy of the Rijnmond region and OMA argued likewise for the spatial development of the region. They suggested that the idea of a second Maasvlakte should be seized upon as a means of conceptually separating the city of Rotterdam and its port.

OMA's contribution is interesting in that it breaks with a particular convention: the office is pleased to announce the end of the relationship between port and city. Proceeding from the persistent idea that Rotterdam is the last modern city in the Netherlands, the city of permanent transformation, the only permanent underlying factor - the port - is ditched to make room for a city concept freed of identity, so that Rotterdam can be the first Dutch city to 'go Asiatic'.[1]

It appears as though OMA have been led on primarily by exasperation about the way the port is now playing a role in city development - as a tourist theme. With an allusion to its heroic period, the port only remains present in the city as a plaque for holiday makers in the 'Waterstad' (the water activity zone in the old harbours on the north bank) and as a 'dash of atmosphere'[2] in the shape of old quays, barges and boats. In the ambitious plans for transforming the Laurens Quarter, for example, the port identity is in fact already forgotten and all efforts are towards shaping a traditional city centre with labyrinthine routes and café circuits.

From the other side, there is an approach that seeks to make the port more urbane by subjecting the buildings in the port area to the same design terrorism as that in the city and by infilling public spaces with specially designed port furniture.[3]

Looked at this way, there are two cities in one, trying to make contact in the most superficial way imaginable.
Yet OMA's decision to forget the port altogether is out of the question: the port is an undisputed presence. References to it are not just a species of phantom pain in a city that has lost its port. Port and city are still part of a single system. In trying to understand what the system means to both sides without OMA-style emotional outbursts, we first have to look at the *reality* of the port.

Port system

Since its construction in the second half of the 19th century, the core of the port has been to provide hardware that enables commercial activity, from the building of company premises, the laying of electricity cables up to and including fiscal constructs such as free market zones. The complexity of the resulting activity generates systems to coordinate it and look after common interests. The port is more a network than a hierarchical structure, a network consisting of repeatedly changing configurations of municipal services, government policy, infrastructural hardware and business activity. When one of these factors changes, the port changes with it. The cause of such changes lies mostly at a distance, in any case far beyond the Netherlands. The nationalization of oil companies in Iran in the seventies or the closing of the Suez Canal in the fifties were developments that lay wholly beyond the control of the Port of Rotterdam but to which it could respond quite adequately. The global economy resonates here in the most concrete terms: on a local level in full view of everyone. A revolution of unprecedented impact was the introduction in the sixties of a standard box for the transportation of goods by truck, train and ship: this was the container. The latest developments are informed by a general tendency towards globalization, with the harbour transformed into a 'network port', a logistics centre in a deconcentrated port region stretching from Rotterdam to Venlo. Every time such an incident occurs it signifies a radical spatial reconfiguration of the entire port layout.

Nevertheless we may identify a certain continuity: the port has its own commercial culture, with its own rules and modified laws which make its organization more similar to that of other ports elsewhere in the world such as Pusan or Hamburg, than to cities in the immediate vicinity like The Hague or Amsterdam. This global identity, however, is filtered through the fact that the port is not a free state, but part of the local and national territory. The port exists as part of the global economy of goods, money and information, but also of local circumstances with an enormous pressure exerted by nature, dwelling and the environment. Rotterdam central city is, in its symbiosis with the port, the centre that each world city needs. In that centre the actual port has become invisible, but inhabitants of Hoek van Holland, Hoogvliet, Vlaardingen, Maassluis, Spijkenisse or Schiedam (all together the Rijnmond region, or Greater Rotterdam) undoubtedly think otherwise. There are still the trucks, the office buildings, the smog alerts, the Betuwe slow-freight railway line, the unemployment and the new 'old' port present as signs that the harbour is still there. Continuity also exists in the spatial relationship between city and port. The constants here are the infrastructure of the river and the motorway ring around Rotterdam, which at this moment is being extended with extra cross-river connections, more than doubling the imaginary planning square superimposed on the city to capture the entire port region in a single elongated grid.

The port is still there, only it is no longer found in the city centre. This has many consequences for the way city and port engage one another. Just after the war, the ingredients of the city were configured according to Van Traa's concept of a living-working city, based on a hierarchical model of the 'neighbourhood idea'. Living, working and recreation were arranged in direct interdependence. Hoogvliet looked out on the smoke of the Shell chimney, Rozenburg on the fairytale skyline of Europoort's tank parks. Since the seventies, large-scale campaigning for our daily living environment and the environment as a whole have provided for enormous recreational and green buffers along the edges of the port. Furthermore the Rotterdam City Development office had opted for a new expansion model. No longer were compact versions of Rotterdam built in the polders, but the existing villages became centres of urban growth. These were the starting points for a massive suburbanization, for an Arcadian habitat geared to the individual. The demarcation lines and compensatory green zones that have arisen around the port imply an altogether different, yet highly intensive use relationship between the voids in the port and the city's inhabitants. In this configuration the port is becoming increasingly independent of the urban work force, but not of the residential and leisure-seeking urban population.

OMA give evidence of an uncustomary conservatism in focusing on *identity* in terms of *city*. The eccentric location of the port is for them an argument for removing it entirely from the city's self-image. However, we should realize in this respect that Rotterdam's identity has not been fixed by the centre for a very long time now. Only a minority of Rotterdammers live in the 'real' urbanity of the centre or Kop van Zuid. Rotterdam is defined more by its access system and the fields these form than by a central city, no matter how much cappuccino they serve there.

Revolution

Each change in its operational management has far-reaching effects for the port's physical appearance. Before the invention of the container, ships were unloaded on the quays and the freight stored in sheds or conveyed further by train or truck. The crux of containerization was that general cargo could be handled as another form of bulk cargo.

The effect of this revolution was that the transport world demanded new machinery that had to fit into the uniform container system of measurements, hooks, codes, securing systems and clasps. Now that even in the most remote corners of the world there are trucks fitted out to receive containers, we can conclude that the first chapter of the revolution has been successfully completed. With the advent of the container, it became necessary to arrange the piers differently: more space was needed as storage and less for buildings. The image of dockworkers slaving away on the quays disappeared along with that of endless rows of harbour sheds of brick, concrete and Stelcon panels. In their place is an alienating mountain landscape of stacked containers, brightly coloured steel cells where to the initiated the RAL colour is a code for the type of goods transported.
The second phase of the revolution which began with the container, was to make transfer more rapid, more efficient and on a larger scale by automating and integrating the machinery. The best example of this is the extension to the terminal of the container giant ECT (Europe Combined Terminals) on the Maasvlakte. Already now the existing Delta-Sealand terminal is a state-of-the-art transshipment company. The transfer of containers is effected seemingly without people, just with bar codes, unmanned vehicles and a gigantic concrete platform simply bristling with electrodes.
The last development to visualize the port as an anonymous, synthetic environment has taken place in three 'Distriparks' (Maasvlakte, Botlek, Eemhaven). The buildings housing the expanding distribution section are predominantly of the shed typology in ever-increasing sizes. These are buildings better described in hectares than in square metres. Whenever architects are asked to contribute, these are always individuals unknown in the world of architectural magazines. Until the sixties, when familiar Rotterdam offices such as Groosman, Van den Broek & Bakema and Maaskant designed harbour buildings, the city and the port were a dual entity residing in the consciousness of architecture and planning. At the moment the profession is absent from the port's construction and that explains a certain helplessness to the designs of today's port buildings.
The hundred-metre-long walls of the un-decorated sheds have mostly blind elevations faced with some kind of panelling. At best the colour of the box refers to the logo of the firm, or the firm's name is advertised on the building. When Reebok submitted a design for a bright blue steel box of four hectares for the storage of sport shoes on the empty expanse of the Maasvlakte, the municipal amenities committee, used to assessing designs in terms of their contextual surroundings, found it an impossible task and their standard criteria floundered in quick succession. These are buildings meant to last until fully paid up, and no longer. Everything in the port is designed within an ecology of permanent transformation. These changes may be invisible, such as when many times the costs of the

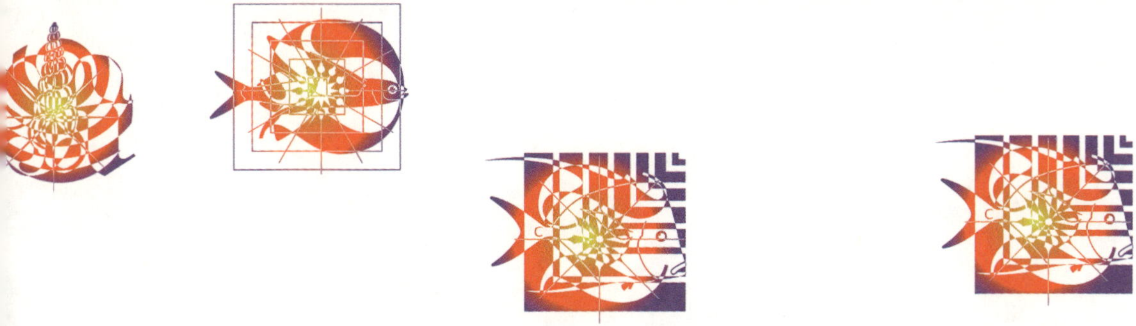

'IJstijd' (ice age), PHOTOGRAPH BY HANS WERLEMANN, 2001. Oudelandse Park, new town Hoogvliet Rotterdam

Typical architecture and atmosphere of the distribution centres

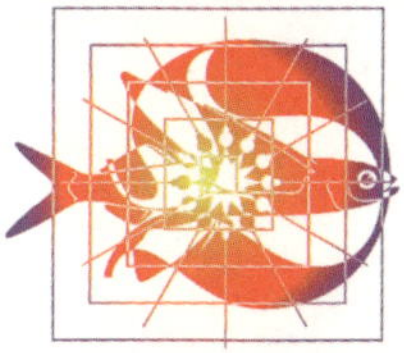

The port of Rotterdam, with the North Sea at the extreme left and the city centre at the extreme right

ロッテルダム港食料品部
ロッテルダム港では95ヘクタール(230エーカー)を果物、野菜、ジュース、冷凍食品などに割り当て、積み替え、配送に備えています。

航空輸送コネクション
ロッテルダムからアムステルダム国際空港(スキポール空港)までは、わずか70キロ。さらにロッテルダム空港も控えて航空輸送への接続も万全です。

内陸輸送
ロッテルダム港はその優れたヨーロッパ大陸内への水上輸送接続を誇り、年間17万から19万隻の内陸輸送船がロッテルダム港を訪れています。

輸送と保管

配送機能

工業用地

The pier of container giant ECT on the Maasvlakte

∧ Beach at the edge of the port ∨ Distripark in Eemhaven

Kop van Zuid development is invested by Shell within its own gates. Visible transformations usually involve features that have disappeared: a nature reserve or a few villages that are pulled down to dig a harbour basin. Another example is the port buildings of the above-mentioned Rotterdam offices, where barely thirty years have passed and they have already disappeared. The turnover rate of architecture in the port is many times that in the real city. Buildings are demolished with an unsentimental ease that makes every architect and urban planner drool with envy. As a result, the port is not a layered structure like the historical city, but perpetually different in that its previous version has been erased. If there already is a tradition, then it is the tradition of temporary existence. It resembles the city only in the manner of Rotterdam's city centre of the reconstruction period, before that too became layered to some extent.
City planning in the port is an accumulation of demands by individuals, a succession of sites primed for use without attempting any sort of coherence or harmony. It is a type of urban planning that occurs almost nowhere in the Netherlands, except in other peripheral districts such as industry parks, office parks or Carel Weeber's proposed self-build neighbourhoods. There is a minimum of spatial or visual rules, and a maximum of others: rules fixed by the technology of transport or industry and of course environmental requirements and the Nuisance Act.

Oppositions

The port should in no way be confused with the authority responsible for its running (Havenbedrijf or Port Authority).
Confrontations between national aspects - the national highways of the Department of Roads and Waterways, the goods transportation of Netherlands Rail, the nature policy of the South Holland Province - and international developments that rise far above the scale of the Netherlands, are the reason why port activity is a disparate succession of one-off occurrences. The shape the port has is the result of many compromises, each and every one of which is still physically legible. The elongated form is determined by the southern border established by the province, beyond which the port is not allowed to extend. The continued presence of the Brielse Lake and the Rozenburg and Pernis housing enclaves are examples of nature and housing respectively that according to the Port Authority really don't belong in a port; examples of situations in which the Port Authority had something in mind but was not allowed it by the Urban Planning department or the provincial government. Yet it is precisely this type of enclave that makes the port an environment of uncompromising juxtaposed oppositions. This accounts for much of its fascination.
Nature's position in the port adds to the image the port has of an environment of improbable overlappings. Simultaneous developments of infrastructure, city and

agriculture have led to stunning combinations of nature, dwelling and industry, of images, functions and uses. The unprogrammed fields of green space are used by Rotterdammers for sports and hobbies and a welter of other types of recreation that one did not even know existed. The down-to-earth anarchy of this exploitation has already been fully charted by Adriaan Geuze of West 8 Landscape Architects. Simultaneously the green zones are technical spaces and illustrate a type of double land use. Running under the clay shooting runs, the golf courses, or the scrambling area are pipes, glass fibre cables and all manner of underground infrastructure.

The electronic port

When describing the reality of the Port of Rotterdam, we tend to use terms that seem to derive from the Asiatic city: permanent unsentimental transformation, the juxtaposition of opposites, the limited importance of architecture, city planning that breaks away from the European tradition. There is an enormous programme and a great concentration of activities incompatible with a large built mass. The port appears slow, but it is swift, it seems empty, but is full. We see the occasional oil tanker, a mountain of containers, and many stationary and a few mobile cranes behind a motorway with a power station in the background. What we do not see, however, is the criss-cross of tunnels and pipes under the ground where many times the above-ground goods transportation takes place. Nor do we see underneath the concrete a network of electronic wiring and above the concrete surface, a network of infra-red rays along and above which robotic goods vehicles travel like bats. We see just as little of the innumerable scenarios that are enacted most realistically in a multitude of simulation programmes. More and more of the daily workings of the port are determined by the use of new software, so that activities are coordinated and controlled from behind a monitor in an office, far from the place where the event is taking place. One of the most extensive components of the virtual electronic port is the traffic control system. The white-blue-yellow observation posts are the beacons of a complex system with a far-reaching integration of information concerning all ships and their destination, the quays, the cargo and the weather. Stevedores, tugs and clients only have to log into the system to see when their cargo will arrive.
Another system whose aim is to increase the efficiency and speed of the port by directly linking the goods flows to one another is the EDI system (Electronic Data Interchange) which ultimately means that no paper is needed for the endless stream of information, confirmations and checks that direct the journey of the container. Or the Smart Card and the Biometric Handreader, so that truck drivers no longer have to leave their vehicle to hand in forms or get them stamped. The ever expanding databases are used not just to direct reality, but also in sys-

tems simulating and extrapolating disasters and real-life situations. Even before the Erasmus Bridge was completed it was possible to make a virtual boat journey under the bridge in the Maritime Simulation Centre, Norman Foster's building on the Wilhelmina Pier. Captains and helmsmen from ports all over the world arrive in this training centre to be instructed, to navigate a ship from a virtual bridge - a bridge that really moves - under all weather conditions and in all types of ships. Filmed images ranging from the port of Curaçao to that of Singapore are contained in the database and are used for port development studies.
With all these measures of information technology, automation and simulation, the distinction between the real and the virtual port, between hardware and software, is gradually disappearing. The image of the port is now that of a silently functioning, coded landscape, with a specific grammar of colours, bar-codes and signals. For each real occurrence there are tens of simulations with a degree of reality that differs little from the real thing. The entire port has become a smart building with glass fibre lines for data, asphalt routes for goods vehicles, railway tracks for trains and water routes for ships.

Port becomes city

The attitude of the Port Authority towards the accessibility of its domain to people and nature has undergone a drastic change in mentality since the sixties. In those days, green areas surrounding the port were conceived as camouflage greenery, as buffers to hide the docks from view. Consequently the port is only visible from Spido pleasure boats. These days the Port Authority is not as defensive in its ideas as it was. The beach at Slufter, the new nature reserve on Maasvlakte 2 and the seals off Oostvoorne are examples of nature developments betraying a new openness by the Port Authority towards those living in the city and those seeking recreation. It is not afraid to recommend the port as an educational project: the EIC (Educational Information Centre) for schools is being built on the Rozenburg peninsula.
If left to the Port Authority the port would become more 'humane'. This is regrettable, because one of the aspects that makes it such an aesthetic phenomenon is its sublime, man-made, aloof beauty, its character of untamed nature. For all that, the Port Authority hopes to entice footloose companies with an attractively designed port. In the first place they want to design the open spaces, to brighten up the desolate spots in this technological primeval forest.
We can look upon this as an implantation of city methods in the port. We should also acknowledge that the port's desire to look like the city is less interesting than the type of proto-city it is now, where things happen that would be impossible in the city itself. Not because the city, arranged according to traditional planning logic, has had its day but because the areas it has always neglected, such as

the periphery or the port, are interesting *in themselves*. We must therefore desist in stubbornly forcing upon the port the model of the real city. We should sooner consider the opposite: we can take the links between city and port seriously by assessing which qualities of the port are useful for a city such as Rotterdam. The permanent transformation, the apparent emptiness, the invisible congestion of activities, the anonymity without the burden of a fixed historical identity, the fusion of oppositions, planning as a sum and abstraction of its aesthetics - how could these contribute to the task of reinventing the city? In actual fact, these very aspects correspond to the proposals OMA makes for Rotterdam should the city eventually shake off its port identity. OMA should unleash the same fascination it has with the Asiatic city on an atypical city like Rotterdam, instead of merely superimposing the Asiatic model onto it. Behind this strategy, of course, we can discern a rhetorical dissatisfaction with the conservatism of European urban planning, but Rotterdam is definitely no example of this. Singapore is not the only place containing all those aspects that can make the city new, beautiful and exciting - they can be found here on our own doorstep.

Notes

1 Office for Metropolitan Architecture, Nyfer Forum for Economic Research, *Maa$vlakte,* The Hague, 1997, 80.

2 Ole Bouman on the role of information technology and modern physics in the work of Winka Dubbledam, Kunsthal 1996.

3 This and other information I borrowed from an interview with Henk de Bruijne, Rotterdam Port Authority.

∧ **RISC, practice boat for the fire brigade** ∨ **Maasvlakte**

The Maritime Simulation Centre in downtown Rotterdam

Control tower of the ground control system

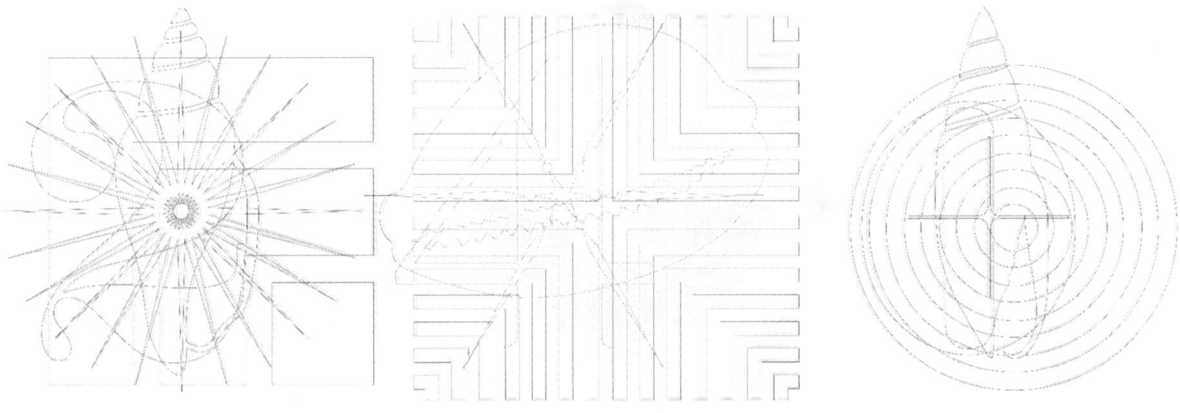

Shiny and bright

The new Dutch landscapes

A car proceeds at a leisurely pace through the Dutch landscape one sunny day. Two fresh lanes of concrete divided by a strip of grass wind their way to the horizon. A windmill on a canal is outlined against a cloudy sky straight out of a 17th-century Dutch painting. Along the way by a traffic sign a few people stand around, another looks out across a meadow dotted with haystacks. An idyllic scene, a 20th-century Ruisdael, that calls to mind roadside picnics, drive-in beaches and Sundays out driving with the family. In the fifties when everyone started buying cars, the motorway slicing ruthlessly through the virgin landscape to join two cities was probably the best way of seeing the countryside and in fact this is still so; the finest view to be had of the old and new Dutch landscapes is from the road.

Of course the motorway is part of those landscapes too. The pastoral ribbons of concrete have grown into an efficient traffic machine, a supremely controlled environment. The individual cars are guided by a sophisticated system of guard rails, white stripes, traffic lights and electronic congestion warning signs which keep both fatal accidents and economic losses down. The roads themselves, with their viaducts, intricate interchanges and flyovers are, at times when seen from the road and always when seen from the air, impressive sculptures. The motorist undergoes the 'voluntary dressage' almost without thinking; his only rebellious act is to up the maximum speed. Many people love the world of their car and have discovered the highway romanticism that in America has led to a true culture of mobility which has left its traces in literature, art and film. But there is no Dutch Jack Kerouac as yet and the American pleasure

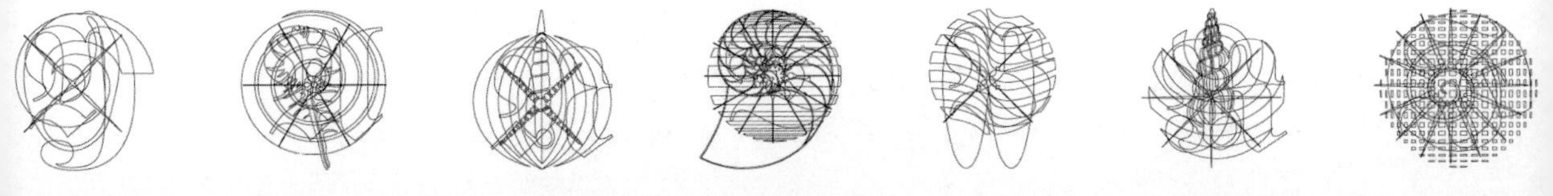

in cruising or the dream of the road movie - driving endlessly through the dark night with music on the radio and a cigarette for company - is quite unknown in this country. Our own culture of mobility consists of tailbacks and masses of traffic. Rem Koolhaas once said that Holland has no great distances, which is why we take our time. The idyllic family get-together at a motorway lay-by is not the enviable pastime it used to be. Its place has been taken by the efficient comfort of air-conditioning, car stereo and car phone. We may have no road movies or Route 66, but we do have the greatest car density in the world. I was made forcefully aware of this upon landing after a trip to Asia, where we had gaped in disbelief at the traffic chaos in so many cities, and then having to spend two hours in the Monday morning snarl-up from Schiphol airport to Rotterdam. It puts Kuala Lumpur to shame.

You can really only observe from the air just how far the motorway system extends on either side of the asphalt of its surface. Then you see that the first thing that belongs to it is a grassy slope, then a ditch, and then you get a no man's land of several hundred metres brought about by the noise and stench of vehicles, where dwelling is prohibited. This is an environment that is not designed but wholly dictated by rules and pollution control legislation. So you get sportsfields, breakers yards, private allotments, clubhouses and anything that is cluttered or of a temporary nature.
It’s not like that everywhere: you don’t find down-at-heel, unorganized residual areas along the motorway at sliproads and major interchanges. On the contrary, these are home to more and more gleaming offices of companies attracted there by the traffic roaring by. There they stand, jaunty splashes of architecture lined up at all the prime

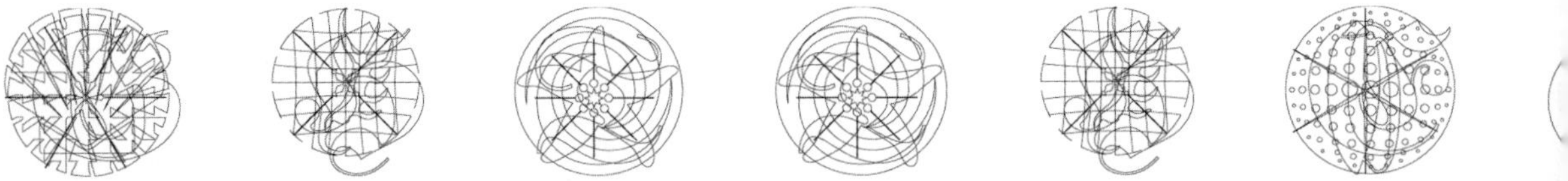

sites, one aesthetic control-sanctioned business park after the other. This environment has nothing of the pragmatic aestheticism of the motorway. Being pragmatic is not good enough for a business park; here you find buildings that have been thought long and hard about, sensitively laid out flower beds and mini-parks, roads with pavements and traffic signs, everything is neatly in place. Looked at thus, the Dutch landscape certainly is a 'well-raked office landscape' as the writer-photographer Hans Aarsman trenchantly put it after spending months on the road in the Netherlands looking for typical 'Old-Dutch scenes'.[1] Despite his distaste - Aarsman is in fact an incurable Amsterdam romantic - his photos and journal show just how surrealistic workaday reality can be, even in a business park. The core of this landscape, then, is its unreal orderliness and neatness without visible human presence. You arrive there by car in the morning, park, go in and reappear at five in the afternoon to drive back home to some suburb.

There are few who don't experience this landscape as boring and monotonous and don't feel a sense of nostalgia about everything that has been swept away in the wake of the motorways: the unsullied landscape, the picturesque villages, the unplanned aspects where time does not pass at 120 kph.
One of the rare enthusiasts who unreservedly applauds the arrival of this new urbanity is the English writer J.G. Ballard, best known to us from the filmed versions of his books *Empire of the Sun* and *Crash*. A few years back he described with relief how the sleepy town in the English countryside where he has lived for 35 years, has been turned into a suburb of Heathrow airport, with all the six-lane motorways, offices and industry this entails: 'For me this inter-urban landscape of marinas, research labs,

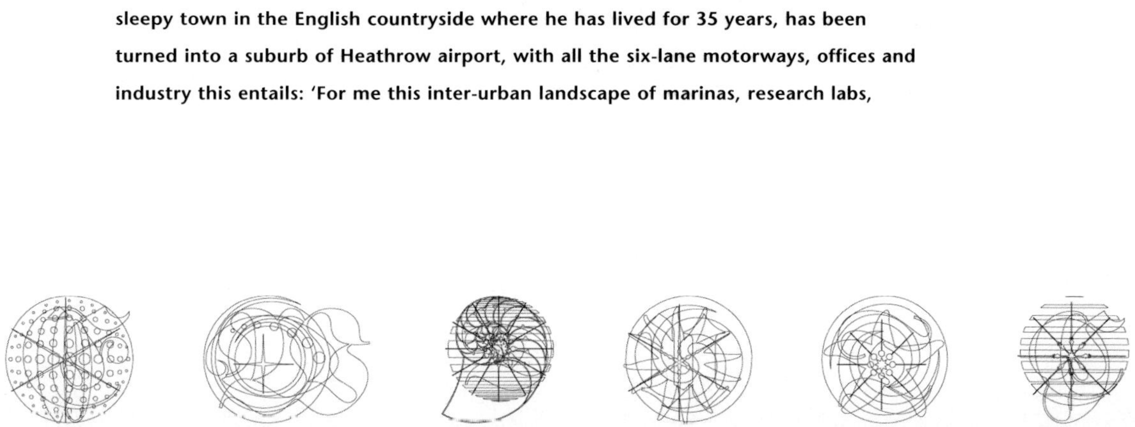

hypermarkets and industrial parks represents the most hopeful face of Britain at the end of the century. The countryside as we used to know it, apart from the National Trust's colour-coordinated nature trails, is now little more than an agribusiness by-product. We live in the TV-suburbs, among the video shops, take-aways and police speed-check cameras, and might as well make the most of them, since there is nowhere else to go.'[2]
The situation he himself describes exists across most of the Netherlands too - even across much of the world. And while it is regrettable that many of these territories are over-organized and over-designed, one also finds landscapes of a sublime beauty, where the otherworldliness of Hans Aarsman's photos is pushed to the limit. A road cutting through a meadow in which a shiny white computer factory stands; a roadside car showroom at night with cars stacked up three storeys in a dazzling white light.

Unquestionably, this slick and anonymous atmosphere is typical of the new (urban) landscapes springing up around us. Such an unreal environment is incomprehensible when pitted against the image of the city we know so well; familiar to us not just from our own experience but also out of countless famous works of the cinema and literature that have featured the city as backdrop or protagonist. Against this, there are few writers who have taken literary cognisance of the new environments of periphery, motorway or port. These evidently have no appeal. Just as Ballard abandons himself to the latest unstoppable developments with a mixture of fatalism and enthusiasm, so too there is a fine task in store for those of us in the Netherlands who wish to sound out these new and unloved landscapes.

Notes

1 Hans Aarsman, *Hollandse Taferelen*, Amsterdam 1989 2 J.G. Ballard, *A User's Guide to the Millennium. Essays and Reviews*, London 1997

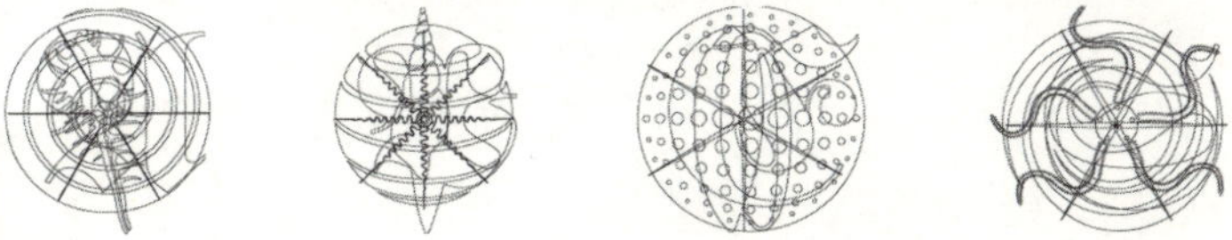

'Lemmer', photograph by Hans Aarsman 1988-1989

HONGKONG AMSTERDAM

Five Asiatic cities in a row shock *us Westerners* by the improbable overlappings of programme and form we encounter there. The physical surroundings and the use of these have a hybrid character that to us borders on the impossible: the clean image of smooth skyscrapers contrasts with the unbelievably intensive use of the street, the laissez-faire economy of shopping malls and international companies with the stalls of small family businesses, the chaos you can see with the strict (social) rules you know exist.

This hybrid character presents itself as the confrontation of the global with the local. It is generally assumed that globalization leads to uniformity in culture and economy, but at this moment old and new are still existing alongside each other. It is difficult to imagine that this hybrid moment might well be a permanent quality of Asiatic cities; surely increasing growth and wealth leads to the old condition being shaken off, as articulated in the gentrification and upgrading now happening in Singapore and Hong Kong.

The confrontation with the local is made most clear when large modernizing operations occur, such as road construction and the building of tower blocks and New Towns. Typologies deriving from the Modern Movement in the West (shopping malls, Corbusian towers in green space, gallery-access flats, Archigrammesque city machines) are taken from their avant-garde background and transformed into totally realistic Asiatic urban models, which differ utterly in their essential use and meaning from the prototypes they derive from. Pressure of land costs, high densities and the time factor have squeezed all theoretical or metaphysical meaning from them. This applies to the Linear City and Putrajaya, to the New Towns of Singapore and Hong Kong, but also to the Haussmannian road widenings in Hanoi, boulevards with no unity in their frontage but boasting individual palaces.

This moment in the development of South-East Asia is memorable in that the global and the local coexist without frustrations in a way that would be regarded as problematic in the West (think of the Bijlmermeer project): a market below a skyscraper, a wedding below a block of flats. Two modes of use, two scales, two cultures, two extremes. What we see here is how the 21st century and the Middle Ages interlock as two parallel universes; we see non-simultaneous phenomena taking place simultaneously. This is a fine thing, in that it enriches city life more than the breaking down, ordering and zoning of functions that we know in the West.

Read Down

27

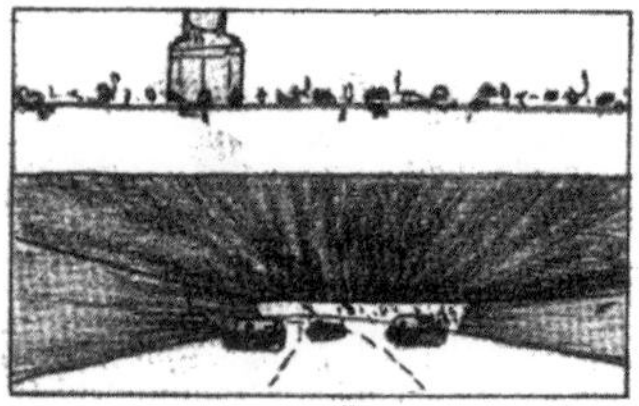
28

29

30

31

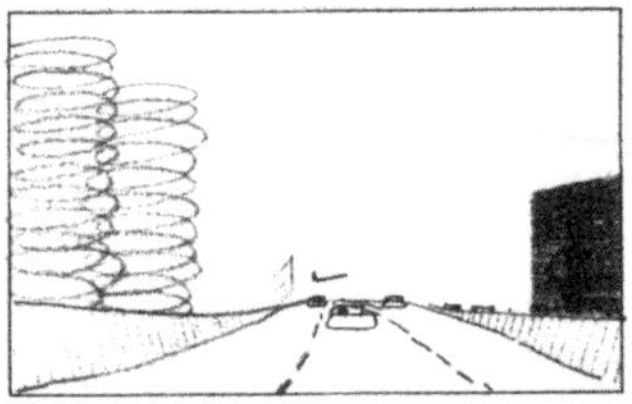
32

33

34

35

36

37

38

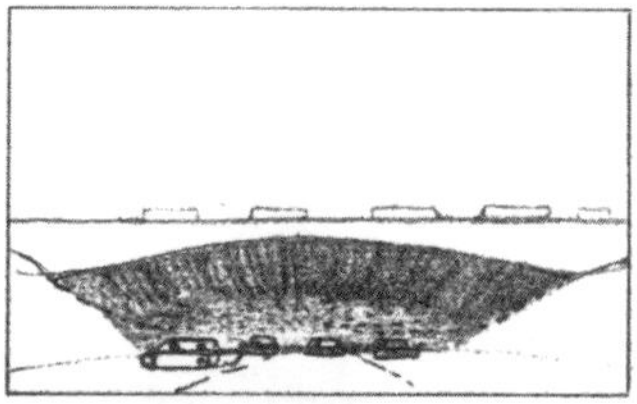
39

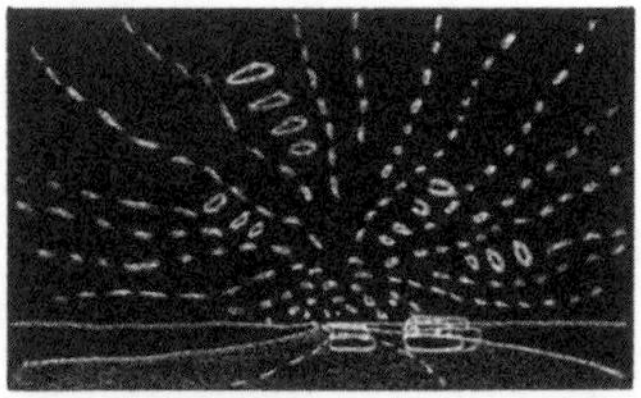
40

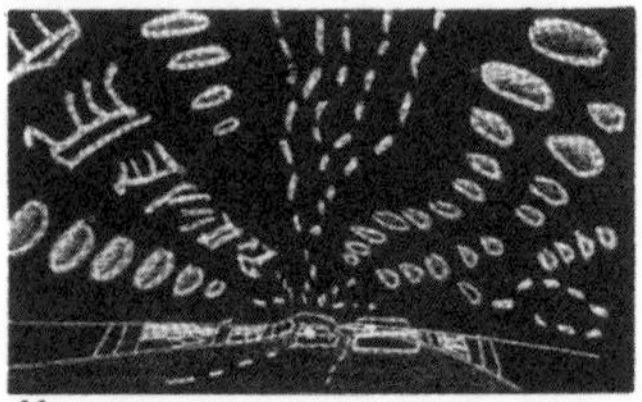
41

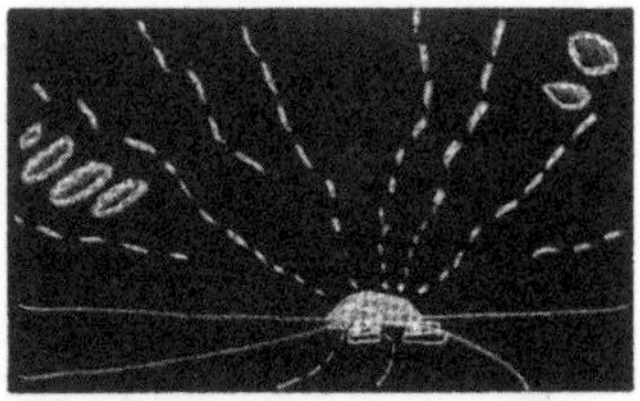
42

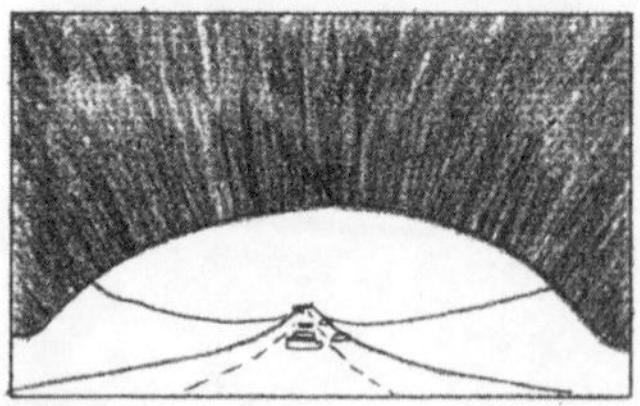
43

The view from the Boston Loop, as imagined by Kevin Lynch and Donald Appleyard

Infrarchitecturbanism

The motorways of the 1960s were designed in a spirit of pragmatic open-mindedness but above all with a clear sense of purpose: the construction of the most efficient and safest road network possible for the benefit of industrialization and internationalization. Nowadays, with the notion of context fully accepted as the basis of every urban design, and with tough environmental laws in place, such a simplification of the task is no longer possible. The implementation of infrastructure has become much more complex and paradoxical as a result of the processes of political decision-making, public debate and environmental protection through which it must steer a course. The combination of all these factors means that the design of infrastructure nowadays is treated as a form of contingency planning; the same operation that was undertaken with pride in the 1960s, is now carried out with a blush of shame. The hegemony enjoyed by technology and engineers in the 1960s has weakened; the critical debates of the 1970s about the need for new infrastructure have ceased and been replaced (in professional circles) by a polite discussion about the form the engineering works should take and the location of the routes. The situation appears to have changed in some essential way now that all manner of designers (landscape architects, architects, artists) have been allowed to take their place at the drawing board. To wat has this led? How is the unavoidable combination of infrastructure and city being given shape?

Since the 1980s when Carel Weeber designed the metro stations at Spijkenisse the institutional clients have discovered that giving form to infrastructure is an architectural task too. Now the railway lines themselves are regarded as a potential subject for design along with the nodes in the network. Now sections of road and their environs need embellishing too and motorways are designed with an eye to blending and harmonizing with the city or the countryside. But what is the value of aesthetics if it is twinned with a defensive strategy exclusively targeted at blending, harmonizing, making things invisible? What a curious idea it is to adapt infrastructure to the Dutch landscape, as if the two were polar opposites, the one artificial and the other natural. On the contrary, one might contend that laying out roads means the opportunity to give shape to an entire *new city or an* entire *new landscape. Is design really the essence of infrastructure? In fact, the current offensive by infrastructural designers seems more like the emancipation of a professional group that is bent on establishing its own kingdom; that wants to bring this last anonymous and elusive piece of the Netherlands within the structure and system of industrial and landscape design. That makes us yearn for more 'laziness', something the architect Willem Jan Neutelings advocates as 'the only remedy to rid us of the overwhelming influx of increasingly cheerful street furniture, inimitable public art objects, permanently modifying traffic situations and the succession of impenetrable city plans'.*[1]

In architecture, good increasingly means beautiful, but what is 'good' infrastructure? Traditional aesthetic and urbanistic notions are not much help in understanding infrastructural works. The same is true of the urban areas generated by motorways: the planning of such residual zones has a logic that is difficult to understand in terms of traditional urban planning. By introducing extensive aesthetic monitoring of the roadscape and aestheticizing office parks in an effort to counteract the banality of the architectural objects, designers and officials are desperately trying to get a grip on these apparently still new phenomena. This is astonishing considering how many historians, architects and artists have long since pointed out how fundamentally different the motorway is. For the most part they were foreigners, and in the first instance Americans: Victor Gruen, who led an offensive against the chaos of the commercial strip in the 1950s with the introduction of the shopping centre; ten years later Robert Venturi and Denise Scott Brown, who disciplined the popular freeway architecture in a design strategy; Edward Ruscha, who immortalized the endless American roadscape in his paintings; and Kevin

The Ruit, the ring road around Rotterdam, built in the sixties and seventies

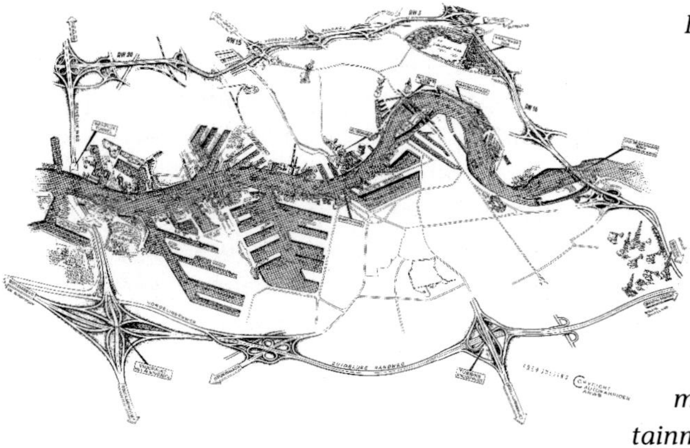

Lynch, who drew attention to the visuality of the motorway and its environs as a starting point when designing them. In England there were the Smithsons, Reyner Banham and Melvin Webber, in France Paul Virilio and Jean Baudrillard.

The architectural historian Reyner Banham paved the way for a vision on mobility as a way of life and as entertainment. In his book Los Angeles; the architecture of four ecologies *(1971) Banham confessed to his fascination for the 'freeways'. This preference, however, had nothing to do with the design of the freeways (the 'freewayscape'), but referred to the visual experience of the motorist and the 'culture of mobility' that was developing on the freeway – the rules and codes evolving in the community of car drivers in the ecology of 'autopia'. Banham did his fieldwork behind the wheel, by plunging into the mainstream of the traffic system. His only aesthetic interest was in the design of customized cars (painted, tuned up, or otherwise adapted to the personal lifestyle of the owner). Banham regarded the highway system as an 'incredibly demanding man/machine system', full of sensation and danger, with ruthless laws to which the driver had to adhere if he wished to escape alive or at least arrive at his destination. But not all examples of behaviour involve pragmatic navigation; some refer to a different way of perceiving and experiencing the city. Take the following quotation: 'The first time I saw it happen nothing registered on my conscious mind, because it all seemed so natural – as the car in front turned down the off-ramp of the San Diego freeway, the girl beside the driver pulled down the sun-visor and used the mirror on the back of it to tidy her hair. Only when I had seen a couple more incidents of the kind did I catch their import: that coming off the freeway is coming in from outdoors. A domestic or sociable journey in Los Angeles does not so much end at the door of one's destination as at the off-ramp of the freeway, the mile or two of ground-level streets counts as no more than the front drive of the house'.*[2]

Analogous to this orientation of architecture towards the highway, the book Meten en regelen aan de stad *(Measuring and regulating the city; Jan de Graaf, Ad Habets and Wim Nijenhuis) was published in the Netherlands in 1981. This was the first time an effort had been made in the Netherlands to understand the highway as a new category of 'non-place' space, an urban system that still required analysis. Unfortunately, this study is rather dominated by the Foucauldian question as to the 'workings of power' and the role of architecture and urban planning within contemporary power relations. The authors tended to regard not only the new ecology of the highway as a medium of political power, but also the democratization movements of urban renewal; it was seen as a strategy to encode and normalize human behaviour.*
Banham had already mentioned the paradox of private car ownership that enabled freedom but also demanded total public discipline: the price of hyper-individualistic, door-to-door transport is the almost complete renunciation of personal liberty during the journey. Whereas Banham regarded the adaptation of the individual to the traffic system as an innocent if far-reaching form of pragmatism, the same mechanisms were appraised as 'voluntary dressage' in Meten en regelen aan de stad*; the associations of democracy and freedom linked to the private car in the 1960s are hard to find here. Against a background of photographs of storks' nests at IJsselmondseplein and the flyovers of Kleinpolderplein, the authors postulate: 'The traffic system is a cybernetic system that normalizes bodies: the interdictions and instructions, the traffic reports on the radio and the acquired driving expertise regulate the direction and speed of progress, the time spent, the physical posture, the motor skills and the visual conduct of the motorist. The straight lines, the flyovers and balanced curves form test-tracks of disciplined behaviour. The freedom of movement is the pre-programmed freedom of binary options: to go straight on or turn right?'[3] Nonetheless, this study is one of the first attempts in the domain of architectural criticism to take the motorway seriously as something new requiring a new vocabulary and a new perspective: a project that has remained unfulfilled up to the present day.*

The American landscape artist John Brinckerhoff Jackson, a pioneer and expert in the field of highway culture, must not go unmentioned. He pointed to the fact that the highway environment is becoming increasingly uniform and offers less opportunity for recognizing or becoming attached to the place where one is currently located.[4] Should the motorist have what Jackson calls a 'sense of place' or is a 'sense of time' more practical in the universe of the highway? Is the exterior still in any way important, or is the car's interior the only context relevant to the driver? Is the highway a liberation from the genius loci*?*

If that is the case, what then is the significance of view and orientation – topics on which Kevin Lynch developed specific theories in the sixties? In the repertoire of the highway, traffic signs have more meaning than the normal panorama. Driving at a speed of 120 km an hour, the human eye lacks the capacity to assess the complexity of a traffic junction. Seeing the travel destination does not mean that one has arrived; it probably means that one has turned off the highway too late.

Despite these incongruities, which make clear just how futile traditional design concepts can be when applied to roads, railways and traffic hubs, designers who have been appointed to regulate matters of infrastructure still cling stubbornly to a Sittesque conceptual structure. Instead of recognizing the identity of the highway, they seek access to the realm of architecture. They try to breach the sameness and tedium of the Dutch landscape from the highway, try to make a place by giving striking form to static structural works. They seek to assign a sense of place to a network that has no intrinsic local identity but is the same everywhere, and has no clear need for a sense of place.

Designing for infrastructure is being increasingly done out of an interest in the static: in the elaboration of roads, noise baffles and road furniture, making use of architectural concepts such as identity, composition and harmony. Urban planning on the other hand is increasingly drawing inspiration from mobility: plans are being formulated as flowcharts and described as dynamic processes. Everything is flowing and running, the static properties of architecture have disappeared; in computer drawings, everything seems made of quicksilver. It is as if the two disciplines have overtaken one another simultaneously.

It is not surprising that the afore-mentioned designers and philosophers wrote out of a fascination with America, the country with the oldest and most deeply rooted culture of mobility*. Automobility does not exist as an attractive lifestyle in the Netherlands; the motorway is simply the dynamic part of the productive landscape; driving is a necessary evil to get from A to B. Tailbacks and busy roads spoil the pleasure of cruising, the American indulgence to which people here in the Netherlands react with envy and have tried in vain to find.*

The heroic ideas of the sixties, linked to car ownership and the opening up of the countryside by means of highways – freedom and democratic openness – have disappeared. The vision the Ministry of Public Works wished to realize at that time was that of 'Netherlands City', where all parts of the country would be brought closer and made accessible through the highways and where civilization could penetrate into the furthest corners. This situation has long been achieved and other methods of imposing civilization – such as the electronic mass media – have proved more effective and sweeping. The ideal concepts to which the mobilization of the Netherlands was linked have now become introverted: the idyllic family outing to the verge alongside the highway is no longer seen as a desirable pastime; the efficient comfort of air-conditioning, sound equipment, and the car telephone are much more in demand. The idea that the highway could be a place where one voluntarily spends some time has been replaced by the idea that the highway is the quickest connection between two places. The Netherlands only has a 'culture of mobility' in quantitative terms. We have no road movies or Route 66, but we do have the highest density of cars in the entire world.

GRAND PROJET

To make a genuine urbanistic project out of the current infrastructural projects – in much the same way as the IJsselmeer Dam or the Delta Works developed from necessary protection and pure engineering work into the 'pride of Dutch civilization' – there are a few things that need to happen. If the planned operations are important enough, they should not be regarded as a necessary evil and camouflaged, or constructed in the cheapest way possible. The issue now concerns the opportunities that are available to convert the unique combination of factors - landscape, urban, administrative, social and economic - that collectively constitute the specific Dutch situation into a distinct form of infrastructural works.

The first cardinal feature of the Dutch situation is the administrative organization responsible for the fact that plans comprising a mixture of architecture, urban planning and infrastructure are so difficult to realize. We now know what highways do, so we can predict and anticipate the tendencies to urbanize that new roads or stations elicit. An obstacle to an intelligent application of this foreknowledge, however, is the Dutch 'orgware': government and legislation, the bureaucracy of specialized institutes, the 'apartheid' among countless departments. The many new Vinex sites show us where an

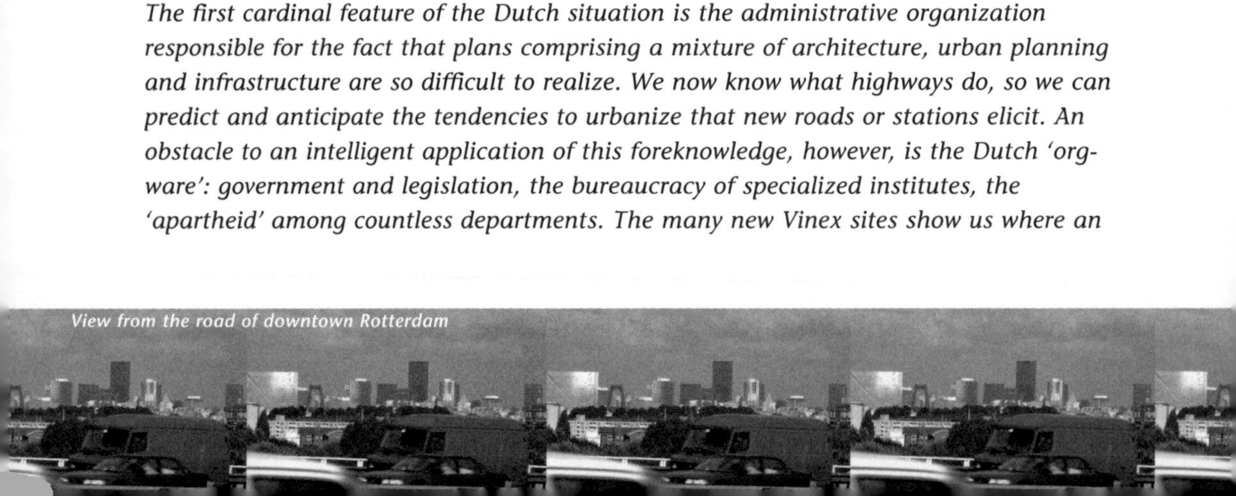

View from the road of downtown Rotterdam

organizational distinction between traffic planning, environmental planning and housing programmes can lead: even before the urban planner has put pencil to paper, the Nuisance Act has already formulated a zoning plan for infrastructure, green zones and residential areas. This specializing is crippling and requires manoeuvres from urban planners that would put an escapologist to shame.

Furthermore, we must accept that there is an essential difference between the first and the second generation of highways. The current infrastructural works cannot possibly become an autonomous structure but that is no reason for despair. Regarding and romanticizing the relative uniformity of motorways as the core of their identity is merely misdirected Americana. In fact, the contrary is probably true due to the proximity of various kinds of environments: the mutual shaping of motorway and context. Uniformity belongs to a different spatial order and a different society. In addition, the simple objectives of the fifties and sixties are confronted with the paradoxical aims and complex resources of today: restriction of the growth of mobility in combination with a flexible throughput, modal split, combicars and Personal Rapid Transit systems, 'penny lanes', toll tunnels and car pool lanes. A variety of roads should connect to these, differentiated according to usage.
If one wishes to assign preference to the motorist's experience when designing roads, to 'the view from the road' as championed by Kevin Lynch, it is impossible to place completely different environments unmediated in adjacency. The view from the car will sometimes be impeded by noise barriers or may even disappear entirely as the driver enters a tunnel. The complexity of the urban environment calls for a far-reaching differentiation of road design, of the roadscape, the view from the road and the view of the road, pragmatically considered from an all-in planning concept. A route can be designed with maximum diversity in the urban environment and simultaneously create its own landscape. The way roads and railways alternately lie underground, covered or half-covered, on a viaduct or at ground level, redresses as a welcome side-effect the existing tendency towards polarization: between the highway romance of speed and dynamics on the one hand and reactionary conservatism and anti-automobility on the other.

The third answer to the question as to how the city and the infrastructure can be interlaced lies in the character of the Dutch landscape. Both the geometrical expanses of the

polders and the picturesque and squat landscape of Randstad Holland are man-made, the result of manipulating the environment and making nature productive. The conquest of nature (by civil engineering works) is one of the few forms of intrinsic Dutch romance, more applicable than the romance of travelling and being on the road that we know from other countries. The combination of short distances and the existence of a maximum speed ensures that in the Netherlands there is no question of travelling, only of driving. In conjunction with the extreme usefulness and artificiality of the existing landscape, this leads us to conclude that the highways do not have literary, mythical or emotional significance, but are simply the conveyor belt in the productive landscape.[5]
As a consequence of its flatness and powers of abstraction, this landscape lends itself excellently to the adoption of large-scale infrastructural elements. It is not difficult to appreciate the attractiveness of this. Dyke tunnels can convert the polder into a landscape of meadows with wrinkles and folds. Highways and railways can advance invisibly and inaudibly, like archaeological lines concealed underground, while all their energy is concentrated around slip roads and stations. The dual use of the ground also increases the intensity of the productive landscape. Whereas the cities in the global network acquire new significance as concentrated nuclei of activity and information exchanges, the surrounding landscape can become greener and emptier. In this way, a unique combination of nature, civil technology and culture can arise; one of invisible yet intrusive presence, both in the city and in the landscape.

As a final and most interesting connection, we find, in the history of Rotterdam, a number of experiments in which the dynamics and the congestion of the traffic are regarded as a concrete phenomenon, one that can be used. Buildings like the Wholesale Building and the gateway buildings show how the pragmatics of infrastructure can be consumed along architectural lines. By studying what infrastructure actually is, what transport, loading, unloading and transshipment involve, new starting points for urban design need formulating, free of traditional rules and regulations. Accordingly, a new interpretation of the city has become possible and something has arisen that we can refer to as 'infrarchitecturbanism', to paraphrase an old-fashioned construct from the Modern sixties.
Cities are expanding, the landscape is expanding, motorways are expanding. Regardless of whether or not one wishes to see the Netherlands as being full, *it remains a fact that every claim on space is debatable within our planning tradition. This relative congestion*

can be interesting to the infrastructure if it is regarded not only as a problem but also as a reason to experiment with new programmatic combinations of architecture and infrastructure. We are already familiar with a number of recent pilot plans: the covering of the A2 near Utrecht at the Leidse Rijn Vinex development, Roel van Duin's proposal to superimpose 40,000 houses on the Amsterdam circular, the municipal plan for offices cum high-speed train station on a platform above the tracks at Rotterdam Central Station, Willem Jan Neutelings' study for the Antwerp ring road, OMA's contemporary versions of the Wholesale Building in the project for the A4 corridor in Rotterdam, and so forth. With these proposals, we can form a picture of how the paradox between far-reaching urbanism and the economic future of the distribution centre that is the Netherlands can be resolved without the cities and the landscape having to endure only damage and nuisance.

RING AND RUIT

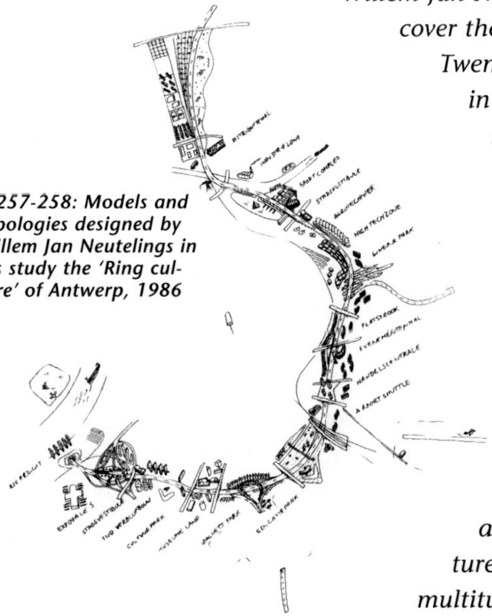

p 257-258: Models and typologies designed by Willem Jan Neutelings in his study the 'Ring culture' of Antwerp, 1986

Willem Jan Neutelings was the first European architect to discover the zones along the European urban motorways. Twenty years after Robert Venturi introduced the Strip in Las Vegas as a reservoir of images for contemporary architecture, Neutelings observed that the most exciting urban development was occurring at the city's edge. He took the parameters of the Ring in Antwerp as a topic of study in order to convert the results into a design strategy. Neutelings interpreted the developments along the Ring Road as a positive aspect of the 20th-century mass culture. He demonstrated how the locations along the Ring, due to their accessibility and central situation (in the agglomeration) were pre-eminently suited to accommodate the programmes that the mass culture demanded: 'With pleasure Neutelings surveys the multitude that indulges its buying power in furniture megastores, shuffles in closed ranks through exhibition halls, descends upon the parking lots [of amusement parks and hasten back to its freezers] with its booty of cutlets and chicken quarters'.[6]

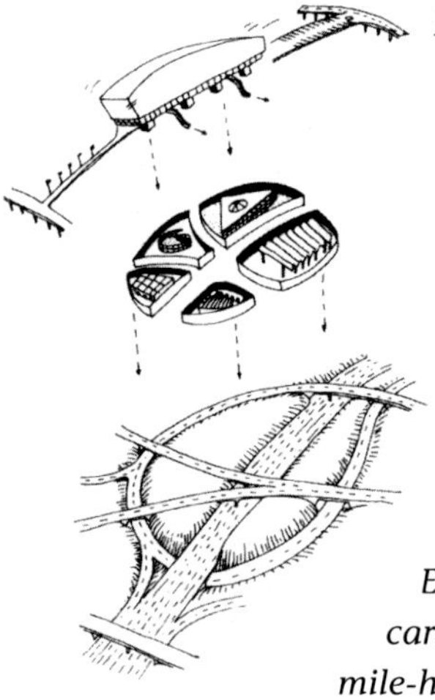

In his Fenomenologie van de Ring, *Neutelings analyses the most important spatial, functional, symbolic and morphological features of the Ring culture. As an extrapolation of existing ordering principles, he designed a developmental model for the Ring as a whole, in which an expo palace, a museum island and an education palace are among the public attractions. A number of new building typologies have been elaborated, apparently with the basic aim of presenting a picture of the enormous programmatic and visual potential of the residual zones along the urban motorways. Neutelings' buildings beguilingly span or stand adjacent to the motorway. Each one enters into an intimate relationship with the road, the cars, the view or the slip roads. In so doing Neutelings breaches a mile-high taboo: the ban on ribbon development, which was unchallenged for decades.*

Is the Antwerp Ring in any way applicable to the Ruit, Rotterdam's tangential structure of highways? What are the constituents of this Grid culture? There are significant differences between the Rotterdam Ruit and other European urban circulars. The Ruit consists of main roads whose primary function is to accommodate through rather than urban traffic. Although the Antwerp Ring was constructed in approximately the same period as the Ruit, the latter is not routed along former city fortifications, between 19th and 20th century urban quarters, but at a considerable distance from the inner city.
Unlike the Antwerp Ring, the surroundings of the Rotterdam Ruit exhibit great contrasts. To begin with, the Ruit is four times as long (40 kilometres). Its north and east sections consist of built-in urban motorways whereas the city is almost invisible behind trees and greenery when viewed from the western and southern roads. Mass culture has already taken possession of the residual zones along large parts of the Ruit, but not by erecting large-scale complexes. On either side of the motorway and the railway line, the embankments have been converted into an Arcadian idyll: hundreds of city-dwellers have created islands of nature in the shape of allotment gardens amidst the bustling traffic. From his

asphalt podium the motorist has a view of the secluded world of small marinas and houseboats on the canal. Elsewhere, where a dozen breakers yards huddle together, stacks of car wrecks are visible as a kind of memento mori. Slightly further up, the shining offices of the 'brain-parks' scream for attention at the high-visibility sites. Nevertheless, some concepts from Neutelings' analysis do apply to Rotterdam. The Franciscus hospital is typical of a whole generation of large-scale construction in the sixties. Situated on a piece of no man's land between two railway lines and motorways, it was designed with the apparent urge to enter into dialogue with the scale and speed of the motorway: The front facade is oriented towards the motorway though it cannot be approached from that side. A simple industrial box, austere lines and the absence of detail determine its architectural image. The essential attributes of this typology are the motorway slip road and the enormous surrounding parking area. The building provides an example of what Neutelings calls the 'density of emptiness' in his Fenomenologie van de Ring: the massiveness of the hospital facilities to which thousands of people stream daily has resulted not in a high development density but merely in a somewhat solitary building, a neutral personality along the motorway, that betrays little of the wealth of activities that take place within.

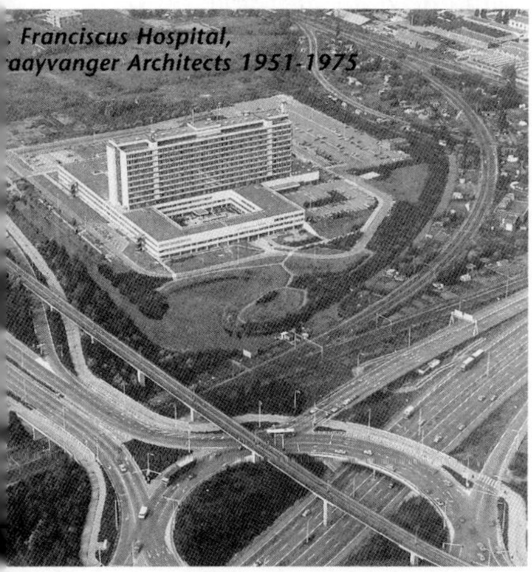
. Franciscus Hospital,
aayvanger Architects 1951-1975

Whereas the Rotterdam Urban Planning and Public Housing Agency (dS+V) is oriented towards ordering and completing elements that are unfinished and unformed, men like Willem Jan Neutelings, Rem Koolhaas and Adriaan Geuze turn their thoughts to sublimating these features in architectural design. The architects find themselves outside the institutional contexts and, from this position, arrive at the most radical proposals, rather like the avant-garde in the sixties. Koolhaas makes the motorways and their nodes a topic in architecture, both from a romantic tendency towards such places and from a certain recalcitrance with regard to the deeply rooted planning bans on ribbon development and the development of Randstad Holland's Green Heart. This is illustrated by the designs formulated by OMA for three transferia along the motorways near Rotterdam.

All three are places of transfer from the one type of transport to another, accommodated in buildings that have lost all free will and blend into the infrastructure of railways or roads. 'Dolphins' have been designed in Moordrecht: tall offices bounded by road and railway junctions and assuming their flowing curves. An outpost of the ECT container terminal has been built in Lage Zwaluwe on the Maasvlakte: a container transferium where trucks can transfer their loads to trains destined for Belgium, Germany or Rotterdam. In and between the traffic flows are a truckers' motel, a hotel, offices and sheds. The third transferium is projected above the east flank of the Ruit, in Kralingen. This time the traffic is linked to all kinds of urban public transport: tram, underground, express bus. The design is a disappearing act: it wishes to eliminate the boundary between the City of Rotterdam and its periphery. Although this boundary has been eroding for years – particularly due to the advances in transport and telecommunications – the physical signs have remained, namely motorways around the old town.

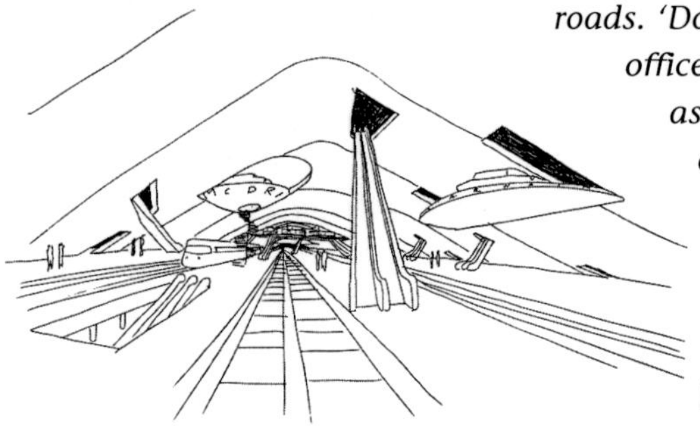

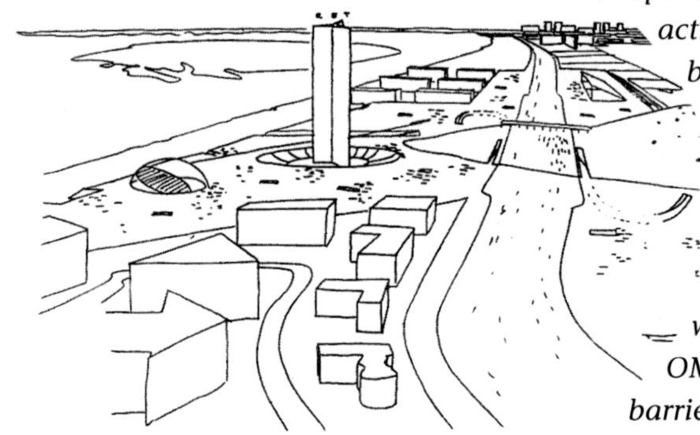

Transferium in east Rotterdam, by OMA, 1992

OMA's transferium is demolishing this barrier with the help of a building that has encapsulated the motorway in an artificial hill. In it there are parking bays in garages and on outdoor lots, and connections to other means of transport: an espace piranesien from the Star Trek era, in which a carwash and a McDrive float like UFOs. The plan radiates the romance of the Smithsons: 'One ought to believe in the future of mobility'.[7]

In addition, the transferium has a latent aggressive side. The adjacent brain-parks, which adorn the motorways like knickknacks on a shop counter, will be slowly swallowed up by advancing parking lots if the transferium turns out to be a success. It is interest-

The mammoth, a social housing high-rise linked to the highway, J.B. Bakema 1953

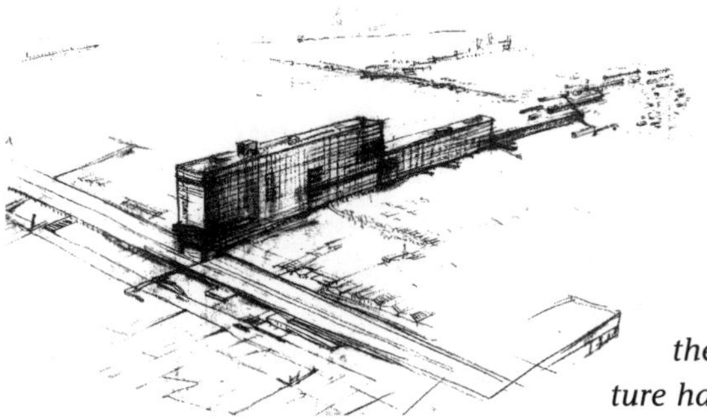

ing that, besides the boundary between city and periphery, that between infrastructure and buildings is disappearing too. With this, Koolhaas goes one step further than Bakema did at almost exactly the same site thirty years earlier. This holds in a visual as well as a logistical sense: with this building, whose function is similar to that of the roll-on roll-off system in the port, architecture has conclusively surrendered to infrastructure.

The OMA design for the A4 corridor takes as its point of departure the continuously modernizing logistics of port and transport, which without a preformulated idea nonetheless engenders new buildings and environments. The plan was drawn up in the context of 'Rotterdam 2045', an event mounted in 1995. An intensive nucleus of all kinds of infrastructure – motorways, pipelines, rail and water transport – was created at Beneluxster near Ridderkerk. In the design, the Container Recombination Industrial Site was a reaction to this 'uncontrollable explosion'. It is a complex of machine-buildings for handling and dispatching containers: hundreds of buildings, each of 70 x 70 x 40 metres. Analogous to the forthcoming ECT site, the motorway traffic and lorries run under these container machines, while the ground level is reserved for the robots (Automated Guided Vehicles) that move the containers. The port strategy and the corresponding attributes have also subsequently been deployed in the other structures that are part of the design: a mega-warehouse with a surface area of 3 million square metres above and under the A4 motorway between Vlaardingen and Schiedam, with a preposterous stacking of traffic and commercial and housing programmes, and a shopping transferium (super-supermarkets atop enormous parking garages) of 900 x 2500 metres and boasting eight towers, at the junction of the A4 with the A12 and the railway line. The quantitative and congestive urban development of the port has been boosted with public functions into a pandemonium of traffic, entertainment and commerce.

The same problems that Bakema encountered with the 'mammoth' he designed for Alexanderpolder in the fifties rear their ugly heads here too. The planning, organiza-

tion and funding of infrastructure and architecture are two separate issues. The architect can indeed include both elements in one design, yet the separate book-keeping presents a formidable obstacle. To eliminate this is an important precondition for a new approach that should be developed with an eye to the great infrastructural projects of the near future. The history of the Rotterdam Ruit illustrates the sheer scope of infrastructural interventions in the city. Their cultural significance ensures that they cannot be exclusively seen as a technological task; infrastructure is linked to a socio-economic or societal vision. The challenge that lies in future infrastructural works consists of allowing these projects to not only reflect political and financial considerations but act as a visionary starting shot for the city of the 21st century.

NOTES

1. ***W.J. Neutelings, 'Over de luiheid, recyclage, sculpturale wiskunde en vernuftigheid', in: B. Colenbrander,*** Mutaties, ***Rotterdam 1996, 13***
2. ***R. Banham,*** Los Angeles; the architecture of four ecologies, ***London 1971, 213***
3. ***J. de Graaf, A. Habets, W. Nijenhuis,*** Meten en regelen aan de stad, ***Sunschrift 170, Nijmegen 1981***
4. ***The two most important publications by John Brinckerhoff Jackson are:*** Discovering the Vernacular Landscape ***and*** A Sense of Place, a Sense of Time, ***New Haven 1994***
5. ***See: M. Provoost, 'A "grand projet" for the Netherlands. The love-hate relationship between railway, road, landscape and city',*** Archis ***1995 no.3, 68-81***
6. Willem Jan Neutelings Architect, ***010 Publishers, Rotterdam 1991, 8***
7. De verdwijning, ***OMA's account of the designs for the transferia (undated, no pagination)***

Used car dump Alexanderpolder

How can infrastructure and the city be reconciled again and profit from each other? This question was raised in Hoogvliet, a satellite town of Rotterdam where the highway has to be extended with all the risks of spoiling the living conditions. Hoogvliet asked Crimson in their capacity as 'programme directors' of WiMBY! (The International Building Exhibition taking place in Hoogvliet) to formulate an alternative to the governement planning...

In cooperation with One Architecture a brochure was made that presented our idea: to turn the technocratic highway extension into the starting point for an urban development of the existing green buffer zone which at this moment separates city and highway. The new multi-use area could function as an intermediary between them and heighten the quality of both the living environment and the driving experience.

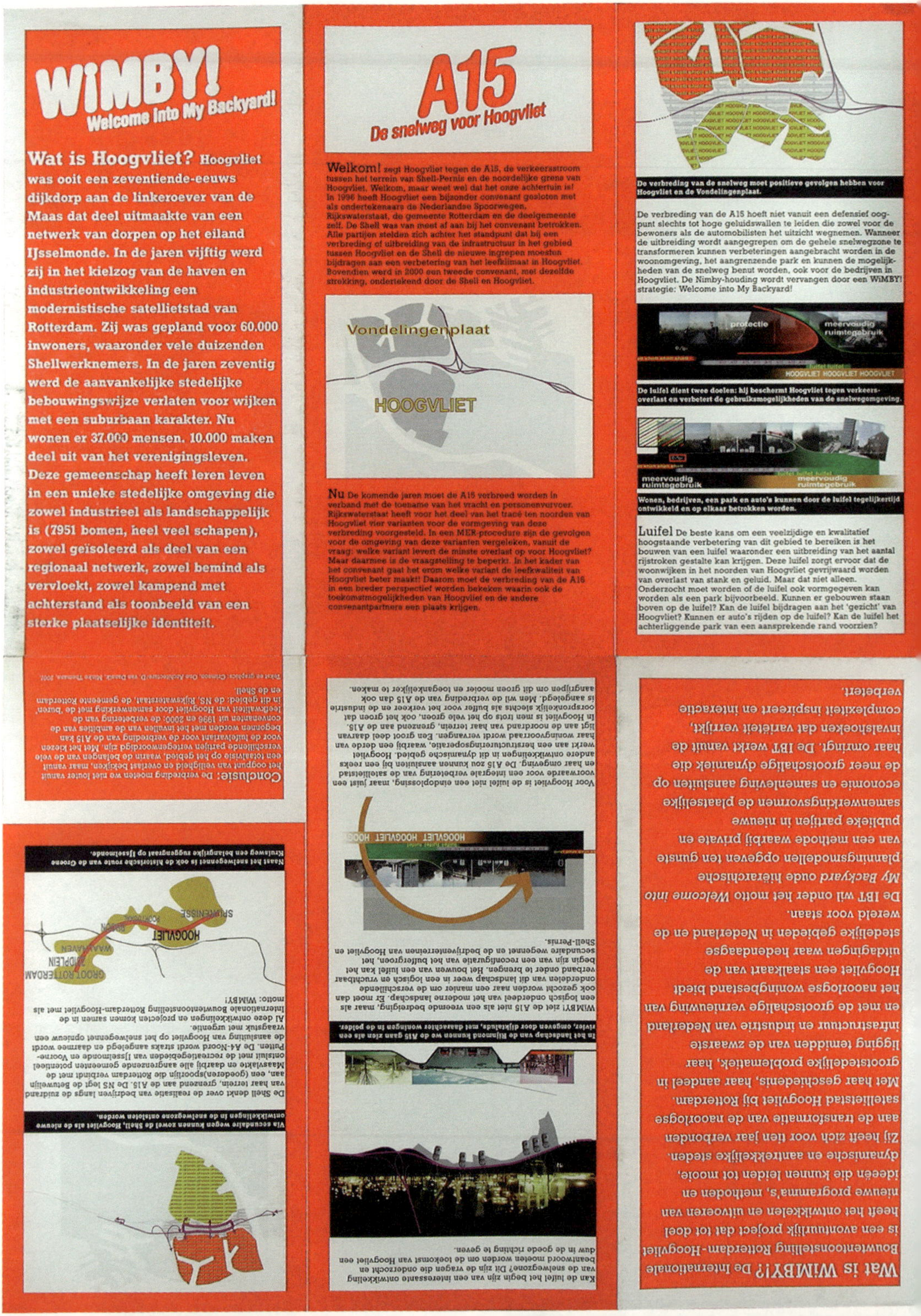

CITY OF INDUSTRY

An Architectural History of Spaanse Polder Rotterdam

The good reputation that Dutch urban planning enjoys is mainly due to the renowned designs for housing estates and urban nuclei drawn up by designers like Berlage, Van Eesteren and Van Traa. These plans that were commissioned by the government and their implementation was itself accompanied by extensive bureaucratic and financial constructs. As a consequence, they are *Gesamtkunstwerke* of planning and politics. In the history books, this brand of urban planning is the only one. Not surprisingly, then, industrial areas scarcely get a mention.

The urban planning generated by an industrial site meets criteria utterly unlike those applying to a housing estate. The ecology of industry consists of a system of machines, turning circles, siding tracks, lorries, canteens, trains. The considerations on which such urban plans are based are literally inhuman – they are about traffic and transport, the choice of site, road and rail access, business management, light incidence.

Planning takes place according to a principle that otherwise only occurs in business centres and left-over zones along the motorway and in other forsaken peripheral areas. It is founded on efficient parcelling and infrastructure, within which companies plan their buildings. This urbanism most resembles that of the 19th century when small-time private developers set up their own modest blocks of houses within plots prescribed by government.

☞ In plans for industrial areas, there is not the steady progress towards completion we do see in those for residential areas, where for example streets are laid out simultaneously. There is a field marked by lines indicating roads, harbours and railways and there are companies that occupy a place here or there. These loose batches of industry reflect the workings of the market, in contrast to the well-lubricated production of mass housing organized by the government.

For all that, Spaanse Polder ('Spanish polder') designed in the 1940s contains more urban elements than other industrial sites and even more than some housing estates. The original design aspired to create, within the limited programme, an urban environment with a centre, recreation fields, trees, vistas, shops, shrubberies and a swimming pool.

There is architecture too. Here renowned architects have erected buildings that were held in high regard by the profession. However, these works have been continually adapted to permanently changing demands. In Spaanse Polder, there is only the tradition of transience. Just as in the port or on other industrial sites, architecture is totally subordinate to economic motives. It has never become an ideal industrial neighbourhood with a high density of bustling social activity, an urban image and character, an ambience of harmony and neatness, Architecture. Thus, Spaanse Polder is a failure, though a failure with the remnants of ideas that are brilliant and idealistic at times and far-fetched at others, with a yen for urbanity and a level of ambition that bodes well for the future of this quietly simmering area.

MAKING A START

Before the war, the urban economy of Rotterdam was largely dependent on the port. The city lived on shipping, not just the loading and unloading but all the allied enterprises and undertakings. The vulnerability of this one-sided economic structure was demonstrated during the economic crisis of the thirties when the transit trade declined to the extent that the city-machine ground to a halt. The lead that Antwerp, with many other industries of its own besides the transit trade, enjoyed over Rotterdam then became apparent. A similar industrialization of service and creative companies was necessary to make Rotterdam less sensitive to global economic fluctuations.

In the 1930s, W.G. Witteveen and L.H.J. Angenot, director and head of research of the council's technical department respectively and later joint motive force behind the first post-war reconstruction plan for Rotterdam (1940), began work in those crisis years on a plan for an expansive autonomous industrial complex on the periphery of the city. In so doing, they were anticipating the large-scale division into functions and zoning that would be implemented after the war.

Within this context, a site like Spaanse Polder, connected to the major traffic arteries and to the radial extensions of the urban nucleus, was an ideal domicile for industry. The first step was expropriation, in view of the fact that the land in question belonged to a different municipality.

It is a well-known fact that the reconstruction of the centre of Rotterdam primarily rested upon a change in legislation and orgware [1]: the unbending expropriation and clearance of the bombed centre enabled a complete rethinking of the city centre. The same new (German) orgware was likewise applied to Spaanse Polder.

Once Witteveen had signed the reconstruction plan for the centre, the expropriation procedure could be initiated. Besides the inner-city areas that were earmarked for reconstruction, there was also expropriation of land designated for new industrial sites and housing. Expropriation hit Spaanse Polder as early as September 1940. [2] This was made possible by special ☞ legislation implemented in connection with the devastation of some 40 hectares (85 acres) of industrial ground in the inner city. An additional advantage was the fact that the costs of this operation were met by the reconstruction fund. At almost the same time (1941) a start was made on priming the first section of Spaanse Polder, which lay 2.10 metres below Amsterdam Ordnance Datum, by adding a layer of earth nearly 2.5 metres deep.

☞ The first urban design for Spaanse Polder, at that time a green expanse with cows and ditches, dates from 1941. It consisted of three zones with regularly parcelled industrial plots separated from one another by a green wedge with central facilities, an attribute typical of Witteveen's urban planning in its form and deployment of green space. The way in which the zones could be accessed determined their quality and their price: by road, water or rail, or a combination of these.

Besides the zoning plans, the road links were the second mainstay of the plan. Spaanse Polder was logged into the national motorway network on which the Roads and Waterways Department had just begun.

☞ The contours of Spaanse Polder were sketched and, within these, both the Town Development and Reconstruction Department and Rotterdam's trade and industry projected their perspectives on the future. Although the urban plan could be described as efficient, modern and pragmatic, the ambitions for the area reached much further. In commercial, social and architectural terms, Spaanse Polder was to become an ideal example of a post-war industrial neighbourhood – 'a complex that has no equal in the Netherlands', as Van Traa put it. The intrinsic conditions and organizational structures needed to realize this idea were tackled from the very first sketches of the area onwards.

☞ As a pioneer at the frontiers of the site, the Van Nelle factory played an important role in formulating the ambitions for the area. This meant that the design of the neighbourhood had to contribute to the social life and emancipation of the workers, that the urban plan had to incorporate the most up-to-date expertise available in the domain of industrial estates, and that Spaanse Polder had to become a pleasant, purposeful and humane environment by means of a thoughtful, functional architectural design.

First of all, these criteria were translated into designing sports fields and a swimming pool in the central green wedge as recreation facilities especially for the workers. Furthermore, a 'civic centre' was planned, in which all kinds of community amenities could be accommodated. The name betrays the influence of the British 'Trading Estates'.

In addition, severe demands were made on the architecture of the industrial buildings. A committee of men of social standing, closely associated with the reconstruction of the city centre, was set up. This committee worked as a Quality Team, establishing starting points for designing industrial buildings with the objective of harmonizing the overall picture in line with an ideal industrial image – functional and not too monumental. (3)

The contents of the guidelines laid down by the committee are not surprising when we examine the examples that most members referred to as being instances of fine, pristine industrial architecture. After all, chairman Kees van der Leeuw had commissioned the Van Nelle factory. Jo van den Broek and Wim van Tijen were both renowned modernists who worked with standardized and industrialized construction methods even in their housing projects. In addition, both had designed factories in Spaanse Polder which, although never implemented, functioned as paradigms for further fleshing out the area. The architecture had to be an expression of the production process, the form a delineation of the various departments; each factory was to be an independent entity with a patch of green on the street, the streetscape an assemblage of these independent entities strung together by a brick wall exactly two-and-a-half metres high to tie down the restless silhouette of the industrial streets. These were all trial-and-error attempts to find the ideal design for an industrial quarter that were then projected onto the rest of Spaanse Polder.

Building

Compared with the speed with which the plans for Spaanse Polder got under way, the actual occupation of the site by companies and factories was somewhat slow going. The first company started operations there in 1948. The photograph of that first domicile, an unsightly house with a hall behind it, smack in the middle of the polder expanse, does not give the most encouraging picture of the urbanity advocated here by the planners. There is certainly no trace of architectural ambition.

The quite intensive, close-knit development as presented in models and drawings and as anticipated by the Quality Team, failed to materialize. There were no close-set streets and blocks; instead, one building after another took up a solitary position within the allocated parcels. In complete contrast to housing, where neighbourhoods were extruded street by street, the 'market-driven urbanism' in Spaanse Polder tended to resemble the image of an American frontier town where small-time developers built here and there in tufts.

Even in the sixties, Spaanse Polder had yet to resemble a well-lubricated, tightly packed industrial site with an urban resonance, a controlled environment choreographed by its architecture and the collective response of the workers. Photographs present a typically expansive, peripheral image of houseboats in the harbours, caravans on empty plots, storage behind unsightly fences and people swimming – not in the pool constructed for this purpose, but in the harbour itself.

☞ Not that the architectural rules of Van den Broek and Van Tijen's committee were not applied. We can find, especially in the southern part of Spaanse Polder, streets dating from the fifties and sixties that display the intended spatial effect of openness and distance achieved by rhythmic spacing of the objects. The objects themselves are invariably extremely simple, rectangular office blocks of a concrete construction that defines the external articulation, with a hall to the rear where required. The offices generally have two storeys, occasionally with a live-in unit on the roof, while the factory hall or garage has only a single floor. Simplicity and sobriety were regarded by the architectural committee as a virtue of industrial architecture and, as such, were encouraged. Any kind of monumentality was soon written off as being 'too much'.

☞ An exception to this is the DAF garage on Schuttevaerweg designed by the engineering and architectural office of A.G. and J.D. Postma, which apparently just got by the committee. It is a combination of utilitarian spaces with a steel frame construction and representative areas in a concrete skeleton.

Spaanse Polder from the south-west, with the central green area on the right

> Montage in aerial photo of 1946 urban plan

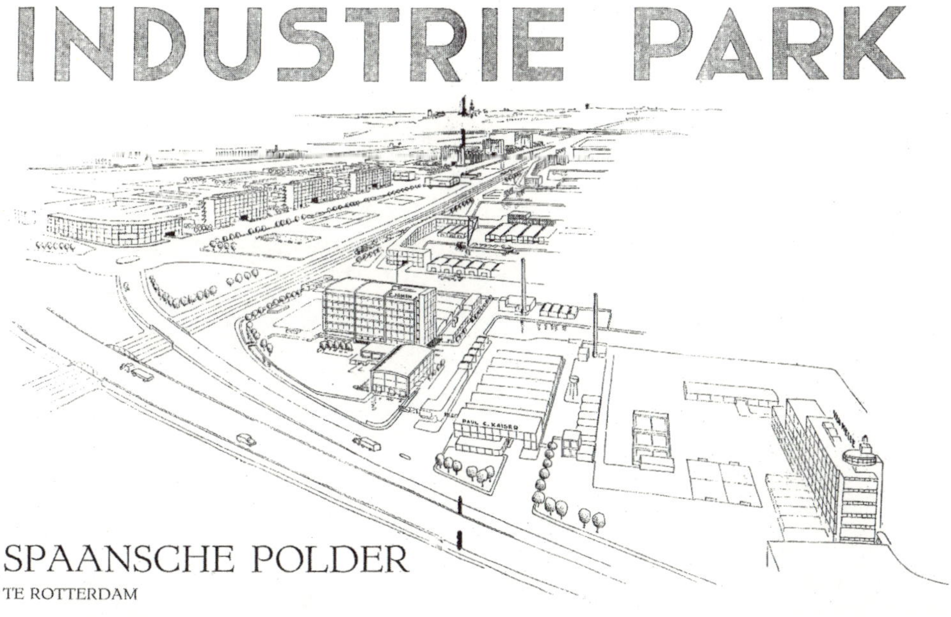

Promotional brochure for Spaanse Polder, with in the front row (left to right): Jamin factory (1941), Paul Kaiser factory (1943), Van Nelle factory (Brinkman en Van der Vlugt, 1925-1931)

Swimmers in one of Spaanse Polder's harbour basins, 1949
The first industrial firm in Spaanse Polder, more polder than industrial, 1948

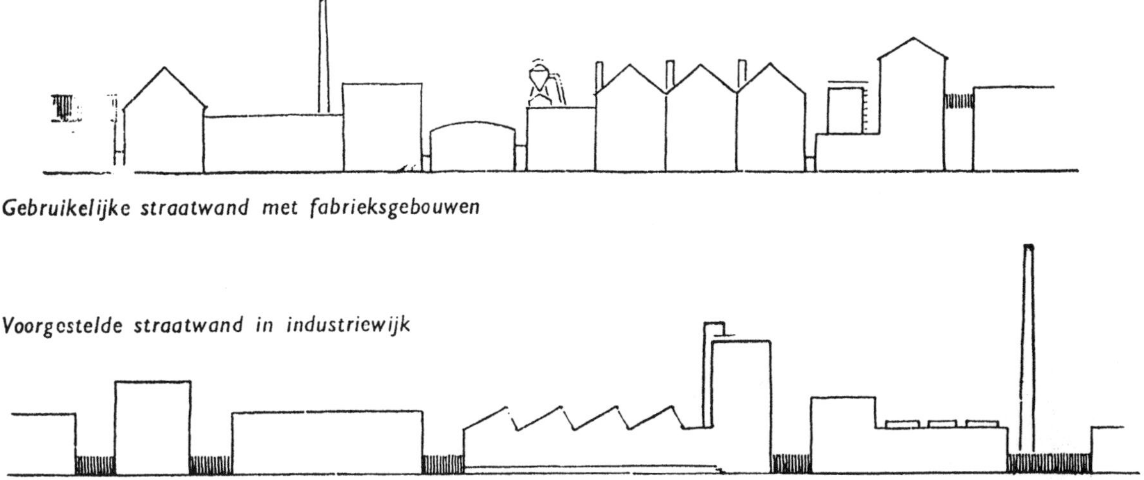

(above) The customary cluttered street facade of industrial buildings.
(below) What the street facades were planned to look like with unifying walls

A street built according to the rules:
autonomous buildings with 5 metres in-between, separated by 2.5-metre-high walls set back 30 cm

The DAF garage with its showroom for lorries, built by Postma Architects, 1958

The Sterovita milk factory, built by Lelieveldt and Hoogerwerf, 1961

The largest element in the complex is the garage, a rectangle measuring 24 x 68 metres that was constructed with steel girders to make up for the lack of supporting columns. It is a simple workplace with concrete slabs on the floor, and extremely lightweight as a consequence of the construction and the long shed roofs. By contrast, the facade has a more traditional look to it due to the positioning of the joltcrete window elements.
The company eye-catcher is the showroom – a grotesque display window for lorries – situated at the corner below an enormous DAF logo. The only access in the front facade is three metres high and is for lorries only; humans have to go to their own entrance round the back.

☞ The horizontal division of a factory into parts housing the various components of the production process, as exemplified by Van Nelle, Paul Kaiser and Jamin, was emulated by many other factories. One of these is Sterovita, a milk processing plant built in 1961 by the architects J.A. Lelieveldt and A. Hoogerwerf. The factory comprises a detached configuration of buildings of which only the office has a respectable position on the street. The slender office slab is connected by an even skinnier footbridge to an enormous, symmetrically configured factory with a tall section set centrally on a low, flat hall. In the high-rise a large void offers the director and visitors alike a view from the observation balcony of the cereal drums on the shop floor.
Only one third of the ground area was built upon, the rest remained empty, reserved for possible expansion, unimpeded due to the autonomous positioning of the office, live-in units and electrical substation. As is common with prestigious industrial buildings imbued with social and cultural ambition, the obligatory facade sculptures, murals and mosaics (a cow) were laid on in the office and in the factory.

☞ The factory that Huig Maaskant designed for the Gilda liquorice plant expresses an antithetical ambition. ④ The various components of the production process were designed as a single unit within a single rectangular volume in the same architectural language.
The different departments are divided on plan by enclosing the production floor between rows accommodating the office and the storeroom. These are linked by a wide corridor which on the ground floor is merely a dividing wall separating the shop floor into liquorice and confectionery processes and above that is crammed with toilet groups and changing rooms. Even the boiler house has been included within the contours of the rectangle.
That the architectural design can be read as various building portions in a rectangle is demonstrated in didactic fashion by the facade. At the front, the areas for the storehouse, the offices, the dispatch area and the canteen are united in the same system by the recurring steel cladding panels and the sharp horizontal lines of the roof, floor and loading platform that dominate the facade. In the side elevation, the depth of the office is indicated by a change in material from brick to concrete strips. These so-called 'vertical slats' keeping out the sun are repeatedly interrupted, as in the front facade, by dark columns in the concrete skeleton that lend a certain vertical rhythm to the facade. The entire building appears to float slightly, the loading platform necessary for the dispatch at the front providing a felicitous touch:

Maaskant saw an ideal of beauty in solid buildings that appear buoyant. The building radiates a certain monumentality created not by particularizing the representative portion, but by the reduction in the composition and the disposition of all elements within the whole; this ensures that the building is read as a single broad gesture of just a few lines.

Lorries and the large-scale

In the sixties, the area's ambitions of urbanity and completeness were traded in for the more traditional values of an industrial site: efficiency, flexibility and maximum use of the available ground. The expansion of road haulage attracted large-scale companies primarily geared to this means of transport. The building that Van den Broek and Bakema designed for the mail-order company Ter Meulen in 1962-69 is a prototypical example of a new generation of industrial buildings. It was a gigantic cube containing the head office, mail-order firm and goods warehouse. During the design process, this upscaling manifested itself in a succession of enlargements in the programme. In 1962, the building was planned to have three floors and a volume of 69,000 cubic metres; in 1964, this had become four floors with the possibility of a fifth; in 1967, there were six floors which could be increased to eight, with a volume of 130,000 cubic metres.[5] By now the limits of the building regulations had been reached.

The concrete facades display a materiality and impenetrability that suggests a solid block but on closer inspection the building turns out to be clad with precast concrete panels as if it were a vertical system ceiling. The construction is a fully flexible and adjustable response: the entire building is prefabricated with a steel skeleton.

The interior is also flexible, so much so that the whole is undefined. The ground plan originates exclusively from the requirements of free subdivision and consists of four empty quadrants separated from each other by firewalls. Four staircases on the facade are the only other fixed elements, together with a tower at the centre containing a cluster of lifts, stairs and services. Although the building is one large block, the rule of the committee of architects ('form shows function') was applied here as well to visually distinguish the various departments of the organization. They are not laid out horizontally here but stacked vertically. The offices are located behind window bands set back in the facade, the warehouses have a narrow, high strip of fenestration and the staircases are enclosed in vertical concrete shafts.

An essential component of the complex was the emptiness of much of the building site: 80 x 32 metres of ground remained untouched and was used for parking lorries, cars and bicycles. From here, the mail-order company goods were taken from the storehouses, loaded onto the lorries and dispatched to customers throughout the country.

☞ Another object that introduced a new scale was the building Jan Hoogstad designed for the firm of H.H. de Klerk en Zonen in 1968. Some of its impact derives from its incompleteness. The heavy volume of the 'Spanish tower' rises above the low, staggered fronts of a typical 1950s Van

Tijen and Maaskant industrial estate. However, the intention was to sit the tower on a platform that would eventually replace the entire industrial estate. From the rear, a slope would carry visitors to a deck that was to function as a parking lot. At the front, as the last stage of the new-build, an office would be built on the platform. So what we see today is just the first stage of warehouses and showrooms only.

This building was another to proceed from the notion of flexibility and growth, being built with a concrete skeleton that leaves the floors as open as possible. They are only interrupted by two solid cores of lifts and stairs that extend so far above the building that another three storeys could be built on if required.

☞ The building is a rare example of Brutalism in the Netherlands, not only through its ungainly placement atop the complex but also in the design and material treatment of the facades. Here too, the various spaces have been shaped in such a way that a keen observer can see what is located where. But, in this particular case, Hoogstad has seized upon and exaggerated the differences in the programme to achieve an uncustomary facade composition. Large holes have been punched in the top of the simple brick-cube shape, behind which are the showrooms. From a distance, from the motorway, the building presents itself as a recognizable company logo. We also encounter the same feeling for drama in the interior where the areas open to the public have been arranged in a rather extreme manner with ponderous concrete stairs that float above the ground, a showroom with an immense skylight and fashionable interiors laid out by the famous industrial and interior designer Kho Liang Ie.

The present

The image of Spaanse Polder as an industrial estate with an urban character, a concentration of buildings of a putative high standard architecturally, a humane and orderly environment and facilities for the social edification of the workers, is an typical idealized image from the 1940s. But the desire to substantiate this ideal seems to have been no match for the forces of economics and business management which the designers sought to subordinate to a higher socio-aesthetic order.

Although it is interesting to see which rudiments remain of that idealism, it is more interesting still to identify the brand of urbanity that does inform Spaanse Polder today.

The planned civic centre in the green wedge never materialized. The place and the role of a monumental symbol of collectivity are now fulfilled by the McDonald's on the edge of the pool along Thurledeweg. Instead of a concentration of amenities, the kiosks and restaurants have been distributed almost casually across the entire area, without conspicuous accommodation and at places uninformed by planning considerations. Nonetheless, they are there: party centres, bars, snack bars, sandwich bars and a petrol station. Potentially, given these catering establishments, there is the opportunity for dual use of these 8-to-4 industrial surroundings. A new public has now made

its entrance in Spaanse Polder. Whereas white Rotterdammers used to populate the factories during the day, Hindustanis and Surinamese now make good use of the party centres in the evenings.
There are other aspects too that one might not expect to come across at a site whose zoning is based on a strict separation of functions, aspects that were originally to the advantage of the surrounding residents but are even more so in the interest of on-site expansion, noise and other hindrance. There are flea markets held on vacant lots, a windmill on Graafstroomstraat, the collective halls of Van Tijen and Maaskant accommodate Turkish businesses; trendy architects' offices, silversmiths and hairdressers occupy the former Ter Meulen premises designed by Van den Broek and Bakema, and houseboats lie in Peltserhaven and elsewhere. It is hardly a typical picture of an orderly urban environment, yet Spaanse Polder does possess urban qualities. These could be enhanced in terms of a more varied programme for more varied users, a contemporary substantiation of the intentions the designers envisaged for the area in the 1940s, without the erstwhile hang-ups of function separation and social guardianship of the collective. Within the current notion of urbanity, Spaanse Polder need no longer be isolated as an autonomous area. The openness of the planning principle in Spaanse Polder, the zoning into neutral fields of varying size, the flexibility of the plan and of the architecture are historical ingredients that present themselves when thinking about the area's future. The flexible structure enables the adoption of major functional alterations that continue along the chosen path of broadening the use of Spaanse Polder. This will undoubtedly be determined by a shift from a few large factories to many small offices, from blue collar to white collar, by the growing presence of consumerism and the retail trade, by the business of selling which prefers cacophonous buildings bristling with billboards to quiet and introverted architecture, by the growing presence of immigrants who make use of other kinds of firms and party centres. Within the neutrality of the plan and the urbanity lurking within it, these current developments indicate the parameters for the future.

Notes

1 Orgware, abbreviation of organization-ware: all factors that have anything to do with administration, organization, regulations, laws and politics.

2 The expropriated ground became a part of the Municipality of Rotterdam due to a boundary change between Overschie and Rotterdam in May 1940, just before the German invasion.

3 Memo from Van Traa, 11 November 1947, Archives of the Department of Urban Planning, box 17, G.A.R.

4 See: H.A. Maaskant, 'Fabriek van suikerwerken', *Bouw* 1959, 1010-1011

5 Folder: *Hoofdkantoor, magazijnen en postorderbedrijf H. ter Meulen,* RKS 1992

The Gilda biscuits and sweets factory, designed by Huig Maaskant, 1957

Showrooms and warehouses for H.H. de Klerk, Jan Hoogstad 1968. Interior design by Kho Liang Ie

'The Cube', building for mail-order company Ter Meulen by Van den Broek & Bakema, 1962-1969

Highways and lorries characteristic of Spaanse Polder in the sixties

Hindu festivities in the Blokhut bar, diving club and windmills: the new inhabitants of Spaanse Polder

URBANISM, STRIPPED BARE

Rients Dijkstra

The circumstances for ground-breaking progress in the field of urbanism are ideal. Holland has a production backlog of sorts, has growth potential, real problems, needy clients, money, experience with the large-scale operation, and almost unparalleled organizational and managerial expertise. If one were asked to outline an experimental set-up devised to boost professional evolution, these are the ingredients that would have to be contained in the Urbanists' Biosphere. It is quite disturbing then, that the recent production and the debate about it are so light.

= One of the issues worth researching is that the Dutch Government (through the RPD, its planning department) promotes URBANITY: compact city, intensive ground use, high-density central urban mixed-use milieus. The Dutch citizen, on the other hand, gravitates towards the exurban, garden-rooted, single-family house. Los Angeles[1] seems to be the only realistic combination of these two inclinations: a compact, working, all-inclusive pancake of single-family houses for 16.7 million people. Los Angeles, on the other hand, is considered to be a detestable city by a large portion of the professional critics. It would most likely be just as appalling to the citizens of Holland, if they were to be confronted with it.

= To escape this outcome, suppose that we drop all instances of governmental or supervisory will. Holland will then become like Belgium, but twice as densely packed, without the Ardennes, wetter and lacking in gastronomy. The appearance of Belgium is a source of continuous ridicule to the Dutch all the same.

= The conclusion has to be that the Dutch, the compromising collective that they are, desire what they despise. In the coming 10 to 15 years, we will be free to build what we want but we will not like the result. What are we doing to prevent this?

Here come the mutants

The world is a hurricane of events with architects, urbanists and planners trapped in its eye. They hear the faint rumble, they notice something different in the light, they stick up their wet fingers: 'It sure is a perfectly quiet day today'. Some attempt to develop suitable theories to catch up with the rapid changes that happen to our cities and our nature. But these theories only come in the shape of applets or service packs that cosmetically patch up 'Ye Olde Theory'. 'Ye Olde Theory' is a blend of classical pre-mobility urbanism ('the centre is dense and is in the middle') mixed with equal amounts of congestion theory (1978!), Tapijtmetropool (carpet metropolis, 1989) and housing milieus (1990s).

= The common practice is to absorb the events and wrap a theory around them: cling-film theorizing. This has brought forth a shitload of mutant urbanities, to the extent that finally even landscape has been deemed urban. There are four main mutations: Quantitative Urbanism, Socio-Economic Urbanism, Image Urbanism and Experience Urbanism.

= Quantitative Urbanism implies that something is considered to be urbanism based on HOW MUCH is happening. It is Manhattan, Bombay, Los Angeles, Tokyo, and traffic jams, pop festivals or refugee camps. Social Urbanism is based on WHAT HAPPENS (between people). It is Jane Jacobs, street life in warm countries, all sorts of socio-utopian models,

New Urbanism (although critics maintain that it is Image Urbanism). Image Urbanism is based upon a plaster-mouldable, marketable recycling of popular urban images. It is what Jon Jerde's work is made up of (sometimes so intensively that it turns into Experience Urbanism), it is New Urbanism (whose founders claim that it is a brand of Social Urbanism). Experience Urbanism is to urbanity what experience economy is to retail. It is urbanity played out as events, manifestations, riots, demonstrations, Olympic Games. ═ Recently we have been asked, twice, to give OUR opinion about urbanity.[2] We wondered what would happen if we were to resist proliferation and instead try to uncover the axioms of the urban: Urbanism, Stripped Bare (hereafter referred to as USB).

CITY = MAN + ARTEFACT

Quantity. At the heart of our definition of urbanity is a marriage of amount and size. To be urban a thing needs to be able to house a minimum amount of people and artefacts. It needs a minimum size too: anything smaller than 1 km^2 should not be called urban. Surface and quantity determine density. There should be a lower limit to this too. We need minimum lifespan but that is being taken care of by the artefacts: a city with enough stuff will not have a short life, for obvious economic reasons. The artefacts are there to protect the people, to provide them with a network and to make sure that they don't leave too soon.

═ Only people: not urban; only artefacts: not urban; everything in a computer: not urban, cyburban at most. Small isolated settlements: not urban due to a lack of people and artefacts; large settlements with a low residential density: not urban, but suburban (Broadacre City, Auckland); large settlements with a low density of artefacts: not urban (pop festivals, refugee camps).
═ Until now, this definition lacks a social component: urbanity already starts as soon as 1 km^2 of surface is inhabited by, say, 10,000 people in need of a lot of buildings and infrastructure. A large number of the existing definitions begin with the social component. In 'Ye Olde Theory' and all of its derivatives and additions, the social component comes in the form of a preferred type of intense human interaction. (This is what links Jane Jacobs and the celebrated Mr. K: urbanity of young and old people, people who dwell and people who work and all of them mixed up in densely built, busy neighbourhoods.) I will propose an alternative soon.

The third reason

Why worry about the definition at all? Is there any reason left to WANT urbanity? What can you achieve with urbanity that cannot be achieved with other means? Do the advantages outweigh the disadvantages? There are, still, three really good reasons to want urbanity (these are not globally true, but in the first world countries, they are): First reason. Because there is a need for it. Because some people want it. They are willing to pay for it. This is urbanity based on the human need for input, experiences, opportunity, social contacts, hope. ═ Next. Urbanity stimulates cultural production. A large part of the cultural production of

any nation takes place in its cities. A country needs this culture for reasons of identity and economy. It is the city as a factory (of cultural products): urbanity creates economic value.
═ The third reason. Urbanity restricts the consumption of surface. Raising density, for instance, is the only way to limit the size of the city. This is urbanity used to control what kind of surfaces (urban, suburban, man-made nature, nature, etc.) a country has in stock.
═ What is hugely underestimated, by urban planners and ecologists alike, is that a sloppily built city has an enormous impact on the surface that is not used by the city. We have discussed Vinex and how ugly that turned out to be (to professional critics; inhabitants seem to like it), but we have forgotten to look at the effect Vinex (and all other substance built at the same time) has on its surroundings. The sloppily built city brings about related amounts of sloppy, un-urbanized landscape.
═ Countries with abundant nature do not have to be fussy about the third reason for urbanity, yet. But in all densely built-up countries, like Holland, one of the most important reasons to build urban substance should also be the value it has for the landscape.
═ The third reason works both ways: good landscape is of vital importance to the city. The third reason for urbanity - better cities for better landscape for better cities - forces a valuable parameter into the definition: the typology of the urban plan (its shape, its spatial characteristics).

CITY = MATTER^3 x NETWORK

Back to the social component. The recent history of urbanism clearly shows the dangers of blueprinting certain types of social behaviour in urban matter. Not just that: the demise or constriction of the 'proper city', the good cities that were long believed to be absolute, is because we anticipated certain types of living too strongly.
═ 'Ye Olde Theory', too, is stuck with a nostalgia for the classic European City (Berlin, Paris, Prague). When large numbers of people started to return, from the city, to the country, to build their cities away from the congestion, they were expelled by urbanites and urban theorists. Their urban product, the suburb, was never granted a front seat in the debate.
═ Because our specialism is surface and not social interaction, because it is naive and dangerous to try and freeze a certain class of social activities in built form, we should refrain from moral judgement and concentrate on the spatial needs of (any kind of) social interaction. We should refrain from attempts to stimulate certain types of social behaviour and suppress others. All we should do is study ways to accommodate social behaviour, whatever form it may take.
═ The obvious solution is: provide for connections and you provide for social behaviour. (Restrict connections and you restrict social behaviour. Take Bijlmermeer as an example: it was definitely urban on the basis of its size and population number. But the network was flawed. No serious study has been made yet of the demise of Bijlmermeer because of a NETWORK FAILURE.)
═ An efficient network is a prerequisite for and great stimulant of urbanity. This is not to

say that connections are all you need to produce urbanity. Ten million people spread out over the globe with mobile phones, free calling cards and each other's numbers are NOT a city. This 'community' lacks stuff, lacks density, lacks temporal stability. The common belief is that they are networked, because they could all get in touch with each other, but they are not. What is the equivalent of a riot in this community? (10,000 people all calling 5 other people at the same time, shouting: 'we want bandwidth! we want bandwidth!'. They in turn are called by 200 policemen who tell them to stop it. Next, things get out of hand?) This so-called network lacks the possibility of complex interaction.
═ Sloppily built city spoils landscape. Sloppily networked urban tissue reduces the opportunity for that tissue to become urban. Compact shape and network are mutually enforcing. It is hard to build networks using isolated, fragmented or linear bits of city. It is easy to build networks in omnidirectional and compact tissue. One of the best and most beautiful examples is Los Angeles.

GONE

This definition of urbanity, stripped bare, seems harmless. It emphasizes size, quantity (of people and of stuff), density, shape and network, notions that are implied in almost any definition of the urban. Axiomatic quality can be claimed because it excludes all other categories, there is no further speculation. But, if this definition is unleashed on all manner of existing notions of urbanity, then it turns out that many of the familiar ingredients of the city are gone. The definition says nothing about centre, says nothing about modes of transport, nothing about programme or mix of programmes, is not specific about social programme, says nothing about culture, nothing about building typology.
═ To see how it works, it is interesting to look at one of the most controversial urban constructs of the 20th century, using the new USB definition: the gated community. It is considered to be one of the worst urban inventions ever. According to USB, it is not. It adds to the size, the amount and the density like any other neighbourhood. In the morning, it spits out people that will contribute to the urbanity elsewhere. A gated community houses dwellers, workers and culture-producers like every other neighbourhood. Its biggest flaw is that it does not contribute to the network; in fact it is a hole in the network. In that way it is like a fenced park, closed after dark. Most gated communities look like parks from the outside. Parks and nature can also be defined using USB; it is no people, no artefacts (and therefore no network, except for plants and animals), sufficiently sized. In USB terms, raw, non-recreational nature is a gated community too, for animals. Let's define Urbanism, Stripped Bare and start from scratch.

Notes **1** Los Angeles County, Riverside and Anaheim. **2** The commissions were issued by the RPD (Dutch National Spatial Planning Agency), who needed input for the discussions surrounding the Fifth Report On Spatial Planning, and by Stichting Hoogbouw (the High-rise Foundation), who wanted to renew the foundations of their programme for propagating high-rise. **3** Matter, in this formula, includes people.

LA: a satellite image showing 85 km x 52.5 km of **LA**. Image scale: 1 cm = 5.667 km.

	S= (km2)	R= (km1)	people x 1E6	people / km2
Mulberry Bend	0.011	0.06	0.0057	**505848**
Jane Jacobs	0.004	0.04	0.0002	**56832**
SanFran North Beach	2.6	0.9	0.08	**30888**
Manhattan	60	4.4	1.54	**25802**
1E6 on 100 km2	100	6	1	**10000**
Tokyo	2186	26	11.9	**5444**
Hong Kong	1040	18	5.5	**5323**
LA city	1200	20	3.8	**3167**
Leidsche Rijn	25	3	0.07	**2800**
LA county	10600	58	9.9	**934**
Randstad	6970	47	6.0	**861**
Nederland 2050	34000	104	20.0	**588**
Nederland 2001	33883	104	16.1	**475**
India	2973190	973	1030	**346**

the best weather is just a few clouds.
(18 · SEP 2007 @ 18:00 DUBLIN SKY)
(on the plane?)

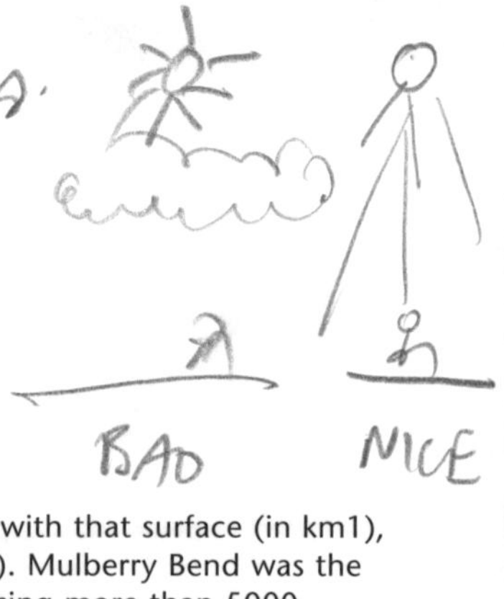

sizes and densities: the surface **S** in km², the length **L** of the side of a square with that surface (in km1), the number of people (in millions) and the resulting density (people per km²). Mulberry Bend was the most infamous slum in 19th century New York. A little over 1 ha in size, housing more than 5000 people, it is one of the highest population densities ever recorded anywhere.

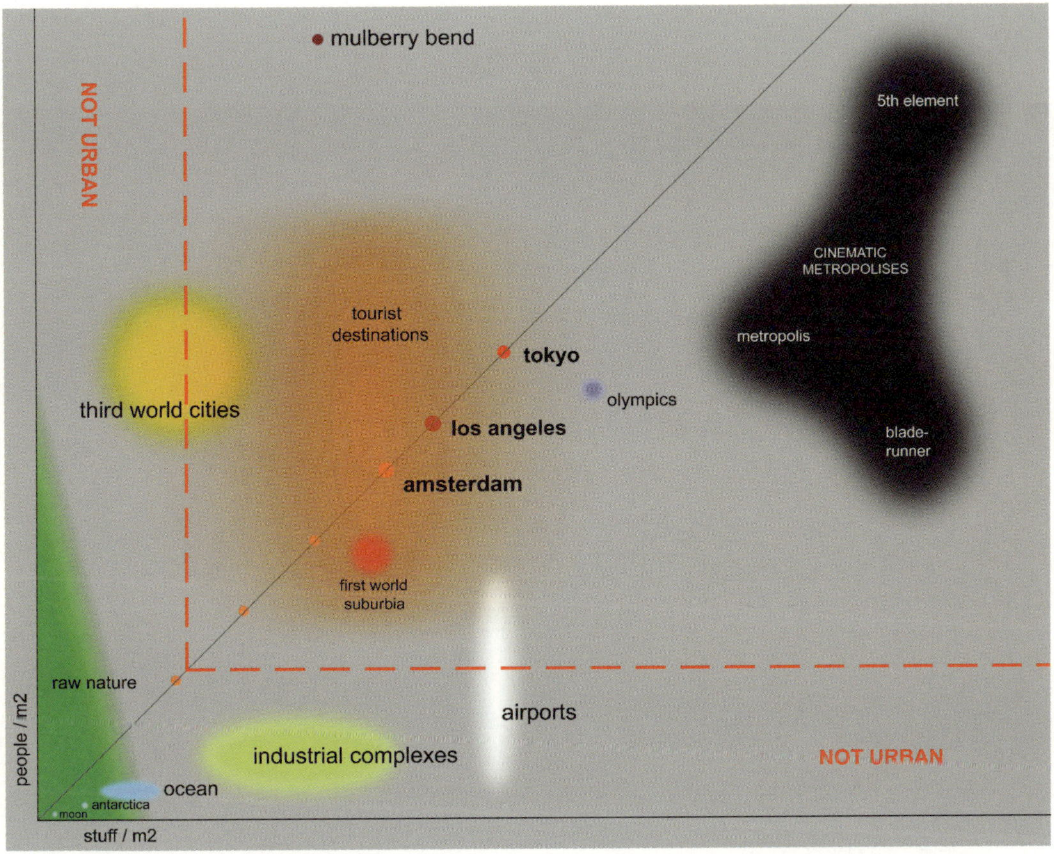

people and matter: the USB diagram of urbanity, focusing on matter only (amount of people, amount of stuff). To the left of and below the red dashed line: **NOT URBAN**.

DeltaMetropool: a satellite image showing 85 km x 52.5 km of the Deltametropool. Image scale: 1 cm = 5.667 km.

there goes the neighbourhood

The first urban renewal

Apart from the large and prestigious projects in the pipeline for Rotterdam (the high-speed rail link or a new airport), apart from the records the city seeks to hold or break (largest port, most modern centre), there are 600,000 Rotterdammers living in ordinary residential districts. Nothing much ever happens in those districts, they are maintained with small unobtrusive and fragmented projects and keep a low profile. Having said that though, 25 years ago they too were part of a celebrated project, a familiar Rotterdam export product: urban renewal.

The first urban renewal programme was enacted within the existing physical contours of the districts. It was an enormous project involving the building and redeveloping of 70,000 dwellings yet it presented itself as a collection of small interventions, as a dissemination of prefab roof units, bay windows, mansard roofs, cycle racks, flower boxes, benches, railroad sleepers and composite cladding boards. But all this concealed a major operation, that of withdrawing a gigantic quantity of real estate from the complex ecology dominated by private owners and landlords. Just as the jerry building districts in their day had sprung up with the arrival of mortgage financing, so too was urban renewal facilitated by financial innovation: urban renewal funds, the 'interim balance ruling' and individual rent subsidy. This meant that as of 1974, the year that Rotterdam gained a left-wing council and urban renewal shot to the top of the list, Alderman Mentink could spend millions buying properties from the landlords, the successors to the small-scale private developers of yore and just as unpopular. The previously vilified districts of jerry-building were transformed into government-managed complexes of public housing; this was a more sensitive blow against the unplanned city than any dealt by modernistic urban planning. As a result, the districts were purged of every notion of market, economy or profit.

This centralizing of the possession and management of the old districts was implemented by decentralizing the municipal services. The city was divided into eleven urban renewal districts. Project groups were set up in the centre of each, manned by officials and residents and *not* by property owners. The project groups decided which properties were to be demolished and which retained, where a local square was to be and which architects were to work on a project. They were led by young designers from the Town Development Agency, those who some years earlier had been fleshing out immense satellite towns at the instigation of agency director Lotte-Stam Beese. Now they were being sent into these eleven districts to 'build for the neighbourhood' and construct traffic-calmed residential precincts (*woonerven*) in deliberation with the residents.

Besides the colossal transformation of the city's 'orgware' (the assemblage of organizational, policy-making, administrative, financial and legislative structures), urban renewal ushered in a large-scale transformation of its software, the notion of city. This was a strategy best attested to by its slogan: building for the neighbour-

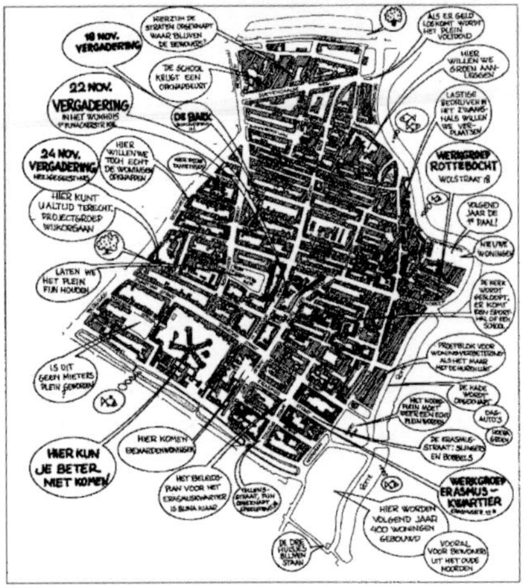

Urban Renewal 'planning' scheme for Noordsingel area, Rotterdam ca. 1975

hood. Urban renewal was presented as giving the city back to its inhabitants by presenting plans not at the scale of the city as a whole but at neighbourhood level. The neighbourhood, not the city, was regarded as the unit of social life. The city was written out of the narrative; it imploded in a cluster of neighbourhoods, each of which would embrace collective life separately.

The second urban renewal

The successes scored by urban renewal in terms of the house and its immediate surroundings were considerable, and this permanent cycle of use, dilapidation and improvement of city districts had to continue. But we must look also at the limitations of urban renewal. True, politico-ideological and psycho-social ambition have departed urban planning since then; yet the transformations from the urban renewal era in organization and in the basic idea of the city live on. The city, city planning and the idea of urbanity are still divided into enclaves that coincide with neighbourhoods and/or sub-municipalities in the hands of project groups. Plans for the city as a whole are at most inventories of the various neighbourhood projects. Even today the urban agglomeration falls beyond the horizon of urban planning, as a single large field.

Since the advent of urban renewal, planning practice has been directed inwards and large visionary schemes for the entire city were no longer feasible within the new conception of what urban planning entailed. And since the denouncement of Plan 2000+, the last major scheme to wrap port and city in a single concept, the port was not the inseparable part of the city it used to be, but something the city needed to defend itself against. The relationship between city and port was broken. There were protests against the construction of a number of motorways for the same reasons of noise, stench and danger. The legislation on pollution control subsequently ensured that port, motorways and districts, and therefore also industry, companies and houses, were kept at a safe distance from one another.

In addition urban renewal also functioned as a sprucing-up project *within* the districts. The existing commercial activity was sacrificed to the snugness of neighbourhood life; to guarantee a street life like that of the 19th-century Jordaan district in Amsterdam the small workplaces and businesses that might be inconveniencing in some way were moved elsewhere or closed down. The same went for residents who failed to fit this 19th-century snugness such as illegal guest workers, garage proprietors or prostitutes. This way, the ideal residential district was created within the contours of the old jerry building, under the aegis of government and the corporations and purged of commercial activity. So despite the fact that urban renewal virtually coincides with its historical context, we could regard it as a Modern Project in an urbanistic-historical sense, one that meets the division into functions as set down in the Athens Charter just as well as Ommoord in the north-east of Rotterdam or Bijlmermeer in the south-east of Amsterdam.

Meanwhile the disadvantages and impossibilities of this approach have become evident: districts that were renewed in the 1970s are now ripe for renewal again. High-ranking government officials are now even criticizing urban renewal because for them it has only spawned poverty-stricken areas with unemployment and deplorable social conditions. Urban restructuring and urban conglomerate policy are the way to fight such problems. This means supervisors for youth hangouts and keeping porches locked at night; social renewal as a means of tackling the symptoms. Post-renewal urban culture has in a way become oversensitive and exclusive. By defining the city in terms of neighbourhood and dwelling, more and more urban aspects are shaping up as a threat: local commerce, mobility, addiction, informality. These components - there whether we like it or not - are not part of an urbanistic project, which is why they present major problems. At which point camouflage and disaster prevention plans are the only possible reaction on the part of city council and city planning. These have exaggeratedly innocent expectations of today's city.

The City of Rotterdam calls these spasms of social renewal and revampings of post-war and urban renewal districts the second urban renewal. Actually it is nothing other than the next instalment of the first, but then without a specific ideal. The first urban renewal had been a revolutionary undertaking, a massive project that operated at the smallest scale, entailing an intense organizational, political and financial transformation and underpinned by an idea and a narrative about the city. As far as we are concerned, the real second urban renewal, in the light of today's city and today's briefs, should be kick-started as a separate project with its own idea and its own narrative regarding the city. That narrative must be about how Rotterdam functions at the turn of the millennium, how it is run, how it is used, what it looks like. It starts not with the house but with the city as a whole, and all the beautiful and ugly things that go on in it.

One of the greatest problems in the old districts besides unemployment is the depleting level of amenities, and the resources of 'classic' urban renewal are no match for this. Where most people live there is simply too little to do. This has to do with the fact that the extent of available amenities is still rooted in the existing blueprint. So the number of inhabitants gets translated into the number of activities and the amount of programme on site. This is a relic of both the 'neighbourhood concept' and the concepts of urban renewal, in which the neighbourhood is wielded as the measure of all things. But there is no longer a homogeneous neighbourhood life, and street life is light years away from that of a convivial 19th-century district. There is a rear guard action raging against a city structure that is getting more and more fluid and a city-dweller who is becoming more and more mobile. The neighbourhood boundaries have long stopped functioning as a limit to the activities of their inhabitants. These may live in Oude Westen, work (or draw social benefits) in Alexanderpolder, keep fit in Ommoord, party on the Maasvlakte and shop in Schiedam. Urban life can no longer be enhanced within the borders of the neighbourhood, nor within the ancient hierarchical scale-system of a city centre surrounded by numerous sub-centres. The second urban renewal should be about building not *for* but *against* the neighbourhood.

The city as a whole

If we stop looking at the city purely in terms of its neighbourhoods, we discover, counter to all generally accepted ideas, that Rotterdam is a city that can be better understood from its coherence than from its fragmentation. This coherence is, to begin with, the product of the very thing that is supposed to have fragmented the city: its industry and infrastructure. Rotterdam extends from the most westerly point of the Maasvlakte to Capelle way across in the east. From the late 19th century to the post-war period, the coherence of this expansive area grew in tandem with developments in the port and the urbanization processes attendant on such developments. With the digging of Nieuwe Waterweg, the North Sea connection, Rotterdam all at once found itself with a coastal annex when the new Hoek van Holland was declared part of Rotterdam's territory, even though the two settlements were ridiculously far apart. After the Second World War an umbilical cord of urban substance grew between annex and city generating a double belt city on either side of the river.

On the south bank this took place in a process that had got under way back in the 19th century. The existing fishing villages of IJsselmonde, Katendrecht, Charlois, Pernis, Hoogvliet, Spijkenisse and Rozenburg were held captive by the port's advances. On the north bank the existing towns of Capelle, Rotterdam, Delfshaven, Schiedam, Vlaardingen and Maassluis bled together along the railway

Proportional diagrams of Rotterdam boroughs
Hel = PORT AND INDUSTRY

inhabitants

jobs

surface

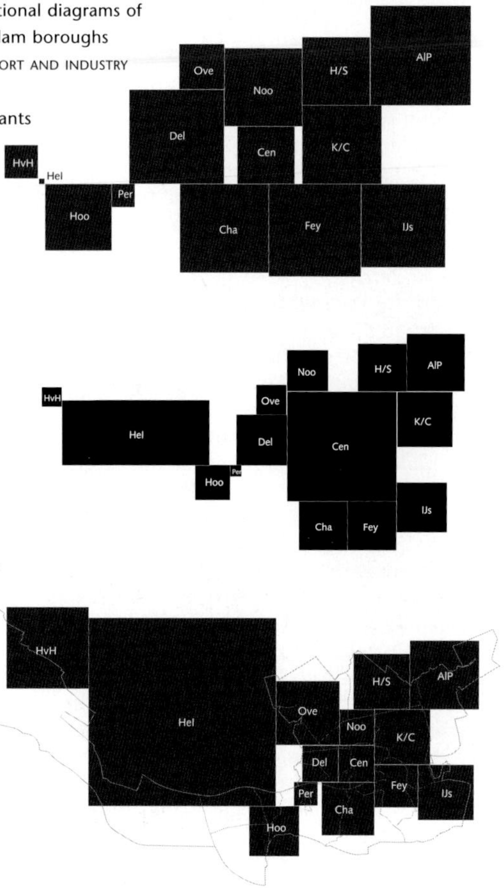

line to Hoek van Holland. This accretion among the villages and towns proceeded in parallel with the expansion of the port landscape which flattened out to the west accompanied by a decreasing sense of scale. The outcome was an urban field strewn with centuries-old villages, modern lines of transport, oil drums, fortified towns and large ships. That this seemingly muddled assemblage of villages, towns and harbour basins was in fact interrelated only became visible in the 1960s with the construction of the Ruit, the tangential highway network around Rotterdam's central city, which rallied all the region's components under a single system. The autonomous geometrical grid of motorways laid over the city threw up a number of lengthwise and transverse connections which tied all the villages and towns together. At that moment a continuous (or virtually continuous) urban area could be discerned, with the Ruit supplying it with an even spread of energy.

Of course the port these days is all but invisible from the city centre, but inhabitants of Hoek van Holland, Hoogvliet, Spijkenisse, Maassluis or Schiedam (all components of Greater Rotterdam) no doubt see things differently. For them the lorries, the office buildings, the smog alerts, the Betuwe rail freight link, the unemployment and the 'new' old docks are there as signs of the Port. It's still there, the port; it's just that it no longer sits in the centre of town. Its eccentric alignment can hardly be a reason to erase it from the self-image of the city. Rotterdam's identity has long ceased to be defined by its centre. Only the tiniest minority of all Rotterdammers lives in the 'true' urbanity of that centre, or on Kop van Zuid. The urban potentials of Rotterdam are determined more by its system of access and the fields this forms than by a centrally sited inner city, no matter how much cappuccino gets served there.

Residual tracts

After the ideal neighbourhood-city of the first urban renewal we now see an ideal city issuing from the physical structure that gives Rotterdam its cohesion. As this structure consists of three or four systems - landscape, city, port, infrastructure - simply dropped one on top of the other, each made and used according to its own logic, there is much that grates and jars on the spatial and programmatic fronts. Space is the only conceptual notion that can unite the impossible heterogeneity of the city's hardware, software and orgware. The space created by the urban development specific to Rotterdam requires an empirical approach as it cannot be compared with the space we know from the 'real' city: we first have to find out what it looks like, what it is made of and what were the mechanisms that gave rise to it.

Where the different systems touch they generate no man's lands together constituting a gigantic basin of residual tracts of land, urban antimatter. These areas owe their character solely to the impossibility of managing or naming them; they are between zones, between city and non-city,

The future PortCity in the middle of the 17th century

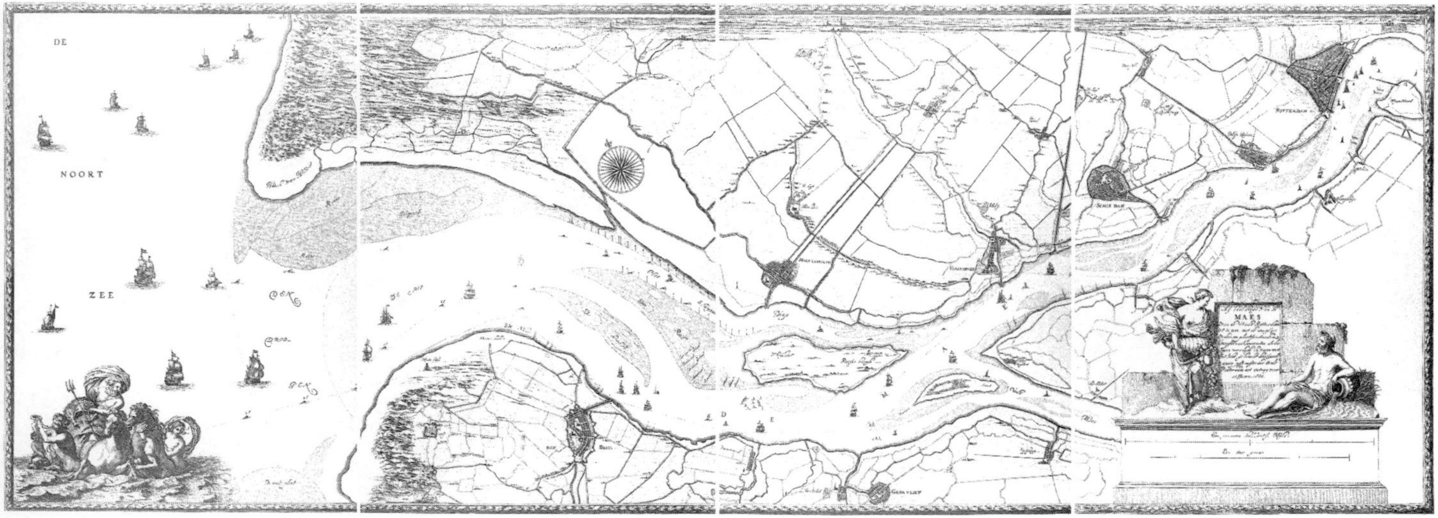

Red Haze I, in red: the areas between port and city

Red Haze II, in red : port and city

Network of Second Urban Renewal Proposals

multinational company and municipal district, motorway and residential area, port and landscape, sports association and Netherlands Rail, industrial site and suburbia, public administration and private interest. They consist on the one hand of the elements that brought them about: large-scale infrastructure like motorways, railway lines and harbour basins. On the other hand they are filled with activities that had no place elsewhere, functions frowned upon in the 'real' city as being untidy, temporary or undesirable in some other way. Here you find weekend chalets, personal allotments, breakers yards, clubhouses, sportsfields, marinas, youth clubs and playing fields. Yet these areas are a faithful reflection of the city's reality, in the same way that the contents of a rubbish bag at the doorstep reflect the household behind that front door. The programmatic and spatial structure of these areas is not unplanned, but constitutes the negative side of planning: everything rejected at some other place can be found here. Much of what happens in these areas is tolerated at most, and seldom desired. This is not to say that they are marked by an informal or anarchistic use of space. The sex'n'drugs toleration zone for heroin prostitution at a post-industrial site on Rotterdam's Keileweg shows how the municipal services are able to develop physical structures for the most abject urban programmes, structures that are just as detailed and well-supervised as a local park or square, or a street channel in the central city.

Besides the smaller-scale infills of these residual areas there are parts that sprang exclusively from exploitation of the optimum accessibility and visibility of the strips along motorways or areas near stations. These have nothing of a destitute and (seemingly) unplanned environment; on the contrary, they are home to more and more gleaming offices of companies attracted there by the steady stream of traffic passing by. There they stand, jaunty splashes of architecture lined up at all the prime sites, one aesthetic control-sanctioned business park after the other. This environment has nothing of the pragmatic and individualistic use of the allotments and sportsfields. Being pragmatic is not good enough for a business park; here you find buildings that have been thought long and hard about, sensitively laid out flower beds and parks, roads with pavements and traffic signs, everything is neatly in place. It is a monofunctional environment, of an unreal orderliness and neatness, without the visible presence of human activity. People arrive there by car in the morning, park, head for the office, and reappear at five in the afternoon to drive home again.

There is a third category of areas along the motorway, mega-facilities like the Alexandrium furniture boulevard, the discotheques, Feijenoord football stadium, the Franciscus hospital, Brielse Meer recreation area, Ikea, Hoogvliet sports centre and so on. Peripheral zones make the best places for sheltered mass culture. There is space here for large buildings with a large car park where large numbers of people daily gather, without the intensity of the use of those buildings ever being visible on the outside. This holds as much for hospitals as for the distribution centres in the docks that deal with masses of containers instead of people. All you need is a motorway exit and billboards showing the way. That one facility is in the Delft area, another in the sub-municipality of Hoogvliet out in the southwest and a third officially belongs to the Port of Rotterdam is no big deal for those who visit them. Local life has expanded way over the borders of neighbourhood and sub-municipality and fanned out across the entire city and region, following the force lines of the port agglomeration.

The characteristics of the residual zones vary from an untidy environment defined by individual use, to a perfectly ordered commercial site, from a green no man's land with gigantic mega-facilities hidden among the green buffers, to an outlet for otherwise inconveniencing drug addiction and sexual frustration under hyper-surveillance. When the rails and roads first arrived they figured mostly as autonomous elements on the edge of town, but through the expansions to Rotterdam following the war they have since ended up among its districts. This has left a continuous strip of left-over spaces of such size and with such quirkiness of form that there is no district in Rotterdam that does not abut one such area. Not just that, the proximity of these 'bad' areas is something all the 'good' areas of Rotterdam have in common.

This varied infill gives a programmatic diversity and an abundance of activities that has more to offer the neighbourhood than urban renewal, competitive sprucing-up and Urban Conglomerate Policy rolled into one. Look behind the thornbushes and the concrete fencing and it is like lifting up a stone and being amazed by all the bugs milling underneath.

Red haze

The residual areas have always remained outside the focus of urban planners and administrators because they came about through a negative process, whereas urban planning is always couched in positive terms. This explains why such a gigantic area of the urban territory falls outside the conscious thinking and acting of designers and politicians. These areas merge in a red haze before their eyes. They are *not* the outcome of a thoughtful, well-wrought design or of single-minded political ambition; they *are* for a large part the consequence of the 'paper city', the city of orgware: the Nuisance Act, municipal regrouping, or the sub-municipalities. Avant-garde architects - champions of the periphery - see them as an alternative for the city, as a romantic, history-less, anarchistic, context-less, untamed futuristic zone. In fact they are the side effects of an immense surplus of surveillance, policy, legislation and definition. They are united in a large dysfunctional family through their shared formlessness, unknowingness and impotence. They are a product of the excessive sectoral conventions of the urban actors; of the division and distance between the land owned by Roads and Waterways, Netherlands Rail, Shell, the city.

The potentially exploitable cohesion these areas impose upon the city is never understood as such, nor made a point of departure for an urban project, once again because this cohesion falls outside the urbanistic and administrative paradigms. They cannot be described in conventional terms of spatial or visual coherence. Even more important is that they take no notice of the administrative borders of sub-municipality, municipality, even of the region. Their cohesion is not designed, but issues from physical structures imposed by others than the city authorities, such as Roads and Waterways. In part Rotterdam's structure just happened to it.

The red haze envelops districts where the first urban renewal is now being enacted, the project that tackles the neighbourhood from the scale of the sidewalk. Our dogma, *building against the neighbourhood*, means seeking to conquer a domain that has something to do with the city as a whole. It transforms the districts *in spite of* their scale, *in spite of* their identity, *in spite of* what underlies them. The province of the second urban renewal is the red haze. Abutting the residential districts like a long ribbon, it is invariably closer to them than the city centre. These interstitial areas are as a result potentially better suited as centres than the centre itself. The red haze can unfurl as an elongated centre that flows around the entire city so that the urbanistic exchange normally only possible in the city's centre can take place throughout. This would mean, there is more of everything than you yourself could have imagined, you can profit from the attractiveness your area possesses for so many others. That is what is sensational about the city: living in something that is bigger than you, that has a longer life than you and that can offer you more than you need.

Figures

The potential continuum of the red haze we see on the map of Rotterdam, consists in reality of various fragmented and mutually isolated areas. For each of those areas we have formulated an idea and a programme that differ in that the areas themselves differ. The programmes are based on an extrapolation of what there is now, what will be and what might be. By rearranging, exaggerating and expanding existing urban attributes in a simple fashion we have compiled new urban figures. For this we use the existing hardware instead of merely adding a programme and a building mass that would be just as convincing at any other place. The figures join in a series, or rather a horizontal archaeology, of the potentials for a new urbanity of ideals in the no man's lands of the red haze.

By reconfiguring the red haze it becomes possible to once again regard the city as a totality when seen from all of the parts together constituting Greater Rotterdam, a place where port and industry, villages and motorways, polders and airfields all belong. We discovered that the red haze, flowing like a river through the city, can also flow into the parts that enclose it and can irrigate the barren fields of the old neighbourhoods and post-war districts. Using a process of exchange, the programmes of the districts and the interstitial areas can revitalize one another.

The new figures function as evidence of the possibilities inherent in this area, their aim being to focus the attention, not only that of designers but of administrators too. The figures in the red haze are in the middle of political and administrative no man's lands and as a result are obviously controversial issues, planning outcasts by their very nature. They invariably straddle fences and partitions between services and companies, inhabitants and engineers, trees and cars. The figures could be an inducement to regard these in-between areas as centres, as central zones, as the common ground where the various urban players could concur on a clearly stated objective, namely constructing urban areas which attack the organizational depth of the agglomeration to return it in a compact form to the public domain instead of screening it with a buffer of green space.

The urban figures proposed in the plan are only a fragment of an endless selection of possibilities. They do proceed from what it is that physically exists in those areas, but also from a radically unorthodox if already existing culture of urbanism: one that does not primarily draw and design but through its negotiations with all the various players, intervenes in the arena of urban transformations.

Bospolder/Tussendijken • Spangen • Marconiplein • Vierhaven

Reprogramming the post-industrial fringe areas allows the once-declining districts to rotate 180 degrees and face the city as a whole, not just its centre. The important thing here is to find an all-encompassing solution for the residential districts and the as yet isolated margins and edges abutting them by exchanging programmes and opening up dead-end areas.

In the far west of Rotterdam lies the sub-municipality of Delfshaven, one of the most jobless, heavily immigrant, right-wing and doped-up sub-municipalities in the country. Along the through roads it is a functioning, bustling district, but immediately beyond that it is one big tenement block for the poverty-stricken. From here the centre of city activity, linked to the district along one tenuous vein, seems light years away.

In truth Delfshaven has a stronger bond with the bundles of infrastructure surrounding it than with the city centre. If these infrastructural areas were to be orchestrated in unison with the residential districts an urban area could be developed that could profit from what up till now has been regarded as a position on the sidelines.

The new football stadium for Sparta (Feijenoord's local rival) is one object that could help boost this part of town; the same can be said of the Van Nelle factory, soon to boast a cultural and public use form.

But publicness exists by virtue of accessibility; which is why a Sparta station should be built at the place of the three bridges over the Schie canal. On the other side of the Schie lies Roel Langerakpark, a park with a great many large-audience facilities, such as an events hall (Energiehal), a baseball stadium, a mosque and the Oceanium belonging to Rotterdam Zoo. A bridge station could convey in and out the football fans, those visiting the Van Nelle factory, the hardcore house brigade at the Energiehal, the inhabitants of the Spangen district and visitors to De Schie penitentiary.

At present Marconiplein is a gigantic and inextricable 'traffic square' with a metro terminus and four office towers for the council planning agencies and the port authority. This administrative hub has contact with the car park and metro stop and nothing else. The entire square can be transformed into a public area that also includes the Marconi towers as the immense underlying canteen area will be opened to the public. What is now no more than a bookshop and a hairdresser's could expand into a special version of the underground shopping malls that are two a penny in other countries.

◉ The large port pier behind Marconiplein is at present occupied by fruit storage sheds and old warehouses colonized by artists and small companies. Further up can be found some wholesale and DIY businesses. In the middle of the pier stands a disused gasometer, a power station and masses of empty space. The most striking item on the agenda is the sex'n'-drugs toleration zone, which transforms the pier at night into a Vegas-style strip with hundreds of cars cruising slowly past the red-tubelit canopies of the heroin hookers.

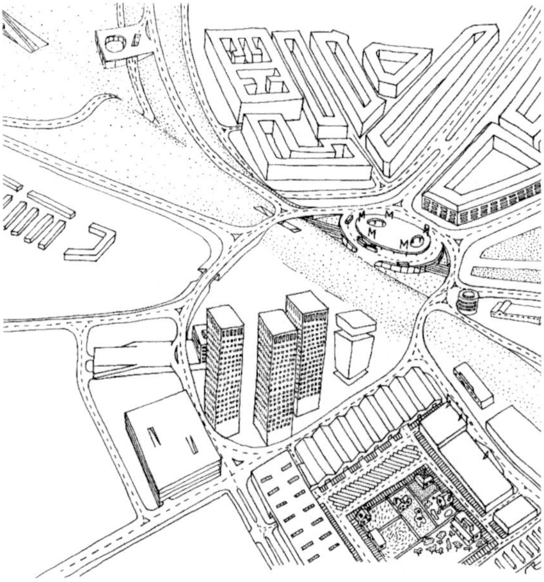
Marconiplein underground shopping mall

By revamping the pier into a number of exceedingly large city blocks, an urban fabric can be created that is an automotive version of Katendrecht, Saint Denis or Soho. The programme consists of industry, trade, dwelling and sex, along broad streets between low, large buildings. The broad pavements are used by the prostitutes; the 'service' areas would be located on waterside plazas. By mixing the toleration zone with the 'upper grade' of the sex industry the former can be stripped of its purely negative air and integrated into a traditional urban environment gone automotive: a bustling street where you can live, trade, work and whore.

◉ The railway embankment west of Bospolder can be transformed through a strategy of zoning and exchange into a park of great significance for the adjoining residential district. The many old school buildings can be moved from the district to the elongated park. The new schools can be spread like railway carriages across the embankment turned park with direct access to a gigantic green playground.
The old school buildings in the area are eminently suitable for the informal activity currently housed in the buildings lining the railway embankment: traders in second-hand furniture, architectural practices, garages, workshops and the like. By exchanging the one programme for the other, district activity will pick up and the schools can profit from a park conceived of as a long line at the scale of the entire city.

Combination of bridge, train station
and soccer stadium, Delfshavense Schie

The sex'n'drugs toleration zone, Department of Public Works, Rotterdam

Charlois ❁ Waalhaven

Waalhaven fuses with the existing city in a new breed of city, a collage of two broken-down systems that are no longer able to continue fulfilling their originally sharply defined functions. Thus an unbroken fabric can be assembled from two fabrics that have forcibly been denied each other for the past three-quarters of a century.

When Waalhaven harbour basin was dug at the beginning of the 20th century it gave the city an impressive body of water with mooring buoys and piles for hundreds of inland craft arriving to pick up their cargo from the grain elevators and floating coal tips.
Piers were erected at right angles to the quays of Waalhaven, each shot through by a broad public road attended by rails and with a necklace of warehouses to either side. With this simple system all the different modes of transportation were organized across this harbour and a clear distinction was made between the public area and the privates grounds of companies along the quays.
Round Waalhaven lay a thick bundle of infrastructure and small businesses and beyond these, at a safe distance from the docks, the residential district of Charlois. Built at the same time as Waalhaven, Charlois was in part laid out in the then new typology of open row development. While providing better houses and a more open and green urban structure, it also marked a deterioration of the residential programme. Whereas the 19th century blocks filled up with workshops, car service garages and other commercial use forms, in the open row housing this got no further than a shop on the corner. The urban renewal of the 1970s onwards went even further in erasing trade and small-scale industry from the residential areas. The upshot today is the complete absence of a local economy or a sense of urbanity.

The edge of Charlois, 1997

● At present the state-of-the-art port is beating an inexorable retreat from the pre-war city. Waalhaven will also be abandoned by the port, beginning with its east side which will transmute into a business park of urban stature, with a fairly small-scale flow of activities. This is a strategy which makes integration with the adjoining city areas a very real option, conceivably generating one large urban region stretching from the old quarters to deep into the harbour basin. To achieve this, the existing structures of both harbour and residential area will require transforming with great care. The network of roads, quays, sheds, tracks, dykes and buildings can be reparcelled to accommodate a multifunctional urbanity.

● The sheds on the piers can be used for transport and industry, for wholesalers and retailers too but also for housing. Since the quays are no longer needed for transshipment they can be made public and dedicated to cyclists and pedestrians. The central loop can then be used for lorries and cars. Each building is made accessible from two sides: from the cycle/pedestrian quays and from the lorry/car route.
The head of each pier should be graced with a super-monumental public object, something that draws the neighbourhood life of Charlois into Waalhaven, say a mosque with four tall minarets.

● Then we come to the residential component, where both the alternation of light and

Industry back in the City, Charlois

heavy traffic and the mix of functions can be continued. This can be done by opening up one half of the inner courtyards for modest businesses: sheds, service garages, workshops. These streets have to be accessible to company vans and lorries, while the blocks of housing on the other side give onto a street for pedestrians and cyclists: a *woonerf* or dwelling compound, only without parking spaces. Like the dockside buildings, the housing blocks are accessible from two sides as much for cyclists and pedestrians as for business traffic.
At the end of the *woonerf* you can see vans and lorries on the move; the many visiting truckers generate a corner café, snack bar and restaurant; you can park your car in one of the sheds and proceed on foot along the quay; the plaza around the mosque can also house a market. These are residential surroundings that are defined not by 'dwelling' but by the vagaries of the vicinity and by the activities as these occur in the city as a whole.

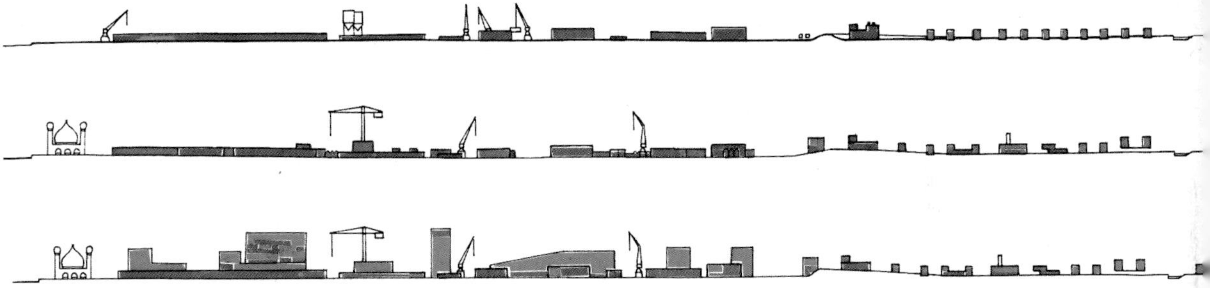

Blending from of pier and city

Terbregge ● A20

The domestic culture of suburbia is fundamentally linked with the motorway, as is the current domestic culture throughout the Netherlands. Yet the house and the motorway are nonetheless regarded as incompatible elements. With the urban configuration outlined below, the motorway and suburbia are able to coincide instead of having to be defended against one another. It could mean that the mediaeval Bergse Linker Rottekade could retain its character; the circulation of cars need not reach it, and from the dyke one could look out on the landscape of court-houses and motorways.

● Between the A20 and bends in the river Rotte lies a pristine polder. On one side is Bergse Linker Rottekade with its fine-spun ribbon development atop a dyke, on the other the prodigiously busy A20 and the railway to Utrecht. It is an area effectively cut off by infrastructure.
There are at present plans to fill the polder with a government-designated Vinex expansion scheme (now in full swing), to widen the A20 and to double the railway line to Utrecht. Sportsfields along the motorway and tall screens are to shield the houses from the audiovisual presence of the A20. The district cold-shoulders the heavy infrastructure, turning instead to the market-driven living-along-the-water conditions being recreated on the land immediately behind Bergse Linker Rottekade.
A better idea perhaps would have been to stick to an urbanistic strategy in which the factor dominating the area - being encapsulated by heavy infrastructure - is not a problem but its greatest advantage. The entire area can be seen as nestling in the crook of the main traffic interchange (Terbregseplein); the 'centrifugal geometry' of the motorway traffic could be augmented in an planning framework for a suburb wholly targeted at mobility. Kilometres-long sliproads can be tapped from the A20 and A16,

just as tracks have been tapped from the railway line to Gouda to constitute Rotterdam-Noord goods station. Immense dolphin-shaped blocks will emerge, between which you can drive at almost motorway speed. The blocks are literally framed by the physical attributes and materials of the motorways, slip roads, guard rails, road signs, filling stations, stopping places etc.
The building blocks can be issued for fleshing out with an as yet unrealized house type: the motorway house. Whereas the widest range of typologies already have motorway-specific mutations - Chiesa dell' Autostrada, filling stations, motels - the house has always been held clear of the motorway whether as an environment or a culture. The most compact description of a motorway house, perhaps, is that of a suburban villa you can pull into at speeds usually reserved for petrol stations. This type can be developed on the basis of the Miesian 'court-house' for car owners, where the house's orthogonal geometry is distorted by the curving geometry of the arriving vehicle.
Another attribute that might be mutated to meet motorway conditions is the gravelled driveway. In hilly regions of France, gravel-filled troughs are placed at slopes in the road; lorries breaking into a skid can leave the road where it makes a gentle curve, and continue in a straight line into the trough, safely coming to a halt in gravel several metres deep. A less drastic version of the above could be installed in front of the motorway house. The car would approach the house at 75 kph, roar up the gravelled drive - symbol of a suburban lifestyle - and grind to a halt in decimetres (rather than metres) of gravel. The occupant obviously is the proud owner of a four-wheel drive with a winch, so exiting again the next morning will present few problems.
The public amenities in this residential area as we see it are asphalted expanses like those at the Dutch national border and in America with banks, garages, cafés, restaurants and so forth amidst a sea of parked cars. These motorway squares would make this area the most opulently programmed stop-off point in the Dutch road network; with such speed at their fingertips residents would only be seconds away from facilities geared to millions of cars passing daily.

Kralingse Bos ● A16 ● Alexanderpolder

The enclaves along the motorway are at present monofunctional, non-urban areas with masses of unused public space. By reprogramming them with, say, sportsfields, gardens and dwellings a new figuration emerges, one that manages to unite a number of seemingly irreconcilable functions.

● Since the war, the eastern flank of Rotterdam has developed into a string of large-scale and extensive units set in a course-grained infrastructural network of motorways. The enclaves within the grid are inward-looking. Where they differ from other post-war introverted urban enclaves is in their great spaciousness and strongly developed visual identities. There is the Rivium business park with its brand image culled from the Roman Empire of Asterix & Obelix. There is Prinsenland, the residential district with a neo-modernist habitat designed by Mecanoo and deriving from the modernism of Jacques Tati; there is the so-called Brain Park with its Silicon Valley inspired office bungalows grouped round a reflecting pool, there is Lotte Stam-Beese's elementarist city Het Lage Land with its open rows and slabs, there is the wooded parkland of Kralingse Bos, there are 'Van Traa's kidneys', a rare example of post-war reconstructional hedonism in urbanistic form-play, and of course the lengthy green barricade of sportsfields without end along the A16.
● The zone between Alexanderpolder and Kralingse Bos, given the right configuration, is capable of becoming a new brand of urban area with a mix of buildings

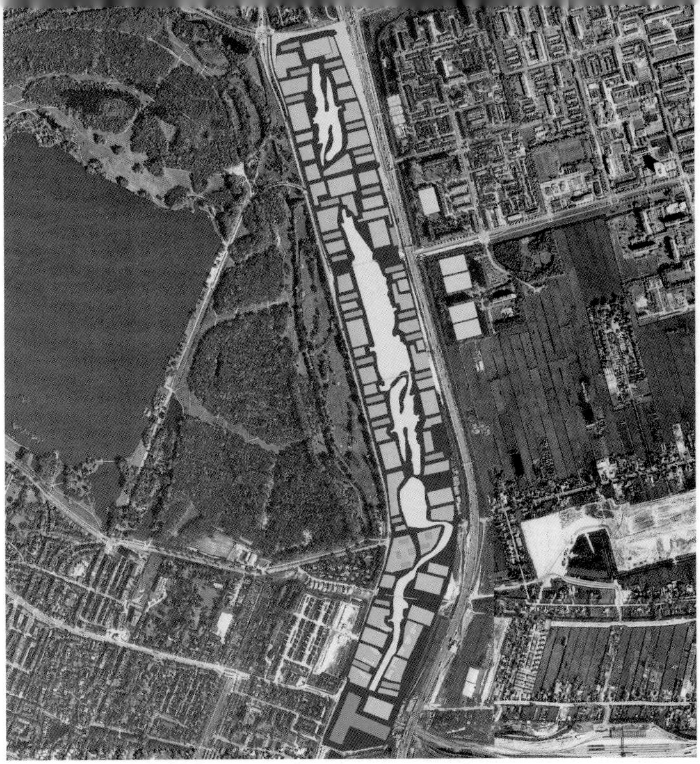

Business park, housing estates, soccer fields and allotment gardens around golf course paralel to A16 motorway, Alexanderpolder

instead of monofunctional enclaves. This area is wedged between a 'traffic square', a transportation exchange centre or transferium, a motorway with beyond it a residential estate, and a park. Potentially, then, it is an ideal residential setting, an ideal high-visibility location and of course an ideal sports venue at the same time. It is furthermore possible to combine all these elements within one figuration. Right next door, in Kralingse Bos, can be found the largest imaginable sportsfield; a golf course. In sampled form, this can become the centre of the new enclave. Following the Asian model the golf course could be used to whip up an attractive environment for business transactions but also for dwelling. The other factor is plainly the motorway plus transferium for guaranteed accessibility. To allow the area to continue functioning as a sports park for the residents of Alexanderpolder, the existing sportsfields can be rearranged at right angles to the golf course. Once there are office buildings and housing blocks standing along the golf course, the motorway and the park, the sportsfields will ensure a view through to the park and the motorway. This gesture will be backed up by several dozen leisure gardens mixed into the programme.

Within this simple figure, the area can fulfil a number of what in conventional urban planning would be conflicting use forms. It makes space for a modern 'ribbon development' of offices on ring roads. It creates a themed enclave where offices share a common denominator, not metaphorically like 'Rome' in Rivium, but through the overriding presence of a golf course. It offers a residential setting on a park accessed from the motorway yet fulfils at the same time a local role as the place where sports days, tournaments and training sessions are held.

The system's unconventional common sense is demonstrated by the ease with which existing buildings and land use slip into this programmatic reconfiguration. The whimsical, flexible form of the golf course worms its way between the blocks of flats and office-villas, stitching them together here in 'Putt City'.

'Putt City'

Second Urban Renewal 'Planning' scheme for area around Feijenoord Soccer Stadium

Groot IJsselmonde

Groot IJsselmonde is opened up to the programmes that have been enacted up against its borders. In a process of exchange, the excessive space between houses is programmed with sportsfields. The space thus freed is used by the park cum high-visibility location. The bond with the rest of South Rotterdam is restored.
The effectiveness of these interventions is inversely proportional to their magnitude in the three-dimensional structure of city planning. It is a virtually non-physical proposal for opening up and reprogramming.

◉ The sub-municipality of Groot IJsselmonde is surrounded on all sides by infrastructure and industry: in the north by 'Little Belgium', a strip of business premises on the river Maas, in the east by the A16 and a traffic interchange (IJsselmondseplein), in the south by the A15 and in the west by the railway embankment, fringed by minor industrial activity and sportsfields. Nestling inside this thick mantle is Groot IJsselmonde, laid out on the basis of a hierarchic road network, a configuration typical of reconstruction-era expansion schemes.

◉ The principal object in the vicinity is Feijenoord football stadium, which in the first instance is scaled to the city as a whole. This explains why a station was specially built for it with an immense pedestrian bridge and stairs giving onto the stadium. There was, besides, a local reason for building the stadium here: most manual labourers and most football fans lived south of the river. Building the stadium to the east of the railway was an attempt to encourage urban expansion in that direction. But post-war developments resulted in the large-scale zones on both sides of the tracks becoming a gigantic barrier with only a handful of crossing points along its length of 3.5 kilometres. This came about primarily because after the war the railway embankment became steadily broader and more and more impenetrable. More importantly, the urban planning concept for Rotterdam had changed. The 'neighbourhood idea' led to parts of town being developed as introverted units, clearly separated from one another by infrastructure laid out in green parkland. The design for Groot IJsselmonde is an example of this strategy.
By redeveloping the districts surrounding Groot IJsselmonde we can bring the sub-municipality back into contact with the rest of the city. By these means it can regain something of the bond it enjoyed with Rotterdam before the reconstruction drove wedges into the city.

Panorama of IJsselmondde, 1997

• The first means with which to address this issue is the potential park-like quality of the area. Sitting on a bench on the edge of the Hillesluis neighbourhood, you see trees, lots of empty space; Feijenoord stadium looms up and the odd train flashes by. Cross to the other side of Stadionweg on the rim of Vreewijk and the picture is the same: trees, emptiness, a train and across the way a hospital (Claraziekenhuis). This gives rise to the idea of a latent park, an open zone with sundry large-scale amenities. But it still has to become reality. There are too few visual and physical links between the two parts of South Rotterdam on either side of the railway.

• The immense intermediary zone of the marshalling yard can be optimized in a way that profits from its post-industrial status. In doing away with the old docklands on Kop van Zuid the railway embankment has been reduced in size, and a market now suggests itself of modest clusters of offices and businesses targeted at the motorway. If this area were to be made permeable, the zone could be developed as a high-visibility location. Above all else it means that a scattering of discrete objects can spread across the new void - objects that mark the expanse all around and strengthen the sensation of a virtual park.

• Following a process of exchange, the local green space between the rows of houses can be programmed with the relocated sportsfields. Through this exchange the former green space can be used and maintained and the district extricated from its monofunctional isolation. The sports clubs would not only pay for the upkeep of the green space, they would also introduce elements that would benefit the locals; the local café would reappear in the guise of the football canteen.

We can follow a point-by-point strategy as they did with the urban renewal programme in the 1970s, only this time we will be building against the neighbourhood.

> Cheap yet effective ways must be found to cross the railway
> The green buffer is to be drastically cut back, so that the area can once again figure as a whole
> Sportsfields are to be relocated to local green space
> The space thus freed will become a B-grade location (i.e. good general accessibility for labour-intensive companies)
> The marshalling yard will become a park, an empty space with objects in it
> The Twee Heuvels park will be programmed for organic cattle-breeding which unlike the time-honoured factory farming can be done in full view of the public. Free-range pigs root for truffles in the park.

Supporters club, skyboxes, social housing and soccer field, IJsselmondde

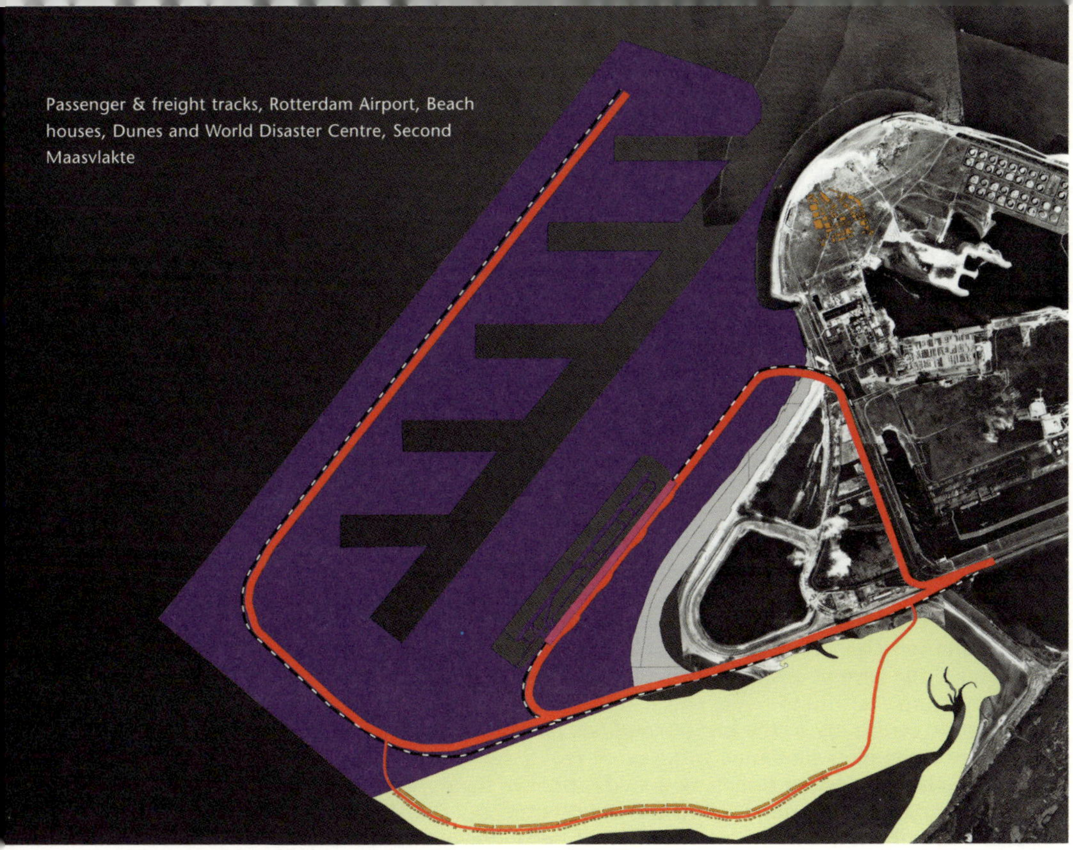

Passenger & freight tracks, Rotterdam Airport, Beach houses, Dunes and World Disaster Centre, Second Maasvlakte

Maasvlakte I and II

Expanding the port with Maasvlakte II will not further disrupt the contact between city and port but can further strengthen the cohesion in the urban region. Once the Maasvlakte has multifunctional programming it can be the second central pole in the city and bring a new definition of urbanity to bear.

● The project for a second Maasvlakte will expand the Port of Rotterdam with 1000 ha. of new land wrested from the sea. This would seem to reinforce the model of Rotterdam as a port and city steadily growing apart. But the second Maasvlakte will also have enormous repercussions for the immediate hinterland: these include the Betuwe rail freight link, the extension to the A15 motorway, the arrival of Distriparks and tunnels under the Nieuwe Waterweg, not to mention 750 ha. of new 'natural' surroundings scheduled for laying out around and against Maasvlakte I and II. In other words, expanding the port into the sea means its ever greater presence on land.
Now is the moment, then, to look at a development already under way for decades from another perspective. The port's expansion will exert an increasing influence on the cohesion of the urban region as a whole. Hence it is possible to regard the programming of the new Maasvlakte as the development of a second urban pole. Which is why we should be looking at the urban - and therefore multifunctional - potentials of this port component.
● The second Maasvlakte should be able to bring together a number of elements of the city. There are two existing developments that could make of the Maasvlakte a centre of urban activity. First, there is the airport. If Zestienhoven in the north of Rotterdam

were to be split into a hobby aerodrome and an airport for freight and passengers, and if Schiphol were to contemplate expanding onto the Maasvlakte for freight and charter flights, the idea of an airfield on the second Maasvlakte would make sense. The Betuwe rail freight line would then have to be continued up to the airfield and primed to receive passenger trains as well. It would also mean that the A15 could be used much more by private cars. In short, this area of the port would have become urbanized.

Once the dunes of Voorne are extended as planned along the lower edge of the sludge storage basin (Slufter), the beachside living of Oostvoorne and Rockanje can likewise be expanded along the southern rim of Maasvlakte II. A kilometres-long beach boulevard can branch off from the motorway. On the beach side this boulevard can give access to drive-in beach houses with their feet in the sand. Across the boulevard will stand several taller buildings with shops and cafés on the ground floor and flats on top with a view out to sea, and of course across the Maasvlakte.

The fundamental anti-urbanity of the Maasvlakte - in the sense of things that are against the city mentally and physically, literally and metaphorically - culminates in the World Disaster Centre. This is where they stage catastrophes. Behind a huge fence we see the burnt-out shells of cars, buildings, ships, planes and lorries. Here an endless stream of firemen, anti-terrorism teams, police, armies, state police and Red Cross organizations from all over the world are trained in all manner of rescue techniques. Yet the incidents simulated here are isolated as if in a Petri dish from the unpredictable effects of the complex urban context in which they would really occur.

So instead of the current set-up, the disaster centre should have as its context a mock-up of Rotterdam's central triangle. This can trigger a condition on the Maasvlakte that lends historic continuity to the transformations of Rotterdam: the constant upscaling and outward accretion combined with a very real memorial to the destruction of the city centre. This destruction is then exploited further as the onset of a culture of emptiness, as a symbol of the conceptual liberation of central city thinking, and as an appropriation of the urban-disaster theme, to be presented to the global economy in the form of know-how and knowledge production. Flying and sailing into Rotterdam, one is immediately confronted with the fact that destruction and constant transformation are conditions that this city may perhaps not have chosen but have certainly made it what it is. Seeing the city burn for the umpteenth time, the traveller sits back, fastens his seat belt and sighs, 'home again'.

Home again

Credits Texts & Projects

Chapter 1

History

Substance and Tenacity in:
Martin Aarts (ed.), *50 jaar wederopbouw*, 010 Publishers, Rotterdam 1995

Rotterdam 1940-1960 **panorama 1**
contribution to exhibition *Post Rotterdam, Architecture and City after the tabula rasa,* Porto, 2001. Catalogue: Pedro Gadanho (ed.), *Post Rotterdam, Architecture and City after the tabula rasa,* Porto 2001 SA, Porto/010 Publishers, Rotterdam 2001

Emptiness *in: 50 jaar wederopbouw,* 010 Publishers, Rotterdam 1995

What If? exhibition at Boijmans Van Beuningen Museum, Rotterdam, 1999

Re-Arch New Designs for Old Buildings in: Crimson, *Re-Arch: Nieuwe ontwerpen voor oude gebouwen,* commissioned by Stimuleringsfonds voor Architectuur, 010 Publishers, Rotterdam 1995

Free at last! Noordsingel Prison, with Sofia Vyzoviti, commissioned by Wijk Ontwikkelings Maatschappij, 1998

Old and Improved Delfshaven Rotterdam, with Fenna Haakma Wagenaar, research assistant Lonneke Bakkeren commissioned by Wijk Ontwikkelings Maatschappij, 1997

One Nation Underground Mont des Arts Brussels, in collaboration with Maxwan Architects and Urbanists - Rients Dijkstra with Eva Pfannes, Estefiana Julian and Harm te Velde (CAD)- design project for the project Vacant City, Brussel's Mont des Arts Reconsidered, a coproduction of Bruxelles/Brussels 2000, Onderzoeksgroep Stedelijkheid en Architectuur K.U.Leuven, Koning Boudewijnstichting/Fondation Roi Baudouin, BBL. Publication with the same title by NAi Publishers, Rotterdam/Bruxelles/Brussels 2000, Brussels/OSA K.U. Leuven, Leuven 2000

Chapter 2

Obsession

A Compulsion towards the Real IN: WIEDERHALL, NO. 19, WIEDERHALL FOUNDATION/010 PUBLISHERS, 1996

Rockbottom OMA builds house in Bordeaux IN: Harvard Design Magazine, NO. 5, SUMMER 1998

Northern Soul IN: De Architect, NO. 7/8, 1995

Oh Heavens IN: Wiederhall, NO. 19, WIEDERHALL FOUNDATION/010 PUBLISHERS, 1996

Brave New Office Building the Tomadohuis by Huig Maaskant EXTRACT FROM FORTHCOMING MONOGRAPH ON HUIG MAASKANT

Gizmoism and Gadgetry the world of Reyner Banham IN: Harvard Design Magazine, NO. 5, SUMMER 1998

Dr. Jerde's Urban Rejuvenation Center

IN: Harvard Design Magazine, NO. 12, 2001

Urbanism as an Act of Deliverance
Bakema on Mont Blanc by Ed Taverne
IN: GERRIE ANDELA, COR WAGENAAR (EDS), Een stad voor het leven, Wederopbouw Rotterdam 1940-1965, UITGEVERIJ DE HEF, ROTTERDAM 1995

Chapter 3

Top Down

Rotterdam 1960-1970 panorama 2, contribution to exhibition Post Rotterdam, Architecture and City after the tabula rasa, Porto 2001. Catalogue: Pedro Gadanho (ed.), Post Rotterdam, Architecture and City after the tabula rasa, Porto 2001 SA, Porto/ 010 Publishers, Rotterdam 2001

Mechanization Takes Command Building Rotterdam Harbour 1870-1914 extract from forthcoming monograph on J.H. van den Broek

Rotterdam PortCity This article is the continuation of a text that was written for the jury of the Rotterdam-Maaskant Prize 1997. The Port of Rotterdam was nominated by the jury, but the committee of the Rotterdam-Maaskant Foundation failed to award it the winner. in: Archis, no. 10, 1997

Shiny and Bright The New Dutch Landscapes in: Panorama Nederland, boekenweekmagazine 1998

Hong Kong, Amsterdam entry for the exhibition on study trip to South-East Asia, Fonds voor de Beeldende Kunsten, Vormgeving en Bouwkunst, Amsterdam 1998

Infrarchitecturbanism research assistant Chantal van der Zijl extract from Asfalt, Automobiliteit in de Rotterdamse stedebouw, 010 Publishers, Rotterdam 1996

A15 the highway for Hoogvliet with One Architecture and Minke Themans (graphic design) for International Building Exhibition Hoogvliet-Rotterdam WiMBY!, 2001

City of Industry An Architectural History of Spaanse Polder Rotterdam extract from research project for Haven- & Industriegebieden, commissioned by Stichting Comité Wederopbouw Rotterdam, 1998

There Goes the Neighbourhood with Fenna Haakma Wagenaar, research assistants: Chantal van der Zijl and Lonneke Bakkeren proposal for the second urban renewal of Rotterdam, commissioned by Dienst Stedenbouw + Volkshuisvesting, 1997-1998

Origin of Images

t=top/b=bottom/l=left/r=right/c=centre

Aeroview/Dick Sellenraad p. 232b
Alvar Aalto Foundation Helsinki p. 128 tl and b
Anti-Slavery International p. 92t
ANWB p. 240, 249
D. Appleyard, K. Lynch and J.R. Myer p. 248
Architectenbureau Jan Hoogstad p.278
Academy Editions, London /Architectural Design p. 110
Architectural Review p. 133b, 134-136
Archiv für Kunst und Geschichte, Berlin p. 66
Atelier Van Lieshout p. 302
Beatrix Potter/Penguin Publishing London p. 109
Dienst Stedenbouw + Volkshuisvesting p.254-255
G.A.R. (Municipal Archives Rotterdam) p. 13, 14, 15, 16, 22, 23, 24, 37b, 39, 46b, 47, 85b, 86b, 212, 213, 214t, 216, 221t, 222-223, 270, 271, 272, 277, 279t, 293
Gemeente Archief Groningen/Aerofoto Eelde p. 69
De Ingenieur p. 215
The Jerde Partnership International p. 181, 182
The Laser Vaginal Rejuvenation Center of Los Angeles p. 174
Maxwan Architects and Urbanists p. 93, 94, 96, 98, 100
Museum of Finnish Architecture Helsinki p. 125t
NAi Archive p. 45
Willem Jan Neutelings p. 257, 258
New Society (March 20, 1969, p. 439) p. 166
Office for Metropolitan Architecture p. 70b, 111, 112b, 260
RISC p. 237
Alison Smithson/Architectural Review p. 110
Stadsarchief Dordrecht p. 149
Madelon Vriesendorp p. 70b

Photography

Freek van Arkel p. 232t, 239b
Hans Aarsman p. 245
Wout Berger p. 262
Matthijs Bouw p. 141c
A. Carré p. 47
Crimson p. 48, 59, 60, 61b, 71bl&r, 77, 117-120, 133t, 141t&b, 142t, 144, 167, 168, 173, 184, 224, 230b, 279b, 280, 303, 308b, 309b
Rients Dijkstra p. 108
John Donat p. 165
Cor Geljon p. 278
Gerard Hadders p. 70tr, 71tl, 71tr
Kim & Wendela van der Hoeven p. 126-127
Arie Hooijmeijer p. 38
Suoman Ilmakuva Oy p. 125b
Hiroyuki Kawano p. 175
Dennis Keeley p. 183
Mischa Keijser p.72
Maxwan p. 93, 94, 96, 98
A. Meijer p. 21
Marcel Molle p. 64b
Charles Le Noir p. 176t
Oy Sääski p. 125tr
Göran Schildt p. 128bl
Simmons/Del Zoppo Photographics p. 176b
Tim Street-Porter p. 165r
Rauno Träskelin p. 128br, p. 128tl
Arnoud Verhey p. 238
Jan Versnel p. 150, 151, 152, 157, 159tl&b, 160
Robert Walker p. 143
Hans Werleman p. 229

CREDITS

THIS PUBLICATION CAME INTO BEING UNDER THE AUSPICES OF THE ROTTERDAM-MAASKANT FOUNDATION ON THE OCCASION OF THE PRESENTATION OF THE 9TH ROTTERDAM-MAASKANT AWARD FOR YOUNG ARCHITECTS TO WOUTER VANSTIPHOUT ON MAY 17, 2002 IN THE BURGERZAAL OF ROTTERDAM'S CITY HALL.

— DE OORSPRONKELIJK IN HET NEDERLANDS GESCHREVEN TEKSTEN VAN DIT BOEK ZIJN INTEGRAAL TE LEZEN OP WWW.010PUBLISHERS.NL EN WWW.CRIMSONWEB.ORG.

— WAIT FOR THE SEQUEL: VERNACULAR SPECTACULAR, AND FOLLOW CRIMSON'S ADVENTURES IN DUTCHNESS, SMALLNESS AND POLITICS.

EDITING

Crimson; Ewout Dorman, Ernst van der Hoeven,
Michelle Provoost, Wouter Vanstiphout & Cassandra Wilkins

Image research

Annuska Pronkhorst

Translations

John Kirkpatrick and George Hall

Graphic Design

Gerard Hadders - BLH, Schiedam
Barbara Dijkhuis, Amsterdam

Scenes

Threesome; Michiel Kluiters, Maria Pask, David Powell

Printing by Lecturis, Eindhoven

ISBN 90 6450 466 0

ckbar
ARMY

Tropical
De Slegte